Uncanny Cinema

Uncanny Cinema

Agonies of the Viewing Experience

Murray Pomerance

BLOOMSBURY ACADEMIC
NEW YORK • LONDON • OXFORD • NEW DELHI • SYDNEY

BLOOMSBURY ACADEMIC
Bloomsbury Publishing Inc
1385 Broadway, New York, NY 10018, USA
50 Bedford Square, London, WC1B 3DP, UK
29 Earlsfort Terrace, Dublin 2, Ireland

BLOOMSBURY, BLOOMSBURY ACADEMIC and the Diana logo are trademarks of
Bloomsbury Publishing Plc

First published in the United States of America 2023
Paperback edition published 2024

Copyright © Murray Pomerance, 2023, 2024

For legal purposes the Acknowledgments on p. xiii constitute an extension
of this copyright page.

Cover image © Moira Shearer in *The Red Shoes* (Michael Powell and Emeric Pressburger,
The Archers, 1948). Digital frame enlargement.

All rights reserved. No part of this publication may be reproduced or transmitted
in any form or by any means, electronic or mechanical, including photocopying,
recording, or any information storage or retrieval system, without prior
permission in writing from the publishers.

Bloomsbury Publishing Inc does not have any control over, or responsibility for, any
third-party websites referred to or in this book. All internet addresses given in this
book were correct at the time of going to press. The author and publisher regret any
inconvenience caused if addresses have changed or sites have ceased to exist,
but can accept no responsibility for any such changes.

Library of Congress Cataloging-in-Publication Data

Names: Pomerance, Murray, 1946-author.
Title: Uncanny cinema: agonies of the viewing experience / Murray Pomerance.
Description: New York : Bloomsbury Academic, 2022. | Includes bibliographical
references and index. | Summary: "An in-depth study of several films and television
shows to demonstrate the difficulties of conveying the experience of viewing cinema"–
Provided by publisher.
Identifiers: LCCN 2022014191 (print) | LCCN 2022014192 (ebook) | ISBN 9781501398742
(hardback) | ISBN 9781501398780 (paperback) | ISBN 9781501398759 (epub) |
ISBN 9781501398766 (pdf) | ISBN 9781501398773 (ebook)
Subjects: LCSH: Motion picture audiences–Psychology. | Television viewers–Psychology. |
Motion pictures–Philosophy. | Television–Philosophy. | LCGFT: Film criticism.
Classification: LCC PN1995.9.A8 P66 2022 (print) | LCC PN1995.9.A8 (ebook) |
DDC 791.4301–dc23/eng/20220414
LC record available at https://lccn.loc.gov/2022014191
LC ebook record available at https://lccn.loc.gov/2022014192

ISBN: HB: 978-1-5013-9874-2
PB: 978-1-5013-9878-0
ePDF: 978-1-5013-9876-6
eBook: 978-1-5013-9875-9

Typeset by Deanta Global Publishing Services, Chennai, India

To find out more about our authors and books visit www.bloomsbury.com and
sign up for our newsletters.

Is it because of this that the spectator (sustained by the hope of an unknown body made of antennae of emotions or feelings) would be some part of this turning machine, thrown into what has already been recorded? The spectator seeks this point of gravity (this center) lost only because the body that accompanied it has vanished . . .

–Jean-Louis Schefer
The Ordinary Man of Cinema

A procession is effective by the way it unrolls, turning to a mere mob if all of it passes at once.

–Henry James
Preface to *The Spoils of Poynton*

There are higher languages than that of the toiling mind, deeper intuitions that can be overtaken by the microscope or telescope, even a space one. They require metaphors, and mixed ones at that.

–William Golding
Foreword to *To the Ends of the Earth*

I will not cease from mental fight.

–William Blake

In the ornamental density of this presentation, the distinction between thematic and excursive expositions is abolished.

–Walter Benjamin, "Interior Decoration"

Contents

Acknowledgments: For My Teachers   xiii

Prelude: Bright Experience   1
Thinking about bicameral man and our experience with film; *Cape Fear*;
Wife vs. Secretary; *Vertigo*

Lost Voyagers   7

1. Sidestepping   9
   Thinking about small performance and small observation; *The Crown*; *Forms of Talk*;
   Singin' in the Rain; *Bringing Up Baby*; *The Band Wagon*

2. Unforgettable   16
   Thinking about star personae; *A Star Is Born*; *Negotiating Hollywood*;
   I Love Lucy; *The Hunchback of Notre Dame*; *Some Like It Hot*; *Casablanca*

3. Banquet   23
   Thinking about labor and the viewer's attitude; *The Real Thing*; *Reversal of
   Fortune*; *Hulk*; *From Russia with Love*

4. Plastic Surgery   30
   Thinking about cinema and advertising; *The Long Goodbye*;
   Samson and Delilah

5. Registrations   36
   Thinking about stars and registrations; *The Nutty Professor*; *Gentlemen Prefer
   Blondes*; *Waiting for the Barbarians*; *The King*; *Personal Shopper*; *Good Will Hunting*;
   Dark Passage; *Conflict*; Dustin Hoffman; Harrison Ford; Marlene Dietrich;
   Lee Marvin; Arnold Schwarzenegger

6. Great Expectations   43
   Thinking about the future of cinema; *The Philadelphia Story*; *The Bourne Identity*;
   The Manchurian Candidate (1962); *The Lonedale Operator*; *The Portrait of a Lady*;
   Joan Fontaine; Vera Miles

7. Naming of Parts   52
   Thinking about cinema's embodiments; *The Cranes Are Flying*; *Hugo*; *Strangers
   on a Train*; *Citizen Kane*; *Silence*; *Psycho*; *Pan's Labyrinth*; *Fellini Satyricon*; *Invaders
   from Mars* (1953); *Syriana*

8	**A Flicker**	58
	Thinking about images and moments; *The Quiet Man*; *The King of Comedy*; *North by Northwest*; off-camera reality; snapped shots; *Jaws*; *Kramer vs. Kramer*	
9	**Being Alive**	64
	Thinking about cinema and mortality; *Chinatown*; *Being There*; *Magnolia*; *Cries and Whispers*; *The Shootist*; *East of Eden*; *The Bourne Supremacy*; *Dinner at Eight*; *War of the Worlds*; *The Third Man*; *Mildred Pierce*; *The Bad Seed*; *The Karate Kid*; *Carrie*; *The Entertainer*; *Marriage Story*	
10	**For Your Eyes Only**	71
	Thinking about cinema as seen; *Life*; *Alien*; *2001: A Space Odyssey*; *Saboteur*; *The Astronaut's Wife*; *Jaws*; *Imitation of Life* (1954); *Rear Window*	
11	**Hands**	76
	Thinking about onscreen love; *The Theory of Everything*; *The Band Wagon*; *Howards End*; *Empire of the Sun*; *Twentieth Century*; *Blade Runner*; *The Lonedale Operator*; *Stairway to Heaven*; *The Big Sleep*; *Birth*; *F for Fake*; "Life Lessons"; *Vertigo*	
12	**A Logical Gasp**	82
	Thinking about seeing what characters see; *The Horsemen*; *The Kiss*; *Some Like It Hot*; *The Thomas Crown Affair*; *Annie Hall*; *Saturday Night Fever*; *A.I. Artificial Intelligence*; *Perfume: The Story of a Murderer*; *Big Night*; *The Graduate*;	
13	**Vigil**	89
	Thinking about submarine cinema; *The Command*; *On the Beach*; tin cans; *20,000 Leagues Under the Sea*; *The Wolf's Call*	
14	**Privileged**	97
	Thinking about cinema and intimacy; *A Most Wanted Man*; *Laura*; *Rebel Without a Cause*; *Stage Fright*; *Sunset Blvd.*; *The Incredible Shrinking Man*; *The Egyptian*; *20,000 Leagues Under the Sea*; *Peter Pan*; *Dr. No*; *Sabrina*; *Forbidden Planet*; *Three Days of the Condor*; *The Talented Mr. Ripley*	
15	**Ting-a-ling-a-ling**	105
	Thinking about the *acousmêtre* and the telephone; *Lili*; *The Errand Boy*; *Being John Malkovich*; *The Conversation*; *The President's Analyst*; *Wait Until Dark*; *Dial M for Murder*; *The Thirteenth Guest*	
16	**Unheard Voices**	112
	Thinking about vectorless sound and narrations; *Bullitt*; *Lawrence of Arabia*; *F for Fake*; *The Magnificent Ambersons*; *The Hospital*; *The Ten Commandments* (1956); *Titanic*; *The Maltese Falcon*; *Casablanca*; *Gaslight*; *Dr. Mabuse, der Spieler*; *On the Beach*; *The Birds*; *Rebecca*; *The Age of Innocence*; *Winnie the Pooh and the Blustery Day*; *Men in Black*; *The Revenant*	
17	**Remote Control**	120
	Thinking about film performance and spontaneity; *Who's Afraid of Virginia Woolf?*; *On the Waterfront*; *Shane*; *Donnie Brasco*; *Klute*; *When Harry Met Sally . . .*; *The Laundromat*	

Spectator, Watch Thyself   125

18   Paranoia   127
Thinking about binge watching as neverending surveillance; *Bosch; Narcos: Mexico; Homeland; Giri/Haji;* the optimêtre; *Gone Girl; Mindhunter*

19   Quote Me   139
Thinking about visions as shadows, sounds as echoes; *Vertigo; Conflict; Tempest; La mariée était en noir; Marnie; J'ai épousé un ombre; No Man of Her Own; Nouvelle Vague; The Barefoot Contessa; F for Fake*

20   The Magic Touch   147
Thinking about seeing a world I cannot feel; *Marathon Man; The Sound of Music; Rear Window; One Day in the Life of Ivan Denisovich; Manhunter; The Incredible Shrinking Man; Star Wars* (1977); *Blow-Up; Marriage Story; The Kiss of the Spider Woman; Psycho; Devil in the Flesh; The Dreamers; Commando; Grease; Fight Club*

21   Exeunt omnes   155
Thinking about how they leave and we cannot follow; *American Graffiti; Casablanca; Diva; Jurassic Park; The Graduate*

22   Throw It Away   162
Thinking about simple watching becoming impossible; Robert De Niro; Acting as being; *The Train; Red River;* Impressionistic sight

23   Who Are You?   168
Thinking about how seeing is not knowing; *Bunny Lake Is Missing*

24   The Walking Cure   175
Thinking about the camera returning us to childhood; *Paris, Texas; Gerry; North by Northwest; Marathon Man; Rebel Without a Cause; Fahrenheit 451; The Bridge on the River Kwai, The Man Who Knew Too Much* (1956); *Day for Night*

25   The Picture Dances   181
Thinking about what film music can be for us; *The Sea Hawk; Psycho; 2001: A Space Odyssey; Jaws; Catch Me If You Can*

26   Taboo   185
Thinking about film, limits, and every offering being a denial; *Blow-Up; Blade Runner;* 1939 General Motors Futurama; Disneyland; *Until the End of the World*

27   Only Connect   190
Thinking about films as theories; *Dog Day Afternoon; Forbidden Planet; Shane;* purity and danger

28   The Impatient   195
Thinking about the viewer's forward gaze; *Ugetsu monogatari*

29   At the Party   200
Thinking about eventful and uneventful encounters; *Annie Hall; The Party; Notorious; Top Hat; Mystic River; Saturday Night Fever; John Wick; Flying Down to Rio;*

His Majesty O'Keefe; Tootsie; The Big Chill; Top Hat; Goodfellas; Play It Again; Sam; Romeo + Juliet

30 O! 208
    Thinking about seeing more than a characters sees; *Blow-Up; Somewhere in Time*

31 A Sight for Sore Eyes 212
    Thinking about waiting with breath abated; *Vertigo*

The One-Eyed Stranger 217

32 It's Like This 219
    Thinking about actors and aging; *The Irishman*; performance and visibility

33 Taking Off 223
    Thinking about discontinuity; Harold Edgerton; contiguity and non-contiguity; *My Dinner with Andre; Lawrence of Arabia; The Phantom of Liberty; The Return of Martin Guerre; Source Code; Interstellar; Pillow Talk; The Big Store; All the President's Men*

34 Topographies 231
    Thinking about the view from above; *They Live by Night; West Side Story*; the Haussmannized city; *8 1/2*

35 Forget Me Not 236
    Thinking about erosion and the *field of the previous*

36 Inspired 238
    Thinking about cinema, the real world, and REALITY; *Munich; Official Secrets; The Philadelphia Story; Jaws; Peter Pan*

37 Shades in the Dark 243
    Thinking about how watching film is social and not social at once; *The Purple Rose of Cairo*; cinema and the mass audience

38 The Jitters 246
    Thinking about language and the shape of action; *6 Underground; 21 Bridges*; systematic discontinuity; fugue; action cinema and attention deficit

39 Irrational Space 250
    Thinking about the power of the irrational; *The Maltese Falcon; Rope; Kiss Me Deadly; The Incredible Shrinking Man; Vertigo; Blow-Up; Zabriskie Point; Chinatown; My Dinner with Andre; sex, lies, and videotape; Birth; Personal Shopper; A Ghost Story*

40 Spaced Out 256
    Thinking about crossing the axis; *Blow-Up* and Consort Road

41 Rabbit 261
    Thinking about watching the *animus* of the screen; *The Red Shoes*

42	M'm! M'm! Good!	267
	Thinking about film viewing and judgment; "good" and "likeable" films; *Cries and Whispers*; *Rabbit of Seville*; *L'Avventura*	
43	Brotherly Love	271
	Thinking about watching in companionship; the camera-friend and the production camera; *Crossfire*	
44	The Star's Twin	276
	Thinking about the star's doubling; *Honey Boy*	
45	Wink Wink	280
	Thinking about famous-performer walk-ons; *Charlie's Angels*; *Sunset Blvd.*; *The Night of the Hunter*; *Blade Runner*; *Blade Runner 2049*; *Battlestar Galactica*; *Planet of the Apes* (1968); *Planet of the Apes* (2001); *Mary Poppins* (1964); *Mary Poppins Returns* (2018); *War of the Worlds* (2005); *The War of the Worlds* (1953); *West Side Story* (2021); *West Side Story* (1961); *West Side Story* (1959)	
46	Filmic Is Filmic	287
	Thinking about how film is not text; *The Jungle Book* (1942); *Rebecca*; *Gone with the Wind*; *Who's Afraid of Virginia Woolf?*; *The Ten Commandments* (1956); *Empire of the Sun*; *Top Hat*; *Singin' in the Rain*; *Murder on the Orient Express* (2017); *Citizen Kane*; *Clash of the Titans*	
47	Read This	295
	Thinking about the writer onscreen; *Finding Forrester*; *That Certain Summer*	
48	Time This	299
	Thinking about moving through four times; *My Dinner with Andre*; *Carnage*; *2001: A Space Odyssey*; *Barry Lyndon*; *Night and Day*; *The Right Stuff*; *Halt and Catch Fire*; *Nick of Time*; *Irréversible*; *Memento*; *Betrayal*; *Still of the Night*	

Postscriptum: Must I Know What I See?   304
Thinking about knowing film; *Blow-Up*

References   307
Index   311

Acknowledgments

For My Teachers

Evelyn Eby Bedford and Reginald Bedford gave me music, in ways far more profound than my ears and fingers understood at the time, but taught me, too, how some of the very profoundest beauty can reside in what is unknown.

Dorothy Foster was at once hilarious and demanding, the first quality tempering the second so that I never stopped wanting to satisfy her (to me at the time) incomprehensible need for precision.

Gary Michael Dault challenged me with a surprise and an intoxicating riddle, *The Four Quartets*.

I would not have been able to write these pages without having benefit of an extraordinary educational experience with Edgar Z. Friedenberg, who showed me gracefully and brilliantly how to look twice at a phrase.

My friend and teacher Paul Goodman was generous in untold ways, but two lessons stand out clearly: that it is all in Nature; and that it is never finished.

From Steve Miller I learned that there is nothing wrong with standing up for what you believe, and pronouncing it with a smile.

Virginia Rock taught me what an editor really is.

Kenneth Boulding showed me how play and its delights have nothing whatever to do with age. He fed me peanut butter sandwiches while displaying a mind of truly astonishing lambency.

Arthur Vidich said I should learn how to stutter.

Norman Lloyd taught me how the past is always alive.

I feel grateful in a very special way to my charming colleagues at Bloomsbury: Katie Gallof, Stephanie Grace-Petinos, Jonathan Nash, Venkat Perla Ramesh, and Eleanor Rose whose many talented labors in the making of this book were vital, caring, and sweet but, as with so much labor in publishing, remain untold. Daniel Sacco has been very generous with time and effort to help me. Nellie Perret and Ariel Pomerance have born with my agonies in the best of spirits, and persist in being sources of blazing illumination always.

Prelude:
Bright Experience

Vertigo *(Alfred Hitchcock, Paramount, 1958). Digital frame enlargement.*

Turning and turning in the animal belly, the mineral belly, the belly of time. To find the way out: the poem.

Norman O. Brown

It is credible that everything I write in these pages, eager to stop it from dropping into the river of Time, you have already experienced or that it will be your experience soon enough. You don't know me. Why should you strain to lean my way? Are you straining, perhaps, now as ever, to be in the same situation whatever that could be, to join by sharing, and only because you sense a voice? Do I strain forward this way, insatiable, because "I heard voices"? Or is it all graphic instead, the form of the words as etchings?

We watch movies together, in the dark, you and I, and wonder together what is happening there, what we could be doing in staring at it. There are no flavors in the mix we would not bring into focus, could we taste as deeply as the sea. "*Todos fuentes la Fuente,*" Julio Cortázar wrote: "All Fires the Fire." Knowing not what you have watched, dear reader (and not what vast collection of pictures has been watchable for you) and nor recognizing you in the street, *"mon semblable, mon frère,"* might I be permitted to say, "All Cinema the Cinema"? *Todos los cines el cine.* All cinema the voice.

It may help to listen to Julian Jaynes—to listen with the ear and heart as well as read his words: "Bicameral men did not imagine; they experienced" (371). In the "bicameral era," voices—of the gods, of nature, of humans, of the world—had not been separated or pushed away by the advance of text, by the reception of the tablets on Sinai as a replacement for the burning bush. To repeat: when text advances, the voice is pushed away.[1] For Jaynes, and arguably for all of us, what we think of as "consciousness" is a "vocality" far greater, more diffuse, more encompassing than the "text" we think of as "thought," and indeed the very idea of thinking about film—film, my subject here—of framing ideas or postulates or hypotheses or arguments or observations or notations or conjectures or issues or significances, the very thought of such thought, the belief that one can subsume and encompass the problem with words, must miss a great deal. Text pushes the voice away. And I am of course hoist on the petard of struggling with words to point to this problem. Jaynes challenges us to pick up two dissimilar objects, one with each hand, and decide which of them is the heavier; but then he asks, beside the fact that we know the objects and know the feeling in our fingers and know the pull of gravity being different in both, still, *where* is the thinking about which of them is heavier? Not *which is heavier* but *where is our asking and deciding which is heavier?* Not, says he, in consciousness (on the page).

Here, I have tried to write about cinema not as I expect readers will already have found it as history, statistic, technique, or political argument but instead as it is in experience, when it is filled with voices and a "thousand twangling instruments," as Caliban says. While I have been obliged to write about it, I have tried hard not to write it. What can be written can be imagined; what can be imagined can be written. But seeing film is something else. Sometimes in life language breaks off. *There are times in life when we all need a little help.*

Taking in a vision of the world, or taking in a picture, is effectively a way of listening to sight, hardly the same as taking in a written statement, a text. Jaynes writes, "What had to be spoken is now silent and carved upon a stone to be taken in visually" (302). Text, the voice turned and made accessible to the eye only, not addressing the whole person whose eyes wonder and wander. Let us say that the screen is both softer and more extensive than a stone upon which text can be carved, and that the image, in light, is neither carved there nor laid by pressure, nor daubed by the hand, while never ceasing to be for heart's eye. To see film is to return to a distinct form of "the spoken," to hear the voices with the eyes. Think of Scorsese's *Cape Fear* (1991) and the way the entire film crumbles away into powder as we are confronted with Robert De Niro's mind-bending babble in the river, the tenor of the voice invoking not only air and music and lung and expression and confounding and coalescing but also what cannot be inscribed, what resists even circumlocution, what sinks. And when it sinks where does it go?

In silent film one heard the voices, but in sound film words took over, were inscribed, were made memorable. In the act of seeing film, memorability is dissolved, order as we

---

[1] On repetition consult Kirkegaard, and also Beethoven, Symphony No. 3 in E-flat, "Eroica."

know it is dissolved, consciousness as we call it is laid aside to rest, and we experience with a deep fullness we do not describe, cannot describe, cannot account for, cannot even recognize until afterward, in some pallid diminished substitute. There is a music to our experience, and this music is not to be scored.

Think of music as breathing, rather than as performance of a score. We can think of an actor's performance much less as a subservience to a script and a set of dictates and much more as a freeing and imbibing, an entrance and a penetration, a touching and a public gift. Say, an actor arranges for some cue cards so that he can play a scene before the camera without being disabled by his inability to "remember his lines." This is how a stranger on set might see it. But the actor, first of all, has no intention of remembering his lines, or of paying attention to himself speaking at all, or of the thing we call "lines in a script." He knows his character must seem mentally weak, unstable, fragile. The key word is "fragile." And to be fragile he reminds himself of being fragile by calling up fragility itself, by knowingly and intentfully straining to read a cue card (that will be off-shot) while he says what his character would say. Yet, even when he does this, there is a confounding together of at least two voices, the character's voice and the voice that is of the utterer's own body, a body that has no need or use for a script or for lines, and also a body that has no consciousness of itself as even such a body, once it has plunged into the action, once the swimming has begun.

Jump with me now to the vivid days of yesteryear, 1936 specifically, when a theatrical trailer was released for MGM's production of *Wife vs. Secretary* (directed by Clarence Brown). "A comedy drama" was the billing, with lots of pretty and bright close shots of the three major stars, Clark Gable, Myrna Loy, and Jean Harlow. The plot has Gable caught between the women, both of them stunningly beautiful. In shot after shot of this trailer, a narrative voice—filled in by way of superimposed white text (usually in capitals, and in a fashion entirely conventional at the time)—points to a portion of the story and literally spells out to us what is happening. The film clip beneath is selected so that the overlaid text will harmoniously illustrate a smiling face, a wry wink, and so forth. All of this image-text combination is par for the 1930s trailer course. The shots we see, with only a few exceptions, are star portraits, with delicate key-lighting, perfect coiffure, romantic pose. But the trailer plays a game of particular interest here:

We find ourselves being directly introduced not to the three major characters but to the three major film stars who portray them, and offered at the same time, on an accompanying visual plane, images of the star bodies in action. (The star is well known by this point as a box-office trigger; these three were epitomes.) All three seem star-*like*, because of the lighting and poses, but they are also, because of the text, in fact (and recognizably) stars. Yet, the proposition is that characters are doing things, and we are being given a special view. We thus come away with a double realization. First, this is a story about three personae, and it runs along with a certain arc and resolution. Second, this is a story of the involvement together of three stars. Every line of spoken dialogue, neatly cut in, applies to both character "realities" and star "possibilities," the latter to be understood by way of the kind of illuminating press releases about stars' private lives that flood the audience's consciousness so that offscreen romances are continually conceived and conjectured in just the form we see.

The trailer begins with the film title, and then:

[1] Character/actor portrait, "Clark Gable."

[2] Character/actor portrait, "Jean Harlow."

[3] Character/actor portrait, "Myrna Loy."

[4] A three-shot: "3 Great Stars"

> Many in the audience will already know what they are here being told, but just in case, here's blunt identification of Gable, Harlow, and Loy as, first and foremost, movie stars already elevated to greatness.

[5] Gable partially exposed between the two women: "Could any man choose between them?" . . .

> A direct invocation of the story skeleton. But also a direct implication: if he were given to choose, how might Clark Gable (already linked and soon to be married to Carole Lombard) select as partner either Harlow or Loy?

> . . . "Especially if that man is Clark Gable."

> A completely direct assertion that the man making the choice (about which the film plot spins on) is not some hitherto unnamed character but Gable himself. That is, a man we are to take as Gable, or a man whom we could take as Gable with complete appropriateness.

[6] Gable is embracing Loy, and speaks: "You know, someday they're gonna put us both in a wheelchair. And then, when my lumbago isn't bothering me, honey, look out!"

> The foretelling, again openly asserted in the Gable voice and from the Gable figure onscreen, that they (not only the characters but also Loy and he) will age, fall out of public favor (metaphorically be put in wheelchairs, or, indeed, together in *a* wheelchair). But even weakened, debilitated, severely afflicted (by his lumbago) this twinkling male archetype Gable will not shirk from giving the beautiful Loy a (playful? tender? erotic?) squeeze.

[7] Gable in a long-shot action with Harlow, teasing her, "Keeping true to me?" And this text boldly onscreen: "CLARK GABLE ROMANCING AND SKYLARKING WITH JEAN HARLOW"—

> The skylarking and romantic innuendo are stated in the scene clip, and so the textual out-spelling is part of a conventional identification pattern by which audiences were thought, stunned as they were taken to be, to require hand-holding through the movement of a story. (To "skylark" is to frolic.) But the

key to this little bit is that we are being told bluntly not that one character is romancing and skylarking with another but that Gable is doing so with Harlow. Is this a view into their private lives? Or a view into their "private lives" as configured and retained by the delighted viewer on the secret instigation of Hollywood publicity? Was he skylarking with her on set?

[8] Gable and Loy kiss:—"AND MYRNA LOY IN THE SPARKLING COMEDY DRAMA THAT DELIGHTED MILLIONS OF READERS OF COSMOPOLITAN MAGAZINE"

> This is a fabricated tale, originating in a popular woman's magazine presumably read by many who sit to view. Thus, an audience is conceived to be familiar already with the gist of the story and eager to see, not what happens but, Gable, Loy, and Harlow involving themselves in it.

A double voice, a double awareness, a double experience. The characters are falling into an imbroglio, and watching them squirm and strain will bring a kind of *Schadenfreude* to the viewer wishing, perhaps, to project herself in some real relationship of her own. The comedy drama lies in the proposition of the conflict and complication, and in its final resolution. But simultaneously, the actors have fallen into a situation where they must come into contact in intimate ways, and as these are attractive people believably engaged in love affairs (with such types as one another)—surely affairs of some kind since here they are—we can easily take the pictures and texts to be alleging secret liaisons, hidden from some judgmental public sitting on high elsewhere yet made available here, specially, to us.

Every syllable from Gable is his character's and his own, his own and his character's. And every syllable from Loy. And every syllable from Harlow. All speaking for unavailable strangers and speaking for the selves we have dedicated to them through the star process.

We know that the classical movie star was always available to the audience as construction, never wholly disappearing inside a character. But here one receives blunt evidence that the star needn't have even tried to vanish, that the star presence in tandem with the "official" guise of a character presence was the treasure the audience sought to find again and again in that dark room. Everyone in the theater knew about the actor/character formula, in other words, and everyone in the theater considered the character little more than a pretext permitting the licensed appearance of the performer-favorite, already cherished, already seen a thousand times, already and still the object of a profound hunger (since no completely satisfying picture was ever offered; and also since no picture at all can be completely satisfying).

But if film stories as they unfolded were being figured out by persons known as (albeit glamorous) working selves, every act of viewing the story film was at once a submission to the narrative and a fascination with the production, was both of these at the same time. Another way to say this: the audience saw and heard a communicated text about a dramatic tension posed and resolved but was understood as well to be swimming in the depths with a strange laboring substance never clearly explained, never accurately touched or weighed, and always elusive. As the black indeterminate shape says, floating up into the tower at the very end of *Vertigo* (1958), "I heard voices."

Is that a nun, by the way? The first we see, it is a dark ghost, a pure Being, and as we see no face when we hear the speech, the speech is a completely acousmatic thing, emanating from we-know-not-where. Or, if it is a nun, is she tied by bonds of love and fealty to the institution of the Church and its postulates, complaining here of having detected "the wrong" voices for a place like this. Another librarian. Another harbinger of social form, organization, control, primacy, dictation, and order. Or wait: she is born from Sister Clodagh in *Black Narcissus* (1947), a black flower herself facing black emptiness, almost thrown off the Himalayas at Rajput. "I heard voices." And the action now is very swift, horrifying, unshaped, and unstoppable, as our figures pull back from this Thing. "I heard voices," yes, past tense.

Voices from elsewhere, to be sure. From Beings of great magnitude, in far-off places, engaged as the gods would have been engaged in fights and squabbles, battles and blessings. Voices as we are catching them, strangely amplified, traveling from a galaxy far, far away. Bodies lit as though by angelic light. The boundaries of nature toed and crossed, flipped and stretched. Colors earthly and unearthly, earthly things with unearthly color. The world of human connection vital, instantaneous, feelingful, ambiguous, as sharply limned as it is blissfully vague.

Norman O. Brown: "Turning and turning in the animal belly, the mineral belly, the belly of time. To find the way out: the poem." But never to forget that before it found a way into cuneiform, onto parchment, onto paper, into a book, the poem always was what it always remains, a song.

Lost Voyagers

{1} Sidestepping

{2} Unforgettable

{3} Banquet

{4} Plastic Surgery

{5} Registrations

{6} Great Expectations

{7} Naming of Parts

{8} A Flicker

{9} Being Alive

{10} For Your Eyes Only

{11} Hands

{12} A Logical Gasp

{13} Vigil

{14} Privileged

{15} Ting-a-ling-a-ling

{16} Unheard Voices

{17} Remote Control

1

Sidestepping

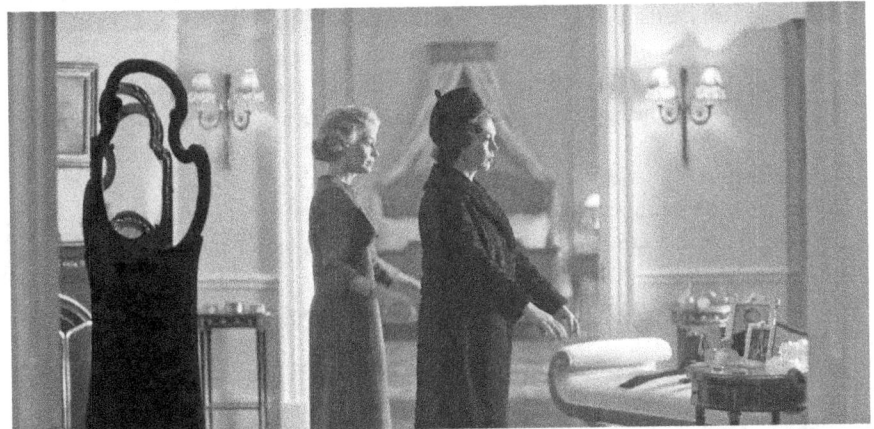

Olivia Colman (right) with Pippa Winslow in The Crown *(Left Bank/Sony, 2019). Digital frame enlargement.*

Midway through her début episode as the Queen of England in Season 3 of Netflix's *The Crown*, Olivia Colman makes an exquisitely tiny, summarily noteworthy gesture. The Queen is in the last moments of preparation before leaving the Palace for the funeral of Winston Churchill. We see her in a full-body medium-long shot, profile with face to screen right, as a dresser finishes helping her on with a stylish black overcoat. The Queen is gazing forward as into a mirror, and the dresser steps away. The royal arms are dropped to the side, but just before the shot concludes, Colman gives a tiny shake of the wrist and fingers, the sort of move that would settle the arms of the coat properly.

An eccentric little move. To note:

- The Queen of England wears new clothing that is expressly tailored for her. Very little that she puts on has been worn before, by her or by anyone. Nothing she puts on doesn't fit. She knows this. Therefore,

- With or without her little gesture, the Queen will be ready now to exit the Palace. The dramatic flow of the moment (get the Queen dressed; get her out of here) is neither interrupted nor embellished by the move.

- Colman is a much accomplished actor with legion screen credits of all kinds. She is not "nervous in front of the camera." (At least, here no more than ever.) The little gesture is in—not out of—character.

- Neither here nor in subsequent action of *The Crown* is the coat, or any other element of the royal costume, given dramatic prominence at all. There are no moments centering on this coat, beyond this one, and one could not even seriously claim this moment centers on it, either.[1]

- The Queen has not been discussing her outfit with anyone, and so we are given no dramatic hint that she is wondering whether this is the right coat, or whether she should wear a coat of this kind, or any such thing. She is merely being dressed in the coat, as a finale to a dressing ceremony. It has been decided she will wear it. She is wearing it, merely. She could be, this Queen, an actor getting into costume.

- Finally, aside from the dresser, who backs away graciously and who would not, in any event, make comment, there are no characters either present on the scene now or brought into the action subsequently to make reference to, or comment upon, the Queen's garb. Notwithstanding that, in reality, it would be a huge breach of protocol for anyone to make such comment; still, here in the composed drama no one does either.

What can we say is happening as Colman flicks her wrist? How may we regard this tiny moment? Unless we choose to look away, it will be there for us to see.

When I note that her gesture is the kind of tactic that would settle the arms inside the garment, especially, perhaps, settle the arms inside a new garment hitherto never worn (as we might expect this to be), I mean to indicate a functionality that is utterly common and utterly understandable, far outside the precincts of any palace. Anyone might put on a new shirt or coat and flick a wrist to settle its lining against the wrist. Thus:

[1] The gesture is not in itself regal, though here it is being exercised by a regal person. A regal person is performing an unregal gesture, but in her regal capacity. (I am addressing the Queen of England as configured; not Olivia Colman, who is not, I think, regal actually.)

[2] Moreover, the gesture is elemental as gestures go, involving the shape of the human body and the shape of the garments tailored to fit upon it: body and cloth. No such shaping can ever be presumed perfect, try as a royal tailor might.

[3] Here and more generally, this particular little gesture is given no articulate significance. Nobody intends to signal anything by doing it, only to make the self a little more comfortable and accustomed to the novelty of the coat. But, too,

---

[1] For a vivid contrast regarding royal clothing, see *Spencer* (2021).

in this increase of comfort nobody is trying to openly proclaim, "I am making myself more comfortable." It is taken generally as a given and unimportant matter that a person will try to make the self as comfortable as possible in circumstances. One will adjust the body into its circumstance: anyone, with any body, in any circumstance.

But:

Benjamin Caron, the director of the episode, and Peter Gordon, who wrote it, are both entirely aware that the shot in question will look as it does (they see it before we do) and in letting it run long enough to include this gesture, the editor Yan Miles is aware that he is giving us something to see. Briefly, then, the production *is* making something of this gesture even if "Her Majesty the Queen" is not, this picayune gesture that in everyday life nobody would turn into anything significant. This instant is *significantly insignificant.*

And so it seems reasonable to wonder what this cultured insignificance signifies? By "cultured" I do not mean that it was the producer, the director, the writer, or the editor creating it by intent, because my approach here takes the actor, Colman, to be responsible. Colman makes the judgment to execute this behavior or, indeed, permits herself an unjudged, unmonitored physicality. The director does not ask for the shot to be retaken without it; and the editor does not see a point in cutting the shot before this happens. What are we to make of this performance, then? Even more, what is this *kind* of performance, in which, with lightning speed, we cut beneath the façade of the character, Elizabeth II's queenliness, to something else. And what, indeed, is that something else? Sometimes even the tiniest flicker of light illuminates a landscape.

A very broad theme of the entire *Crown* series, an enigma and a supreme challenge, is here stated boldly, if in miniature:

- That the Queen's regality is separated from the everydayness of civilian life, say, British civilian life over which she rules and which is displayed to us orbiting around her all through every episode. This life, *as* life, is something she shares with other people to some degree because, after all, she lives inhabiting a body that takes its nourishment and breathes its air in London, as happens with millions of others. The Queen of England is an English woman. And, at least "now," a Londoner.

- That the Queen behaves according to duties associated with a role assigned through primogeniture. She does not invent the monarchy or its (many) restrictions.

- That the Queen feels obligations to her role and believes these obligations to supercede her personal desires, whatever they might be. She has personal desires, then, confessedly. While her humanity is the humanity we all share, still, her behavior onscreen—what she does and the context in which she does it—proclaims again and again, "I am not a person like all other persons." Meanwhile, circumstances in which we see her (especially when Claire Foy plays the role during Seasons 1 and 2) often call for a human, not a regal, response; for feeling that is simple and genuine; for the outplaying of touch and want. This distancing of person-ality from regal-ity is emphasized through the delicate and somewhat obtuse rituals imposed on those who meet her, their being forbidden to touch except in certain ways and only after she approaches, the language they must use—even such high-and-mighties as the Prime Minister and even, through tiny curtsies, the adored younger sister (Vanessa Kirby; Helena Bonham Carter).[2]

Put simply, as *The Crown* posits, the Queen is a role being performed: performed in a very extensive theater where the curtain can be up twenty-four hours a day and in all locations, and performed according to prearranged rules and proprieties all carefully designed, part of the inheritance of royalty. Further, as *The Crown* also carefully posits, the performer playing this role is a person, in this case "Elizabeth Windsor"—that is, the character "Elizabeth Windsor" not the real Elizabeth Windsor who in fact rules as I write and who does not necessarily watch this program—who was born one day, who grew up, who played as a child, who felt the weight of the crown tumble upon her when her dear father shockingly died.

In the program itself, this *performer* Elizabeth is given to us in three ways: first, the Stage and the Backstage Queens. We see a Backstage Queen, standing well away from the glare of publicity and the stares of the adoring public, a Queen in privacy, even behind the screen of the room in which she confers with her Prime Minister. A family Queen, a singular Queen, an embodied Queen, a Queen who gets the news, who can appreciate a joke, reflect upon a rumor, utter an opinion about people she has met—just as any of us might do in our own lives. She lives a life. The creators of the show take great care to balance moments in which the Backstage Queen is shown (revealed) against public theatricals in which the Stage Queen is on full view (live or through the media). They make sure that the Stage Queen gains sufficient prominence for us, that every instant of seeing the Backstage Queen is a special moment in the wings of the other show, a pleasant surprise, a pungent aroma of fact, because we are to know that the Stage Queen is the glory. Were the program to be balanced in the opposite way, it would become a soap opera.

However, there is also a Human Queen, surely backstage yet showing still another offstage aspect, and she is shown with the most singular rarity. Let us say, she is backstage of the backstage. We never see her at all during Season 1 or Season 2, not for an instant. All the private moments are clearly acted (by Foy) as instants in which the public front is being let down inside the bounds of a clearly demarcated (and, for some key advisors, enterable) private scene—such as a private aircraft with Philip or a

---

[2] I know this distancing intimately, having been asked once by a bobby (in 1972), while I stood on a paved street ready to cross it, to please, sir, stand back on the sidewalk (because, as he told me, standing on the road himself, no one [no uniformed one] may stand on the road when the Queen's car passes; and her car then did pass, with her inside it). Even when decades later I stood in a hotel lobby while François Mitterrand walked through it, I was required only to back away, not vacate the floor beneath us.

huge bed in her royal bedroom. In all of these momentary instants, the Queen is, and never stops being, the Queen in Private. One is never to forget who she is, who she *truly, deeply, really* is when she is not in public: never to forget that not in public she is still the Queen.

But in this little gesture by Colman, the first of its kind on *The Crown*, we meet that someone backstage of the Backstage Queen, the someone who had to think and imagine her way to becoming the Queen in the first place, who was going to be required to be both Queens, on the stage and off—in the end, two faces of the same coin—someone who *truly, deeply, really* is a woman who was a girl who grew up (too fast). A girl who lost her father and whose mother was somewhat distant. A girl who stands in the warm sunlight. A girl who, being helped (by anyone) into a new topcoat, would flick her wrists to settle the arms. However genius this acted moment is (on Colman's part and on the part of the others who did not disband or eliminate it), it does not promise, and surely does not attempt, to bring us to the Olivia Colman who is all the way beneath even that show. To the identity of that person (perhaps her closest friends know it) we are given no clues. We do not chance to meet her, though we may wish it. Even in "backstage" interviews as she chats about "playing the Queen," we do not meet Olivia Colman herself but only a staged "Backstage Olivia Colman" who gives interviews as arranged by publicity agents and as marshaled through the complex agencies of bureaucratic media outlets. In all of this, we do not "bump into Olivia in the street," as it were, where either she or we might indeed settle our arms inside our own clothing.[3]

Colman's onscreen gesture of giving us, briefly, the Human Queen: I think of it as a case of *sidestepping*. She moves away from both facets of her formal role, but in such a way that a return is entirely possible and entirely void of difficulty. A bizarre link: in baseball, a pitcher will sometimes, for a breather of whatever kind, step off the rubber for a second or two, breathe, reflect, then step back and line up for the pitch. The only rule is that he cannot do this after he has started to wind up: that is called a balk. But he *can* do a "sidestep" and would not be balking. Colman does a *sidestep* and avoids committing a balk: she does this by tacking the gesture onto the very end of the phrasing of her action at the instant, not inserting it inside as a misleading interruption or ornamentation, even for a breath.

There is another, quite delicious, feature of the Colman sidestep. For most viewers it leaves behind no trace. I rhapsodize about it here only because I am now, and have long been, obsessed by riddles of performance. This is the kind of thing that tickles my neurotic fascination. Anyone who just jumped into *The Crown* and became engaged with this Queen would probably have seen nothing particularly interesting. Here, then, is a statement of real significance that can be forgotten, elided, even erased by the viewer with no trouble. The performed instant thus speaks wholly of the actual moment in which, casually, we engage with a gesture presented before us. François Truffaut wrote in his *Journal of Fahrenheit 451* of a brief—but importantly dissimilar—

---

[3] On "performative layering," see Sobchack and Pomerance, *Depp*.

thing (on which I have commented elsewhere): that taking a break from shooting his film in England one day, and sitting at a Steenbeck to watch *Singin' in the Rain*, he was astounded at one instant (the Steenbeck permits frame-by-frame advancement) to see Debbie Reynolds, in the "Good Mornin'" number with Gene Kelly and Donald O'Connor, drop her hand to flick her skirt to cover her knee, out of what Truffaut smilingly calls *pudeur*. Here one might mistakenly think Kathy Selden is dropping out of Stage Persona (and dance beat) to show us the Kathy who walked into the soundstage (the film and the number are set at a movie studio), thus giving a clue of the Backstage Kathy. But she is not the one doing the dropping out, not Kathy. As Truffaut has seen, it is Reynolds who is doing the dropping out, the Reynolds behind Onstage Kathy and Backstage Kathy as well. In this moment of *Singin'*, then, we go past the performative world as depicted into a world beneath the performative world, this time *inadvertently* depicted. But *The Crown* does something else. Colman isn't showing us Colman—an actor unaccustomed to the costume the producer has arranged for her to wear, an actor beneath the television role, onstage and off. By the exact exquisite swift roundness of her manner, she is showing us the Queen.

It is not Colman who is making this gesture. It is the Queen of England.

(In short, the actor is here openly showing us a character, indeed a character with elevation, performing a perfunctory gesture in role.)

A very delicate analysis of techniques like the one I am calling the sidestep, but involving talk not physical action, is given by Erving Goffman in his analysis of *footings*, in *Forms of Talk* (1981). Curiously, the cultured person engages in changes of footing and in interpretations of other people's footing changes, ongoingly and in numerous different ways relating to momentary situational variables. But when we see acting onscreen, the change of "footing" which is implicit in, but not fully equivalent to, the sidestep tends not to gain much attention critically. It may be that support for Colman's gesture is given by the overall series theme I mentioned, the duplicity of the Queen's existence, and the creators' desire to stress it in several ways again and again. The sidestep might become paramount in such a case, whereas in other dramas, where such duplicity is not invoked (even if it could be), an actor could feel no motivation to make one.

As will be imagined easily, other cases of sidestepping in the same vein as the Colman example, yet more openly declarative, could be adduced. The typical Hollywood "backstage" musical form is full of opportunities for a visible and noteworthy sidestep, because not only are we given access to both the Stage Persona and the Backstage (or Offstage) Persona attached to the same body but we find ourselves, too, sometimes looking at a third Persona further interior, a human being who took up the trade of performing and gained a career and is now on show in this film: on "show," then, in the dressing room, then on show again. The muscular strain in play when a singer/dancer holds a finale pose (holds it in order to demonstrate that it belongs to a finale) can work as a sidestep when we see it, as with the upraised arms of Gene Kelly at the very finish of the "Broadway Rhythm" ballet in *Singin' in the Rain* (1952). Yet here, it is not Kelly whose musculature we discover but the "performer Don Lockwood" underneath the famous DON LOCKWOOD we have been following, in his onstage and in his offstage life. Kelly sidesteps more clearly, and very beautifully, with Mary Young in the "By Strauss" number of *An American in Paris* (1951). Sidestepping can be withheld boldly and dramatically, as when, in *Bringing Up Baby* (1938) Susan (Katharine Hepburn), while being harassed by the goofy, even half-demented David (Cary Grant), signally fails at any expression of annoyance or complaint, very private annoyance or complaint, giving just a quarter-breath pause that allows the annoyance to pass over to the viewer instead of him. This isn't Hepburn pausing, it is Susan; Hepburn herself doesn't sidestep, as far as I can recall, ever.

Many cases of sidestepping could be called "theatrical," appertaining to characterological personae who are defined as performers in the first place (the achievement of their depiction thus requiring a performance of performance). In *The Band Wagon*, take Tony Hunter, Onstage Tony for a relatively short time (for instance, "I Guess I'll Have to Change My Plan") while the Backstage Tony (Fred Astaire) is all over, rehearsing, sitting at a party, playing "theater," as in "That's Entertainment," musing as in "By Myself," and so on. But the Human Tony underneath these has a non-professional ego and a sense of dignity, not addressed in stage and backstage work, and his deep self emerges in sidestep when these other two are wounded, as in the Plaza Hotel room with Gabrielle Gerard (Cyd Charisse) as he stands surrounded by his Impressionist canvases in gilded frames. Because the musical form is generally more caricatured than so-called realistic drama (as in *The Crown*), sidestepping will perforce be comparatively extended and emphatic. And because of the need for polish, the person beneath the actor beneath the character will *not* be sidestepped to reveal a being resting beneath. What is surprising, even enlightening about theatrical sidestepping is that the deep performative self is almost never given to be encountered, some (albeit faked) everyday "real" of the superstar emerging (suddenly, and apparently without fakery) from someone especially known (and esteemed) for openly faking.

Again—to catch Debbie Reynolds, Truffaut had to sit at a machine where he could pause at a single frame.

To return briefly to the Colman sidestep: it has an ancillary effect of *almost but not quite* sliding away from role, and had it been extended (in the editing), we might have lost sight of both the Regal and the Backstage Queen, seeing all of the, in this case normative, surface as only sham. Colman's achievement is to retain fully a command of the Queen's separateness, elevation, and particularity, in all circumstances, while letting us have a soupçon of her—the Queen's, not the actor's—true embodiment. Absent such a soupçon, all the Queen's backstage moments, so vital to the drama, might read as sickeningly disingenuous.

2

Unforgettable

(Left) Charles Laughton in The Hunchback of Notre Dame *(William Dieterle, RKO, 1939); (Right) Marilyn Monroe in* Some Like It Hot *(Billy Wilder, Paramount, 1959). Digital frame enlargements.*

It is a truism that in the classical age the Hollywood star system operated in large part by marketing an individual's recognizable features to a hungry public. The star's name was itself constructed as a commercial glyph linked to the facial image (see in *A Star Is Born* [1954] the transformation of Esther Blodgett into Vicki Lester), intended to lure the attention of strangers and provoke the memory of previous satisfactory encounters with it, much as with the brand name of any commercial product. In *Negotiating Hollywood*, Danae Clark gives a meticulous analysis of the system and mechanism by which this "stardom" was achieved and perpetuated. Quoting Barry King's comment that actors could conduct themselves in public "as though there [was] an unmediated existential connection between their person and their image," she goes on to point to a career challenge handily met:

> While this strategy complied with the studio expectation that actors would develop "personalities" for purposes of public visibility, actors who initiated this process could claim some degree of control over the form their representation took. Similarly, actors attempted to control the details of their film performances in order to claim credit for their work. When successful, this strategy created the identity of a "good dramatic actor" as opposed to a "popular Warner Brothers [sic] star," thus allowing the actor (instead of the studio) to receive recognition for his or her own labor." (22)

The same mechanisms of extension, repetition, and prolongation that grounded the "star presence" in classical Hollywood, whether powered then by actors individually or by studios systematically or by both in interrelation, are in practice today, facilitated exponentially by promotional possibilities offered through the internet, streaming services, and so on. Presumably, we love *that face*. We love *looking at that face*. We love the very thought of being attracted to *that face*. And, equally, to the name (the word combo) attached to that face as represented in images. BAFTA eagerly Instagrams birthday portraits and huzzahs, Facebook celebrates the birthdays of stars no longer alive to have them, the media treats happenings involving stars as politically and economically important.

It was of course vital that in every new iteration of the classical star persona—virtually unimaginable now in the absence of studio-controlled portrait photography—a trail of earlier iterations be picked up or invoked, since the power of the star image, quite beyond its beauty and apparent "perfection," lay in the vibration of memory, in the fact that it called up the past.[1] Photographed in a new, and perhaps eccentric, role for advertising a picture, the star's embodiment had to call up similar embodiments in earlier roles, no matter how different they were. The twinkle in the eye, the cast of the head, the angle of the hair so tellingly lit, or, for off-camera poses, the style of clothing this person purportedly "likes to wear" beside the swimming pool all contributed, and to a marked degree such conventions persist. To boost his performance in *Joker* toward Oscardom, *Vanity Fair* published in November 2019 a full-color cover image of Joaquin Phoenix, clothed in an expensive white shirt and black necktie, standing wet in a turquoise swimming pool. The advertising image constitutes a performance in itself, a playing out to an eager spectatorship of a physical form determined by producers for economic gain. Garbo. Barrymore. Angelina Jolie. George Clooney. Elizabeth Taylor, Paul Newman, Ansel Elgort, Kristen Stewart. In *Vogue*, *Vanity Fair*, *GQ*; on TCM and CNN and "everywhere" else.

But alluring presentation and memorability are not sufficient to account for the star presentation. Also involved is something that works even on first exposure to prod the viewer's attention in a special, novel way: the look of the person, as given in visual exposures of whatever kind, is provocatively *abnormal*, the body or face separated out of the *boue* by artful exaggeration of some kind. Especially long hair, especially aquiline nose, especially wide temples, especial scarring or muscularity, ... There are many ways to accomplish this separation of the unique from the mass, and make-up artists, dressers, photographers, and directors are constantly at work practising them, to such a degree that the business of exaggeration becomes naturalized, unreflected in itself. Consider the extreme hairstyling of Sophia Loren or Farrah Fawcett, Julia Roberts or Kerry Washington; the extraordinary facial gauntness of John Carradine or Robert Pattinson; the hyper-pouty expressive lips of Joan Crawford or Timothée Chalamet; the broad, sailboat grin of Mickey Rooney or Michelle Yeoh or Cuba Gooding Jr.;

---

[1] Kenneth Boulding gives a rich examination of the relation between image and knowledge in his book *The Image*.

the enormous, wondering eyes of Marilyn Monroe or Johnny Depp; the telltale facial wrinkles of Kirk Douglas and Ian McKellen. These kinds of features are the same ones that could crop up in everyday life, as one met, and later remembered previous encounters with, friends and associates, but with the star construction in order to make for instant and profound appreciation the characteristics are carried further and given especially concentrated exposure. Since they are so easy to recognize, finally, stars are our friends; perhaps even more recognizable than our friends.[2]

If the star looked like "any other person," it would be difficult to establish a rationale whereby special attention, special reward, and special status could be explained. The star as a *figure* has to be the sort of being to gain a glimpse of whom people would flock from far and wide. A site of attraction on one hand, and a reason for attraction on the other, a sufficient reason for the viewer's turning away from the everyday world to considerations of extraordinary possibilities—possibilities so extraordinary that storylines by means of which the star's appearance can be coherently organized seem "naturally" worth special consideration and preeminent devotion of thought. In professional terms, the movie star would make a very bad spy, since in espionage being lost in the crowd is so vital. That on film spies are played by famous stars is both charming and ridiculous.[3]

In everyday discourse, we apprehend the balance of features on a person's face as a way of coming to "know" them, a mode of operation now systematized mechanically in "facial recognition software" yet always present in the brain's filtrations and selections.[4] It is not specifically the shape of the brow alone, for example, that we recognize, or the color or distance of the eyes, but the relationship between the eyes and the brow, the eyes and the nose, the nose and the mouth, any or all of these and any other combinations. The assemblage, as perceived and, on the basis of the perception, retained is "the face" as we know and recollect it.[5] Much of the world is perceived and recognized by virtue of such assemblies, even down to the window on one's computer, its proportions, and the colors and array of the desktop behind, all of which work to convince that this is my computer, my desktop, my point of contact. Perceiving assemblages does not by its nature lead to the concentration upon particular features that is present in encounters with the freakish, the special, the noteworthy. Like any person anywhere, the star has eyes and a nose and a brow and a mouth, etc., and taken together they do form an assembly, yet it is not the assembly *as assembly* that is noticed or stored in memory in star discourse: it is particular and idiosyncratic individual

---

[2] In *Charade* (1963), Audrey Hepburn's character asks Cary Grant's, noting his dimpled chin, "How do you shave in there?"

[3] Martin Ritt's *The Spy Who Came In from the Cold* (1965) was designed for a "realistic" approach to espionage. It is salutary to inspect the makeup (or lack of it), costume carriage, and lighting in this film with the same in Joseph L. Mankiewicz's *Cleopatra* (1964) to gain insight into the laborious transformation of the glowing, celebrated Richard Burton into Leamas, a deplorable and shabby figure whose life was led in the shade.

[4] And not only in human brains. Barbara Clucas has studied crows' ability at the same type of recognition.

[5] Deficits and inabilities can inhibit recognition. Oliver Sacks writes about FRA (facial recognition aphasia). See my *The Film Cheat*, chapter 1.

features standing out from the ground of the assembly and associated with published promises of pleasure. In our selecting or noticing particularities, in our regarding their exaggeration and exaggerating them further through attentiveness, and in our cultivation of affection for or against them and the pleasures they have been connected with in the past, as far as we remember, the individuality of the star is conjured. This conjuring could vary generation to generation: for movie fans of the 1930s Lucille Ball was a pair of elegant legs; for fans of *I Love Lucy* (1951) she was a mouth. Through idiosyncrasies the star can be successfully represented in cartoon (represented so as to be instantaneously recognizable—the cartoonist-epitome is Al Hirschfeld [1903-2003]), and through idiosyncrasies the star exists and perdures, aging be damned. The star is not only discernable and memorable, recognizable on the spot, but also in a particular way sweet: a taste, recollection, and promise of candy.

By a system of aesthetic organization predominantly under the aegis of publicity agents and operatives, the notable feature of the star's presentation is made a principal under which other features of the embodiment are subsumed and regulated. The broad shoulders of Rock Hudson do not compete with the sterling squareness of the jawline and the rocky, yet polished surface of the jaw and cheeks that identify him. We see the shoulders but we relegate them to subservient status. Marilyn Monroe, as an image, may call up for many observers emphatic and elegantly shaped breasts, but her breasts were always regulated under the aegis of her lips, even beneath the gaze in her eyes. The lips dictated to the eyes, and the eyes dictated to the body as a whole. Watching her one held oneself in anticipation at every moment, as though out of this mouth some astounding (perhaps ironical) philosophical insight was about to flow. Scarlett Johannson is formed as a star image through a similar pronunciation of the lips, more generally the mouth, but her body is trimmed and her eyes retreat rather than moving forward. She definitively sees, but does not look, and so in publicity photographs we find an expressive mouth reacting to something she apparently notices by gazing outward at us; we can find this in *Lost in Translation* (2003), again in *Vicky Cristina Barcelona* (2008), again in *Under the Skin* (2013). By contrast, Timothée Chalamet has brilliant and lambent eyes, always lit to emphasize the brilliant, optimistic lambency, yet he does not appear to see; he opens himself to being seen. However expressive he makes it, his mouth is entirely subservient to his eyes, even to his prominent, very finely sculpted nose. The receptive eyes dominate his star presence.

With any of these descriptions, admittedly overly shallow here, one would have to go further in carefully detailing shapes, nuances, tendencies, implications, associations, and formal properties. That the Johannson mouth, perhaps oddly, seems dry when we look at the lips. Whereas the Monroe mouth does not. That the Hudson eyes, articulate as they must be, seem not to be there in light of the torso. That the Chalamet torso seems subsumed by the hunger of the eyes. These attitudes and qualities are all parts of constructions, not inherent features of actual people in their privacies, to which we have no access. Lighting does a lot to help achieve such construction, as does camera angle, in combination with the scripted moment as performed and the fullness of the form as shown in the shot composition. Once we have a young man who appears eager to be seen, he can play a significant role in one film after another in which his character is eagerly seen, or else is hiding from being seen. Once we have an attractive blonde whose lips appear always to be whispering, we can configure a drama in which her character (say Sugar Kane in *Some Like It Hot* [1959]) whispers confidences and desires. Just as the feature makes possible the fictionalization, the fictionalization helps lead us, seekers all, to isolate, frame, and mentally organize features. For the system of construction and recognition, the outside container is a myth packaged and sold widely in the culture that stipulates the star face and personality are necessary guideposts by which one navigates the cruelly deceptive pathways of life. "Who is your favorite movie star?" is a question that is presumed always to be answerable.[6]

Could it not be considered, then, that his Quasimodo in William Dieterle's *The Hunchback of Notre Dame* (1939) is not only a key figure in the parade of Charles Laughton's (1899–1962) stardom but also a signal model of stardom itself? What is Quasimodo most deeply but a collection of astounding deformities packaged in one supplicating, accepting, humble soul?

> Something in the part and the project drew him hypnotically towards the pain it contained. This was over and above the pain of Quasimodo's predicament, his sense of ugliness, his sense of rejection, his physical suffering. It was all of these, with which Laughton could of course so readily identify—but it was something more: some kind of world-pain, world suffering that was sucking his soul out of him. He was not conscious of political events, but even he was aware of the impending conflagration. His memories of Flanders, 1919 were still vivid and frightening, and informed the emotional state that was welling up inside him. (Callow)[7]

That huge lump between Quasimodo's shoulder blades: it is hidden so very frequently as the bell ringer moves around, not only because he knows it to be shameful but also because he feels—and the performer recognizes—it is not the signal regulating feature of his being. That regulating feature is the misshapen cheek and corresponding misaligned eye, the twisted face as it were—for Simon Callow "that famous mask of mangled features"—that he cannot successfully tuck away and that proclaim his noteworthiness wherever he goes. He cannot but be attractive, even seductive to apprehension. We cannot forget that face, even long after seeing it, and even if, in remembering, we twist and stretch it even further than the make-up artists did with Laughton on the set. He speaks, but the voice is forgettable—in a way that, for example, with Roger Livesey, an affable-looking man whose face is more likely to be forgotten, the soft raspy voice is very distinctly not. And since his voice is forgotten so is what Quasimodo said. But the desperate look in that misplaced eye! That beckoning: "Do not see me only as this figure. Do not reduce me to this eye!" In advertising, the eye, the cheek, and the hunchback can all be either emphasized (advertising in 1939 was by way of artist's cartoon rendition, if visual at all) or de-emphasized in order that the

---

[6] It is fascinating to see self-taught cinematographers making Instagram flicks pick up the "right" angles for candid shots of stars "out in public."
[7] Laughton was gassed in the First World War.

experience of watching the film could be made surprising.[8] But in performance the eye remained central to the configuration, and the actor knew that above all concerns was his flexibility in controlling that eye and manipulating it expressively.

If we can gain some appreciation of Quasimodo as a recursive reference to "the movie star" epitomized, we can open a door to understanding how, since the Victor Hugo novel was perfectly composed and richly consumed in its own right, a particular, additive consideration could be made in converting the story for the screen. The film is not only a way of bringing the Hugo work to a wide (and perhaps even comparatively illiterate) audience, a democratizing, but also a way of subtly reflecting upon itself, suggesting to audiences eager for belief what it is that they are eager to believe in and, indeed, what their eagerness is. Dieterle's film is full of audiences in its own right, multitudes raptly attending to this "star" and his various moves, surveillers considering his moral status with readiness to act upon him (just as, in the 1930s and still today, crowds are eager to take action upon the stars they adulate). The film is both a tale of Paris and one of its denizens and an accounting of his fate, but equally an announcement of what is happening as audiences flock to see notable figures on the screen. The screen becomes the public square or the cathedral within it. The plot the wheel.

"Quasimodo, the object of the tumult, stood in the doorway of the chapel, gloomy and grave, letting himself be admired," Hugo writes (68). The doorway of the chapel; the framed limit of the image. Gloomy and grave: the actor's offered rationale for standing perfectly still and permitting close focus.

The selection of a pope is in progress:

> A mob comes together, as here for instance, then each in his turn goes and puts his head through a hole and makes faces at the others; he who makes the ugliest face according to general acclamation, is chosen pope. That's our way, and it's very diverting. . . . The grimaces commenced. The first face that appeared at the hole, with eyelids turned up to show the red, cavernous mouth, and a forehead wrinkled like our hussar boots in the time of the Empire, excited such an inextinguishable burst of laughter that Homer would have taken all those boors for gods. . . . When this sort of cyclop appeared on the threshold of the chapel, motionless, squat, almost as broad as he was high—"squared by the base," as a great man has expressed it—the populace recognized him at once by his coat half red and half violet, figured over with little silver bells, and still more by the *perfection* of his ugliness—and exclaimed with one voice: "It's Quasimodo the bell-ringer! It's Quasimodo the hunchback of Notre Dame! Quasimodo the one-eyed! Quasimodo the bandy-legged! Hooray! Hooray!" (61, 62, 67; emphasis added)

Note the artful circumlocution and reticence of the authorial gaze, both dictating and leading a circumlocution and reticence in the reader's *jouissance*, "the perfection of

---

[8] Many of the artist renditions had the character in silhouette, many in semi-profile to emphasize the hunchback and to align the vision of it with the word "hunchback" in the title; thus, the warped face was reserved as a special pleasure for paying viewers of the film.

his ugliness" being given as a phrase without accompaniment by a detailing rationale; "the bell-ringer . . . the hunchback," as occupations and epithets, but not visions; the "little silver bells," a gorgeous poetic substitution of a tinkling (charming) sound that announces a hideous—though for this crowd already customary—figuration.[9]

When the star persona is powerfully configured as a vision, it is unnecessary that the star in role should utter pregnant dialogue, most especially in portrait close-ups where the features of the form are on carefully modulated display. In fact, for the star's career to profit, and for the box office to sumptuously recompense the producer for a given film, it is preferable either that memorable dialogue should be elided or minimized or else that scenes of memorable dialogue should be balanced against other scenes of pure pictorial expression. It must finally be what the star looks like, not what the star said, that clings to memory. If Humphrey Bogart standing on the tarmac with Ingrid Bergman and saying, "Here's looking at you, kid," is a case where the tone, the fluency, the timbre, and the softness of an expression combine for an undying echo, still Bogart's tenderly smiling eyes in his half-lit face will anchor this voice to metaphysical bedrock. The Bogart eyes, the thick Bogart lips, the stolid peacefulness of the head position all configure Bogie regally, and the voice falls in line, obediently, beneath the distinctive tonality that emerges, that must emerge, from *this* form: from a form like *this*.

---

[9] To be noted: even for Hugo in the beginning, Quasimodo rang bells in two resonant ways, one through his occupational link to the bells of Notre Dame and one through the little bells that tinkled wherever he went, like tiny mockeries.

3

Banquet

Miles Malleson (left) and Conrad Veidt in The Thief of Bagdad *(Michael Powell and Emeric Pressburger, The Archers, 1940). Digital frame enlargement.*

To have the dream of being invited to glory: sit calmly at a long, even horizonless table polished to shine like a precious stone, set with flowers in tufts tall enough to reach Jack's giant. Spy silverware manifold and shimmering in candlelight. Note the magnificent plates, embellished with gold filigree, painted over with hares and huntsmen, coats of arms and seafaring ships, forestial glades and sumptuous fruits. Watch the footmen in livery (scarlet livery!, apple green livery!) bend gracefully past one's shoulder to lay down roasts and stews, soups and puddings, cheese and bottomless goblets of wine.

To linger and be served.

Yet how very disenchanting all this could be, the more conscious one became of the boundless labor behind its production and the devious turnings by which that labor had been hidden; the more one could detect the elaborate devotion of care and attention through which a feast is arranged, just so that appetites may be served this way. To be conscious, indeed, even at the instant of being served, as the arm of the footman stretches over one's shoulder with a crystal goblet of stewed apricots! To see the food and the sweaty kitchen labor—in one cubist view. And then also, to be conscious of having this consciousness blurred by a veil that has been guilefully superimposed.[1]

Cinema is a banquet. Whoever be the folk one sits with "to table," they are presumably of like social status, brought together (with you) only because they have been summoned (lured) to this event, only because some force behind the event has drawn them in by operating as though, of all creatures, they—and only they, since every audience imagines itself original—would be especially responsive to an invitation. While viewers may find enjoyment in one another's presence, *mutual* enjoyment is not the purpose of the gathering, so that its absence causes no blot. It is the array that is to be enjoyed above all, the array only; the muttering unknowns sitting all around constitute only a feature that by its inclusion explains the elaborateness and extent of the arrangements evident onscreen, the investment of wealth and thus the supreme availability of resources, the magnitude of the frame (the gilded frame) in which splendor is held and offered as sacrifice.

To be brought, in effect, the gifts of the Magi: a show of capacity; an encounter with touching strangeness; a regard directed by lighting *from above*; a music of perfectly timed strokes, humorous or disarming or placid but always incessantly sung. So exquisitely marvelous are cinema's designs, performances, visions, implications, and rhythms, so stirring and so renovating, that in absorbing them all one would have an impossible challenge either in believing them the results of careful preparations, *arrangements*; or else, anything *but* arranged. Both sides now. Recall the Dutch floral still lifes of the sixteenth and seventeenth centuries, the Huysums, the Bosschaerts, the de Heems and company, every collection modulated by the highest principles of Matthew Arnold's "sweetness and light" to show each petal, each insect wing, each bead of light in the glass vase set with unwavering sureness into a picture of truth. Cinema cannot but overwhelm in this way. When I first saw it, I could not have been more than three or four years old, sitting close by and gazing uncomprehendingly up at a gigantic silvery space, flooding over with blacks and grays and whites and blazing opalescence and sheen, faces, faces coming close, enormous faces, the faces of giants: sheen and opalescence.

To be in a theater and engage with acting on a stage is a very different matter indeed. There is an electricity in the air, metered by the pattern of actors' living breath. There are lungs working to project speech, one can see or feel the breathing. The settings are entirely false, speaking out not only this hollowness of verisimilitude but also the emphatic importance of the beings circulating before them so nobly. The postures, the pauses for audience laughter, giveaways that the actors know we are there and want to touch us with their concern. The mounting thrill with each phrase and each flare of an arm. In the theater one senses an event happening *now*, now and only now, here and

---

[1] See on this camouflage, Orwell, *Down*.

only here. Benjamin's use of the word "aura" only vaguely approximates the experience one has taking it all in, with the high and godly proscenium, the velvet curtain drawn away, the phrased lighting, the graceful bodies not as models of the body but as, and only as, bodies. On Broadway in 1984, performing Tom Stoppard's *The Real Thing*, the body of Jeremy Irons embracing the body of Glenn Close, embracing, touching, except that she is very very tiny and he is immensely tall, so that an irony [sic] was produced, like static, with even just the connection between them together, at once, at the same moment, face looking up or down at glowing face. Onscreen in 1990 as Sunny and Claus von Bulow in Barbet Schroeder's *Reversal of Fortune*, these two give an entirely different taste, a more cultivated taste simply in the sense that one can sense it as prepared for delivery. Onstage with actors the only preparation for delivery that one senses—that one can sense—is the preparation taking place onstage in front of you just now, just as the lips part. However much rehearsal there has been, still for each syllable and each gesture preparation is needed, an upbeat before the downbeat. In cinema there are no upbeats.

But in place of upbeats there is a flow of splendor.

The splendid flow, concocted for us, readied for us, delivered to us, as though it is proper that we should be at this banquet:

> Before he could finish, the cock was brought, and Trimalchio ordered it stewed in wine. Daedalus, that same expert cook who had made fish and birds out of pork a little while ago, hacked up the cock and tossed the pieces into a pot. While he drained off the boiling broth, Fortunata ground pepper in a little boxwood mill.
>
> When we had consumed this tasty dish, Trimalchio took a look at the contingent of slaves around us. "Huh? You still haven't eaten? Get out, and let the others do their shift." (Petronius 57)

As though we should be served, by the anonymous.

While in a certain abstract point of view all film partakes of the form of Film, just as every banquet is The Banquet, and while a myriad films exhibit incalculable variety and richness, eliciting a wide range of responses and thoughts, still, no matter the film, there are certain qualities of expectation, certain attitudes the viewer will bring:

[1] An open and even insatiable readiness to be, as the French say, *bouleversé*. This is perhaps especially true—but certainly very notably true—with contemporary Marvel action films and their relatively young audiences. Rather than taking a preparatory breath, one plunges headlong into conviction that the film will fill one with "pure air," will pronounce a kind of sweeping movement that catches all anticipation by surprise, will offer promise, the hyperbolic expectation that everything one is about to see will be magnificent. (Magnificent if only in being incomparable to so-named wonders that can have been seen onscreen in ages before: Von Trier's *Dogville* [2003] or Kaufman's *Schenectady, New York* [2008] or even Ang Lee's *Hulk* [2003]).

[2] Expectation of relocation. The cinematographic realism of setting gives at least a pictorial sense of traveling, of being in places one did not know, regardless of whether they are densely pictorial and amber-hued (Istanbul's Basilica Cistern in *From Russia with Love* [1963]) or matter-of-factly smudgy with reality (London by night in *Night and the City* [1950]). Places *far from here*. In stage work one never leaves the location of the theater except by virtue of a will to believe, which is always accompanied by our cognizance of it. Film takes us off, reveals vistas and corners, elevations and extensions. Though we may know very well how true this is in general we are never fully set for the startling view that suddenly flashes. To remain where the breathing actors are: this is a fundamental desire in theater. To get out of here: that is cinema.

[3] Attunement to a vision composed as an array, whether colored or on a gray scale: elements that are saturated, mixed, conjoined, and abutted in unanticipated and unanticipable ways, an effect very similar to what is achieved in painting. The cinema being painterly in this respect, one feels the eyes *being opened anew*. Special (because unfamiliar or unrequested) perspectives, outlandish speeds of travel.

[4] Readiness to encounter strangers. Whether they are noble or base, innocent or venal, gorgeous or hideous, modern or dated, and of any and all complexions and purported backgrounds, we will meet persons we did not know before (even in films that are sequels of other films in which the same characters played), persons who model unkenned relationships in odd and characteristic ways (odd so as to lure and characteristic so as not to constitute the strangeness we would find in the street). To meet "other people" is to confront the limits of one's own humanity and one's own experience; to see the boundary of a self and the chasm between selves; to both identify and be alienated in finding a creature who is "similar to me" in this way but not in that. A conspecific bond that goes only so far. We shift between sensing solitude and sensing the crowd. We witness talents and inventiveness as well as crippling incapacity. We are as though tiny children again, brought into confrontation (and, though we may not yet recognize, alignment) with so many "goodly creatures" we did not know, all of them swirling around in a "brave new world."

[5] Interest in, and patience for, a new kind of time, that can proceed in many different directions and that can unfold by slow measures, by skipping, by retreating, by moving into and out of transitional phases like memories and warped memories. Space can be traversed at lightning speed. The clock can stand still figuratively (*Groundhog Day* [1993]) or perceptually (*Stairway to Heaven* [1946]). One begins to see how Tenniel's illustrations of the timepiece for *Alice in Wonderland*, with a rabbit in a waistcoat holding it in his hand querulously, and, derived from them perhaps, Dalí's melting clocks are all, in their plasticity, accurate representations—like untouched photographs—

of cinematic time. Much scholarship on cinematic time, such as Mary Ann Doane's brilliant *The Emergence of Cinematic Time*, tends to elide the spectatorial challenge taken at its broadest and most extreme, the widely experienced anticipation that in going to the cinema we will be entering a veritable time machine.[2]

[6] Sharpening of the senses for detection, at least since the development of a strictly narrative cinema after, say, 1911 and progressively more so ever since. Not only the direction and divagations of the story but also the secrets hiding beneath the cultivated surfaces we see. In the classical era, characters often looked like the types they turned out to be (this originating in the "types" of stage melodrama) but in noir and later film ironic contradictions came to be normalized, to such a degree finally that it became impossible to know the moral status of anyone onscreen, regardless of their attractiveness. Indeed, the attraction of the screen personality is more and more frequently now posed as a mask, albeit a fulfilling one for the audience. The viewer engages with filmic narrative by attempting to move past its surface, either in a quest to decode moral messages or in a quest to find the terra firma under the character glitz. When moral evaluation becomes so complicated as to disempower the viewer, the grounding sought is that of the actor beneath, slippery though it be.

[7] Employment of an empowered gaze—far more special and amazing than the mere power to use the eyes—from a masked situation of privacy for spying on, ascertaining, bounding, measuring, evaluating, and finally controlling the world. That gaze, call it *the direct gaze*, is surely something we come to terms with, but then finally stop noticing. It is not that we lose the ability to be self-conscious or self-critical, but that in its manifestly offering so much to look at, and avowedly so, cinema elicits the gaze, and we offer it, in mere response, as though in a nervous arc. But the empowered gaze is provided by the speciality of the camera mechanism principally (and aided in editing): we can glide, we can pop, we can zoom in or out, we can entertain not only close-ups but macro-close-ups, becoming quasi-scientific in our study of action. Going to the cinema implies picking up new eyes, then. And even more, having the ability and the opportunity to see what—or analogies to what—would surely be forbidden in everyday life.[3]

---

[2] Doane very interestingly theorizes the cut as an indication that we are not in the fluid pre-edited time of the "autonomous, unfolding scene"; and goes so far as to suggest that editing creates a "Freudian time machine" "repudiating the role of cinema as a record of a time outside itself" (224). The implication, I think, is that cinema itself, the illumination upon the screen, is not a time machine already.

[3] In the early 1980s, Philip Morrison challenged our preconceptions of "natural" size in a brilliant book called *Powers of Ten*, but this book stimulated reflection in significant part because it was a book, an object that already participated in a broad (educational) discourse about text and the meaning of reading. We see cinema more playfully. Charles and Ray Eames' *Powers of Ten* (1977), the film that preceded the book, offered a rush instead of reflection.

[8] Willingness to engage in a moral moratorium, a kind of holiday from convention and expectation, from permission and denial, from enrichment and debasement, this at least while we are looking, because in the looking is a moving action of commitment and delirium. Later, thinking back (we like to say "looking back" but of course we cannot look back), we can with great facility pick up our moral lives again, become judgmental, even close the door. But watching is something else again.

[9] Mental flexibility with pictorial flexibility, since the screen frame in which one's visual target is held has been extremely magnified (all through the classical era, from the Academy-ratio films of the 1930s and 1940s through to widescreen in the 1950s and onward [see Pomerance, *Eyes* 113–14]) or else (after the beginning of the twenty-first century) radically contracted: the immense screen with figurations so much larger than human scale occupying a spatial world the magnitude of which is almost impossible to determine from shot to shot; and then the tiny handheld device with the downloaded picture so tiny it is as though one has traveled to a theater in Lilliput where all the characters one watches are no larger than insects.[4] What one knows in advance of all the films to be seen is that the proportions of everyday life will be set aside, or abandoned, in the seeing. Cinema thus teaches us subtly to regard the proportions of everyday life without conviction.

[10] Comfort with, acceptance of, distance. It is always the case that the creatures of the screen are held at a reserve from us, that we do not and cannot meet and know them in the way that we meet and know people around us, although at the same time they are capable of sharply *resembling* people around us. An effect of this is that in watching we learn to be at ease with a particular form of recognition that is activated in the absence of knowledge. Seeing what we can name, we can be deluded into thinking that because of a resemblance to what we have already catalogued this sight is understood or understandable. This all without our being given real access, real touch. If it is true, as Ortega claims for mankind it long was, that we recognize as *real* only things that offer resistance to the hand, nothing in cinema is real. But to grasp the pungency of the cinematic moment: unreal as it is, everything on the screen seems real as we watch it, because we have the sense that we *are* touching by way of the eye. The eye as hand.

[11] Above all, a feeling of safety before relaxing surveillance on the surround and allowing oneself to dive into engagement. This means the film will be taken as no direct threat to the spectator's life, health, or constitution, notwithstanding

---

[4] For a challenging foretaste, long before technology made this possible for the everyday viewer, see the scene in Powell and Pressburger's *The Thief of Bagdad* (1940) in which the Sultan of Basra (Miles Malleson) gleefully shows off his collection of toys, the acme of which is his tiny theater in which a team of miniature acrobats perform. The image at the head of this chapter shows it in part.

that images become ideas and ideas can have influence. The viewer will be in a position to think and evaluate afterward, she knows, but she will not be thrown into existential panic by the film, no matter its aggressiveness or violence.[5] Nor will the film experience lay any obligations on the viewer for future action, any demands for further participation. Sometimes further participation is possible (licensed marketing) but one need never engage. Ideally, all of one's attention goes to the screen when it is lit, and no attention is called for when the film is over. Called for. Required. Obliged. The film is a gift, once and for all. Given, handed over, made available, opened up, released for an audience that does not know the depths of its own hunger.

[12] And then, secret but supreme, a sense of the self as both virginal and prehistorical. Everything that affects me in this film does so because I have never been affected in this way before. I am untouched and pure, I have been waiting for contact but I have not learned how to find it except in facing such a brilliant panorama as this. Every contact both eludes and overwhelms me. I am turned over, and my upending completely monopolizes my concentration. Also, no one I need attend to has ever been here before, my sigh of pleasure makes the first indentation in the snow. I see this as no one has seen it, as no one could possibly have seen it, because it is to me, for me, of me, and in terms of me. It is my vision, my experience. (Box-office figures be damned.)

---

[5] Broad-based moral panics have led more and more to admonitions about violence and sexuality now appearing on the screen, but these are intended for an exclusive segment of the audience already roused (by what Becker calls *moral entrepreneurship*) to an antipathy for exactly such effects; moral panic emerges from a kind of perception by preconstituted group. There apparently being no preconstituted "groups" averse *in principle* to seeing, for example, aerial shots of cities, we do not find the phrase "aerial photography" included in the warnings producers affix to advertisements, but moral entrepreneurs could conceivably change things.

4

Plastic Surgery

For Samson and Delilah *(Cecil B. DeMille, Paramount, 1949): (left) contemporary newspaper ad (note the emphatic chin); (center) contemporary theater poster (note Samson's tightly drawn mouth); (right) set still with Victor Mature.*

We are living today, to speak of motion pictures, in what might be termed a "post-surgical" universe. Surgery, as I invoke it here, refers to a transformation of the body—often the corpse generally or only the torso but most particularly the face—that makes screen images of it look both vaguely similar to and discernably different from the picturing in the advertisements that came before. Between the reality on set and the artist's realization in making the ad, a "surgery" is performed (which, textually and graphically, must always suit the context in which it will be found). Between the advertising poster in the newspaper or magazine, or the advertising billboard outside the theater, and the image inside on the screen, a surgery is performed, too. A plastic surgery, not only in the sense that facial features are reshaped and realigned but also in the sense that operation is made upon a real substance that exists for us in plasticity, derived through the plasma of the image and its construction. When I say we live today in a "post-surgical" world, I mean to point to the fact that because advertising and discussion of films proceed with excerpted *actual* film clips (or, only rarely now, stills), no plastic rendering is performed except in the case of comic cartooning (for instance, certain posterizations for *The Long Goodbye* [1973]). The face one sees in the hype and the face one sees on the screen have become one and the same face, the package accurately representing the contents, although which is the package and which the contents, promo or picture, is often up in the air. Compare two comparisons: Katharine Hepburn's look in *Sylvia Scarlett* (1935), posterized and filmed; and Rosamund Pike's in *Gone Girl* (2014).

The "surgery" is very apparent in regards to Cecil B. DeMille's *Samson and Delilah* (1949). At the time this film came out, in moving—both physically and mentally—from the film as experienced by viewers to the commercial representation of the work, that is, to an artist's rendition of a persona of the filmed person, a transposition was required and easily (even unconsciously) made. It is necessary to acknowledge the difference between two forms, their basic lack of resemblance. But it is also necessary to accept as hypothesis that one image is intended to be a *representation of* the other, the poster or ad as stand-in for the filmic moment. Artists had technical limits to work with, and thus had to transpose from the camera's imagery. But the viewer was then also required to transpose, seeing and later remembering the film while noting posters and ads that didn't quite represent it faithfully. Making such a transposition when or after one saw a film was an invisible and uninvoked element in the filmgoing experience through at least the end of the 1980s, even later. The viewer knew that she would be seeing figures in a picture after moving through a lobby crammed with advertisements, lobby cards, sometimes merchandise. More recently, viewers know they will see films after seeing television ads, or internet trailer releases now accessible through Instagram in the palm of the hand. This transposition differs from what is required in relating Cézanne's pictures of apples and oranges to actual apples and oranges in a bowl on one's table. The painter is always bounded by limits of his art, and his genius is in contriving within those limits and even revealing them: how far can representative urgency go? In films, verisimilitude is not the same kind of problem. The camera lens can obtain an image that seems to bear acute verisimilitude to real objects without showing their reality as we would see it off the screen. Yet in the classical era, the advertiser had to work without the filmmaker's lens entirely at his disposal. Film advertising required graphic artists then, and the graphic artist's picture came from the hand.

When audiences flocked to see *Samson and Delilah*, they had been lured to leave home and parade to the theater by advertisements in local newspapers. It was the newspaper that linked expectation to film experience. Only much later did audiences gain the habit of leaving work and heading directly to the theater, so that for the most part, in 1949, the movies were an entertainment for which people *left home*. A fundamental division between the home and the world.[1] These ads were printed in black-and-white half-tone, designed by artists skilled at representing the human body and thus experienced in working with models or photographs. It would have been conceivable for the film's star Victor Mature to have posed at the studio for artists, yet even though it would have been the studio's own art department responsible for advertising images the artisans there could have used any suitably muscular male, and a paid model would have cost the production considerably less than Mature. There

---

[1] On which, see Gunning.

would have been plenty of facial portraits of him in the studio files, for the purpose of copying. Beyond its (obvious) mixture of graphic and textual elements (in effect, without text the piece is not an ad), the graphic was quite normal in consisting of a meld of scenic moments arranged together artfully inside a vertical rectangle, all these positioned around, and in relation to, a single overriding heroic image, in this case the figure of Samson holding the pillars of the temple with his bare hands. A moment like this would be selected for being highly dramatic, graphically powerful, diegetically telltale, and susceptible to illustration. It would not have been the only such moment possible; nor would any one poster have necessarily been the only advertising choice, since press kits were routinely filled with a variety of select ads featuring different drawings or drawings aligned with other graphics and with text in different ways so that the newspaper's layout staff had a freedom of choice.

Making any and all of these drawings or paintings, artists and managers were aware that they would be the sorts of tease that would helpfully lure a viewer ensconced in the cozy safety of the home, a signal requirement if the picture was to have success. This thing we are picturing—of which you are getting no more than an intimation here—is inestimably superior to this piece of newsprint on which you see it pictured.

The lure of the advertisement owed something to the frame structure of advertising in general, the tendency of all ads everywhere to convey as a basic message that here—"here": that is, in a space presently unavailable but "nearby"—was a product put up intentionally for sale and especially worth acquiring. Acquisition was the mode, until the consumerist decade of the 1950s arrived and using things became as important, or more important, than getting them. The piety of use inculcated two values: the product was expended and required replacement, so that every use became a prelude to a purchase; and use taught desire for action, provoked hunger for taste, in that for the acquired object the thrill of delicious utility became greater than the thrill of buying and owning. *See this film*, then; *register having seen it*; and *see films again*. In the typical movie advertisement, the attraction came from the graphic alignment of the central body (or bodies) in the picture, the little story their postures instantly told there and then about the kind of dramatic action viewers would find in the filmed story if they took the step of acquiring a ticket for it. Here is Mary Beth Haralovich on this representational trick:

> Poster art was crucial to ad campaigns, and in fact newspaper advertising based on posters was a primary use (if not *the* use) of pressbook materials. Pressbooks offered posters in a range of sizes: the familiar one-sheet, larger three- and six-sheets, a gargantuan twenty-four-sheet. Also, variations on the posters were offered in the form of lobby cards, slides, mats in various sizes, and more. Poster ads transmitted the essential attributes of the film, generating viewer expectations.... Posters identified the genre of the film and placed its stars/characters at a point of narrative suspense. Poster graphics often linked head shots of stars/characters to each other *and to a central narrative enigma through glances and tag lines.* (196–7; my emphasis)

Outside the theater itself, and confronting prospective viewers in moderate proportions or blown up to gigantic size and mounted over the marquee, would be a colored poster image, sometimes an oversized cardboard cut-out, showing a similarly plastic and similarly dramatic character pose. The message here was that inside this building, beneath this marquee, and past this box office was to be found the actual Surprise hinted at by the colored rendition. Lobby cards would be designed to fall in line with the producer's sale points, and a series of glossy set stills would be provided for the display windows outside the theater—each of these purportedly showing a "film moment" but in fact bearing images of the star actors taking still poses for a set photographer. For the (still for several decades almost always naïve) would-be viewer, these stills could be imagined as scenes snipped from trailers into stunning freezes, but without the overlay of text so prominent in trailers of the time. The poster was a step beyond the newspaper advertisement, being in full color now and very often gargantuan. Not a pitch for the film, but a piece of the action! "You have found it!" was the subtle proclamation. "Yes, this is the place!"[2]

If the actual images in a film did not precisely correspond to advertising imagery (yet without violation of law), there were lines of connection. There is a scene in *Samson*, for example, in which, just as shown in the advertisements, the hero does stand between the pillars of the Temple of Dagon (in the Bible, beit-Dagon), chained at the waist, and he does exert himself in full force trying to cause the Temple's destruction. There is carefully etched *angst* on Mature's face, exaggerated through the use of makeup and lighting. The scene captures him at the end of his tether, an emotional situation that can be conjured but not replicated in the advertising. For instance, what onscreen appear to be massive stones are in drawings lines and shadings.

In looking at the ads for titillation; in finding titillation there and proceeding with growing excitement to the theater; and in entering to submit oneself to the power of the actual imagery, filmgoers routinely underwent a kind of crusade, not just in the way that disconnected emotions and expectations were tickled and raised but also in the way that comparative judgment was brought into play for rationalizing the juxtaposition, in relation to one single motion picture screening, of so variant a set of displays as advertising provided. It was taken as a given that the film itself would not directly replicate its advertisements and posterizations, that the "surgery" executed in order to convert the "Samson" of the ad to the "Samson" of the screen could be taken as a given. Or, to think it in reverse, that the "Samson" of the screen would of necessity,

---

[2] One small example of legion lobby exploitations from the Classical era. Archie Mayo's *A Night in Casablanca* (1946) was a United Artists Marx. Bros. vehicle with a rather large pressbook, included in which was an exhortation to theater managers under the headline "Some More Loonie Lobbies That'll Have 'Em Swarming Into Your Theatre":

> 2. Crystal Ball Gag: Set-up a crystal ball on a velvet covered table in your lobby a few days before the playdate. The copy behind the ball should read: "There's a laugh-riot in your future when you see 'A Night in Casablanca' on [opening date]."

Also suggested were having cashier and usherettes dressed as harem girls, rigging up a section of the lobby as an Arab tent "complete with cushions on the floor" (Pressbook 9).

and of course, have been operated upon in order to reduce him to the "Samson" of the ad. There is no doubt filmgoers knew (at least vaguely) about such transformations, saw the evidence of them (routinely), and took to heart each part of the transposition as authenticity itself, even in light of a pattern of changes and developments. Yet, though it was transparently clear that the ad was not representing the picture it was selling in a pictorial way—the key way in a pictorial medium—there tended to be no complaint, no cry of fraud, no problem at all. Of course required modifications have been made! Of course the people who made the ad aren't (and have no fealty to) the people who made the film! Of course the ad is *only an ad.* Which is to imply, the film stands on a plane far elevated, a supramundane plane. And these things that were *only ads* did in fact *only bring in business.*

Routinely, then, in moving from the moment of desiring to the moment of actually seeing a film, viewers were witnesses to heroic reconfigurations; in fact, viewers took reconfiguration as a necessary and natural part of the experience. It was inimical to act as though such transpositions were peculiar, or as though transposition was not crucial in making films appealing. Again to pounce on Cézanne: the person who wants to eat an apple does not need to use one of his paintings as a preparation, and would never expect an actual apple to seem *exactly* like what is represented in the paintings. But this hungry person would also not rehearse eating an apple by looking at a Cézanne. Moviegoers *do* rehearse their upcoming experience of a film by examining, judging, and appreciating the advertising imagery that precedes its screening. And they make judgments in full knowledge of fabrications, stretchings, misrepresentations, and plasticities of all sorts. When in 1977 passersby saw erected on Times Square a block-long white billboard containing nothing but the text "A long time ago in a galaxy far, far away . . .," they were not only made eager for what was coming next but also powerfully confused, since whatever would be found in that galaxy was given no pictorial representation whatever and they received no other premonitions.[3]

What is the accommodation viewers make in working through the contradictions of, on one hand, knowing that film images will not be versions of the imagery that seduced them and, on the other, yielding to the seduction of the images not only as images but *as indicators?* In terms of the weight of the viewer's commitment to the filmed drama, this is not an unimportant question, since one obvious resolution of the dissonance between actuality and promise would be to deny the entire operation as artificial at best and duplicitous at worst, to think in advance of a touted film as no less concocted than the (obviously) concocted ad. Even if all advertising misrepresented all cinema (virtually true for decades), still, it would be possible to deny cinema by thinking of it as nothing but a fraud dependent upon lies (an "opiate"); viewers didn't—and still don't—deny this way. Of course (they well know), they are about to see images the likes of which were never more than vaguely hinted at in the ads, but this resolving of hint into experience is taken as an essential part of viewing. Being

---

[3] An early case of advertisement through proclaimed secrecy. A different form of secrecy was used in promoting Hitchcock's *Psycho* (1960): "IT IS <u>REQUIRED</u> THAT YOU SEE PSYCHO FROM THE VERY BEGINNING."

inferior, ads cannot do what film can do. Or, being more Olympian, film can exceed advertising incalculably. That the film isn't what it was promised to be is interpreted as a delectable signal that it is, and will continue to be, *more* than it was promised to be; although of course it would be conceivable (though it was never popular) to read the discontinuity the other way, to fall in love with ads themselves and then sigh with desperation that everything onscreen was sadly less. A fundamental assumption made by the audience is that a film in its visual promise (as well as in other ways) would be transcendent, that, in effect, any renditions that appeared before the screening—ads, posters, lobby cards, all of it—existed only to guy the audience for something ineffable and immeasurable to come.

Early representations of cinema are thus read as (only) a skeleton, *greater than which the actual film promises to be*. Each quoted comment is a bare-bones summarization of something substantially greater and more involving. Each printed phrase of text—"timeless, tumultuous, overpowering"—is nothing but a cue to the complex feeling that will come from the viewing experience itself. In light of this formula of systematic aggrandizement film watching, generally speaking, was exciting. One was excited because of what was onscreen, but also because the work-up imagery both promised an excitement bigger than itself and was perceived principally in terms of an excitement it could be understood as promising.

To see films after noting their advertisement through screened clips; or after noting them by way of downloaded interviews with the director and the star—in short, getting an actual piece of the projection in advance as a teaser, a teaser, not a trailer, issues more a confirmation than a thrill. In front of the film one thinks, *I am seeing it now just as I saw earlier that it would be*. Viewing as recognition, not discovery.

5

Registrations

The wrong Bogart. Conflict *(Curtis Bernhardt, Warner Bros., 1945). Digital frame enlargement.*

*In this particular case anyhow it was not only the
artist who was taken on but his famous and long-known
name as well, indeed considering the peculiar nature
of his performance, which was not impaired by advancing
age, it could not be objected that here was an artist
past his prime . . .*

Franz Kafka, "The Hunger Artist"

The star appears and appears again, as though in Kafka. We detect a continuing self.[1] In a way, the very repetition is the stardom. To think of a "star career" as a smooth chain of appearances is to look back at a line of performances; we must meet the challenge of seeing these in the order in which they were committed (in which the work was done), not the order in which the films were released (since very often it can happen that a film is held "in the can" for a long time after being finished, before distribution). But as viewers are hardly meticulous in general, the phrase "star career" is widely taken to mean "all of the performances by this actor that can be called up at the moment." In any event attention fixes on an actor's working out a film role as part of an arbitrary collection of labors working out film roles.[2] One may associate the actor with one particular role, in this way the role and the actor conflate in the imagination. Many, for example, see "Robert De Niro" as the character he played in *Mean Streets* (1973) or as the character he played in *Raging Bull* (1980), and link his persona onscreen in other films to one of these, or to some amalgam of characteristics drawn from both. We could say that one *registers* De Niro in a kind of catalogue, and that he is *registered as*, for example, a "Johnny Boy" or a "Jake LaMotta" type. To actors, casting agents, managers, and publicity agents this registration process is no surprise. Film viewers even register performers without knowing they are doing so, as though exercising a natural perception.

Jerry Lewis's performance as Julius Kelp in his film *The Nutty Professor* (1963) is so perduring it is often the basis of his registration, fascinatingly so, since from this same film he could be, but almost always is not, fan-registered as Buddy Love. Registration as trademark, derived from the pointedly unforgettable performance. Barbara Stanwyck: a "Stella Dallas." Joan Crawford: a "Mildred Pierce." Marilyn Monroe: a "blonde" as in *Gentlemen Prefer Blondes* (1953). Sean Connery: a "James Bond." For some time Johnny Depp had a rich and chameleonic career, until he played Cap'n Jack Sparrow and became "locked in," especially with a young generation of viewers about the same age as his kids, who persisted in maintaining that registration. The star of *Waiting for the Barbarians* (2019) could not possibly have been Johnny Depp, not *that* Johnny Depp.

It can be a supreme challenge for a star to escape a registration, or for someone to become newly registered, for two reasons. Star labor involves many other people in many phases of work, the performer hardly being in complete control of the way his character looks onscreen as a tease for registration. And fan registrations can be rigid, even imprisoning, no matter the star's attempts at freedom of action. Some examples

---

[1] Celebrated actors who are not major stars tend to be thought of as morphers, people who can always be subtly recognized beneath makeup and costume as identical to beings who looked differently in other films; the actor's presence is negotiated by the viewer by way of the multiplicity of surfaces presented over a pattern of film appearances. The star is different, always discernably the same no matter the characterization.

[2] Even actor biographies and autobiographies fail generally to escape a certain arbitrariness, since even if all the performances are treated, and in exact or rough historical order, the reader can never count on a discussion that will be revealing of much more than the film's plot or the performer's ordinary duties at the time.

of this registration freeze: neither Kristen Stewart nor Robert Pattinson found it easy to escape the registration they obtained in the *Twilight* movies (2008 and onward), and continue to labor against that registration, astounding people about "how talented they *really* are"; in *The King* (2019), for example, Pattinson is so very gruesome as the Dauphin he is unrecognizable as "himself." So many fans and detractors were attached to the Stewart of *Twilight* they denied themselves the ineffable thrill of her work in *Personal Shopper* (2016). If Jerry Lewis went relatively unnoticed in Scorsese's *The King of Comedy* (1982), living there under De Niro's shadow because, of course, really he was "Julius Kelp," in *Max Rose* (2013) his alteration was even more pronounced and thorough, and beneath notice. John Wayne could never escape the lumbering cowboy, even in military films, where he was a lumbering cowboy gone into the Navy, and so on—see *In Harm's Way* (1965). After *Good Will Hunting* (1997), Matt Damon was registered as "a genius," and in all his further roles this "genius" has lingered deep inside his characters. Bogart was a secretly wounded and profoundly noble spirit caught in dirty circumstances, and it was very difficult for fans to accept him in negative light. Thus, *Dark Passage* (1947) was passable, since his character was not in the truest of truths a miscreant, only a man mistaken for one, but *Conflict* (1945) was much more problematic, even impossible to watch as long as one clung to the Bogart registration. This is one reason the film is forgotten.

By contrast, a registration *category* may suddenly become unstable. Take the curious case of young Dustin Hoffman who in 1967 became instantly famous far and wide because he had played Benjamin Braddock, the awkward and innocent twenty-year-old seduced by his girlfriend's mother in *The Graduate*. A new star. A shining light. (As the mother, Anne Bancroft, earlier a recognizable and recognized star, now took less screen time and filled out a smaller, though vital, role.) But almost immediately afterward, Hoffman made it clear he intended to be an actor, not a star, and took the bizarre role of Ratso Rizzo in John Schlesinger's *Midnight Cowboy* (1969). Here he displayed rotting teeth, a signal gimp, decrepit suits, and a whiny petulance unseen previously with him onscreen; he thoroughly disappeared inside the character. Thenceforward he had to be the shifting, variable, Dustin Hoffman morph. Just after that, for Arthur Penn, he filmed *Little Big Man* (1970) in which Dick Smith aged him from early manhood into advanced old age, a veritable play upon transformation in which the aging process itself became a systematic actor transform. Registered as a morph, Hoffman worked onward through a brave and strange progression of parts, but his reception value became simultaneously less predictable. The more he was an actor the less he was a star.

The registration process, flowing out of an intensive momentary engagement with a figure of the screen (all registrations begin somewhere, and with cinema "somewhere" is momentary), involves assigning a personality to a face—assigning moral weight, an imagined history, and an emotional range in connection with a particular arrangement of shaped body parts: eyes in relation to nose, ears, cheeks, chin, and mouth. This "persona," a product of actorial performance in union with script, is then given a fix, an embedding into some aspect of the viewer's worldview and memory space that turns it into a kind of landmark. Later on, other instantiations of this landmark, this face, are associated immediately with the embedded personality, so that this new facial personality, this personal faciality becomes an echo or twin of the original. And on and on. As long as the face bears the identifiable characteristics in recognizable array and as long as the array is affixed to a memorable story type, the personality template can be applied. When people speak of "typing" an actor, of "type-casting," and of "casting against type," they are referring to registration taken in a looser, more general sense, in the way that one performer and some identifiable others can be grouped together as similarly exhibiting what is called a "personality type." Type-casting rests upon registration, and registration is the systemic operation by which the star face becomes iconic. From a viewer's perspective, once one has made and fixed a registration it is supremely difficult to watch an actor at work without seeing a fit: Clark Gable no longer a lothario in *The Misfits* (1961); Elizabeth Taylor no longer a princess in *Who's Afraid of Virginia Woolf?* (1966); Damon no longer sweet and innocent in *Suburbicon* (2017), "no longer" in each case being a way for the viewer to see distinction yet pin it to a contradictory and underlying, even uncannily persistent presence.

Clearly, variations will arise in at least two important areas:

[A] It will sometimes happen with an actor that the face changes over time, due to maturation (say, Leonardo DiCaprio) or a scarring accident (say, David Warner). *Dark Passage* is something of a play on this theme. The new face almost matches the old one but not quite, so that the new performer can be recognized as a *converted* version of the old, a *sequel*, perhaps even a sibling. Accidental scarring, or hereditary facial refigurements present from the start can lead to registrations that persist, always thereafter expectably present: Stacy Keach, Joaquin Phoenix, Reginald Nalder (all males, notice). But actors whose faces are transformed in aging are recognizable as *derived from* the person they once were and, due to circumstances beyond their control, no longer are. An actor like Harrison Ford has aged considerably as we have watched, from, say, *Star Wars* (1977) when he was thirty-five through *Blade Runner* (1982) when he was forty-five to *Blade Runner 2049* (2017) when he was seventy-five and *The Rise of Skywalker* two years on, but Ford, as would be said colloquially (and, I think, strangely) has "aged well," by which is meant, "has aged without especially seeming to have aged," has maintained his registration: looking his way, we can still "see" him without change of body mass, exceptionally visible wrinkles, apparent frailty. By contrast, consider Macauley Culkin, a ten-year-old phenomenon in *Home Alone* (1990) but a different type altogether in *Changeland* (2019); or Marlene Dietrich, thirty-one in *Blonde Venus* (1932) and fifty-six in *Witness for the Prosecution* (1957); or Haley Joel Osment in *The Sixth Sense* (1999; eleven years) and *The Kominsky Method* (2019; thirty-one). To watch Veronica Cartwright as Cathy in *The Birds* (1963) one night and then as the bedridden Irene Saxon in *Bosch* (2014) the next is to lose a sense of continuity altogether. Maintaining star gravity has tended to mean holding onto one's registration with audiences, something Ford has been able to do but so many others have not. What makes Dietrich an enduring icon is not a perduring stardom but the figure she presented in her early work of the 1930s, principally for Von Sternberg, with some later appearances invoking that earlier work principally because of her name alone (as in *Touch of Evil* [1958]). With star alterations, if we see the work consistently enough we can find it possible to see the line of development, and marvel, "Oh my, notice what so-and-so looks like now!," but that is not what is done in catching, recatching, recatching, and endlessly (it seems) recatching a star's perduring registration, always available: Liam Neeson, Renée Zellweger, Hugh Grant, Faye Dunaway.

When an actor suffers refiguration, there can be an attempt to maintain and extend registration, this working by way of identifiable body parts that have remained unaffected and that can be stressed in performance to override the effects of scarring elsewhere. One thinks of Mark Hamill's work before and after his car accident, not only in terms of his shifting over to voice work largely but also, in the earlier years, in his continuing to exhibit the optimism, verve, and sweetness with which he was registered before his face changed. By contrast, some refigurements can destroy a registration, or call for radical reconstruction. This happened with Christopher Reeve after his horse-riding accident. Here was the old dashing hero now transformed into a dedicated, indomitable spirit keeping up the act, although with far less star power and by way of far more pain and obvious inabilities.

[B] Some actor faces were not clearly marked in the first place, because they were presented to the public inside an elaboration of makeup and design. While a name can be associated with the figuration, by anyone who wishes to take the trouble, that name tag does not have the power to call up a particular characterological personality or face, and indeed, as the actor moves from film to film, it is likely that the facial presentation will be radically altered again and again. These sorts are the workers we call "character actors": in effect, they never present the same character twice and achieve substantial performance careers without ever gaining a registration. Whereas the star face must always be recognizable on the instant, the character player's face must not. Eugene Pallette could be registered because his body shape became a kind of "face" and was recognizable instantly. Claude Rains was harder to pick out. Alice Brady harder still. And Helen Broderick. And Una O'Connor. And Thomas Mitchell...

In order to maintain an uninterrupted single registration, it is not necessary for an actor to play the same kind of role over and over although admittedly if one looked at a case like John Wayne in *Stagecoach* (1939) and *Red River* (1948) and *The Searchers* (1956) and *Rio Bravo* (1959) and *The Man Who Shot Liberty Valance* (1962) and *El Dorado* (1967) and *True Grit* (1969) one might think otherwise. It's not the role alone that establishes the registration (in most cases other actors could have been cast) but a relation between the moral demands of the role and the moral status of the performer identified with a particular (and familiar) physique and front. Lee Marvin was an interesting example. Playing the title role in *Liberty Valance* we see him as a grizzled, apparently inebriated type to be connected with meanness and vulgarity and egotism. In *Cat Ballou* (1965), we have the same registration, although now his Kid Shelleen is a decrepit has-been who can't even keep his horse standing up—pure parody but from the same registration. Soon later, as Major Reisman in *The Dirty Dozen* (1967), he is bullyish, demanding, tough, and propelling but again a man conceivably masking a vulgar meanness and egotistical streak. As Walker in *Point Blank* (1967), he executes a paradigm of the registration, slickly dressed now, couth if angry, but there is only one Lee Marvin under this character and he is the same by-now-very-well-known Lee Marvin. A kind of reprise is shown in *The Big Red One* (1980), this time with Marvin playing against a supporting cast of bright-eyed, smooth-faced young soldiers who count on his savvy for their survival. I mention only some of Marvin's many articulate performances. He extended a serious star career, what one might call a *shadow* career since his character was never softly and tenderly illuminated by sunlight but always on the other side of propriety. A brilliant character player like Ian Holm extended a career of similar virtuosity, but never as a star, and never more brilliantly than in *Big Night* (1996). With shorter careers thus far, ditto Giovanni Ribisi and Rooney Mara, Toni Collette and Tom Hardy.

A performer can sustain multiple registrations at the same time, a primary registration occupying and directing the professional image while all along a secondary one, perhaps configured by viewers as a "dream" version or a "wish," lies lurking beneath. Gregory Peck as well-intentioned and brave onscreen, well-intentioned, articulate, generous, and kind off-. Lauren Bacall, elusive and seductive onscreen, intelligent, committed, and witty off-. Or, a performer can puncture a registration: associated with serious, adventurous, and life-threatening roles over and over and over he is transformed into an action hero; and then suddenly he switches to comedy. When the switch is made he finds his fans accepting his new screen self with the greatest enthusiasm, quite as though all along, watching him do battle, they had been secretly chuckling at him for being so over the top. (Such muscularity, such violence, such sneering articulation can only be a self-parody—at least a parody of a registration). Consider the case of Arnold Schwarzenegger moving from, say, *The Terminator* (1984) or *Predator* (1987) to *Twins* (1988) or *Jingle All the Way* (1996). Looking at *Jingle* or *Twins* or *Last Action Hero* (1993) or *Kindergarten Cop* (1990) or *Junior* (1994) and positing that Schwarzenegger is being "cast against type" won't come near to accounting for two important features of his performances: first, that the comedic work isn't singular but stretched over a significant number of films, creating, actually, a second Arnold Schwarzenegger, a man inside the man; or a man inside of whom the other man was. There is an entirely new type here, but if Schwarzenegger lives through both types, one cannot say that actors are associated, each, with *a type*. Second, audiences are more than willing to accept, identify, and project the new persona not as a replacement but as an alternative performing self, as though the actor is registering a schizophrenic doubling. He'll do action cinema again, until he needs another comedic holiday. Whereas in action film he was a type, in the comedies he's another type, not an anti-type. Actor as juggler of star personae.

Interestingly, then, what we like to so casually call "movie stardom" is finally a kind of negotiation between the much-studied complexities of construction, on the part of producers and actors in tandem, and a delicate viewer labor to accept featurings, to grope at understanding them in context, and to relate visions to memories of visions similar or radically distinct in an experiential history with the movies. When the star is made up to look like herself, the artist doing the facial work knows what viewers are likely to entertain as recognizable and what they are not. The complex processes of casting and performing take into account actor histories and the likelihood that repetitions or stark contrastings will make for profit at the box office. This, whether the "box office" is in front of a theater on a city or town street, with a very large screen; or in an online membership page for a download package that will show up, finally, like a small candy. In any sort of event, we are coddled to recognize what we saw before, and in this way to make our current pleasure an adjunct of our memory.

6

Great Expectations

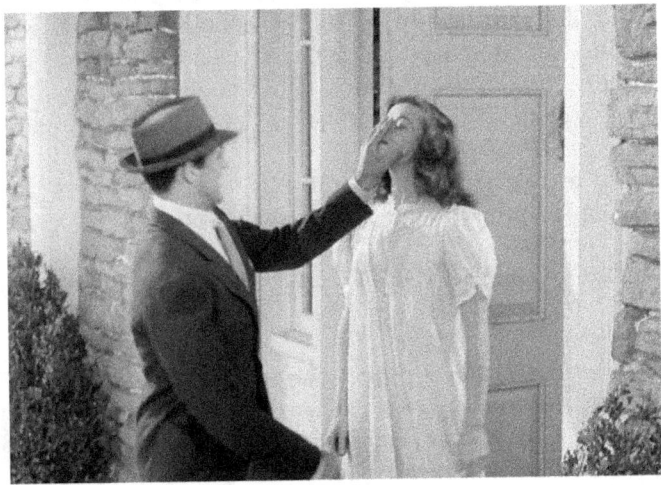

Cary Grant and Katharine Hepburn in The Philadelphia Story *(George Cukor, MGM, 1940). Digital frame enlargement.*

I have been afraid to think of any future.

Charles Dickens

Because the unspooling of film is a continuous one, we could think endless, a perduring sense of expectation thrills viewers, an unresolved wonder as to what will happen next. The irresolution of the wonder makes it uncanny. Every happening is about the next happening. Film cannot pause to reflect, to daydream, but it may present some reflection or some daydream as the next happening. And we may withdraw into daydream ourselves, of course. Printed text does not run on this way, because although the reader's eye progresses along the text line (as with film the viewer's eye progresses, too), the line itself does not progress past the reader's eye. (You may read that sentence again.) With every cinematic edit, every movement, the viewer questions where we are going, what will happen there, yet one never experiences an arrival because in moving forward one is continually coming to wonder where the path leads and what may happen there. Every instant on film is thus a pretext for a subsequent one, to be seen or to be speculated upon.

For a case study that has its own peculiar charms, think of the (rather bizarre) opening moments in George Cukor's *The Philadelphia Story* (1940). The door of a mansion opens and a handsome man (Cary Grant) stomps out carrying suitcases, which he deposits huffily on the drive. When he turns back, a handsome woman (Katharine Hepburn) is moving through the door and tossing in his direction his full bag of golf clubs, first extracting one of them. The bag crashes near him. She takes the single club, and with a gestural flourish snaps it in two against her thigh, tossing the pieces at him as well. He strides up to her, places his hand on her face and, giving a sharp push, flattens her on the floor of her own atrium. Fade.

(As you look at the frame enlargement above, reader, note how very perfunctory it is as an image of what I have just spelled out. Something came before, leading to this. This is going to lead to something else. This instant is but a node, and as a node has no special meaning.)

What do we have here?

[1] A very costly residence (pictured just earlier in the credits sequence through a line drawin3g), for people who are presumably very rich. AND:

[2] A disgruntled resident, thoroughly fed up and closing the door of his mind. AND:

[3] Suitcases, to indicate bluntly and irrevocably that he is moving out. Thus, he had been *in*, and whatever arrangement put him there is now terminated. As to that arrangement: given the decorous house and the nappy clothing, given that things seem "upper," we can work on the presumption that he is exiting a marriage. AND:

[4] The woman involved, whom we now instantly take to be the wife, is as fed up as he is, if not more, and wishes him nothing but "Good riddance," which she signals by throwing out his "most valuable" material, the golf clubs (a marriage union now split). There is information hiding here, but not so difficult to spot. If it is these golf clubs, but not something else, that constitute his object of supreme value, he is committed to a particular kind of landed luxury, not to say a too debonair casualness about his marriage bond. In his soul, *apparently*, he is but a man who spends considerable time walking around grassy areas in search of a little white ball. He is trivial, his clubs are trivial, the marriage—clearly an error—was trivial. She is only too happy to wash him out of her hair. BUT:

[5] Just to be sure she has made her point, because, being male, he is clearly too dense to catch the drift of it on his own without help, she has reserved one holy stick and now in a little ceremony of warlike aggression snaps it so that it will never be functional again. This is all symbolic, because for people of this class the problem of purchasing a new golf club is picayune. She is one who not only makes points but wishes to be certain of their sharpness. She possesses that slight self-consciousness and that grim determination. AND:

[6] Having been amicable enough about her reciprocating his abrupt departure with an abrupt toss of the golf bag—no point losing your composure over the mere fact of things making an exit—he has considered the club snapping just one immodest step too many, a slap in the face. A challenge. A crossing of the border with tanks. Honor requires revenge. SO:

[7] The purposeful stride up to her, the hand on the face to exhibit both (a) the right to touch and (b) military acumen, and the push that ends the battle for the moment. She gives a little expression of defeat coupled with amazement coupled with doubt.

What polishes off this little scherzo is not, and need not be, stated openly. That is the fact, blatantly obvious, that we are talking about the ineffably smooth Cary Grant going to battle with the ineffably articulate and svelte Katharine Hepburn, in short, two major star figures in all-out war, and, as the display indicates, out of nowhere. The glamour of the participants reduces to comedy what in other circumstances might be read as bald aggression.

(Many fans and scholars who have discussed George Cukor have neglected his talent for comedy, if grotesque.)

Note how at each node it is easy enough to fully incorporate and understand the gestures here, to read them to a depth; but also how one cannot avoid wondering what could be next. Where are we going with these two? What will happen? As the ante goes up, what is the next level? Since this whole scene operates as the opening of the picture, Tracy lying on the floor looking upward opens the question, *What can possibly happen now with her?* And what can happen, needless to say, is what the film shows happening, moment by unfolding moment. As all films perduringly ask *What can happen?*, this film displays itself asking this question and in this way has the beauty of the recursive.

All film: stating and unfolding simultaneously, being and becoming, posing and promising. Anticipation is not a quality of cinema, it is a condition. The problem is not event but eventuation, the advance of eventfulness, the looming happening, the reality-to-be. Editors work with this principle stubbornly in mind. Each transition (cut or fade or dissolve) involves not only the problem of terminating a present depiction but also the memory of how that depiction came onto the screen and the structuring of the viewer's anticipation of the depiction that will follow. Also, the memory trace that will follow with what follows. So, *what will follow?* is a key question, dependent inevitably on the details of where we are now and what led us there. Given the technical possibilities of film splicing, of optical printing, and of digital manipulation, any shot at all can go to any other shot at all. But some possibilities are logically marginal, perhaps even confounding, not that an editor will fail to see value sometimes in producing confusion or in mounting the scathing danger of an unprepared jump. The tendency in the classical era (both in film and in music) was to prepare transitions carefully, to avoid illogical moves. In the commitment to logic, to evenly flowing continuity, lay the audience's comfort in knowing that every leap forward would make some kind of sense given events at hand. ("Logic" was convention.) Modernism of course changed all that.

The so-called jump cut was a transition forward in the unspooling, to a vision entirely unanticipated, the viewer being forced to join the past to the present in such a way as to make a (poetic) link. This is Eisensteinian *montage*. If there is a conceptual gap produced by the jump, the viewer fills in that gap, and the filling-in becomes, finally, the event. I think the idea of *montage completion* on the part of the viewer holds nicely as long as there is a lingering cultural memory of continuous development, a memory that incites viewers to recreate "continuity" from discontinuity if discontinuity is directly presented, and that, beyond inciting, offers a kind of stockroom of typical possibilities drawn from a cinema experienced and digested so early as to be part of the body now. After some time, an edited discontinuity between two visions can be entertained for and in itself as a "natural" movement; that is, nature can be thought discontinuous. (Arnold Schoenberg's so-thought "unpredictable" interval leap in the twelve-tone was analogous.) Often now, the fill-in invokes theories of "memory," "memory lapse," "dream," "fear," or some other emotionally laden supra-perceptual experience, something far beyond what a character (and a viewer empathizing with the character) could imagine in a state of what, in an age of continuity, one called *reason*.

Some idiosyncratic forms of eventuation:

[A] *High speed.* The cutting can proceed through what David Bordwell has called "intensified continuity," with (i) radically displaced viewpoints, joined; and/or (ii) very, very, very short average shot lengths, in which the join links visions that last onscreen for, perhaps, no more than a quarter of a second (six frames or even fewer). In terms of a viewer attending to cinema with augmented expectation, the high-speed sequence sets up a condition in which two effects manifest themselves:

- The perception of the current instant is not only shortened in persistence but also made utterly fleeting, so that seeing it clearly and fully enough to generate expectation or prediction is threatened.

- It begins to seem easier to eschew the hope of framing precise expectations shot by shot—the shots link up so much more quickly than the viewer breathes—and to hold instead what amounts to a broad expectation that the entire speedy sequence will end, which means considering it while it transpires as an *active blur* that, although internally integrated, will lead to something quite different, a state of relative peace (signally slower movement forward). To experience such an editing style, hold the breath.

A very helpful example is the Parisian apartment fight in Doug Liman's *The Bourne Identity* (2003). The agent-hero Bourne (Matt Damon) is with his rescuer and new friend Marie (Franka Potente) in a very modern, stylish apartment on the *rive droite*. For reasons the film has already spelled out fully enough, Bourne does not know why they are there, of all places, that is, how he came to know about this place. Perhaps it belongs to him? He has very serious amnesia. Suddenly a stranger has burst in and the two of them must battle to the death, with Marie standing by in rigid fear. The battle is filmed in such a way that the editor can cut it in very short bursts, the camera (the viewer) jumping all around the place. It is never possible at any gulp to know exactly where one will be next, inside the apartment space, or exactly what move will be committed there by either party. The brutal sound effects emphasize the pulsing of the action. But a certain cushion is provided to the viewer, a certain upholstery, as it were (see Schivelbusch 122–3): the illumination is essentially produced by outside daylight flooding in through immense glass doors leading to a balcony, so that the place is brightly and evenly lit; there is no spot in the place that does not feel and seem like a spot *in this place*; no matter the jerky bodily movement and threat of death, one never doubts that one is in a Parisian apartment or what is ongoingly happening. Although the scene is cut in tiny jumps, apparently incessant tiny jumps, one can relax in the knowledge that one isn't really jumping at all, at least not jumping out of a particular rendition of place. The views from and toward which one jumps all give focus to specific spots on human bodies in motion, so one is already prepared to give up hope of isolating any particular pointing.

[B] *Metamorphosis.* The paradigm here is a celebrated scene in John Frankenheimer's *The Manchurian Candidate* (1962) in which we are watching the playing-out of a central character's (Frank Sinatra) nightmare during the Korean conflict. A pleasant and flowery room in an isolated country hotel, where a group of elderly women have gathered to hear a lecture on hydrangeas, delivered by a speaker whose language on the podium is emphatically precise and grammatical, not to say tedious (Helen Kleeb). The lectern is flanked by a line of chairs on either side, and in these sit Marco and the members of his platoon, all drowsy, yawning, listening only vaguely. The camera gently tracks rightward, from the speaker in her flowery dress across the cluster of soldiers, to the edge of the platform and then off it, into the audience of fascinated women in flowery dresses, all concentrating as avidly as soldiers receiving a briefing. Along and along and along we track, past the aisle and past the listeners on the other side, slowly, methodically, and then the other edge of the stage, and gently up the steps to the soldiers left of the podium now utterly groggy, but as we pass through these and come to the lectern again, we see that the speaker is a bald, stocky, mustachioed Asian man (Khigh Dhiegh) spieling about a new technique in what he calls *brain washing*, that has been employed on these men. Exceptionally literate language, wit, perfect enunciation. Cutting now to the reverse, we see that we are in a vertically structured lecture theater, possibly in a medical facility because everything is antiseptically clean, and the audience is composed of grim-looking military types. The transition from the garden club to the military briefing is entirely seamless, this because we have been watching one single shot, made in one long take with the scenery and performers moving silently off-camera. Frankenheimer's long history with live network television drama had prepared him for making very elaborate shot constructions like this. Because the transition that is involved here takes place *without editing*, it is entirely surprising, in the way that dream transitions can be. Our sense of time is shocked, until we rationalize that we have traveled from inside the men's induced consciousness to an "actual" reality.

We are prepared during the hydrangea lecture for one outcome but offered, in the fact of it, another quite unrelated one. Here the formula of expectation and forward-gazing is employed ironically, to produce a kind of displacement in the viewer.

[C] *Jumping in.* An especially involving forward movement is produced through the insertion of close-ups. Whereas in their earliest uses (Griffith's *The Gay Shoe Clerk* [1903], *The Lonedale Operator* [1911] and onward) close-ups functioned to offer the viewer helpful information that it was otherwise difficult to apprehend, such as the detail of an object or object relation that on a screen composed through tableau shots was too far away or too small for satisfactory perception, the insert close-up has gained new functions. Here is a strange little case:

In Jane Campion's *The Portrait of a Lady* (1996), an old man (John Gielgud) lies abed, probably dying (the character is dying in fact, but at this moment we haven't learned that). His son enters. He whispers a question: "Is anyone else here?"

The answer is no. "Cigarette," the old lips whisper.

Now, in macro-close-shot, we see the son pulling out a cigarette and lighting it, and in a jump to a second macro-close-shot we see the old fingers placing the cigarette to the lips and inhaling, then blowing out a cloud of smoke. (There is nothing particularly abnormal, in the late twentieth and early twenty-first century, about insertions like this.) Fingers. Cigarette. Lips. Smoke. What is happening here?

- Since it is in a slowly tracking medium-shot that we see the old man revealed, we recognize him as being abed and in bad shape. And we know who he is, in relation to other characters in the story. The son's entry is also in a clear and revealing medium shot. In short, there is nothing of dramatic importance in this little sequence that is either being held back or placed too far away, or too small, to be seen. We see it all. And it is all about etiquette and helpfulness, about pausing and yearning.

- We do not see cigarettes early in the sequence because when he enters the son is not smoking, and if he has cigarettes (a fashion at the time, diegetically speaking) he mostly likely has them tucked away. We have never yet seen the old man smoking, so when we see him in bed we can have no thought, can project no expectation that he will be wanting a cigarette.

- By the time of the setting of this story, the late nineteenth century, cigarettes of this type had been around for considerably more than two hundred years, so that even if the audience had been lulled into taking the point of view of the characters, there would have been nothing surprising or illuminating for them in the appearance of a cigarette. Thus the close shot of the fingers withdrawing the cigarette gives only slight information. The son possesses cigarettes (but the father's request implied that already). The son knows how to fetch one (obvious). The son is willing to oblige: although for this, any reasonably placed shot will suffice; there is no call for a close-up.[1]

- The father takes special pleasure in his inhalation, because in the macro shot we are given to see his expressive lips (a Gielgudian feature). Yet again, an actor like Gielgud could have demonstrated pleasure in many ways without a close-up: holding his breath before exhaling; making a little sigh; looking beatifically out the window, even mouthing "Ahhhhh."

- The smoking is a signal that the conversation to ensue will be very personal, very confidential, and very important to the story (a cue for specific expectation). Yes, but again, the actors could convey this in so many ways. What does the close-up do here but distract from their poses and relation, and in fact decorate the moment?

The close-ups here do not give us information in a particular and characteristic way, at least they do not give information we already do not have or cannot glean elsewise. But they do suggest something that could be given light and emphasis in no other way, a link between the son's hand and the father's mouth, a link never elaborated in the film in any way. Hand to mouth. Mouth upon hand. This is Cronus (Saturn) who devours his sons. And here is Jupiter, who will be saved. This is Jupiter touching the mouth of Saturn. Still another function is fulfilled extradiegetically, a function that is perhaps far more elemental to contemporary filming than has been credited. The close-ups show off the filmmaker's "unique" capacity for special views, the filmmaker's "possession" of the close-up lens, the filmmaker having the "bright idea" to jump in for an exquisitely formed, uncannily close detail. This is close detail functioning as *close detail*. The filmmaker says, in effect, "Viewer: I can see this moment better than you could without my help." Or, "Do not forget that I am here, helping you. Making an offer you will not refuse." In the sense that jumping to a close-up like this, a sporadic eventuation, is self-revealing for the filmmaker and for the production, it is recursive. Quite beyond showing action, one shows oneself showing action. The showing of a showing. In this way the fact of visual capability and perspective outweigh the object viewed, even the filial cigarette taking its place in the old man's mouth. In the actual movement forward, from the medium shot of the bedroom to the extreme close shot of the fingers with the cigarette, one jumps not only from (a) an old man asking for something to (b) a sight of what he is asking for but also (A) from an old man asking for something to (B) a vision of *our ability now to see* what he is asking for. The effect is that of a mirror suddenly being put up between the camera and its subject, so that without warning, in

---

[1] The viewer is unlikely to imagine another possibility: that a medium shot was taken, just once, of the son withdrawing the cigarettes, but that a performer error or technical error made it unusable, so that an optical blow-up was used instead.

a swift flip, we see *our own ability to see* (as well as the thing focused upon). Perhaps it is because we are watching that Saturn will not devour Jupiter.

[D] *Time warps.* In classical editing, the transition out of "everyday perception" into "dream" or "memory" is achieved by means of a signal system (for a further discussion see my *Eyes* 19ff): the screen seems to flutter or wave, or lines are imposed and disappear, or some other bracketing is used to bound off the metadiegetic moment. But it has become very fashionable now to transition (often to leap) into (a) dream, (b) hypothesis, (c) memory, (d) false memory, and other transparent states with no signal at all. A simple cut is inserted, as it would be in moving from any knock on any door to the door opening, but the ensuing material is *only retrospectively* identified as non-existent in the present context of "everyday reality." Thus, the viewer can be presented with a double shock: first, the transition from "A" to "B" can seem oddly discontinuous, disturbingly disorienting, confusing, unexpectedly challenging; and then, afterward, "B" turns out not to be a continuation forward in everyday time from "A" anyway, but some other version of the dramatic universe, very often something that happened before the story began and of which, in truth, we could have had neither a vision nor a suspicion; or something out of a fantasy version of events. This happens in a culture settled into rapid and interminable change: "Precariousness leading to an ultimate loss of temporal structure: this is the key experience associated with the impression of accelerated change" (Gumbrecht 402). Movements "in and out of dream" all indicate time-travel stories, of course, although only the most conventional of these are actually labelled that way and involve some displayed "time vehicle." The cinematic effect for the viewer is realization that the film can and will take us anywhere in time, far forward, far backward, somewhere else at the same moment, anything or everything, and, perhaps most affectingly, *without signaling itself* doing so in advance of a retroactive clue (that is, what retroactively becomes discernable as a clue). In short, cinema goes; and as there are no limits as to where or how speedily, we must be willing to follow, come what may. At the same time, any of these travel moments, these leaps, say, back a dozen years or forward a dozen more, occur for the viewer in the context of normal forward-moving eventuation. To go back in time, we go forward. To go forward in time, we go forward. To go sideways, forward. To remember, to dream, to guess, to notice, to fail to notice, to think, to see oneself thinking: move on.

> Not fare well,
> But fare forward, voyagers.
> (Eliot, *The Dry Salvages*)

[E] *Doorways.* As a metaphor for transition we have long used the *door*. The door to the future, the door to possibility, the door out of here, the door we have archly been shown—"Show them the door." A character walks up to a door and either (a) places a hand intentfully on the knob (Joan Fontaine in *Rebecca* [1940] or Vera Miles in *Psycho* [1960]) or else (b) knocks and waits to be answered or merely opens and moves in. The touching of the doorknob or the knock would be understood in real life to have different implications, but in diegesis they inform the viewer of much the same thing, that the character wishes to make entry. If in real life when approaching a door one thinks soberly of the figures on the other side and what their reaction could be, in film one is concentrating only on the character approaching the door and all else is for speculation, not consideration. Who will come to the door? What sort of person, with what intent? What is inside, what will be discovered there? In short, *what can happen?*

The finale of Denis Villeneuve's *Enemy* (2013) has Jake Gyllenhaal knocking at an apartment door and, as it opens, discovering something quite horrifically other than he (or we!) could have dreamed. There are some wonderful door moments near the beginning of *North by Northwest* (1959), first when Roger Thornhill (Cary Grant) is escorted from a limousine into the vast Townsend estate on Long Island by way of the elegant front door, opened to a knock by a decorous wife who has a genteel way of showing him and his captors inside. Then they give a knock on an interior door and are beckoned to open and enter, and we find ourselves in a beautiful study laid over with framed landscapes and plush furniture. Things do not go well for Roger here, and, to come quickly to it, he is forcibly inebriated and put behind the wheel of a car on a treacherous cliffside road. When by miracle he survives and bumps into the rear of a police cruiser he finds himself in court, and not long after, having claimed that people tried to kill him, he is escorted to that estate again, this time by a detective and his lawyer and his omnipresent mother. When they knock, the door is opened by the same woman, this time smiling graciously at "strangers she has never seen before." We are given a prompting here that Roger is about to be confounded in his accusation and, surely enough, inside the interior study he can find no trace at all of what happened the night before, not even a bourbon stain on the back of the sofa cushions where he was pinioned and force-fed. The vision of characters at a door resolves into a sensible "picture" only when the door is opened to permit passage forward to a discovery, any discovery, every discovery.

* * *

These (albeit limited) considerations of filmic eventuation distinguish it from our forward-gazing in the everyday. While we make plans for "the future"—a voyage, a meeting, a date, a movie screening—our experience in the moment is not a continual posing of possibility against the uncalculated probability of happenings. Say, one sits in a coffee shop with a nice latte, sipping dreamily and occasionally checking one's email, and this with no special thought that someone will come through the door; or that an email will be surprising; or that the proprietor will have put something in the coffee so that a physical response will now develop. One simply drinks. To our action we bring no special anticipation. However much everyday life may seem like a story, it is not one. Film—any and all film, narrative or otherwise—is storylike in its perpetual, incessant eventuation, its pressing us forward. And one of the telltale features of the cinematic experience is precisely this sense of the pressure to wonder, to hope, to progress somewhere . . . to not be here.

7

Naming of Parts

Strangers on a Train *(Alfred Hitchcock, Warner Bros., 1951). Digital frame enlargement.*

This is the safety-catch, which is always released
With an easy flick of the thumb. And please do not let me
See anyone using his finger. You can do it quite easy
If you have any strength in your thumb.

Henry Reed, "Naming of Parts"

As I sit to write this, I have a sense of living in, with, for, by means of, and through a particular and homogeneous body, one that I have, at least in my conceits, made my own, and one with which I tend to think myself familiar. It is an organic entity, unified, extended, both reaching and shrinking, a body in which, as the old song so happily goes, the right arm is connected to the left arm, the thigh bone is connected to the shin bone, and so on to—as I esteem it in my ignorance—no end. I have no headache suspecting that, as Jorge Luis Borges once wrote, the world around takes the shape of my own self:

> A man sets out to draw the world. As the years go by, he peoples a space with images of provinces, kingdoms, mountains, bays, ships, islands, fishes, rooms, instruments, stars, horses, and individuals. A short time before he dies, he discovers that the patient labyrinth of lines traces the lineaments of his own face. (Epilogue to *Dreamtigers*)

And I know, too, that if ever anybody comes close enough to me to get a decent focus, and looks at, say, my right hand, that person can glide up my arm and see my face, or glide down and see my knee, can walk behind me and see my shoulder blades. I am inspectable entirely at the will of the other, at least under normal circumstances when I do not hide part of myself behind a blind as, say, a professional might, using the desk in his office. Julio Cortázar:

> The doctor finishes his examination and his conclusions are very reassuring to us. His cordial and somber voice precedes the medicines, prescriptions for which he is writing out at the moment, seated behind his desk. Every once in a while he raises his head and smiles, to cheer us up. We don't have a thing to worry about, we'll be better inside of a week. We sit at ease in our easy chair, happy, and look idly and distractedly about the room. In the shadowed area beneath the desk, suddenly we see the doctor's legs. The trousers are pulled up to just above the knees and he's wearing women's stockings. (*Cronopios* 9)

No, not me. I do not normally hide, but instead feel myself and exhibit myself, simultaneously, as a single undivided presence. I make the assumption that when I am looked at, the subsuming eye envelops me, takes into account anything and everything that is available and in ensemble.

Notwithstanding that when I see a photograph of myself, especially one made a very long time ago, I jerk back in bewildered tension to realize that somebody else actually is, or was, looking at this object the photographer gave my name.

How awkward I think it, and how bizarrely thrilling, to see those gigantic Roman plaster casts of noses, hands, or feet sitting on polished mahogany Restoration tables in the grand houses, or even the castrati posing innocently in the British Museum, or that graceful muse standing demurely with half her arm ripped away and her eyes wondering. Body parts. And of course in *Gray's Anatomy* (not the TV show, the book!), the form of the body is subdivided in order to make possible a long, delirious chain of partial studies, unit by unit, system by system, since the whole thing, seen from the inside, is so much more complex and involving than anyone is presumed to be able to digest (!) in one view. The section on the hand, for example, shows all of the muscles, tendons, bones, arteries, veins, and nerves in interrelation, so that by the time one has finished learning it one can say one *knows* the hand. Notwithstanding, of course, that one knows nothing at all, from this sort of thing, of what the hand can do, does do, hopes someday to do. David Sudnow calls his little book, in which he tells us what happened to him as he learned from scratch, as an adult, how to play jazz piano, *Ways of the Hand*.

The unitary body. The mystery of the fleshly terrain, its hilltops and forests, its rivers, its encampments.

In film the body does not work this way.

If, as in the very early days of filming, we see an entire body, that is, a body with space below it and on top of it, this view is called a *tableau* and we find inevitably that the person is so far from the camera the identificatory features are lost to us. For this among other reasons, screen performers were not known as identities (as names) until such time as shots came to be made closer up. The birth of stardom as recognition. Typically now bodies are shot as fragments, entirely according to the dramatic needs of the moment. A finger pulling a trigger. The lower spine lifted in orgasmic spasm. The ear when somebody is saying something interesting. The eye at the moment of revelation or, as in *The Cranes Are Flying* (1957), death.

The most clearly assimilable version of the person is the facial portrait, typically in a close-up and typically made after a tremendous amount of consideration (see Davenport). Makeup on the skin, surely, but then, too, very delicate manipulation of lighting from all angles in order to create a sculpted persona. Where do the shadows fall, and what will be their shape? How radiant will be the highlights, and will they suggest gleaming metal or soft flesh? Interestingly, in film stories about robotic futures, the robots are almost never photographed with facial close-ups, since presumably no one of them has any particular—certainly no perduring—identification. A telling exception is Martin Scorsese's *Hugo* (2011) in its reveal photography of the automaton (but Martin Scorsese the director is also a film scholar).[1]

The face is more dynamic when shown at an angle, although the calculation of the precise extent of the angle remains a challenge for cinematographers, subject by subject. Too much angle sharpens the nose and lips, and changes the "identity" the filmmaker wishes to project for the character, not to say for the performer whose career will hang to some degree on the way he or she looks doing what we see. What lens is being used, and how will the choice of lens alter the space of the face once it is composed? Wide-angle lenses—40 mm, 38 mm, 35 mm, 28 mm, 24 mm, 18 mm, 9 mm—increasingly spread and warp the facial features and round them, and this process can be helpful in characterization. See Tom Hanks, Tracy Letts, or Michael Stuhlbarg, as shaped in Steven Spielberg's *The Post* (2017, photographed by Janusz Kaminski). Or Faye Dunaway and Jack Nicholson in cramped spaces together in Polanski's *Chinatown* (1974, photographed by John A. Alonzo). Much serial television expands dramatic space (and warps faces) by continual use of wide-angle lenses.

---

[1] In their very informative *Visions of Light* (1992), Arnold Glassman, Todd McCarthy, and Stuart Samuels have an interview with Charles Lang bemoaning that when Greta Garbo died there was so little reference to William Daniels (1901-1970), the cinematographer who used light to sculpt her (famous) face.

In a normal medium-shot, the viewer will see the head, torso, and sometimes the waist of the character; in a medium-close shot (for over-the-shoulder conversations) one will see the head and shoulders only. The vision is parts of a body. What does one do here in order to make sense? Obviously, given the choice of accepting a character as possessing and inhering in a head and shoulders only, literally as having nothing else to boast of, or of building in one's imagination various extensions downward from the shoulders to include the torso, the waist, the arms, and the legs, most conventional is to choose the latter. We fill in either by dragging back, from short-term memory, visions of the whole body from earlier in the film, or by assuming the character, like the actor playing him, is enough like us that we can, from our own self-perception, sketch a body at present missing from view; sketch or take as sketched. In the Cortázar doctor's office referred to above, the fictional patient already does this "fill-in" all the way through, and is therefore not only shocked but shockable by the punch line at the end. But if one sees an over-the-shoulder medium-close shot by means of a "fill-in," if one watches by imaginatively figuring an extended body that one does not see, then watching a film at that instant is contradictory to understanding it. One's understanding proceeds exactly from not accepting what one sees, "*not* accepting the world as it looks," as Susan Sontag writes. But understanding: are we to take it as a greater act than looking? Here, as often elsewhere, seeing is confounding but is it bad to be confounded?

It is easy to rationalize: head and shoulders: a medium close-up, being made by the cameraman. But to see surpasses rationalization. A head and shoulders is a head and shoulders and not a reference to filmmaking technique.

The walking legs that open Hitchcock's *Strangers on a Train* (1951) are either seen as such, legs walking, or they form the basis of an imagination of the bodies extending upward from them—bodies Hitchcock is quite competent to show, and that he will show when he thinks the time is right. When we see his shots of legs we are meant, I think, to consider legs *as bodies*.

In *Citizen Kane* (1941), in the celebrated shot of young man Kane reading in the Thatcher library, the part of the body, the hand, nearest the manuscript is easily thought connected to a person sitting nearby, extending the arm. Or take the finale moment in Hitchcock's *Spellbound* (1945) when a hand reaches out from the camera holding a gun. The divided, fragmented body raises to critical consciousness the important difference between seeing and not seeing, between the use of the brain and the use of the eye—or more clearly, the use of the optical area of the brain and the use of the cognitive area. The film image of a partial body can show us how when we see we actually do not calculate. Seeing *is thinking*.

The hands of a pianist playing Chopin in *A Song to Remember* (1945).

In *The Man Who Knew Too Much* (1956), the fingers of a conductor quickly reaching down to turn the page of his score in mid-beat.

The hand of the artist at work, say in Scorsese's "Life Lessons" or in Orson Welles's *F for Fake* (1973) or in Jacques Rivette's *La belle noiseuse* (1991). Hand . . . color . . . canvas.

The hungering buttocks of the lover in, say, *Devil in the Flesh* (*Diavolo in Corpo*, 1986) by Marco Bellocchio.

The well-shod foot of the killer on the mountaintop in *North by Northwest* (1959).

To the degree that we make to comprehend the close-up as an insertion of important information, we read (= see) the shot in relation to the context, and filling in the remainder of a body is no great challenge. No great challenge, that is, to the patterning rationality. To the eye, filling in is a profound challenge, since without advance notice the eye is moving very close into only a small part of the foregoing vision, picking up, as it were, a thread from the character's costume to examine it for revealing detail. *Oh, I wasn't able to see that, but I can see it now!* The inserted information can bring the audience into the thrill or tempo of the moment, showing *yet another* view of the many things going on at once to compose this eventful instant. Or it can make plain a clue that without close vision would be impossible to detect: an ink blot, a tiny insect, an odd position of the foot upon the floor. But still, in all this informativeness there is presumed an audience ready and waiting, here and always, to be informed—informed by projecting beyond the vision—an information-seeking viewer, rather than someone who was fully caught up with, satisfied by the sight on offer just before the close-up and who therefore did not expect to jump *in*. To be fully caught up and then suddenly relocated is, to say the very least, disturbing. The relocation itself is internalized, and the viewer feels a self in motion (if without reason).

Two alarming and unforgettable visions:

- In *Silence* (2016), seen from high above, a Japanese official's sandswept courtyard, with a man standing alone and small, when quickly another rushes up with a sword and lops off his head. For a moment the body stands, almost a figurine, and then it keels over and factota rush in and drag it off-left by the feet, the blood streaming out into a carmine trail on the beige ground. One sees this, even incorporates it, swiftly—before the word "beheading" comes to mind.

- In *Psycho* (1960), that perhaps-too-familiar little moment when Norman Bates goes up to his wall, draws aside a framed picture of Susannah and the Elders, and peers through his peephole. On the other side (we will see what he sees: it's a bathroom and a woman is disrobing there) there is quite a lot of brilliant light; on his side there is shadow. We get a stunning profile shot. No shoulders, no head even, but, very close, the gazing eye at left, looking rightward, and staring back at it the very radiant hole in the wall. The hole in the wall is not unlike a living aperture, glowing fiercely against his slightly darker eye. The eye seeing an eye-like shape, the eye looking at itself, the hungry eye to be sure, the eye whose treasure will be slashed across, just like that horror in *Un chien andalou* (1929), and also just like Juan José Padilla when, in Zaragoza, in 2011, a bull gored him, forcing defenestration, and also like Bataille's "I" with his eye, unable "to see her burning buttocks under the skirt, dipping into the cool milk," which glyph became Godard's egg-sitter in *Weekend* (1968), and yet also the swirling eye, pit of the stairway to the Underworld in *Black Orpheus* (1959) and later on Morgan Delft's strange eyes, peering out into a mirror from beneath his gorilla mask in *Morgan: A Suitable Case for Treatment* (1966). This shot in *Psycho* wouldn't work at all if we saw the full body, or if we saw the kind of action engendered and inspired by that eye and its seeing (as, in Gus Van Sant's remake, we do). The operation is by way of the fragmentation, the *only-ness* of that eye and its twinned hole in the wall. The hole carved in advance, in preparation, in longing, and in the shape of the organ that will kiss it.

Or else, in torso and head crop, with the arms raised up in some queer salute, the white-faced phantom in *Pan's Labyrinth* (2006) with its huge pink nostrils and its gaping black mouth and the two eyes implanted in the palms of its hands.

And the horror in *Fellini Satyricon* (1969) when in a little Roman theater, before an inebriated crowd, a thief is led onstage, quivering, smiling, smiling, quivering, and on a butcher block his hand is chopped off. He is led off, still smiling. This one is a full-body shot, seen from far enough off that he is not fragmented *by us*, but of course he is fragmented while we stare at, and digest, the fragmentation produced by others.

There is a repeated moment in *Invaders from Mars* (1953)—as a child of seven, this chilled me to the bone, so much that I have never been able to let go of it—in which the Martian invaders, not very nice creatures, having strapped a guileless human into a chair device, use a metallic needle affair to penetrate the nape of the neck and make an insertion there (of some item that will, of course, turn the unwitting earthling into an automaton under Martian control). The neck, the unwitting neck, the slender hairs draping over the nape, the protruding device, the journey all the way into the darkest reaches of the interior of the jungle of the mind. *Heart of Darkness*.

Or, and I think it wise to leave the discussion with this grisly pointer, the moment of agony in *Syriana* (2005) when George Clooney, duct-taped securely into a rickety metal chair, has his fingernails drawn out by very tranquil Mark Strong. The calm, almost reassuring, insidious voice as we see the hand in macro-close-up and the pliers grabbing and deplacing the nail, and the abysm of screams, yet at the same time the absolute medical placidity and formality of the shot, the arm, the hand, the fingers, the nails, the plier tool moving forward, its teeth opening and closing on the nail, the sudden force of withdrawal. This is like a lesson in surgery, but of course it is dramatically framed as a lesson in torture. Not to fret too much: Clooney's Bob Barnes will heal enough to forget playing in this scene and will triumph. But we: we do not manage to envision the body at the other end of that arm. We do not construct the full person, alas.

It can be that every framing-in, every loving focus on a part for the whole, let us say metonymy itself, is a torture, and we save ourselves by way of that strange pleasure of using the library of our experience to fill in the artful gaps.

8

A Flicker

(Left, from left) Francis Ford, John Wayne, Victor McLaglen, John Ford, and Barry Fitzgerald in Galway filming The Quiet Man *(1952); (Right) Jerry Lewis (left), with Robert De Niro off-camera on* The King of Comedy *(Martin Scorsese, Embassy/Twentieth Century Fox, 1982).*

A photograph appears, showing a group of people posed together in a nice quasi-familial huddle, in the sunshine, with some scattered buildings behind. Aficionados of cinema discover soon enough that they are looking at John Ford and his brother Francis, with John Wayne, Victor McLaglen, and Barry Fitzgerald in a photograph that was made while the company shot *The Quiet Man* in Galway in 1952. Or Jerry Lewis off-camera with Robert De Niro as they shoot a scene for *The King of Comedy* (1982) in a New York studio. Smiling? But yes, and in an open, unhesitating, generous way, also demonstratively, as though to confess (and publicize) how happy they are to be in one another's company at this moment. They are surely aware that quite beyond the quarter second in which the camera's aperture was open here, and beyond the minute or so ahead of time when they arranged themselves so neatly, and perhaps the few minutes afterward when they stood around chatting this session to its end, the photograph was always destined for a more eternal reception, that it would become part of historical fact, a "true document," and would be unearthed in ages future and incalculable as evidence of an event, an association, a pattern of organization, and residue of a specific project involving, as will be interpretable, general affiliation. Any or all of the "evidence" may be used for investigation, consideration, and conclusion by strangers. "Here we are," not only to friends and relatives but to everybody anywhere anytime.

Photography, Roland Barthes warns us in *Camera Lucida*, participates in a "fatality" by virtue of never being without something or someone. Thus, with every photograph, a plunging into the disorder that objects yield in the world, objects here and there, and why, after all, these objects seen in this way?

If the posers are conscious that this photograph they are making together will have wide accessibility, they must acknowledge themselves to be, either singly or in company, the kind of people who would merit study and attention in so wide a theater as that. Significant folk, perhaps even famous folk, perhaps even living markers of time and memory.

What does such a photograph say, an abstraction from the labor of filmmaking, a token, a clue? The people off-camera, that is, in the place where the camera is but not being gazed at by the camera, by *that* official camera.

[1] First, most elementally and most powerfully: "we" are here together in this place at this time. That is, we see fit not only to gather in association but to be seen by you in our joint relations. Each of us is happy enough, nay proud, to be linked to the others gathered here now. These other people merit my company, and I believe myself to merit theirs. Further, by our postures we are demonstrating a complete absence of malice or loathing between us. At this instant, this is how we are.

[2] Further, we recognize that we are standing in two places at the same time. We are here, before a photographer's camera, clustered to fit his frame, as he busies himself making this picture (and, possibly, other pictures, too). We are in the frame. But also, we are here in Galway or Astoria, making a film on a location or set, and we have paused during the work of making that film. There may or may not be telltale signs of the geographic locale inside the frame (the Irish-style whitewashed buildings, the lights on the set). By allowing this moment to be fixed in the photograph, we are inviting you to be here, too; here in the way that we are here. Not that in order to be here you wouldn't have to travel backward in time.

[3] Our presence in this spot is a temporary one. We are not inhabitants of this place, nor do we visit it frequently in the (day-to-day) personae you are seeing represented here. We have agreed to stand as we do partly to help the photographer, to whose purpose we yield and whose taste (or employer) we admire, but also because we have agreed already to be in this place generally, that is, on this location for the purpose of this project. We have traveled to be here, and when our project is done we anticipate traveling away, each of us to a separate home (a home, actually, that these others probably do not know how to locate). This co-presence is for the instant. It is as though by being caught here this way we form the place as well as the moment.

[4] The intent of our conjoining here is a kind of celebration, a celebration of each of us standing among these others and a celebration of the thing—the project— that has assembled us all. The project is something we are happy for others to

know about, and happy to signal ourselves "happy for others to know about," and also something of which we are each proud and happy (and willing for others to know that). We want to express, together, this mutual joy at being called to engagement together.

[5] More tacitly: we do know there is something called a "group photograph" and that such a thing might be made anywhere on earth where folk are gathered together at work, as we are here. (In his marvelous book *When Two or More Are Gathered Together*, Neal Slavin presents some very strange—and captivating—photographs of working groups unheard of and hardly imaginable [such as the Staff of the Grand Canyon posing at the lip].) Not only are we workers, then; we are workers eager and delighted to be known as such. This is surely not a tea party. (Yet there is a marvelous photograph of Cary Grant and James Mason enjoying their afternoon tea together at MGM, while shooting *North by Northwest*; both Englishmen, one from Yorkshire, one from Bristol, they had to have their teatime, and they are using proper china cups—it's a Hitchcock set after all.)

[6] But, should anyone mistakenly think to be seeing something here that touches on a reality removed from the artifice of performance, we wish to assert that these are still professional faces, whole and in place. We know as well as the photographer does that any photograph of such folk as we are, made in such a circumstance as this, might play in a publicity scheme, and so we are always—both on- and off-camera—set for giving a public face. Bluntly, on- or off-camera we are always *on*. These are our public off-camera faces, different from the faces of the roles we play when the film camera is turning. And, you may be sure, different from our faces at home in the kitchen.[1]

Not that one could propose that such busy folk as these would actually take a moment to make all of these assessments (and more). They live (and work) in a photographic age, where taking pictures of people is omnipresent, under extremely variant conditions. This is just—and nothing more than—"doing a picture." "Let's do a picture over there." One simply gets on with it, never articulating to oneself all of the tacit statements the photograph will inevitably make to those eager for reception. This hypothetical picture is only a quick shot between takes or at the end of a day's work, and because such people are photographed all the time they may very well never see this shot printed up and never remember they stood here to make it. Part of what they do for a living is to submit their faces to the camera, to *face the camera*.

Yet when the actors involved in such a photograph go to work, they do not change visibilities. They do perforce adopt different postures with regard to one another. They utter lines of dialogue written by someone else. They are prepared to repeat

---

[1] There is a charming apocryphal tale about John Wayne being discovered early one morning cooking scrambled eggs in the kitchen of the Formosa Café (on Santa Monica adjacent the former Warner Bros. Hollywood studios).

gestures and moments, if necessary, as many as a hundred times or more until the commanding presence says it's right. They are taken to be not themselves, in any sense, but instead the characters whose names they have been assigned. In order to make a scene work, each of them agrees tacitly to accept all the other players on camera at the same time, and not only to accept them as co-workers worthy of respect and courtesy but also to accept them in their roles. To believe those roles are not roles. To believe that they are interacting with *people*. Each accepts the existence of, and believes in the presence of, the other "people" in the scene, by name and by status and in complete denial—apparent denial—of the performance being created. In *King of Comedy*, Jerry Lewis is Jerry Langford, host of a late-night talk show on network television (à la mode de Johnny Carson), and De Niro is Rupert Pupkin, a delivery boy schlemiel from New Jersey who is fixated on the idea of becoming famous. "Jer"'s becoming the conversational Langford in this context, especially tricky given the fact that Lewis had indeed hosted late-night television, involves fully accepting and knowing Rupert's Rupertness, knowing this bumpkin in the way that Langford would know him, and never for a breath thinking of this specimen, while they are on camera, as anyone but Rupert, though of course he is completely aware that "Rupert" is "Bobby," Bobby his friend and protégé here. When one of the shots for the film is completed, and Pupkin is transformed for Jer back into Bobby, there is only scant effort involved on either side, the shift has been done so many times it is second nature. But the work involved here goes beyond memorizing lines in a script, to include actual mental processes which aid in the performance. Sometimes backstage or off-camera, actors will chat with each other using character names. In the picture here, are Jer and Bobby calling each other Jer and Bobby or Mr. Langford and Rupert? Can we tell from the faces?

The off-camera "reality" photograph would include actors, not characters, whereas off-camera publicity shots often replicate poses from scenes and mean to depict actors in role. One way actors could have of showing off the fact that they are not posing in role is by placement. A person playing a villain could stand next to, rubbing against, even arm in arm with a person playing his opponent in the film (as in the teatime photograph I cite above).

I mean here to point to an astonishing and potentially troubling aspect of cinematic production, namely, that the briefest and most unformalized of moments can be extended through time to make a representation far beyond what anyone could possibly intend in any one instant.[2] The snapshot—the snapped shot—can have a life. And conversely, one lives a life through moments, and a moment through instants, and an instant through the briefest of flickers, but any flicker can find its way into a record the application of which to some greater context, a personality, say, or a pattern of work, is a potentiality in other people's control. The posed off-camera photograph seems to have been something the poseurs know they are helping to make, since all of them look at the camera. With candid photography, the matter of whether or not a subject

---

[2] Well aware of this capacity of photography (and backstage filming) to stretch momentary breaths into solidified status tableaux, politicians, especially leaders of nations, often contrive poses and mutual regards in a session exactly to foster the illusion of relational permanence.

would have the legal right to see such material before it went public would be part of the contract negotiation, and with stars such negotiation would be detailed; but with lesser performers the contracts are simple and do not tend to include such prophylaxes.

But what lies deeper under the skin of the screen is more exciting and more confusing, still:

The film camera is not different from any other camera in that when its aperture is open and light streams in, it captures an array on a strip of film. Even when a cameraman is shooting digitally, with a high-res camera, the image, pixillated, is instantaneous, and here as with all shooting the resultant footage can be subdivided editorially for the purposes of making transitions and assemblages. Exactly in the way that a still camera off-set could perpetualize a swift instant's expression, so does a camera on set perpetualize, too. What we finally see onscreen are instants of a worker's life chained together, before us. But any one of these instants can be revealing (can be claimed revealing) in a way the subject (the actor) wouldn't have thought to countenance at all.[3] Or more: an expression of the instant, slipping in, as it were, can cause a filmed moment to glow, can enrich both a scenario and an aesthetic construction and a star career beyond anyone's wildest dreams. Such are so-called unscripted gestures that the camera can catch and the director choose to preserve. These sorts of gesture are not exactly inadvertent, in that because the actor/worker is fully conscious in front of the camera she knows what is happening with her body, and senses her inability to modify it; yet, they are as likely to be unexpected and unmapped by others, as not. Roy Scheider's gulping comment, "You're gonna need a bigger boat," in *Jaws* (at the instant he first sees the shark, and up far too close) is a legendary example. Scheider did this while the camera turned; he knew as he did it that he was doing it, and that the line was not in Carl Foreman's script; yet he may well have had no advance thought of doing it; so that it was a kind of tic, a spontaneity, even, perhaps, a goof—yet, of course, as we all know, a goof that became serious history. Another example is Dustin Hoffman's behavior at the lunch table with Meryl Streep in *Kramer vs. Kramer* (1979) as he suddenly smashes his glass of white wine against the wall. Part of what a director can do on set is bring an exceptional quality of openness and receptivity as actors work, so that something surprising can happen and when it does its marvel can be sensed on the spot. Yet sensing is not preserving; there can be surprising moments that don't make it onto film.

I want to take this one turn further.

In conventional, normal performative work in front of a camera—the making of a shot, and the doing of this through however many repetitions are called for—the performer is once again emitting behavior, is conscious of emitting this behavior, is fully willing to let the behavior shape itself or to openly act to shape it, and may never have thought of behaving this way, in advance. One does not have to plan every conscious moment. Every take is an event, therefore. And one can have no reason for believing that in take after take performers repeat themselves exactly. Indeed, there are plentiful reasons why they do not. The blocking will be repeated; and the dialogue, more or less.

---

[3] The important early contributor to this reader theory of interpretation, by which what an expressor intends to mean defers to what a perceiver interprets, was Wolfgang Iser. See *The Implied Reader*.

But the way of the behavior will be spontaneous and original to the moment always, because no one has any option but to be original to a moment. A depiction will finally result in a number of visible versions, all of which—errors and patches to the side—the filmmaker will watch critically with the aim in mind of selecting one, call it "the best" if you will but what it is, is the take that, at the moment of making the selection, strikes the selector most evocatively. We will see onscreen all of these judiciously *selected* takes, arranged in "proper" sequence, but many times performers will later on recall that they did something in other takes here or there that they considered to be better. The politique on set is that the director's considerations outweigh the performer's, although there is often give and take about this since a disgruntled performer is somebody no one wants around. Yet the actor's "best" version and the director's may not be the same.

(This kind of judgment is offered both immediately after a take, when the actor steps away and breathes satisfaction or dissatisfaction; and/or in the screening room, where the dailies go up.)

Actions, expressions, momentarities: these are not subject to precise repetition. And as every repetition happens at a point later in an actor's life it must of necessity have a difference, must reveal an accretion.

However the film is worked out, the moments of which it is structured are all idiosyncratic moments, there being no other kind, and because they are idiosyncratic they resemble the moment I hypothesized above, the posing in an instant of time before the off-camera photographer's lens. "This is it, now," such moments say. When motion picture actors migrate to the (Broadway) stage, if they have no previous stage training they can be put off-balance to realize that each idiosyncratic moment of their stage work will be, at this performance, the *only* possibility, whereas on set at a studio they were able to work things again and again with variation. Strangely, perhaps, the still photograph will work more in the way that stage acting works and less in the way that cinematic acting normally does; the moment of the shutter release will be the only version of its type and not so many such moments will be recorded (although with the automatic shutter release photography can become more like cinema in offering multiple "takes"). If another shot or two or three are made, each will be taken as different in that poseurs will not be feeling the obligation to replicate facial and bodily expression here, as they might feel on set. Where there are repetitive takes of a shot on set, the repetitions are taken as being equivalent to, even identical to, one another.[4] Certainly no vital character business can be allowed to show up in only one of several dozen takes, with the result that, however problematic it may be otherwise, this one-and-only take must be selected or the story falls apart.

So, the actor lives in the knowledge that every seen instant may be trapped and remembered long after and far away. But we are all in this position in the moments of our lives, doing while prone to being seen doing. For most of us, however, no one is watching, although the Instagram age might change all that.

---

[4] For *Star Wars* (1977), George Lucas paid for the development of a computer-controlled camera system which could produce mechanically identical camera movements for any number of successive takes; as long as in front of the camera there were only objects, not people, takes could be duplicated. David Cronenberg used a similar system for *Dead Ringers* (1988), but with an actor.

9

Being Alive

(Left) Joan Crawford with Ann Blyth in Mildred Pierce *(Michael Curtiz, Warner Bros., 1945); (Right) Adam Driver in* Marriage Story *(Noah Baumbach, Heyday/Netflix, 2019). Digital frame enlargements.*

Not long into *Chinatown* (1974) a private detective named Jake Gittes (Jack Nicholson) is caught nosing around a sluiceway for the California Aqueduct by a local thug (Roman Polanski), who teaches him to mind his own business by slashing his nasal septum. For almost the entire remainder of the story, Jake sports a pristine white gauze bandage on his nose, an artifact that converts a debilitation into a disfigurement and a disfigurement into a badge of honor. The distinction between disfigurement and debilitation can be crucial. In Jake's case, fictional though it be, disfigurement would involve interference with his presented appearance, that appearance being a principal method of signaling status (and of attracting other people's attention). Debilitation would produce difficulty at taking in air and, because the membranes of the nasal passage figure centrally in it, cutting off his taste. For a "dick" of his type, taste is operationally critical; he sniffs out clues, but now, of course, he won't be able to. Yet, for all the technical seriousness of his injury (the healing would require minor surgical attention, hence the bandaging in such professional terms), the oddness for the film's viewers is that Jake is never, in his bandaging, treated as other than decorated. Very soon the bandage ceases to remind us of his perils and his troubles and becomes a part of his recognizable self, a kind of beauty mark.

The character made fragile becomes onscreen a notable feature of the dramatic environment, but not a weakened agent of change. Through the period of injury his inherent strengths are sustained if not altogether enhanced. We see vigor, enthusiasm, perceptual acuity, appetite for solutions, zest for labor, in short distinctively embodied health. Psychoanalytically speaking, Jake's masculinity should be impaired if, as Robert Paul has suggested, the nose is an upper phallus (in an embodiment where the genital area is a "lower face"), but it is not; the wounded nose isn't a partial castration, it's merely a sartorial fix, like a change of necktie. A similar sustenance of capacity visits many screen figures who are posed for us as physically disabled, the sustenance suggested in many different kinds of display. In *Being There* (1979), Melvyn Douglas's Benjamin Rand is an aged multi-millionaire slowly dying in his rural castle, but for all his sickness he retains inordinate strength and vitality in being the target of a presidential visit (in full motorcade), the single dominating source of advice on whom the president (Jack Warden) counts in a difficult moment and the patient, generous host of the strange hero of the film (Peter Sellers). Rand's potency and vivacity are also signaled in repeated images of the gigantic and delicately manicured estate that stretches for miles in every direction like the manor house of a British lord, and in the cardinal obedience of his staff. A very sick man treated by all those around him, very notably, as though he is still altogether hale and in control.

The staging of Earl Partridge's (Jason Robards) incapacity in *Magnolia* (1999) is managed dramaturgically, since it is in a stupor that we find him lying abed, his energies and powers sapped away by disease. But his spiritual strength is echoed by, or projected outward into, the youthful vitality of Frank T. J. Mackey (Tom Cruise) and the nurse Phil Parma (Philip Seymour Hoffman) who attend his bedside. In Bergman's *Cries and Whispers* (1972), Agnes (Harriet Andersson) lies at the brink of death under starched white sheets while all around her, in a vast room entirely coated in vermilion, the color of burgeoning, of force, of intensity, her sisters whisper and migrate. Death as stage drama. In Don Siegel's *The Shootist* (1976), aged gunfighter J. B. Books (John Wayne) cannot die of his disease until he has paid courtly respect to his landlady Bond Rogers (Lauren Bacall) and passed on the secret of masculine nobility to her young son Gillom (Ron Howard) in scenes where the old man's presence, portrayed as only a diminished version of what it once was, is shown as a kind of reflection of the strength and endurance of Bond and Gillom. The last moments of the very frail patriarch Adam Trask (Raymond Massey) in *East of Eden* (1955), lying motionless in bed after a severe stroke that has warped his face, are made tonally vigorous and feelingful through the presence of his alienated son Cal (James Dean), who now tenderly bonds with his father again. The mortality is a dramatic set-up for the reunification, which has a glow. We can think of the dignifying regal formality surrounding the decapitation of Mary, Queen of Scots (Vanessa Redgrave, 1971); the extraordinarily energetic pursuits, challenges, and confrontations that follow from the accidental shooting death of Marie (Franka Potente) at the beginning of *The Bourne Supremacy* (2004); the austere but magnificent dramatic elaboration (taking up the space of an entire film) that is produced through the death of Kane (Orson Welles, 1941), whose final breath, albeit vitiating, is still powerful enough to articulate a single word that engenders a mystery story; and the suicide of Larry Renault (John Barrymore) in *Dinner at Eight* (1933), staged with all the panache a master of the dramatic can manage, with spotlighting, props, and a proper turn-out to an eager and hopefully adoring audience.

Cinema repeatedly escorts us through the gates of mortality in suitable decor:

- The dying or exceedingly ill figure is ennobled, raised, strengthened, and intensified by virtue of being played by a performer of significant reputation, notable fame. The grander the performer's reputation, the grander may seem the affliction. "O, what a *noble* mind is here o'erthrown!" (*Hamlet* III.1.150; emphasis mine). An epitome is powerful Richard III embodied by Laurence Olivier (1955).

- The depiction of illness or passing is extended through being made dramatically significant in itself, crucial for the unfolding story (no better example of which is Scorsese's *The Last Temptation of Christ* [1988]). Debility or illness is a signal and event-inducing aspect of a character's presence (the mother in *Now, Voyager* [Gladys Cooper, 1942]). Great energies of expectation, fear, and anticipation are associated with dying or being rescued from death (Georgie's beloved mother in *The Magnificent Ambersons* [Dolores Costello, 1942], Alicia Huberman after being poisoned in *Notorious* [Ingrid Bergman, 1946]). Frailty and vulnerability to pain are made the center of powerful expressive moments, even of emphatic bodily gestures (Ellen throwing herself downstairs to abort a foetus in *Leave Her to Heaven* [Gene Tierney, 1945]; Judah's mother and sister as targets of his undying love and long, beleaguered search as they fester in a leper colony and are healed after the crucifixion in *Ben-Hur* [Martha Scott, Cathy O'Donnell, 1959]).

- Telltale effects of debility are elided onscreen. In place of wounds or evidences of tricky body management such as seepage we are shown, through dramatic contiguity, mechanical devices associated with repair. Ron Kovic's (Tom Cruise) wheelchair in *Born on the Fourth of July* (1989), or Sheridan Whiteside's (Monty Woolley) in *The Man Who Came to Dinner* [1942]) or, of course, Jeff Jefferies's (James Stewart) in *Rear Window* (1954). Elaborate bed rigs for broken limbs, complicated, colorful, and expensive emergency resuscitation equipment for sudden cardiac troubles, even ritual surgical garb and ritual surgical tools as in the scarlet gowns and weird devices in *Dead Ringers* (1988). All these metonymies are triumphs for set decorators and property managers, and special trouble is taken to illuminate them crisply and feature them in shots. Mildred Dunnock wheelchair-bound in *Kiss of Death* (1947); Eddie Redmayne in *The Theory of Everything* (2014); Ray Liotta in *Hannibal* (2001).

But deeper and more delicate than these arrangements and the fictive situations they help render for the screen is the ongoing, breathed, experiential vulnerability of the body, those "thousand natural shocks/That flesh is heir to" (*Hamlet* III.i.63–64), that all of us endure on a regular basis through pain, limping, and dermatological sensitivity. Not to mention the frailty of thought: "Present fears/Are less than horrible imaginings" (*Macbeth* I.iii.50–51). A character's wariness, her anxiety, her remorse, his confusion, his nerves: Bergman in *Notorious*, Ronald Colman in *Random Harvest* (1942), Russell Crowe in *A Beautiful Mind* (2001), Doris Day in *Midnight Lace* (1960), Natalie Wood in *Inside Daisy Clover* (1965), Adam Driver in *Marriage Story* (2019). The tender body, the tender mind, and also the tender spirit: Bruce Willis in *The Sixth Sense* (1999), Lillian Gish in *The Night of the Hunter* (1955), Charles Laughton in *Rembrandt* (1936), Angelina Jolie in *Changeling* (2008), especially in the nonpareil moment on the railway platform when she walks bravely toward her missing son. The living of life is a precarious endeavor, and a subtle, charged, intimating, and vulnerable ongoingness. The sense in which one knows—especially with age—that one can never be certain, that there is no certainty (not even of the single death that awaits), that one's measurements and calculations are all subject to gravity, and that gravity is subject to the speed of travel in relation to the speed of light, and that the speed of light is something that can only be stabbed at. Imagine the legion films we have all seen in which characters speak definitively, boldly, assuredly. "We'll always have Paris."

The presentation of real tenderness and vulnerability is so often circumlocuted and circumscribed, the image composed by moving around—perhaps away from, but never into contact with—the responsive skin of life. We are in a cellar in Steven Spielberg's *War of the Worlds* (2005) where desperate Tom Cruise and mad Tim Robbins are circling in the dark shades as little Dakota Fanning crouches for her life, all in the presence of the intruding spotlighting tentacle which is an extension of the alien Martian automaton. Around and around it snakes, turning corners, beaming its "gaze," while our tender characters creep and race to skirt its path. Fanning is photographed to reveal terror, Cruise to reveal unstopping urgency, Robbins to reveal a mind out of control with fear, yet through all of this the dominating force on the screen is the slithering silver mechanical weapon, the eye of the killer, confident, motor-driven, immortal. Or take that considerably celebrated moment in *The Third Man* (1949) when from a gondola of a Ferris wheel at its apogee, Holly (Joseph Cotten) listens to Harry Lime (Orson Welles) glibly point at the "ants" down below and speculate as to how unimportant and unnoticeable it would be, in the grand state of affairs, if all of them should perish of a tainted serum he is black-marketing. Death by scores, even thousands, yet all of this swept away for the instant by the spectacular view from on high, Harry's tranquil and marvelous face and intoxicating (Orson Welles's *always* intoxicating) voice. Holly's horror, and the imaginary agonies of the "ants" below are all replaced, circled away from, by Harry's presence.

Are there moments possible when the quick tenderness of living can be revealed openly, directly, with no shield or filter of mannerism interceding between the show of it and our gawking eyes? There is hardly merit in hunting with no hope of success. Here, I think, are some moments of what could be called *liveliness*:

[1] Mildred Pierce has come up to her bedroom to tuck her teenaged daughter Veda in and wish her goodnight (Joan Crawford, Ann Blyth, 1945). Soft bedside lamplight, Veda in a flannel nightie. The mother sitting on the bed and being soft-voiced. A tender moment between mother and daughter. Why, Mother, Veda wants to know, won't you marry Wally, who has proposed, because it would be nice to have a bigger house and a maid. "I . . . don't love him," Mildred answers, just a tiny bit dislocated—not quite shocked—to realize she's being quizzed

this way, and by her daughter of all people. You wouldn't want me to marry someone I didn't really love, would you? But, Mother, we could have. . . . Selfish, self-centered, altogether narcissistic Veda. Now Mildred leans over to give her daughter the normal good-night kiss and Veda says, "Oh, don't let's get all sticky about it." Mildred pulls herself up, inhaling, as Veda turns away (thanks to Michael Curtiz's splendid direction, the camera is on the side of the bed to which she turns, so that now she is facing us). *"Oh, don't let's get all sticky about it."* And here, in an all but wholly silent flash, is a moment Crawford shares: just a little hesitation, just a hiccup. The hiccup of Mildred suddenly understanding that her daughter doesn't have feeling for her, not true feeling, that for the girl the mother-daughter relationship is about provision, not emotion. Veda, in short, is only a kid, still entirely dependent for her upkeep on the adult she lives with, and this adult is but a person who is older and under whose umbrella she still lives: we can see Crawford causing Mildred to become aware of this suddenly, now, here, as though for the first time. Mildred's subtle regret, however, is not for the loss of her daughter's affection, or even for the sudden suspicion that her daughter never did have affection for her, but for something more provocative that pricks the bubble of her spirit, and this is her own horridly disappointed want—as she sees it suddenly now in the spotlight glare of Veda's turn-off— that Veda should have been her friend. That the love of the child should have had a genuine and equable simplicity. Between these two, apparently now, such an arrangement is impossible, and has always been impossible, and will be impossible always; it is a condition of the social arrangement within which they are forced to live, in America, in the war, now. A world of disorganization and chaos, where for a child predictable stability is paramount above all things, yet also a world in which an adult could feel vitiating loneliness, especially when, as with Mildred, she is living in separation from an abusive spouse. Horrible loneliness, desperate hunger for real affection and love if only for a fraction of an instant late at night. So she is taken by force, entirely without so much as a gasp of warning, before a cold mirror, child as mirror, situation as mirror, and can see—and *must* see—that she is not the person she had wanted to be. *She is not the person she had wanted to be.* All of this given over by the slightest pause, the focus in the eyes quickly sharpening, the hands—and a self—withdrawn.

[2] Veda Pierce and a few other notable examples (like Patty McCormack's Rhonda Penmark in *The Bad Seed* [1956]) to the side, the child onscreen is very frequently seen experiencing events through a fragile and sensitive spontaneity, the face ongoingly giving display of quick—that is, believably authentic— emotional reaction. In the child status, the character is both open to (new) experience and undefendedly prone to being the target of adults' actions. In *Shane* (1953), for example, little Joey Starrett (Brandon De Wilde, aged six) keeps staring at Shane's (Alan Ladd) pistol in its holster, his eyes widening as though in confrontation with a cobra. Shane takes a sunny moment to give the boy some shooting lessons (not exactly with the father's blessing), but the child simply

reaches out with a disarming directness to the older figure and his offering. *So this is what it's like not to be a child any more.* A tender, malleable, even delicate young masculinity is to be seen in Daniel's (Ralph Macchio) deference to his sensei Mr. Miyagi (Pat Morita) in *The Karate Kid* (1984), the boy straining his muscles and withstanding numerous wounds both physical and emotional as he labors to learn the vital (and mysterious) lessons on offer, lessons, finally, not about losing boyish sensitivity but about shaping and guiding it. *So this is what I can do with my posture!* In *E.T. the Extra-Terrestrial* (1982), little Elliott (Henry Thomas) displays his weakness and endangerment most dramatically in competition against a horde of government agents who are chasing him with weapons drawn, but what he brings forth, a quality that more or less obliterates the adults from the scene, is a single-minded purposiveness and concentration, a motive so unadulterated, so strong, if also so impetuous, that it momentarily escapes the bounds of the human. And in her extreme self-consciousness and hypersensitivity, the eponymous heroine of *Carrie* (Sissy Spacek, 1976) is finally brought to an apocalypse of degradation, only there to find some heretofore buried internal strength helping her stand for herself against all odds. All of these young people, and so many more, are defined narratively as only proto-agents, unready for the serious demands of action in the "real" world and, by virtue of this unreadiness, still feeling their way forward with the aid of sensitivities and threatened by vulnerabilities suffered only by the young. The cases I give above are all ones in which the performer's genuineness to the moment, the unpredicted gestures and unrepeatable flickers of feeling, make the moments stand out from the legion dramatic instances in film stories where performers work by giving over routinized expressions and poses, however delicate. The routinization is a signal of performativity, of a certain withdrawal from events at hand, a withdrawal we have no chance to see with Elliott pumping his bicycle to save his and E.T.'s lives or with Carrie under the torrent of pig's blood or with Daniel half-crippled practicing the "crane" move by sunset on the beach or with Joey as he tries to escape the bounds of his own skin in order to bond with Shane.

Routinization dresses, as well as supports, most screen performance, no matter its astounding power and artistic flair. In *The Entertainer* (1960), for instance, Laurence Olivier's Archie Rice, a has-been song-and-dance man in the music halls now facing an uncertain future, is profoundly—yet always—Olivier in character mode, one of his very great numbers, all articulate and glorious in their ways. If Joan Crawford is Ann Blyth's mother in a whole, thoroughgoing, penetrating, even shocking way Blyth never quite becomes Crawford's daughter, except in that she gives us the performative surface professionally and smoothly. The same actor can go both ways. In *Becket* (1964), Richard Burton is stellar, but obviously performatively so. In *The Spy Who Came In from the Cold* (1965), he is lost in Alec Leamas to such a degree, roughed up by experience to such a degree, that his actions onscreen become painfully real, all through the film, offset even by the smart character performances bobbing all around.

In *Marriage Story*, the talented Adam Driver is "giving an act" all through, sometimes tuned up very high and sometimes the opposite but always in performance mode, until an utterly startling moment when at a little bar he stands up at a microphone and sings "Being Alive" from Stephen Sondheim's *Company*, not partially but completely, all the way to the final note. Here, penetrating the irony of performance—because this is a musical number from a stage show, and he is playing a stage director (who may well have starred in, or directed, it once), and he has an "audience" of chums drinking their beers, and he is using a "microphone" (visibly but not really), and he is punching out the song as though on Broadway—is a baring of the most tortured, most sensitive, most human parts of the character and actor's soul. The character's and actor's soul: one soul between them.

10

For Your Eyes Only

James Stewart (with Fred Graham's arm) in Vertigo *(Alfred Hitchcock, Paramount, 1958). Digital frame enlargement.*

We write after speaking and speak after hearing. Hearing is first. It is a terribly strange experience to see a world for the first time (this is what happens when we watch a film) and have no voice. Objects swell and diminish, glide and leap, fade and brighten. The world of these objects, their array, their juxtapositions, not only grows and morphs but also rapidly twitches and confuses, a forest in which one is repeatedly lost in the light. Cinema was not thoroughly acoustic until 1926–7, but it was always pictorial, lambent, changing. Consider how in particular circumstances a filmic moment can be built out of what is visible; aimed to startle or please the eye; reside on the screen as something that cannot be adequately talked about, because what we see is always something around which our paltry language skirts.

One speaks, sometimes, of a film as "a feast for the eyes." Saying or thinking this, we usually mean to make reference to some very elaborate, typically expensive and aesthetically marvelous arrangement, to make which somebody spent a great deal of time, energy, and money. The magical woods in Ridley Scott's *Legend* (1985). Rural England in Stanley Kubrick's *Barry Lyndon* (1975; all shot by candlelight). The chariot race in William Wyler's *Ben-Hur* (1959). Tim Burton's *Wonderland* (2010), a mania of design springing away from Tenniel. Often when we are offered a feast for the eye, our response pays less attention to the eye, beneficiary and trustee, than to the emotion we can verbalize, to the relatively few words that we can find in the mammoth cavern of our heard world.

Notwithstanding that cinema offers sights, insufficient attention has been paid to the onscreen moment *as a sight*. The awkwardness of silence in which we struggle with the image, the always flickering image, the frantic and finally hopeless search for words: these are bypassed in a too-glib summarization that treats what has been seen only as an echo. If the screen is our new sun, our new Sun King, source of light and power and wonder and order (see Jay), we shade our eyes in muteness.

Seven illustrative cases:

[1] In Daniel Espinosa's *Life* (2017), a microbe brought on board a spacecraft far from earth and held inside a transparent protective "cage" begins to respond to touch and then to grow. The film will turn on this ability of the Entity to grow and morph, and on the initial innocence and unfurling panic of the crew (this film is something of a remake of *Alien* [1979]). The audience must be given a chance to experience the thing's changing quite beyond the observations that crew members could report to one another, however dramatically, in suitably written scenes. Using CGI, the filmmaker offers us some shots replicating what we are to assume the most scientific member of the crew can see when through a hyper-powerful magnifying scope he intently peers at the object. The "bacterium," as it were (the initial design is modeled on a bacterium-type form), fills the large-format screen, this in order that the view through the magnifying scope be mimicked. It becomes proportionally larger than any human sitting in a theater watching. As it is so large, its very slightest motion can be detected and noted as an event. Laying aside the whole opera of what happens with this Thing and these crewmen and this ship and this movie, the point is that we are given this extraordinary opportunity to *see*. Not just the depiction of a microscope magnification but this depiction on a large screen itself: a magnified magnification. We are offered the chance to mock up what the scientist is experiencing as he gets his chance to *see*. No matter the advancement of futuristic science (clearly this film is set in the future), what is important can be distinguished from the background hubbub only and principally because *it can be seen in its distinctiveness*.

[2] In *Alien*, a malevolent creature is born out of the chest cavity of a human stretched in agony upon a table (John Hurt). In a view similar to what would be shared by medical students of a surgery in an operating room, far above the incision, we look directly down onto the man's chest, clothed entirely in white, and see pulsing expansion, like a growing balloon, and then puncture—the shirt and the skin beneath it ripped open (incised) from within and spewing blood (blood made all the more visible because of the whiteness of the shirt). A hideous multi-toothed

vermiform entity prods out, sticks up its head, glares (at what is taken to be the surrounding crew members of the fated star vessel *Nostromo* but what also seems to be the viewer's eye, confronted directly) and, showing what definitely appears a combination of surprise, curiosity, and extreme arrogance, leaps away to the floor and races off to hide. Two aspects of this: notwithstanding the design and motility of the "creature" (a plastics-cum-makeup contrivance, hydraulically operated from off-camera), the charge is conveyed by virtue of (a) the rhythmic timing of the eruption, (b) the quantity of "blood" that sprays from the opened chest, and (c) the starched whiteness of the garment in the first place. Getting white clothing is no great difficulty, but the lighting has to be adjusted so that the overall bright spot of the actor's body does not mar the exposure of the shot and make it difficult to see the far darker "thing." Needless to say, the whiteness is the perfect ground for a display of blood. But the most penetrating fear is brought on as a direct result of our cold observation: by the very camera position, our hovering attentively, instrumentally, far too dispassionately over the "surgery."

[3] A long "ape" sequence famously commences *2001: A Space Odyssey* (1968), with a platoon of sociable simians living in caves and interacting with their environment. Since language is fundamentally absent here the viewer's visual capacities are extended, and if ever in the film there is to be a spectatorial hunt for controlling artifice it will be here. To augment the realism of the apes, given that they are on camera for a very long chain of scenes and perform with what seems great (even choreographed) intentionality, arrangements are made for two aids to sight: first, no extremely close shots are made of any of these creatures; second, one of them cradles in her arms a "baby" that is actually a baby, that is, a very young chimp brought into the array for spice. The "adult" simians are all actor/dancers in costume. A not unrelated trick for the eye is used by Hitchcock in *Saboteur* (1942) where he has a shot requiring very long depth of field but must make it on a limited sound stage; for persons to be thought far away from the principals who are near the camera, he employed midgets. With Kubrick, an astonishing vision is offered: we are somehow back at the "Dawn of Man," hanging out with proto-humans in their caves, nestling, observing the day-to-day activities of their lives. Of course this vision interfaces with the viewer's imagination, but the point is that the interface is by way of the composed image, not the action arc of the sequence.

[4] In Rand Ravich's *The Astronaut's Wife* (1999), there is a moment, utterly crucial to the plot as a whole, in which a returning astronaut (Johnny Depp) gives his wife (Charlize Theron) a seductive kiss at a party in a lush hotel lobby. The joke here is that both Depp and Theron were much publicized "sex symbols" by this time, so much so that their joining for a kiss would have been so expected as to be almost invisible. In order to give the necessary highlight not only to this physicality but, even more importantly, to this moment, the filmmaker arranges that as Depp's Spencer Armacost pushes Jillian up against a tiled column and

kisses her, the camera should rotate so that there is an appearance of the world turning and the lovers becoming horizontal. The viewer feels delirious, even vertiginous. The feeling of something important and life-changing is conveyed through the *optical* manipulation.

[5] In *Jaws* (1975), once it has become clear to the town sheriff (Roy Scheider) that a marauding Great White might be in the area and he has briefed the powers that be, we are given a shot of the mayor (Murray Hamilton) arguing that, for business reasons, the island must be open to tourists on the upcoming 4th of July holiday, no matter what. He is clearly both a nervous wreck (because of what the local big money could do for his chances of re-election) and a craven businessman himself, his eyes virtually popping not only with anger at the ridiculousness of the proposal to shut the place off but also with hunger for the money he sees floating in. Two emphases are afforded this untidy man's speech:

First, he is dressed (by Robert Ellsworth and Irwin Rose) in an outlandish sports jacket, as "loud" as "loud" can be, pale blue and dotted all over with white anchors that seem to jump out against the more natural colors of the beach behind him and the blue sky. He is a sailor? Or a weekend sailor? Or merely a fan of sailors? Or merely a desk jockey who likes to decorate himself in the spirit of the sea? He outspeaks himself through his dress; labors (since the mayor "chose his own clothing") to be noticed; works at being heard, being a center of attention, because, we are meant to surmise, actually bereft of talent he is but a pawn on a gameboard being played by much more serious and potent forces. But second, very prominent in the shot, directly behind Hooper the oceanographer (Richard Dreyfuss) and the sheriff and spreading as though to infinity in the background, is a gigantic beachside billboard advertising AMITY ISLAND WELCOMES YOU. On it, in boldly colored cartoon, lounges a teenaged girl resting on a raft and looking out with a seductive gaze. But—"Sick vandalism!"—someone has taken black paint and modified this picture: behind the raft a triangular fin sticks up, and a talk bubble has been hooked to her face: "HELP!!! SHARK." Her eyes have been doctored so that she regards the fin with excited fear. Her mouth is open and she displays glaring snow-white teeth. A white preserve, this little spot in paradise, visited by a white devil, to be sure. (This was all set up in an opening montage where we are at an all-white teenagers' beach party by firelight.) The mayor's particular "whiteness" equates with squeamishness, with a frantic attempt to climb a ladder to success. But beyond the whiteness is the simple function of the billboard altogether, that it proclaims capitalism and capital interests, the jolt of big money hitting the till (presumably summer rentals in Amity are exorbitantly costly). "Look. We depend on the summer people here for our very lives." Mayor Vaughan stands, then, in front of a makeshift backdrop bespoke for a man of his concerns and values, but at the same time centrally sketching the lines of confrontation and plot crux of the film. (If we merely listen to him, we will catch his squeamish panic but miss the explanatory visual context.)

[6] In Douglas Sirk's *Imitation of Life* (1954), we are faced throughout with a visual display of the odd *distinctness* of the faces of the four central protagonists, Lana Turner, Juanita Moore, Sandra Dee, and Susan Kohner, all four being dressed, posed, and lit to bring out quite emphatically the variant colors of the skin. That in their comfortable residence the white woman and her white daughter are accompanied by an African American woman and her mulatto daughter; that the daughters interact, as do the mothers, in contrasting pairs. That one daughter secretly envies the other, and resents her inability to have the same skin. That social class is coded in terms of skin color. Further, that with Turner and Dee one has what were at the time absolute quintessences of white femininity Hollywood style. Kohner slides back and forth in position and status, never quite fitting in, no matter the folk she is with, because her chum is too white and her mother is too dark. The film turns out to be all about domesticity and its implications, in its conjunction with race (and racism) in America, but only to hear it—the dialogue elides references to race and color for the most part—is to miss this principle.

[7] Or, in Hitchcock's *Rear Window* (1954) that Miss Lonelyhearts (Judith Evelyn), a *very middle-aged* woman living across the courtyard from our spying protagonist (and on ground level, where the garden grows), should for an important evening dress herself in rich, vegetative green, the color of the fierceness of springtime. Younger than springtime, indeed, by virtue of her hopes of the appearance she will present as lure and of the trout she may be lucky enough to catch. The green (by Edith Head) is just a little too much like the bride's in *The Arnolfini Marriage* (1434), a little too provocative, too pronounced, even from a distance.

One could go on at very great length, showing how eyefuls are out in the forest to be hunted. Miss Lonelyhearts, green with desire and perhaps too soon to be green with envy and remorse. Susie Meredith somehow incapable of grasping the torment of Sarah Jane Johnson, who *sees* that she cannot fit. The *Jaws* beach scene as a premonition drawn on a large canvas. Spencer and Jillian going out of sync with the rest of our vision of the film when they kiss. The apparently real apes bringing us back thousands, if not tens of thousands, of years into a past we have never been present to image but seem to be present in, now. The exploding chest a clue as to what this alien can accomplish within (and with) the human body. The microbial view of what seems a simple biological organism bringing us, by way of the eye, closer than we dreamed possible: in fact, too close. These are all visual moments. Either entirely or largely, a sound accompaniment is held back so that the play of action is by way of dimensions that the visual apparatus, alone, catches. Size and proportion, precise placement, contrast of illumination or colors, the intimation of color, orientation, and angularity, the frame and its so articulate boundaries within which, and beyond which, someone or something might move.

11

Hands

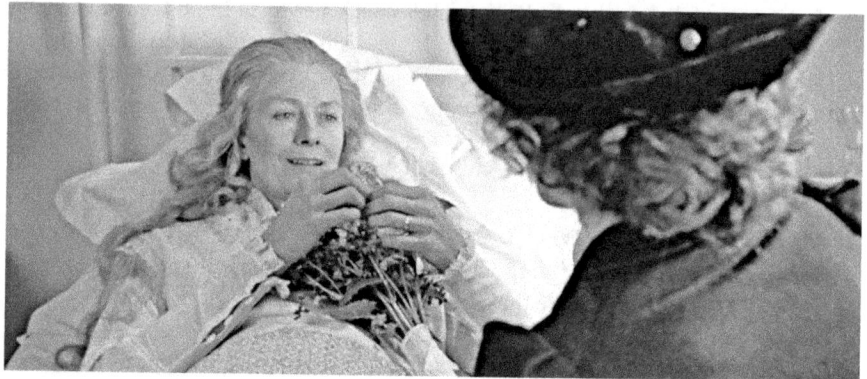

Vanessa Redgrave in Howards End *(with Emma Thompson) (James Ivory, Merchant Ivory Productions, 1992). Digital frame enlargement.*

In our new age of mannerism, in which dramatic displays play so prominent a role in everyday business and cultural dialogue: on the evening news; in the latest Netflix offering; through downloads, through perpetual YouTube, with TCM screening movies from "the past," not to say in theatrical offerings of all kinds, all discussed and argued about, theorized, compended, measured, compared—a world of illusion—it is a hurdle to invoke the idea of sincere love, indeed, to invoke sincerity of any kind beyond *the impression of sincerity*. Love is now conventionally represented by "the love display," in the process fully becoming its own display *as display*: a display of a display of love. Display replaces commitment. Not only display but photogenic display: the face with the glowing smile, the tender embrace softly posed by the fireplace, the stolen kiss by moonlight, and with strings sawing melancholically in the background: if not strings then a haunting lyric by a contemporary band to add layering and piquancy through a language "smartly" distant. And if not tenderness then a vertical wrestling to disrobe up against a wall.

Love takes time, as do the blossomings of other emotions and the securings of other commitments, yet attraction may be quick, and the expensiveness of dramatic media means that time is always at a premium and attraction must always outweigh commitment. Onscreen, then, we will see love develop over a dissolve, even over a cut, perhaps mature in a bopping ballet, and quickly turn corners, too. Love is a racer—a supreme athlete. Thoroughly to confuse our children we make depictions of teenage relationships in which love is accompanied by anguish, surprise, wounding, and loss, all transpiring speedily enough to fit a series episode and all staged realistically enough to give at least the surface impression that everyday life is, or could be, a race like this. "The Race to Get Ahead." Love means tears (because tears work nicely in a scene [and can be done, if necessary, with makeup]). Love is a nice pretext for sex (because sex is always profitable for producers). And love is for paragons: the attractive female with the radiant glow, caught up by the attractive male with the twinkly eyes. The female radiance and the masculine twinkle are the codes that tell us, "This Is Love."

The Theory of Everything (2014) begins this way, Radiance + Twinkle, but soon "degenerates" into a story of lasting commitment between a faithful and serious woman and her very afflicted, then wheelchair-bound husband (Stephen Hawking, played with some authenticity by Eddie Redmayne). To put this in reverse: *The Theory of Everything* is about a faithful and serious woman and her very afflicted, then wheelchair-bound husband but will not function adequately as a popular film unless it begins with an attractive female and her radiant glow, caught up by an attractive male with his twinkly eyes. The typical love story in fictional film is a rationalization for, and opportunity to promulgate, gender stereotypes (still almost always dutifully heterosexual) of the most commercial sort. "I love you, I love you, and also I love you." Vince Vaughn and Jennifer Aniston. Elizabeth Taylor and Montgomery Clift. George O'Brien and Janet Gaynor. Kristen Stewart and Robert Pattinson. Sidney Poitier and Katharine Houghton. Charlie Chaplin and Paulette Goddard.

Onscreen love must either be, or resolve into, a focus upon people, thus seem an affair of the corpus in its agonies and strivings and a ceremony of ritual touches and decorations. A character may love an object, but the love of objects will be forsworn for the love of an appropriate other. A character who loves an animal will grow toward love of a human being, indeed the animal will function as a pedagogical substitute.

Love of a human being:

- Take *The Band Wagon* (1953), a first-class Hollywood musical starring Fred Astaire and Cyd Charisse. She is a ballerina and he is a hoofer, so that when they are cast together in a Broadway production, they must battle to work together. Quickly they conclude they do not like each other. The invocation of disregard followed by its conversion, patiently but inexorably, into adoration (and presumably commitment) is a major theme of the story, here, now, always, and notably with Astaire and his partners.[1] She comes to his suite at the Plaza to make apology for scorning him. Beautiful plain, sincere, immaculate white dress. He is in casual wear (for Astaire, this is always color-coordinated and prohibitively swank) and he invites her into his pink suite laid over, all along the floor, with framed paintings. To put it simply, everybody who is anybody is there, Renoir and all his *amis*, Tony's rooms beginning to take on the character of a gallery. At one point as they go for a carriage ride in the park she makes a comment about him being much the older

---

[1] See Feuer.

and, demurring, he lets her know *those weren't reproductions*. This is sweet but swifter than swift, because we have already left those canvases behind, in fact far behind, being interested in these two beautiful languid poses in the horse-drawn vehicle. They are letting the horse decide where to go, and he delivers them to their final apotheosis inside the park when they perform "Dancing in the Dark," perhaps the greatest single dance rendition on film. But those paintings (which have become nothing as the love pair emerge from the fog) . . .

Imagine Tony Hunter as a man whose films have made him a bundle and who therefore has money to burn. He has gone out and, probably over some time, actually bought these canvases (most likely already framed).

Imagine that this man has had access to canvases such as these (by the painters who were invoked in the stage settings for the ballet "An American in Paris" two years before: the *actual* Impressionists). He knew where to get them, he went shopping. From a number of options he chose these (these and not others).

And imagine that this man is so closely in touch with those paintings, that he cares for them so very much, that rather than entrusting them for safekeeping to a bank he prefers to let them decorate his hotel rooms. What's a painting for, after all, but to look at?

Imagine, then, an artistic man, cultivated, articulate, and mature, who is in love with art. In love with art, with artists, with the work they produced. He does not wish to be apart from it. And for a few moments he shared it with his new friend, who was far too young (and inexperienced) to know a real Renoir when she was gawking at one.

The love of some paintings, then. Yet:

In the film, this love is a trivium to be tossed away with a single flip comment and then forgotten in the wake, while the voyage steams full throttle ahead to reveal the feelingful partnership of Tony and Gabrielle. And it is a splendid partnership, revealed in a splendid way. But also a dominating force that erases what we learn to take as a *lesser* love.

- Or E. M. Forster's monumental *Howards End*, published in 1910 and filmed in 1992 by Ismail Merchant and James Ivory. Ruth Wilcox, married to an aloof magnate of banking and exchange, is now and has always been raptly in love with her country estate Howards End, a comfortable and sedate home of true design and proportion, the treasure of her eye and heart. She comes into the acquaintance of Margaret Schlegel who, with her sister, lives across the way in London, in a house that they can no longer afford to keep up and that therefore must be sold. It becomes strikingly apparent to Mrs Wilcox that Margaret has the same kind of love for her home as she herself treasures for Howards End, and that now Miss Schlegel's love will be broken. Howards End is a very special place, built beside, and incorporating in spirit, a "very splendid tree":

    > "It is the finest wych-elm in Hertfordshire. Did your sister tell you about the teeth?"
    > "No."

"Oh, it might interest you. There are pigs' teeth stuck into the trunk, about four feet from the ground The country people put them in long ago, and they think that if they chew a piece of the bark, it will cure the toothache. The teeth are almost grown over now, and no one comes to the tree."

"I should. I love folklore and all festering superstitions."

"Do you think that the tree really did cure toothache, if one believed in it?"

"Of course it did. It would cure anything—once."

"Certainly I remember cases—you see I lived at Howards End long, long before Mr Wilcox knew it. I was born there." (82)

Ruth makes an arrangement that after her death—which comes, as happens, very soon later—Howards End will devolve not to her husband or children (who don't care at all about it) but to Margaret. Margaret the stranger, only vaguely comprehensible.

Margaret is at Howards End. As time passes, Mr Wilcox courts and marries her, and the novel ends with Margaret living in tranquility in the magnificent house in Hertfordshire, her husband stolidly by her side, but her truest companion of the heart being a memory of Ruth Wilcox and a constantly enchanting view of the house itself, the great legacy. We imagine for ourselves the spirits and feelings of characters in text, but onscreen, once the roles have been cast, we are presented with the inevitable façades of faces and postures and dress and gesture. Margaret is played by Emma Thompson, with a typical querulousness and receptivity. If she perhaps lacks a little style, she dresses with propriety and neatness and has a keen mind—Thompson is very accomplished at enunciation and tonality. Wilcox is given life in a very superior performance by Anthony Hopkins: a stiff-backed fellow, with a view of the world (constantly appreciated through majestic postures), and a very old-fashioned sense of propriety and order. Brittle, let us say, so that if he has feeling it would be something we could only guess at. Will she soften him? Will he give her a framework? Yes, to both questions. But Ruth Wilcox is our concern here, the woman whose heart was given over to Howards End. The very skilled Vanessa Redgrave plays her as, quite beyond intelligent, eccentric. An odd, unexplained and inexplicable turn of the head or gaze. Strange pauses, as in dreams. A very lavish ensconcement among pillows and soft lights, but at the same time an odd fragility—she is not a small person but her strengths are small. And what happens in the film, what must happen if it is to find its audience in the theater (away from the reading chair) is that Ruth's weird love affair with Howards End must suffer conversion, even wholesale transformation, and become, of course, Margaret's odd but solid love for Wilcox and his for her, their redeeming marriage in the train of the marriage that never was.

If all this development is in the Forster, yet the film extends and sharpens it, since the Ruth we meet in London is never quite there—no, she is in Hertfordshire, and this distance is available to us with every glance at her face. Margaret is thoroughly susceptible and Wilcox thoroughly dominating as a shaper of destinies. Hopkins and Thompson together are like a Rodin, whereas Redgrave is a mist, astonishingly beautiful to contemplate but not "to be taken seriously" in the way that they are. Love of an object? The ailing woman's weirdness, her abnormal love, calls for kind charity in Merchant and Ivory's viewer.

Object love is important as a keystone to understanding cinematic arrangements because onscreen a figure's contact with a thing, even a very large thing like a house in the country, can be directly shown. In *Empire of the Sun* (1987) Jim (Christian Bale) opening his little treasure box and pinning an advertising photograph onto the wall next to his pillow. In *Twentieth Century* (1934) Oscar Jaffe (John Barrymore) seizing a hatpin for prodding his supremely recalcitrant actress Lily Garland (Carole Lombard). In *Blade Runner* (1982) Deckard (Harrison Ford) obsessively studying a still photograph by means of a machine that will penetrate its surface and dart around the objects "layered" there. In *The Lonedale Operator* (1911) the station manager's daughter (Blanche Sweet) fondling and displaying her father's wrench, the weapon by which she will be victorious over the would-be robbers. In *Stairway to Heaven* (1946) an entire story (a love story) turns from despair to hope when a figure reaches out and seizes a single tear from the cheek of a sweet young woman: macro-close-up. Yet, all of these object fetishes, as we will learn to scornfully disregard them, resolve into "mature" love relationships between some attractive female with a radiant glow and some attractive male with twinkly eyes.

Indeed, it is conventional in performance to show love by means of specifically focused touchings, a kind of product placement. The body of the beloved is held in a certain way, the face caressed, the hair stroked, the clothing removed—a show of the valuable things. The body as love object is given reverence and adoration through the work of the hand. And when it is necessary for a character to make it plain that love is not on the table, the actor can succeed by withholding touch (Marlowe [Humphrey Bogart] with Carmen Sternwood [Martha Vickers] in *The Big Sleep* [1946]). The transforming power of growing love can be shown by an actor's releasing the withholding of touch, gingerly at first, then more confidently (Nicole Kidman with nine-year-old Cameron Bright, claiming to be her reincarnated husband, in *Birth* [2004]). While special keylighting is hardly ever devoted to it, the actor's hand as an agency of feeling is a central feature of films about love (Kidman's hand near the bath water; Tom Ripley's [Matt Damon] hand near Dickie Greenleaf's [Jude Law] bath water in *The Talented Mr. Ripley* [1999]). It is quite as though the viewer already works with a preformed idea of the hand in its capacity to touch and experience; the actor's hand is brought into focus and prominence simply by the context of a character's relationship with the touchable. As a contrast, in business meetings (typically set in board rooms to code them as "work"), characters may use their hands (upon documents, or shaking one another's) without the hand gaining any particular concentration. In political situations (*Borgen* [2010] is filled with them), the handshake takes on variable significance depending on the momentary context and handshakers. Uniformly love and affection serve not only as invocations to use the hand but as invocations that viewers keep an eye on it.

What is evocatively touched must be touchable, directly or by way of transposition. The love of a poet for language and for the form of his work will inevitably gain a close-up shot of a *hand writing on parchment* or in a notebook. It is not the hand itself that is to be seen but the words flowing from the pen, literally squiggles in ink. Not the devotion a poet has in his fingers (because the poem is finally flowing from the fingers) but his devotion to language (see Omar Sharif as Yuri by moonlight in *Doctor Zhivago*

[1965] or Leonard DiCaprio as Rimbaud in *Total Eclipse* [1995]). The painter seems more variable. The hand working the canvas can reveal passion or frivolity. In *F for Fake*, we see documentary clips involving close-ups of what we are to take as the hand of Elmyr de Hory as he produces (wholly convincing) fakes of Picassos, Modiglianis, and so on. The hand is blithe, lighting swift, almost never pausing for consideration. But in "Life Lessons," his contribution to *New York Stories* (1992), Scorsese has his painter (Nick Nolte) in the throes of emotional turmoil—a girlfriend (muse) is too perversely keeping him distant—as he sweats to finish canvases for a major show. Close shots of his hand sweeping paint over a huge canvas, rushing to lay the paint, hungry and revelling at once, starving for contact with the elusive true surface of things, are brilliantly lit by Nestor Almendros so that one feels a spirit inside the paint crying for contact with surface. There are no other moments in the film when this painter's hands are central to the vision.

A limiting case is reached in *Vertigo* (1958) as Scottie (James Stewart), having managed to climb the bell tower at San Juan Bautista after the fleeing Judy (Kim Novak), clutches the body of his love tightly, beckoning her to stay with him, beckoning with all the force of his will as he intuits the presence of an unknown darkness that is closing in, and suddenly she hears a sound and backs away, away and away and off the edge of the tower. The final shot is made from the air outside the tower opening. Roiling cloudy sky, stolid empty architecture of the tower space. And Scottie stepping to the ledge, looking up, looking down, with his two arms outstretched, palms up, perhaps not quite as though in crucifixion but with an impossibly beautiful expression of resignation and faith, a faith that for him is surrender: greater than love, greater than life, greater than being in the moment. The arms, the hands. The empty hands. The hands that could not hold. That hands that would hold, but have nothing.

12

A Logical Gasp

Leslie Caron (left) and Gene Kelly in An American in Paris *(Vincente Minnelli, MGM, 1951). Digital frame enlargement.*

When a character in a filmed story gazes off at something, a conventional reverse shot following immediately thereafter (a shot/reverse shot construction) permits us to see what it is that the character sees: to see, as it were, *with* the character. We bond this way, seeing the same thing-being-seen, seeing it at the same instant. Acoustics being less strictly directional, when such a character hears—say, hears another character speaking to her—we can typically hear, too, hear what the character is hearing, but hear directly only if the source of the sound is inside the shot and given focus, and even then there is something indeterminate about the sound: sound floats around; vision is in front of us. To see what a character sees; to hear what a character hears; these allegations are entirely arbitrary, and depend upon our making the assumption that the character's optical system can be taken to be as fluent as the camera's, that the character's acoustic system is as fluent as the microphone's. And we do tend to proceed on that assumption. If it is an inebriated character seeing, then, perhaps the image of what-is-seen will be blurred or wobbly to maintain the integrity of the illusion. Also, we operate as viewers faithful to that camera and that microphone. If we were there, not simply "there," we would apparently see the object of view exactly as the character/camera does, with the same acuity, the same openness to registering tone and color, and a sufficiently similar value system as would lead us to privilege the same parts of the visual field as the character/camera privileges. Hearing works similarly. We find ways to "enter" the narrative space by what we conceive as direct apprehension, direct (and directed) sight and hearing. Understood this way, the cinema is a magical probe that lets us into the narrative both sensorially and analytically. Our eyes and ears are at work, as are the eyes and ears of the characters who play to our eyes and ears.

Of course when we look closely at a painted canvas we do not "see" this way, by assuming that exactly what is in front of us is exactly what was in front of the painter (the framing disregarded). The brushstrokes only simulate an artist's experience; the simulation is the treasure. But when we watch movies, we do not tend to see the "brushstrokes." We believe, "The camera does not lie," and think of the microphone as being like a camera. Our servants. Our bearers of truth. One interesting effect: a character who has a hearing problem has a very clear reception of what other characters are saying all around because it is necessary that we should be given a very clear reception; what that means is that the character of focus *not hearing* can be conveyed only through some gestural signs, unless the film distorts verbal sound at the moment and replicates the character's limitation by transferring it to the viewer. One finds visual limitations transmitted to viewers much more frequently than acoustic ones.

As regards the other senses, a viewer's involvement or participation in, or witnessing of, the story is a matter of logical construction. Ortega might call it Impressionist—"Instead of [showing] objects as they are seen, one [shows] the experience of seeing" (124)—since the object of the experience is actually accessible only as a figuration in the mind. I cannot taste the *potage germiny à l'oseille* that the Queen is spooning. I cannot smell the roses and hyacinths in her lovely bouquet. I cannot feel the skin of a diner's cheek as he flicks a crumb away. But rather than claiming separation or debilitation, either of which could lead my commitment astray, I make the claim that I do smell, taste, and feel just as the character does, and substantiate my claim by examining the narrative context and drawing up memories from experiences of my own. I have eaten soup, I have smelled blossoms, I have flicked a crumb. I "get it." ("Get," but not in the way my eye gets what the camera is showing me a character is getting.)

To "get" what the screen action offers.

As to viewing a character's view or hearing a character's received sound, neither of these modes of participation actually makes a connection; one is not brought from one's seat all the way into the diegetic world for direct experience. At the same time, one has no trouble fabricating a tale of connection, one by which the self can be convinced that the eyes and ears of the character are extended out here in the theater. The three kinds of logical hapticity I invoke, taste, smell, and touch work by summoning memory of experience and can slip off-key if (a) they summon an experience upon which we cannot, or do not wish to, draw; or if (b) familiar enough in our experience, nevertheless they are presented onscreen through magnitudes, proportions, dimensions, or warpings unknown and unimaginable to us, since the conditions of their presentation, narratively speaking, are nothing short of extreme, perhaps even mortal: the last cigarette before the firing squad (*Dishonored* [1931]), the smell of cordite in the foxhole (*55 Days at Peking* [1963]), the touch of the limb one is about to amputate (*The Horsemen* [1971]): extremities of extremities that call upon professionally trained appreciations of the sort that exceeds a viewer's in the theater.[1]

Dramatic pungency can be suggested, implied through gestural formulae. A boy meets a girl and they soon fall in love. Nice atmosphere, mist, moonlight, good music. He leans over and plants his mouth on hers. Here, if we have not experienced sexuality yet, is a moment that is both pure balderdash and consummate boredom since, for the innocent eye, it is nothing but what it looks to be, mouth upon mouth for no discernable reason. But for experienced viewers the kiss calls up the form, the shape, the contours, the extensivity, and the limits of an experience, *not one's own* perhaps but something one can legitimately treat as comparable to one's own. *Not one's own*, meaning, *as though they could be one's own, and only one's own*, as though waylaying the widespread fiction that love and attraction are idiosyncratic and the kiss of the lover is unique. Looking at the characters producing "the kiss," as in the little film made by Edwin S. Porter and ongoing for more than one hundred and twenty years, one "grasps the situation," one understands the event as a signal for desire and procedure, one knows to look for tiny telltale evidences of inflammation. Yet this particular, singular, incomparable kiss is something none of us experience (something we might want or not want to experience, being entirely outside). We "read" the kiss through the accepted frameworks of bodily interrelation and contact, culturally learned. But more than being caught up in our distance by cultural limit, more than imagining this kiss as we have learned to imagine kisses, we watch thinking it, and thinking it more than approaching it. The kiss becomes, much more than a feature of our experience, a feature of our understanding. It is only in this way that a scene could be salacious: we understand it as salacious, even without feeling.

Daphne and Josephine (Jack Lemmon, Tony Curtis) ducking under the table at the mafioso's banquet in *Some Like It Hot* (1959): the same oddly abstract mode of receptivity, because we have not been to such a banquet in the 1920s and we are not masquerading in the peculiar way they are. Thomas Crown (Steve McQueen) gliding over the autumnal fields to the extra-diegetic score of Michel Legrand's "The Windmills of Your Mind" (*The Thomas Crown Affair*, 1968). Kane and his wife (Orson Welles, Ruth Warrick) squabbling while they eat their (tasteless) breakfast (1941). When shells whistle overhead we catch the sound, but when they explode nearby we only conceive of the shuddering, the smell, the tremor in the bones, the fright. We see torn dismembered bodies quite clearly, but we do not feel the indescribable give of a

---

[1] I wrote "Recuperation and *Rear Window*" while lying abed in a leg cast, thus with no difficulty convincing myself I had a personal and direct understanding of Jeff Jefferies's condition. One must wonder how much hapticity would have affected the reading of able-bodied viewers, and whether in the climactic confrontation with Thorwald's eyes Jeff's withdrawal would have seemed quite so embodied and quite so desperate (with thanks to Daniel Varndell).

softness beneath the feet as we trudge forward, sometimes stepping on them, even if Foleyed sound cues mean to assist. Do not feel perhaps because we do not wish to feel, to construe ourselves as feeling. Or do not feel because nothing has been given to our feeling. Yet some viewers may wish to feel, and they do claim to feel, in their way.

Imagination filling in for sensation, then. Imagination schooled, rehearsed, and cultivated. A form of mentality unequal to experience. Now, owing to the fact that the viewer's falling back on imagination and falling out of more direct response are both known to the filmmaker, it is a frequent practice to structure scenes in such a way that the withdrawal of direct sensibility is accounted for in advance, even in a craftily subtle way that is beyond notice. A typical dining table where characters we've been following are eating food in one another's presence—as with poor Jewish Alvie Singer (Woody Allen) confronting stoic Gentile Granny Hall (Helen Ludlam)—even discussing the food as they eat it. Here the *actual* incorporation, ingestion, and consumption of food items is gracefully elided, the space filled in with intensified character portrait shots and punchy dialogue. We are meant to grasp that although folks are eating, more important to them (and to us) is saying captivating things to one another. (Ironically, when actors film meal scenes they hardly ever actually eat.) Another example is given at the dining table in *Edward Scissorhands* (1991) where, for at least one participant, eating is a true challenge, and a very classic one can be found at the Manero dinner table in *Saturday Night Fever* (1977): *Mangia! Mangia!* "He touched my hair!!" Were viewers to have a sudden pang of loss, that a character in whom they had taken an intense interest was now putting something into the mouth that apparently tasted wonderful *but that they could not even hope to taste*, they would lose, even for a critical moment, their vital engagement. Pulling away from the food to the face (the expression) or the voice (the speech) brings audiences solidly to the domains of sight and sound, where they can rely much more on what seems their unmediated expertise.

Or the food consumption can be deployed as a rationale for conscious withdrawal, in which case the withdrawal is concocted by the viewer in line with, and as an element of the construction of, the narrative continuity. Take the little "eat your spinach" game played in *A.I. Artificial Intelligence* (2001) by resentful little Martin (Jake Thomas) as he taunts an innocent humanoid robot (Haley Joel Osment) at table. The robot will degrade and his (its) face will melt if food items are placed inside the head. A stunning effect has Osment in full facial close-up literally melt, his cheeks becoming gloppy latex and sagging below his chin as he gamely keeps trying to chew the bright green steamed spinach that is destroying him. Having bonded with him, we pull back from spinach and the idea of eating it, back from the moving jaw, back from our seats at that family table much as having watched *Psycho* we might be eager to pull back from showering.[2] Prince Martin sees the robotic face and presses on with his princely teasing, and, witnessing, we think we are seeing with our eyes just what he is seeing with his.

Aside from comic situations the sense of smell is invoked relatively rarely. In *Perfume: The Story of a Murderer* (2006), we have a character with a special, highly

---

[2] For a detailed discussion of the viewer's position during the *Psycho* shower scene, see my *Voyage* 8–16.

ramified olfaction (Ben Whishaw), but whatever he smells he must use words to name, this producing a story finally reduced to utterables. The 2018 German television series version has August Diehl facing the same verbal challenges. In Leslie Caron and Gene Kelly's famous (and wondrous) *pas de deux* in the flower market, which is the second tableau in the "American in Paris" ballet, we have two central characters in the soft light of *aubade*, surrounded by blossoms none of which they appear to smell, this "disconnection" matching and encouraging our own. It is so perfect—for our displacement—that they should be caught up in dance, not in whiffing. We take special pleasure in the way they move and gesture, reducing the flowers all around to merely colorful décor. Color leaps in (spectacularly) to take the place of smell at Podesta Baldocchi's in *Vertigo* (1958), when Madeleine picks up her nosegay. We are stunned to see the place, albeit she is blasé, but here, too, there's no perfume.

Context can realign viewer and character sensibilities when experiential pinioning is out of the question. A nice case is provided by extra-vehicular activity sequences in space travel films, such as William T. O'Niel's (Sean Connery) in *Outland* (1981), Frank's (Gary Lockwood) pod voyage in *2001: A Space Odyssey* (1968), Spencer's flotation in the void and apparent extra-terrestrial contact in *The Astronaut's Wife* (1999), or the dangerous adventure of Matt and Ryan (George Clooney, Sandra Bullock) in *Gravity* (2013). The prevailing dictate in such scenes, that the floater is in an airtight suit, guarantees that there is no touch to be conveyed, thus no sense of absence for the viewer when one cannot feel what the character cannot be feeling. Outer space has no smell or taste, so that, here ostensibly "with" the character locked inside his helmet, we do not miss not smelling or not tasting. The conditions of the scene work to eliminate, or effectively reduce, everything but hearing (radio communication) and (notably clarified) sight. Or one can find a contextual transform that assists viewers in keeping touch with what cannot be touched. In westerns, for example, characters move around by riding on horses. In fact, one is often treated to some rather spectacular riding skill on display (John Wayne is notable in *El Dorado* [1967]). But when in the offscreen world one rides a horse the experience is bumpy; the body feels it. "The West" is reconfigured as jolt. The horse catches the terrain much better than the rider does, and so the rider is often thrown into surprise by sudden demands on the musculature of the back and upper legs: the rider's musculature is grasping the dorsal musculature of the animal. All of this is almost always elided in westerns by the use of medium and medium-long shots that give the impression horses are merely carriers, merely a local means of transportation. The horse sequence then becomes nothing but a passage from one place to another, and the terms and conditions of the passage become central: will the hero arrive in time to stave off disaster? (Westerns, often called "oaters" because horses eat oats, have been taken over by car movies, where many of the same strategies are put in place diegetically and the road system—often the urban road system—often the densely packed urban road system—replaces the prairie or the hills.[3])

---

[3] An extremely brief long shot in Quentin Tarantino's *Once Upon a Time . . . In Hollywood* (2019) has mounted Austin Butler riding away from the camera, and it artfully replicates both early western riding techniques and the condition of the body being carried over uneven ground.

Or, one is in a professional kitchen where so much food is being prepared on schedule for an important banquet, so much food and so many different kinds of food, that one loses the sense of taste as it is washed away by the urgency, the screaming, the chopping action, the fires flaring up, the gorgeously arranged dishes brutally snagged by a waiter's desperate hand (a very good example is *Big Night* [1996]). In such a case, the viewer's being blocked from tasting is barely noticeable in light of the fact that the *drama* at hand is a race to complete preparations, a race that the viewer is in perfect position to watch. And because both the cooking and the dining will be gestural and characterological, the watching is all. In terms of bodies racing in space, such a situation is like sport.

The distancing of viewers from filmed drama through routines of sensory logic is, perhaps, not the most alarming or interesting of the latent effects of cinema. In live-action films, the characters, whether animal or human, are meant to be understood as living creatures in practical space. But there is no air—none appreciable to the viewer, at least. One *assumes* air, or, in panicky situations meant to be catastrophic, the limitation or absence of air. Think of "air" and "breathing" as pure logical constructs for film watchers. We see a body, we see it pulsing and thriving, moving and acting, and to whatever extent we wish to think of the character being human, in the way that we are human, we wish to believe and take for granted that the character breathes—as, watching all this, we do. There is no question that the actor breathes, but it is not the actor I am pointing to, it is the character. In character space there is room to move (we can see this) and there is an atmosphere to carry sound (that we and the character can hear), and there is light by which visibility is enabled, but air to breathe is superfluous.

In cinema we freely take space as air, but this is interpretive. When Montgomery Clift and John Ireland take pot shots at some tin cans in *Red River* (1948) and the cans go flying off, we see actual cans flying, and the seeing is uninterpreted.

At the end of *The Graduate* (1967), Benjamin Braddock (Dustin Hoffman) comes pelting down the sidewalk toward the camera, in telephoto, and veers off into the church where the girl of his dreams is about to marry a bozo. We see him gasping for air (like a good runner). But the gasping is Hoffman's canny gesture. There is no air for the character to gasp at. Air is not presented, but the sidewalk for him to run on is, and is as visible to us as to him. The church he runs to is there. The balcony chamber is there, in which his screaming "E-laiiiiine!!!" can be heard not only by her but by us. Conclude if you will that Benjamin's scream is carried through air, but we do not directly apprehend air as we directly apprehend his scream; logic is not hapticity. As we can imagine ourselves seeing the world as Benjamin sees it; as we can imagine ourselves hearing the world as he hears it; we cannot imagine breathing the world as he breathes it.

As we are happily, if inattentively, breathing while we watch, we would not choose to imagine creatures who resembled us, stuck in spaces shaped roughly like this space in which we sit, having no air to breathe. Of course, in most films, the dramatic cover for the airlessness of the scene—of all scenes—is an arrangement, a kind of contract, in which characters need not be shown to breathe. (Note the hospital scene, with a patient tubed up in a bed, and a gleamy beeping machine visualizing the breathing for us.) The general absence of breathing as a signal rationalizes a general absence of air, because when characters always automatically do not breathe they also always automatically do not suffocate from being unable to, nor need they try to gulp in the horizon. Editors act to cut out the performer's breathing, if in the chest or face it becomes distractingly visible or irrelevant to the dramatic moment as in, say, the extended underwater passage without equipment. An interesting exception: a character wounded in such a way that he or she must gulp for air dramatizes alarm conditions through "struggling to breathe," but even this is covered by exceptional attention to exceptional details of the character body, the color of the face, the bulbous eyes, the yawning mouth, all of which stand in for trouble dealing with air itself, in these wild circumstances where air is simply not there and our appreciation of the struggle could lead us to be seeing the actor at work. How odd that walking, kissing, sleeping, eating, talking, talking, talking, and talking characters neglect to breathe; or that "taking a deep breath" they become unconventional types in unconventional circumstances so that the non-breathing itself is minor. Acoustic beep as breath; melody as breath. The pilot blacking out when the air is too thin, or the diver having the bends when going too deep—again, logical constructs, and logically shaped performances to accompany.

When a character dies onscreen he is "no longer breathing the air." But as regards the ostensible "performance" of breathing, which usually we did not experience this character doing: now in a key respect he looks just as he did when he was "alive," a present body occupying space but not using air. All characters are ghosts. When a character moves through a doorway and pauses for consideration, in the pause he may as well be dead.

13

Vigil

François Civil in The Wolf's Call *(Le chant du loup, Antonin Baudry, Pathé, 2019). Digital frame enlargement.*

The vacuum of cinematic fiction, its airless lightness, its bubble of vacancy, and its glowing potential, is made iconic in the submarine film. The story of the submarine film is simple and is almost always exactly the same. The state has contrived to produce and enable a fleet of underwater vessels, mostly for aggression in war. Of these, the entire crowd of them are perfectly, often silently functional, deliverers of Fate, defenders of the flag, except one, and this one is the ship aboard which we find ourselves. Far, far from shore. Deep, deep, deep, deep down in the darkness covered by the waves. Something is not working with this capstone vessel, object-star of the submarine film, the something-not-working is the substance of the drama—and the operational failure is played to happen "quite suddenly," because we are to assume (just as the crew assume) that before the craft sailed the maintenance folk did their dailies and all the hatches were screwed tight. Perhaps a depth charge exploded nearby. Or the thing came aground on a rock. Or—not to happen in the Second World War days, certainly, but—of much popularity among screenwriters now is the submarine running on a nuclear reactor that has gone out of control. Berserk atoms! Or—wet melodrama!—there is an enemy sub, nearby, hunting. Or one or another of the crewmen, trapped in this can, is no longer able to handle the tightly regulated normality of the undersea routine and has gone mad. The madness comes to threaten every living person aboard. Or else, paranoiac nightmare, the captain is mad, or disabled, or badly befuddled, or misled, or seriously dubious about something. The crew members are almost all ciphers with a very few exceptions. The faces appear over and over, one of these inevitably belonging to the sonar operator, a "sensory array" of the beast come alive in human form.

The landscape: well, precisely, there is none. Once the film gets going we are incessantly trapped inside the shell of the sub, visiting only a small number of chambers (all familiar to submarine film fans). No matter our location at any instant, given that we are presumably quite ignorant of how a machine like this works, the place and its devices are all arcane. Thus, one chamber is like another, similarly hard to know, colored the same way, filled in the same way with presumable weaponry and presumable aids to navigation, and above all, cramped in the extreme. The only way for a viewer to take it as given that a number of men could be living under these conditions would be—as in fact happens here with us—to have sufficient facial close-ups that one can take one's mind off the body in its too-limited carton. A tremendous choreographic labor is undertaken on set to guarantee that in front of the camera no actor will bump into any other one, this cleanliness giving the feeling of a fluid space through which all well-intentioned movement is straightforward. Unless there is a moment of violence where somebody gets pushed or hit, typically no one bumps a head against a bulwark or an elbow against a lever. The illusion, then, is that the space is large and permissive—contrast the cattle car full of prisoners in *Doctor Zhivago* (1965)—though any and every sub film will have an early shot or two demonstrating how jam-packed things are in here.

In here, but of course not in here, because of all spaces presented onscreen from which the viewer in her theater seat is separated, no space declares viewer/screen separation quite as much as the submarine in peril. Spaceship interiors (post-*Alien*) are designed and built as laboratories, albeit sometimes a tad squeezed. Submarine interiors are tunnels inside a capsule moving inside a tunnel.

While it is ecologically wise to take cognizance of the fact that the air we breathe in this world is not a resource without limit, normal functioning disregards such constraint: I cannot both live and worry that on every exhalation my carbon dioxide wounds the environment. On submarines, however, the air is coming from a bounded reservoir (fish do not breathe air), and can always, in threat or actuality, run out. In *The Command* (2018), an extremely rare case in point, that is exactly what happens to a Russian submarine, and every living person aboard perishes. In other sub films, one is constantly presented with the image of men acting under duress, often "brought to the very limits of their strength and courage," and all this in a depleting atmosphere. Yet, the viewer in the theater cannot be led to the endpoint, a fear of suffocation, for various reasons including the possibility of real medical trouble. The viewer must always know personal placement in an airy space while carefully watching a severely limiting space hold vivacious spirits in, with less air by the minute. The submariner tends to give off a quality of vivacity, even if this is shown through sweating, whining, complaining, limping, gasping, gurgling, even coming close to drowning. The film proceeds without loss of vivacity but depicts a condition we are to take as a serious threat to life.

Tropes:

[A] *"Up periscope!"* The periscope is the "get-out-of-jail" card of the film, the trigger for releasing observation from the containment of underwater secrecy by means of a sudden, sharply clarifying, even seemingly oxygenated view of the water's surface and the horizons in all directions. (If the scope couldn't rotate it might not be half as much fun.) The periscope permits the captain navigational aid, but forget the captain for a moment and think about what the periscope provides *us*. A sudden expansion of space. A social topography, since the existence of the Other is always either invoked or denied (but in either case, stated): a convoy, a battleship, a fishing boat, a coastline, or even nothing but the surface of the sea. A thoroughly remarkable periscope sequence punctuates a key passage in Stanley Kramer's *On the Beach* (1959), as Gregory Peck uses the device to scan San Francisco. Space is expanded in periscope moments generally, but so is permission, since with great frequency the view through the periscope offers invitation to a deck-top voyage. Deck, hatch, conning tower, where vigorous officers spy the territory with binoculars, like the scouts of old-fashioned westerns in "Injun territory."

There is a certain odd pleasure, too, in watching the scope column slide up and down on its servomechanisms, with its little hum, and its seemingly palpable (if invisible) lubrication. "I want to see!" the Captain implicitly calls out, and up slides the device, a kind of robot. A marvelous depth-of-field effect comes into play, because the scope's lens has a definitive calibration, making it possible for the looker not only to see a ship in the distance but also to calculate the precise angle of relation and the exact separation in yards. This is an artificial depth-of-field (about which more, later), operating through a focal change rather than the way depth-of-field is sensed and formed by the natural eyes: periscope as camera.

[B] *"Dive! Dive!"* Perilous moments of one kind or another—warships approaching, an enemy submarine detected too close by—call for submergence, but the submarine must be caused to—thus must be able to—submerge *swiftly*. Bow plane down, angles called out, pictures, from some position outside and undersea, of the craft slanting downward in the blue, the gray-blue, the gray, the gray-green, the blue-green, the green. "Dive!" also functions in quite other narrative contexts as a direction to some character desperate to avoid strafing gunfire from the air: get under that car, get under that veranda, get into that cornfield. Dive into the safety of a zone untouchable in everyday space, a safe zone, a privacy. Ocean depths as privacy. "Those are pearls that were his eyes." Any weaponry that is (can be) used for targeting in such a place produces a busting in, an invasion of private space. "Dive!," get under the surface, bypass that planar boundary that separates the private from the public world. For the actor onstage, and panicking, "Quick, duck over there behind that flat," or, more poignantly, "Hide inside that character": ocean as character worn by the acting submarine. For the negotiating politician at the table, "Quick, keep that word *in* and don't utter it in any event," or, "dive under the cover story," an apt relation because in sub movies the issue is almost always military, military thus political, and the making of the wrong sound is tantamount to revealing a military secret.

[C] *Shhhh!* Metal being capable of producing vibration, and water a perfect medium for transmitting, it is often imperative that people on board refrain from making any sounds at all. Even sneezing. Hitting against a bulkhead or pipe could give the sub's position away to those others out there, passionately tuned into their sonars. But the technical requirement for silence invokes and overlays a religious cloak, turns the military device into a chapel. The praying that one witnesses in adverse conditions is accompanied by quivering silence, as though the Listener is in the water.

[D] *Canned.* The submarine is like a tin can—similarly metallic, similarly shaped, and similarly subject to outside pressure. The first tin-canned goods were produced just before 1813 for the Royal Navy. Tin cans (steel cans, aluminum cans) are made by assembly of pieces, between which extremely secure seals are required—as with a submarine. You can put a can under only so much pressure before it collapses inward. "Dive!" can mean "Go *far* below," but as one traverses new depths, the water pressure concomitantly increases. How far down can one go before the sub just infolds? Can one go all the way down and sit on the bottom? Inside the device, there is no way to *see* the pressure, but the sailors are capable of *reading* it from certain glaring instruments. Shots are intercut: the submarine angling downward, the depth gauge showing footage and the pressure gauge slowly mounting into a danger zone (typically marked in red or with the word DANGER or both). One must imagine conditions for the sailors, who, once inside, are cut off from declarative views. They can watch the dials, they can gulp as the air changes and their eardrums begin to ache, they can look at one another fearfully—macro-close-ups of bulging eyes and perspiring brows—they can look over and see the expression of fierce and intentful concentration on the captain's face (if, that is, they happen to be positioned close enough to the captain). They can see, in short, a structure's internally projected view of itself, thus mimicking the thoughtful civilian having self-conscious wonderings on a street corner. The editor will of course make certain that the panic on the faces is augmented muscularly in accompaniment to the slow movement of the instrument dials upward toward the danger zone. The "danger zone" is thus, practically—as it is given over to us—not a part of the ocean depths but an instrumental figuration, related to, relative of a figuration on the face.

In the interior design of the sub the sleeping quarters, the eating area, and passages for work and movement are all arranged to emphasize the humans being packed in, indeed tightly and efficiently packed, with every tiny dot of space finding its use. Sardines in a can. And like the tin can, the submarine has a "stale date," beyond which it becomes impossible for the thing to support life.

[E] *Skin.* By jumping freely to exterior shots of the sub—the sub traveling normally, the propellers slowing or quickening, the thing angling up or down, marked explosions of surrounding depth charges, the magical transport between the Scylla of a sharp, hull-piercing rock formation on one side and the Charybdis of a sharper one on the other—the film eases us into a divided consciousness, even a battle of perceptions. We are trapped, we are bounded, we are confined, we are crammed in and then we are free not only to jump away from all this on a whim but also, like any friendly shark, to sustain ourselves underwater for any length of time. Actually, on a submarine—not that any sub film is concerned with this—one does not have the liberty to jump outside and watch the thing dive. All of what the craft is doing in the water is made manifest to the crew precisely, delicately, wholly, but only through the instrument panels.

The metallic skin is permeable (to our consciousness and perception) and theoretically impermeable (to water). Our leaps outward gain for us not only information as to the sub's momentary safety against both pressure and the enemy but, importantly too, the pleasure of studying industrial design: the way the thing is shaped for dynamic movement, the position of the torpedo tubes and conning tower, the utter streamlining (futurist décor, a real step beyond Jules Verne, one could love to boast, although his Nautilus was its own future). It is only by logical force that we can exercise a need to link the exterior shape of the sub underwater to the interior chambers in which its crew maneuver it. Very few sub movies deal with passage from the outside to the inside territory, by means of an air lock where pressure can be regulated. The earliest I experienced was Disney's *20,000 Leagues Under the Sea* (1954) in which seamen exploring the ocean floor (for foodstuffs and at one point a funeral) popped up at the lip of a gushing inside tube, their curved wetsuit helmets seen from above forming the basis of the alien skull that would be designed by Carlo Rambaldi for Scott's *Alien* (1979).

[F] *The tubes.* A conundrum of outside- and inside-consciousness appears with the torpedo tubes. The conventional film trope is for the captain to call for a launch, and for the command to be followed, and then for us to actually see a torpedo coming out of the torpedo port and wending its way forward to destruction, giant steel spermatozoon of death. Often we even see the destruction, frequently by way of that magical periscope. One can imagine that sailors in the torpedo room would understand themselves fetching a torpedo, winching it, sliding it over, getting it into place, locking it in the tube, pressuring the tube, and then shooting, but all of this would be seen by us from a position they could not occupy, outside nearby the exit port. (The inside position, carried to comical extreme, is provided with Woody Allen's help in *Everything You Always Wanted to Know About Sex * But Were Afraid to Ask* [1972].) Where the present torpedo is going, how it is going there, why it is going there, and even when it is due to arrive—all this will be an arcane secret for us, and for the crew, except that it will be "soon." This "soon" is what binds the outside to the inside view.

[G] *Say again.* Very often when a drama calls for the motion of an enormous vessel—a spaceship, an aircraft carrier—the pilot has a chadburn whereby he signals his desires to a matching unit in the engine room that registers the command. Perhaps the captain dictates a command and a computer or single voice listening on a sound system repeats it. But in submarine scenarios, language repetition gains new utility. First, the repetition is significant in itself: a command goes from the captain (at the periscope) to his second in command; from the second in command to another officer in the control room, even perhaps yet another officer; from there barked into the adjoining room, then barked further on, then finally obeyed at the end of a long chain of barkers. "FIRE ONE!"—"Fire One!"—"Fire tube one!"—"Tube one, fire!"—"Fire one!"—"Tube one! Fire now!"—"Firing one!"—"One away!"—"Torpedo fired. Twelve seconds to impact."—"Torpedo one impacting, ten seconds"—and so on. The acoustic quality invokes that of the drummers in a marching band, or the choristers in an elaborately syncopated piece by Carl Orff. *It's happening, it's happening, it will happen, it will definitely happen, it happens now.* Followed instantly by, *Yes it happened, it did happen, the happening happened, we are looking back on the happening, we register the event, the event is fully registered and acknowledged.* What are some of the effects of this poetic device? (This device, this device, this poetic device, this poetic, this poetic, this poetic poetic poetic device.)

- Repetitions constitute an echo, as though the submarine is a canyon, as though the voice meets its ghostly brothers hovering in the air. "Hello!" >> "Helloo!" >>> "Hellooo!" >>>> "Helloooo!" Repetitions are reverberations, and reverberations have an intrinsic musical effect, rhythmical and recursive.

- Repetition brings emphasis, drawing the event barked out upward into a special reserve of importance. Not only is something happening, but we see *it happening that* the happening *happens to be* happening.

- The crew as an organized congregation is invoked, even though not all of them are visible in a single shot. Not only can action be seen to have a rehearsed, orderly, even formal aspect, with the carrying out of the command constituting a team effort, but pretext is offered for jump-cutting to various parts of the ship in order that we follow the stages of the repetition (thereby learning the vertical hierarchy of command as it is laterally deployed). Because the act is a team effort it announces the strength and propriety of the team.

- Most crucially, we gain focus. We can easily have a wandering eye, float all over the submarine's intestinal tract, leap outside with the fishes, see another submarine coming, leap back inside, rush down to the crew bunks where someone is stirring in his sleep, and so on, all this producing optical confusion. The repeated command strikes one single, isolated, cohering chord, becomes a bell in a bell tower ringing over and over and over only to announce, *I am ringing, I and only I, I and only I, I and only I.* We can isolate the command, focus upon it and it alone, and follow the passage of the command down a command line until a point of execution. The analogy is the stimulation of a nerve and the passage of the electrical impulse all the way along it, by way of the movement through the nerve tissue, in rapid alternation, of sodium and potassium ions. Just as the stimulation of the eye strikes the retina and through the retinal connection to the optic nerve is passed all the way into the brain, so, here, nervous action in the viewers can register military activity *framed as nervous action.* The viewer sees herself.

[H] *Eyes have they, but they cannot see.* Visual acuity is stipulated and emphasized, shots coming closer and closer as a story wends on. Faces, increasingly haggard and resigned, increasingly tense with the agony of battle as the climax nears, are etched onscreen with graphic power, thanks to the use of wide-angle lenses and startling make-up effects (that seem to age the characters). Instrument dials are shown closer and closer up the more precarious the information they offer. The captain, in particular, uses eyes for discernment, reading the men, reading the submarine, reading the enemy. All this to say, quite beyond the fact that because this is a movie we are given to see everything, still, in this story what we are able to see (and not see) form the very crux of the action and the curve of the arc. Details to be seen inside this container where every hour, every day we look at the same things over and over without relief.

But always the mocking antagonism: what is outside the submarine cannot be seen. Every journey we take for a view outside is balanced by an interior shot showing the desperation of those who cannot join us. *But I'm only here.* To rationalize an alignment between the actions of trapped characters and the logistical and topological position of the container in which they are trapped, it is necessary to provide some signal sensation, some visual substitute for this attention-occupying and attention-blocking visual arrangement, and that is the sonar, anthropomorphized through the sonar operator, a character of typically unique and distinct looks and attitudes. Looks, because we will return to him frequently, as with a cymbal hit by a jazz drummer; attitudes, because he has to have a capacity for focus over and beyond anything else we encounter, else there is no reason for him.

This person listens and by listening *sees.*

He can detect the underwater scape, the pits and the rock formations, even the passing schools of fish. He can surely detect other submarines in the vicinity, and through "reading" sophisticated acoustic patterns reveal whether these are friendly or alien. The sonar operation is dramatically heightened by the plot trope of the "silent-running submarine," powered, usually nowadays, by nuclear fission, profoundly menacing because of the payloads it carries, and sparring beneath the waves, for the most daunting of bouts, with silent runners from the other side. The background hum of the engines can be suddenly cut, on a captain's orders, producing a disturbing silence (like the silence in a crypt) through the density of which the operator strains to listen for audible clues.[1] The telltale *piiiing!* The battering of a metallic object on the hull. The gentle, butterly whir as a vessel passes very nearby. Two blind whales circling to the death in the dark.

To date, *The Wolf's Call* (*Le chant du loup*, 2019) is the most beautiful and also the most stunning depiction of underwater acoustic maneuvering ever put on film, causing all of the submarine films before it to recede into hackneyed convention, although of course when such films first came to audiences' awareness they were similarly stunning in the techniques they used. Here, however, is proposed an operator (François Civil) whose extraordinary hearing, attentiveness, musicality, minute sensitivities, and soulful perseverance are the only means whereby a submarine cruises through peril to safety. What is amazing about this film, far beyond its sophisticated setting and brave performances, is its devotion to showing a person bent over himself listening, listening, listening, listening—to the silence, the silence, the silence, the silence, the silence—"No, wait! Shhh!"—the silence, the silence, listening, the silence, until the very most subtle of blips, a blip that is not even a blip, only the idea of a blip, nothing but an idea, a blip that is the shadow of a blip, the idea of the shadow of a blip. The extent of the strain. The muscular tension. The face in agony with the huge (heroic) headphones coding the future. "Shhhh! SHHHHHHH!!!" The most delicate tissue binding the inner to the outer world, the imagination to the fact, the fear to the event. And all around him, every crew member holding his breath. One can *feel* the pain of the chest muscles holding the breath. Not a cough, not a sniffle, not a rubbing of fingers against cotton, not a step, not a swivel, not a craning of the neck, nothing but statuary. Nothing but silent statuary in the graveyard guarding the watery tombs. And the one living being listening, surveilling, keeping the vigil against those who would roll back the watery stone.

---

[1] Ex-airforce pilot Gene Roddenberry's *Star Trek* enterprise, centered, of course, on the U.S.S. Enterprise, often uses in battle sequences the trope of some (usually Romulan) commander "switching to" a "cloaking device," not unlike the submarine's silent running, a feature that in submarine pictures was not exploited until decades afterward.

14

Privileged

James Mason in 20,000 Leagues Under the Sea *(Richard Fleischer, Disney, 1954). Digital frame enlargement.*

About body intimacies in cinema and encroachments upon them I have written elsewhere.[1] But not all closed behaviors are intimate or exclusive because they focus upon the body and its upkeep, upon our pleasure centers and their elaborate massage, or upon the secrecies of the person or the family. Once society has developed to the point when it is organized not merely by persons but by institutions, there can exist institutional intimacies, secrets or statements that are intended, for various reasons and by various players, to be kept out of the purview of the public eye. When a gang of thieves operate upon a bank vault, they keep their plans and their endeavor in the dark, but when one of them feels a sudden nosebleed and rushes to a bathroom to check it in privacy, the "darkness" is entirely of another variety. Occupational versus bodily darkness. Darkness of the person and darkness of personality (which in high organization is finally status).

One may be given privileged access to considerations, planning sessions, debates, votes, negotiation and deal-making, even elopements, all of these being variations on the public act, the act that invokes public sanction (either because it is widely accepted or because not enough people know about it to frown), gains or avoids gaining public

---

[1] See chapter 15 of *The Film Cheat.*

verification, and addresses, modifies, or circumvents public standards. Think of the board room; or the shady corner of the playground; or the throne room; or the public rooms of the private residences of the high and mighty; or the boiler room of the ship; or the little table of the Czech café where an agent sits in wait for a meeting (*A Most Wanted Man* [2014]). One conceives of conversations and transactions not meant for wide appreciation, yet openly dramatized in locales however removed, thus available for the camera. When the camera goes there—our camera, our treasure—it does not violate the sort of intimacy one would meet in the bedroom, but it does penetrate a well-kept boundary, revealing what had been hidden intentionally, even systematically, and affecting our orientation as viewers by lending us a warming feeling of being invited *in*.

There are also locales that if not forbidden are utterly inaccessible, and so our presence viewing there is not just an intrusion but a miracle. The cockpit of the Spirit of St. Louis midway across the Atlantic (*The Spirit of St. Louis*, 1957). The driver's seat in one of the cars in the French circuit, shown in *Grand Prix* (1966), or the back seat of Thelma and Louise's car as it sails above the Grand Canyon (1991). Joseph Gordon-Levitt tightrope walking between the towers of the World Trade Center (*The Walk* [2015]). Floating and tossing with spacesuited Sandra Bullock in *Gravity* (2013). Standing in the control chamber with Sigourney Weaver and her cat at the ending of *Alien* (1979)—terrifying, but we are on the inside, after all.

Viewer orientation is delicate and involves recognizing and thoroughly appreciating, by its details and nuances, not only the diegetic situation in which screen events are taking place (that is, the situation we are "in") but also the propriety of our "being there" as observers and the delicate sense of comfort or strangeness that befalls us as we sense our own belonging or alienation, fit or non-fit. One is typically aware of "scenes" in everyday life to which one is not being offered access. One knows that one does not have the appropriate membership card, or the passcode, or the pocket history of introductions. A conversation across the floor at a soirée (Judith Anderson observing Gene Tierney and Vincent Price together in *Laura* [1944]). When a location or scene is by definition, and from its origin, open to some wider public—the Boston Common, the lobby of the Museum of Modern Art, a redwood forest south of San Francisco—presence there has the quality of seeming natural. But many non-private spaces are also non-public ones: not the star's dressing room in the theater, but the darkened area in the wings, just offstage; not the doctor's consulting room but the waiting room outside; not the professor's office, nor, perhaps, even the lecture theater in which he talks, but the basement corridor and tunnel through which he walks in solitary thought to keep out of the snow. Films are continually invoking, if not bringing us to, these places of access to which we did not gain, and in everyday life would never gain, actual access.

Case studies:

- For walkways consider the scene in *Rebel Without a Cause* (1955) when Jim is starting out at his new high school and we see the students rushing in (and then, with more discomfort, find ourselves actually in the hallway next to a boy and his locker). As the camera moves we have an odd sense, like Jim, of not belonging where, apparently, we should belong. It's a very apt touch upon the first day at a new school.

- For theatrical wings, the eccentric camera shot in *Stage Fright* (1950) when, as Marlene Dietrich's Charlotte Inwood performs in a hot puddle of stage light we watch from the shadows and see the whole act in lateral profile. Or, in *Sunset Blvd.* (1950), our ascension into the flies of Stage 18 at Paramount when the gaffers spot their old friend Norma Desmond visiting below. Or, in *Citizen Kane* (1941), a similar hike into the flies as the stagehands pass judgment on Susan Alexander Kane singing *Aida*.

- For the practitioner's waiting room, in *The Incredible Shrinking Man* (1957) the space in which Scott Carey (Grant Williams) is given his test results by Dr. Bramson (William Schallert) or, in *Magnificent Obsession* (1954), the empty room in Vienna where Bob Merrick discovers that Helen Phillips has fled—her private room, but now vacated.

In semi-private public areas, one feels anticipation for an oncoming or bordering privacy and also a degree of seclusion from the hectic everyday world, and so the space is transitional. But it is also a definitive space in its own right, since to whatever degree one feels "membership" with respect to its interiority one recognizes that the feeling is justified by social arrangement. In *The Public* (2018), a number of angry protesters take over the second floor of the Cincinnati Public Library as their home.

The quirky privilege of spontaneous presence in hitherto unvisited semi-public spaces can be confusing and disorienting, especially when a depiction is historical. For example, I am privileged to stand in the throne chamber of the Pharaoh (in Michael Curtiz's *The Egyptian* [1954]), presuming that what I see bears some relation to what must have been there long ago. Although I am neither Egyptian nor regal, nor a subject of this Pharaoh, I feel myself welcomed and in place. Immense magnitudes, a ceiling so high up one cannot find it. Opulence, palm fronds, military order among a legion servants and courtiers, the Pharaoh himself (Michael Wilding) garbed in gold. Standing here (as a camera incarnated) I know this cannot be real, because I am watching in 1954, a little boy in a huge dark theater in the West, and this is happening in the Middle East, a place I have heard about vaguely but never visited. I am here now, and this is all "happening" or happening, however I choose to understand, thousands of years ago, so long ago that even with the magic of mummification none of these folk could be here as they seem to be. I am listening to pronouncement, dictate, royal command, and the intonation of echo. The space is far outside the human proportions through which I measure my own experience. The beings are all nobler and more austere than anyone I have ever met. Yet, while I sense the place and its occupants as strange, there does not seem to be threat. I am *permitted* to be here. I have a visitor's pass. Yet even as a pass-holder, I stand to watch in odd circumspection: should anyone prostrate himself before the Pharaoh, I would not feel obliged to do so too. More: if I did there would—deplorably—be nothing to see but the floor and the floor is not what I bought the visitor's pass to see.

Or imagine standing in Capt. Nemo's *Nautilus* in *20,000 Leagues Under the Sea* (1954) and listening to him (James Mason) play Bach on his magnificent organ. He did not invite us, explicitly. But he doesn't mind that we're listening, in fact it's us he's performing for. More: as at the moment we are undersea we are trapped, even imprisoned as his audience, yet at the same time feel entirely at liberty and take ourselves to be his special guests. A narrative conceit, certainly. But in cinema, narrative conceits must be designed visually. Where are we to see this? How do we come here? How do we stand?

Because I am in Pharaoh's court, his space away from the public, I can know of things that will transpire before they transpire, as his vizier does. I am given forewarning of scenes to come. Indeed, I get a preview of the upcoming film. I am let in on a grand secret that is only slowly going to be given official revelation. And if Nemo in his submarine confides to someone, I am there to watch, and in confiding surreptitiously he is confiding to me. I see where things are going because I have been invited to linger in the room where the plans are made. Or there I am, staring at naughty Tinker Bell and prognathically nefarious Hook in *Peter Pan* (1953), as in his secluded cabin he sees on a map where Hangman's Tree must be! "Hop, skip, and a jump across Crocodile Creek!" Neither a bed under the sheets nor a public street corner, but a place where I normally wouldn't be *but I can be* and recognize myself being there in comfort.

Or, take *Dr. No* (1962), the first James Bond film available onscreen. In a motorboat I am escorted by my new chum James (Sean Connery) out to Crab Key in the Caribbean off Jamaica. There I (blithely) enter and (with curiosity) wander through the techno-palace of the secretive and omnipotent Dr. No (Joseph Wiseman), an eloquent and cultured villain I am pleased to "meet" and, given his erudition, especially pleased to listen to. I see his large atria and capacious corridors, I see from inside his lavish living and dining space, both of which are furnished in high modernism and with lots of decorative stonework all around (the designer is Ken Adam). I listen in on the ironic twists of the conversation between these two men and I notice gently unfolding, by way of Bond's sweet prodding, the covering layers of No's malice. I witness (perhaps more than Bond does?) the squinting examination being performed by No upon Bond, his "welcomed" guest, especially the obscure man's seemingly all-detecting eyes, because beside being a bad guy No is also, obviously, a detective.

If I weren't allowed to be in here, I would never have a "homey," a *gemütlich* vision of the villain of the piece; he would be nothing but a mechanical cipher. His final eradication would amount to nothing more than sweeping a game piece off the board. But now, because he is as much my host as James Bond's, I can see that he is fully fleshed out, that he has a personality, even a wit. When the villain has a wit, we feel him inside our skin and would hate to see him vanquished, no matter his evil design for conquering the world.

If not wit, then passion. In *20,000 Leagues*, Nemo's marvelous submarine ship has been rumored to be ramming vessels on the high seas and ripping them to shreds. Various views are shown of the thing, usually only partly surfaced. With its two globular yellow-lit window eyes and its powerfully serrated cast-iron bow crest the thing is a mechanical crocodile (making Nemo [1869] an odd progenitor of Hook [1904]). But now, magically, I am inside the bowels of the thing, and it is shocking to see that, very distant from the mentality behind its mechanical, military design is the mentality of the interior decorator of this thoroughly fin-de-siècle world. Sumptuous velvets and brocades, rosewood furniture polished to a gleam, a silver dining service to assist if not tasting at least participating by observation in the rich meal (all from the sea). Nemo's tour of the ship is guided by a gentle, learned, respectful voice, if also, perhaps, a voice tinged with madness. I can see the foundation of a development to be built later on, that Nemo's impulsive idiosyncrasy and outré sense of order will be taken to some impossible limit, that his sense of civilization, here made exploratory and odd, will finally become utterly anti-social and destructive. Yet, he will never lose his attractive passion for the seductive and incomprehensible world of the sea, nor will I lose mine for watching him thrill to it here in this sweet sanctum.

For a different experience altogether, I am shepherded by Linus Larrabee (Humphrey Bogart), a major New York tycoon, up, up, up, and up into the office suite of the Larrabee Corporation (at the top of the Larrabee Building). Here, I know, I will see power made manifest, and indeed there is a spectacular picture window looking out over the Hudson and a board table big enough to sit a small army. But the surprise is Linus's matter-of-fact tone of voice, his this-is-all-mine-and-I-needn't-think-about-it attitude, especially as he asks his assistant to go to the kitchenette and whip up something tasty. The sheer puissance of the man and the place. Flat, bright illumination. Polished and unrevealing surfaces. No documents lying around, no memoranda, no handwritten notes, only the slicker-than-slick skin of a corporate beast. Perhaps this place in itself means nothing. I must be ready to watch the human interactions, as they will tell all, albeit they could be set almost anywhere—except that up here Linus will feel the extent of his power in the most casual, the most sincere way. A total disruption would be shocking and exhilarating. An abrupt, surprising disruption even moreso. It is imperative that the story at this moment be set here. This space must not look the laboratory for testing out mechanisms of profit that it is, must seem more a distorted residential space designed by some nouveau Howard Roark, in which all the measurements have been stretched to a size beyond the person, beyond his family, beyond even his board of directors. This 1950s design space by Hal Pereira and Walter Tyler for *Sabrina* (1954) mocks up the living room and nightclub interiors Van Nest Polglase designed at RKO for 1930s films, those vast spaces it could take half a minute to stride across (as in *Tarnished Angel* [1938]).

What does look considerably more like a laboratory is the secret Krell headquarters buried inside a mountain in *Forbidden Planet* (1956), designed by Mentor Huebner and Irving Block. We are sped by Morbius (Walter Pidgeon) in a small tram on a long tunneled track, then led across a slender bridgeway over a bottomless aqua-blue chasm of rising and dropping energy orbs, having gained initial access by way of a coded sliding triangular door in a rock wall. Arcane, esoteric, intellectually elevated, far in advance of anything we can imagine, although, to be honest, while I take this little voyage, I do have to remind myself that somebody has actually imagined it all, including room for me. The weird IQ-testing "plastic educator" where you plug a stethoscope onto your temples and when you conceive a form it appears as what we would term a "hologram"—George Lucas would borrow this for *Star Wars* (1977): fantastic!, yet also just waiting for me to approve it. The walls in the background covered from floor to ceiling with machines registering some sort of power by way of shimmering lights (that twinkle for me). The scrolls that Morbius "taught himself" how to read, all those cuneiform wisdoms from the ancient past left as talismans by a civilization entirely extinct (extinct yet somehow waiting for me to connect with it). I have a confounding double sense, with which I must struggle as I watch: the quality and essence of all this is dead, is emptiness, is a vanished past, a whole civilization eroded away, so that some subtle whiff of wholesale decay infuses the atmosphere. The crypt with the Mummy. At the same time, utter presence and empowered utility. The winking of the lights, the machinery in perfect operating order, an illuminated scroll that, though written by ghosts, is still here to be read by the living—*and is readable!* Morbius has learned it, *but it can be learned!* The Krell are present, the Krell are gone. Both at the same time. And in the confusion, I rely on the wise Morbius, but alas, he is a man clearly harboring some secret he does not choose to reveal, a man who is not really teaching me although he gives a very good performance as a "guide."

In *Three Days of the Condor* (1975), I am privileged and daunted early on to be escorted to the interior office spaces of a clandestine CIA bureau in Manhattan. There, to my horror, I witness a wholesale slaughter as a man comes in with a submachine gun and assassinates the entire crew—the only survivor being Turner (Robert Redford), who had apparently darted out to get coffees. I saw, and recognize, the assassin (Max von Sydow), so that considerably later, when Turner finds himself alone in an elevator with this man, I am suddenly brought to the lip of abject terror. Turner is somewhat suspicious in that elevator, but only because he is altogether suspicious at this point of the film. The assassin could not be more courteous, but of course in my privileged position as witness in this public space I am quite certain I am about to see the withdrawal of a pistol-with-silencer and the man plugging charming Turner artfully, silently, and plot-resolvingly. Certainly, I know better, I know I am not at the end of the story and that Turner cannot be killed here. But the lethality of the earlier bloodbath and something about Sydow's blank expression as he stands in the corner of the elevator bring on a wave of terror. He is too professional. Too cool. Far too composed. All this composure can be nothing but a cover. Turner drops something and the assassin bends with the simplest graciousness to fetch it up for him, smiling. Is the graciousness a ploy, to throw Turner off his guard before the kill? The doors open and Turner exits, while the assassin gives an amicable smile of farewell. Whatever Turner feels, I know with certainty that the man has been smiling at me, as though to say, "Oh you! How nice to see you again!"

Not only are most elevators open public spaces, they are *closed open* public spaces, and if anyone can walk in anyone can also be trapped under adverse circumstances. We all know the elevator is a closed system, but we also know we would prefer to be lifted up than to trudge, so again and again we gamble and walk in. Turner is tuned into such contingency much more than the average person, even though for the CIA he does nothing but read books; he's on the inside of the organization, thus presumably briefed. And so here he is, not at all densely unaware, and standing next to absolute mortality. It is like that old tale of the man who meets Death on the road to Samara. But because I have wandered at Turner's side—I like and trust Turner, I care for him, he is the officially designated hero here, he is Robert Redford!—I must be as observant as he is of what surrounds him, indeed the tight space forces me to be observant because the walls are tedious to look at, not to say blankly uninformative, and there are only the two riders beside me. Forced to look, I cannot fail to see the grim assassin in all his grimness. (This is a man who projects grimness when he relaxes the muscles of his face in contentment.) Nor can I miss cheery Turner in his innocent vulnerability. (This is a man who projects innocence when he relaxes the muscles of his face in repose.) So again, the confounding reality of two contradictory positions laid upon me at once. I am happy to be with my hero, watch him, see him move in the game. But I am anything but happy to see his elevator mate, especially because, having been absent from the murder, Turner did not see the assassin whom I did see and he does not recognize the danger as fully, as unequivocally as I recognize it. Agonizing to be here. I wish I could speak to Turner! But of course, if I could this wouldn't be a movie, and more than wanting to save Turner I want to watch this movie. Also, actually: impossible always to be anywhere else than where one is.

Think of my horrible conundrum. To be in the elevator without knowing what I know, that is, to be Turner, and thus to see the stranger as a friendly, genteel, and courteous man would be wholly comfortable yet also boring, as regards the plot. At the same time, to be in the elevator knowing what I know is to ride with a professional killer, configured by Sydow[2] to be so very menacing that I must fear he will kill me (and end my experience of the film).

Oddly, it is in public or semi-public space that my sense of privilege as a viewer is brought to its sharpest point. When I invade the privacy of a character's living space (Dickie Greenleaf's [Jude Law] bathtub), I must feel I have been explicitly invited, because the occupant behaves with a "turn-out" to me (the camera), slightly adjusts his angle of posture (actor pose; camera angle) so that all the important nuances of expression are available to my eye. The turn-out signals that the character not only knows he is being watched but is happy to be seen, in this way giving off a faint aroma of the actor beneath (the being who knows a camera/eye is there; the one who makes a living by being seen). At home with Gary Cooper's Prof. Bertram Potts in *Ball of Fire* (1941), at home with Bette Davis's Maggie Cutler in *The Man Who Came to Dinner* (1942), at home with Davis's Charlotte Vale and her mother in *Now, Voyager* (1942), at home with Eugene Pallette, Alice Brady, and Mischa Auer in *My Man Godfrey* (1936), at home with Lionel Barrymore's Martin Vanderhof in *You Can't Take It with You* (1938), at home in San Francisco with Katharine Houghton and her parents Spencer Tracy and Katharine Hepburn in *Guess Who's Coming to Dinner?* (1967), at home with Bogart's

---

[2] As to Von Sydow's challenge mounting this threat: he need do very little in the elevator because the murder scene, he knows very well, will be edited in as the beginning of the film and by this point his deep character will be firmly set. As to Redford, a career star identity has established him firmly as loveable; he need do nothing to create that quality here.

Dixon Steele in *In a Lonely Place* (1950), at home with Rod Taylor, Jessica Tandy, and Veronica Cartwright in *The Birds* (1963)—on and on and on, I never feel awkward or out of place, never intrusive (though of course I intrude), never uncomfortably resented although I could, and perhaps should, be. And: *I never seem to outstay my welcome.* Just as the home space I have entered is designed for coziness and warmth, so is the narrative presence I occupy designed for coziness and warmth, and not a jot too much. Indeed, I feel so cozy and warm making observation here that I might be a member of the family; yet I am also at enough of a remove to be free from suffocation by the family warmth.

And I am a member of a "family" to which I need not politely apologize when I get up and leave. A family in which I am the child extended all permissions, subjected to no expectations, and talked down to in the very endearing, engaging way that addresses my cares and my curiosities without calling for me even to demonstrate that I understand.

In public space, the family and family intimacies disintegrate. Familial relations become signal, definitional, wholly formal: a subject for passing strangers to identify and respect as such but otherwise typically non-functional. The discomfort, the slightly jarring feeling of being the camera's friend in a public place is derived from just this knowledge that here one must share a "public identity" with the characters; one must be readable in role or social position, as they are. A passer-by—say, a *mere* passer-by—readable even if not yet equipped to read. Just as figures of the screen are made visible, we are made curious to see. Meanwhile, here in this now-darkened theatrical space, we are carrying as well a quite different public identity, that of theatergoer, the one who may lose a self and find it again, the one who voyages in stillness. What we do in joining the characters on their railway platform, as it were, is to fake an identity, to participate in deliberate—or at least conscious—camouflage. Yet, too, if the characters we watch are, in their way, camouflages as well it is also true that the actors putting them on are professionally adept at doing this sort of thing, "being" in public, while our capability staring at strangers is both more casual and more imprecise. We will surely be found out. To be caught watching is always the fear of those who sneak visions in the dark.

Every moment in a public scene, then, is one in which someone is on the verge of turning our way and saying, "Here, you! What are *you* doing?" Watching Michael Caine's classic take on this in *Alfie* (1966), the viewer's first reaction is precisely a pulling away from this sense of having been discovered by him, "him" being either the actor or the character. Alfie's Cockney helps relax us into friendship so that by the skin of our teeth we can escape judgment. In that escape itself there is a distinct *frisson* produced, a thrill of cinematic pleasure. When we watch at home or on our iPhone screen, no public or quasi-public role need be taken up in relation to our seeing characters' pranks; no "wicked offence" be confessed; no chill felt at the imminent discovery of what impostors we are. No chill, then, at the marriage of our discovery and our fear of being discovered discovering. The electric public space degrades, becomes merely cozy, like a bed in which, not dreaming, we need not be awake.

15

Ting-a-ling-a-ling

Doris Day and James Stewart in The Man Who Knew Too Much *(Alfred Hitchcock, Paramount, 1956). Digital frame enlargement.*

The Bells of Hell go ting-a-ling-a-ling
For you but not for me:
For me the angels sing-a-ling-a-ling,
They've got the goods for me.
Oh! Death, where is thy sting-a-ling-a-ling?
Oh! Grave, thy victory?
The Bells of Hell go ting-a-ling-a-ling
For you but not for me.

World War I British airmen's song

Habits will grow old and beg for replacement but not all the time. Here is one that has lingered since childhood but hasn't lost any of its charm. We're watching a scene where some people are in a room, a room full of objects, a room with windows looking out on some trees and a pond. Suddenly the telephone rings.

The device is sitting in front of the camera, f2, and as it rings (rings loudly, shockingly, because so close), we believe we can almost see it trembling with urgency. "Ting-a-ling-a-ling . . . Ting-a-ling-a-ling . . ." Someone will inevitably answer it, and when they do there will be at least one side of a conversation that registers as relatively important, especially to the ongoing process of the story, but before they reach out for the receiver let us just suck in that beckoning jangle, "Ting-a-ling-a-ling," and see what pleasure it can bring in itself. A dramatic scene with a phone ringing—nowadays typically a cell phone: a total narrational habit. Somebody who is not in the *here* of the tale wants to walk in.

The viewer in me thinks like this:

[1] Oh, someone is calling! They must be calling *me*.

[2] That is, I have every reason and every right to know who is initiating this ring, and for what reason. This is *my business*. (Walter Benjamin noted how, somewhat similarly, readers of the newspaper felt they were entitled to have their interests addressed.) Another angle: when the phone is answered and I listen in, there is nothing untoward about my presence. *Of course* I should be listening in, because somehow *I* am the (actual) intended recipient of this call. Anything of import within the call itself will be conveyed to me (dramaturgically speaking, the call exists in the play of action *only* so that information can be provided to me). And while in other circumstances I might well be accused of it, here, there is no doubt, I am not eavesdropping.

[3] Who, I am eager to know, is ringing? Who wants me, wants me now, wants me to know something? The scripted "purpose" of the call would depend on who was making it. Imagine the other party saying, "Come over here quickly!" If this were a total stranger who had dialed a wrong number I wouldn't care at all, and wouldn't budge. In dramatic film, wrong numbers pop up almost always as right numbers that only seem to be wrong. If the caller were a character to whom the character I am bound up with apparently felt close, I might care a lot and feel the desire—at least the responsibility—to be going. So intense a desire or so pressing a responsibility, in fact, that if my character-friend at this end of the line didn't hang up immediately and race out, I might well be disturbed. There are many other possibilities: that the caller is someone the receiver does not wish to be talking to, to be vulnerable to contact from, and so the very fact of the call is an intrusion that riles the plot. In any event, the ting-a-ling-a-ling signals the presence, in the *away*, of an initiating someone out there somewhere else, and because the phone itself signals distance I cannot immediately see or know who (or where) that someone is. Unable to know, I want to know. Unable to see, I want to see. (The ringing phone is like a shot of Vitamin A that opens my eyes.)

[4] No matter who it is calling, especially because I cannot see I want to hear. What are they saying? What tone? What silences? I need the grain of the voice. Someone is essentially drawing my attention, and I wish to attend fully. Speak

to me, speak, I want to hear your voice, I want to know you. Ting-a-ling-a-ling raises in me, instantly, this desire to hear the other's voice and piece together the other's words into a coherence, a meaning. I am *ready for interpretation*. But also, more deeply, I am ready for meeting.

[5] When I hear the ring, I have a very clear anticipation that whoever is making this call *I will recognize* in some way, even as an unknown. If it is a stranger calling, the voice type will constitute a recognizable signal of known unknownness. Or it will be a familiar, perhaps a character to whom the camera has already introduced me, perhaps only someone the other characters have spoken about. But I will cast in my mind an image of the invisible other, I will flesh out the voice with a body and a face (however inaccurately). I will know this distant invisible other by remembering or by imagining. As much as the call is about information transfer it is about the acknowledgment of relationship and about the placement of the other on a map of the self.

[6] Caller, I hope fervently that you are patient, because I would be chagrined if not irritated were you to hang up (change your mind, give up the endeavor) before the phone got answered, or instantly on hearing the voice at this end. *Keep ringing, do keep ringing.* The longer it takes the proximal character to reach out and pick up that phone, *Ting-a-ling-a-ling, ting-a-ling-a-ling, ting-a-ling-a-ling, ting-a-ling-a-ling,* the more desperately I fear that you, Dear Stranger, all the way at the other end, the other end of the world, will not linger. Oh, do linger! Instantly, then, upon the ring, I loathe the thought of a loss of contact that we do not yet have. *Ne me quitte pas!*[1]

[7] I have divided the universe in advance. You at the other end (the "dark side of the moon") will either be identifiable or summarily identified by way of your voice: a person I have met, whom I know, whom I recognize, whom I have already thought about enough to characterize; or else a person I do not identify, a stranger, a newcomer to my space. Strangers and non-strangers. You are (already) in or out. Tending toward in, tending toward out. (Only two categories.) If you are in, I will already have some ideas about the sort of conversation you intend to have, even, perhaps, what you might say. I will have rehearsed the conversation as a type. The dialogue will follow a model already constructed, a model that will not be discarded even if we waver from it a little. If you are an unknown, you will be offering me a blank presence and I will be likely to be taken off guard as my proximal speaker-friend works to place you. To map you. How difficult and uncanny it would be, perhaps for the answering character but most certainly for me, should I not be able to know you yet persist in hearing your stranger's voice.

---

[1] This elevated desperation for contact on catching sight or sound of a signal from afar is a typical trope in the climax of desert-island sagas, reflected as far back as Buñuel's *Robinson Crusoe* (1954). See, for examples, Peter Brook's *Lord of the Flies* (1963) and Robert Zemeckis's *Cast Away* (2000).

[8] This situation takes us beyond the *acousmêtre* invoked by Michel Chion, the voice from off that addresses the ear as a vision plays out (the narrative voice, the voice from the past or the side, some telephone voices). The *acousmêtre* is unknown or unrecognized, but not deeply unintelligible. We know who is making the sound, but we do not see them. Or we know what kind of sound maker this has to be, though we do not see the origin of the sound. Here I am thinking of a more profoundly troubling sound and sound maker, as one might do in standing on a hilltop and hearing thunder. Thunder, the voice of the sky, but with a source entirely ungraspable. This voice on the other end of the phone could be a thunderous voice, in that peculiar sense of coming from something or somewhere inconceivable, even if the sound of it is clearly taken in.

[9] The mechanical ring itself, "Ting-a-ling-a-ling, Ting-a-ling-a-ling," is inherently irritating. *Ting-a-ling-a-ling!* A perduring, not a simple bell. The idea is to rouse me (me and my local pal, with whom I am so tightly bonded I am inside their skin) from a stupor (my self-indulgent stupor) into a state of acute readiness. The ring demands not only instantaneous conversion to consciousness but conversion to sharp and attuned consciousness. Also, the ring directs me to the ringer, the melody to the instrument: that is, the telephone as a piece of equipment, a single item now centering, even commanding the space in which it resides. Everything draws to a focus on this tingling thing, this thing that will not stop tingling until I act to stop it (or my simulacrum does for me). See, for example, Robert Altman's *Images* (1972).

[10] The ring is disturbing (to my placidity) because it seems troubled, in and of itself. It is the bleating voice of a creature in pain. As the device is agonized, it must be the sort of entity that could suffer agony, in short, an entity conscious and alive, or "alive." The phone rings with life. Life and pain. The ring does not sound as though it can signal anything other than urgency, pain, distress: the call for release. "Ting-a-ling-a-ling" means "Help me!" I will have a sense of urgency about a ringing phone no matter where, no matter when, no matter the type of machine it is. The living phone prods me and invokes what anthropologists recognize as a "conspecific" bond. "I am like you, I am the same as you, look at me." If I could understand the telephone as nothing more than a thing I would not be so surprised, irritated, shocked, jolted, or prodded by its ring.

[11] Because it is nothing more than a thing, however, in its ringing, its "Ting-a-ling-a-ling!," the phone masks over its essential nature, jumps into performance (and therefore performative mode). It becomes a device (human-made) pretending to be a human, an object pretending to be mobile and sensitive and reactive—the signs of life. The ring of the telephone thus animates it. And every instant of onscreen telephone ringing, "TING-a-ling-a-ling!!," is an animation. The animator (the being instigating the animation) is the producer, operating through a script-writer and then a props master. But caught up in the diegesis (as I would hope to be), I recognize only the putative caller at the other end as the animator. The person I take to be making this phone ring is bringing the ring of life.

[12] But in not seeing this distant caller I place the figure as off-. This caller is as invisible as a puppeteer (puppeteers are universally invisible in the puppeting even when, as in *Lili* [1953],[2] we see them). The caller is a puppeteer and the telephone ringing is a puppet. And when someone reaches out to pick up the receiver, when a character acts with the phone as I would act, this responsive being is addressing, is interacting with, a puppet. Look at *The Errand Boy* (1961) or *Being John Malkovich* (1999) and find puppets onscreen masquerading as themselves, puppets that look like (nothing but) puppets, but here, with the telephone, *Ting-a-ling-a-ling*, we have a puppet that looks like a tool. A puppet no one will recognize as a puppet when it rings. "Lili! . . . Lili! . . . Over here!" converted to "Ting-a-ling-a-ling." Taking this machine to be not a machine but a creation, not a thing but a life, still we confer upon it the indeterminate identity of a puppet.

[13] And as a "machine" we imagine it having innards that could be drawn out surgically (see *The Conversation* [1974]), and a surface that could be marred (note the numerous contemporary action films in which a cell phone is thrown to the cement, stepped on, tossed in the river). We surmise integration into an operating system that is supreme, that is unknowable, that is an agency of darkness itself (see *The President's Analyst* [1967]). The machine contains a ringer (a bell, a buzzer) and the ringer bears culpability for contacting me, for vocalizing the animation of the thing. (Imagine a Bugs Bunny cartoon fully alive onscreen but missing the vocal participation of Mel Blanc.)

[14] The "wrong number" is a secondary unbroken habit, often a cause of deep chills and anxiety. So many things can go wrong, after all. A slip of the finger will change a telephone number as dialed or keyed, producing the entirely innocent wrong number. "Ooops, sorry!" Or one has the wrong number that is a "wrong number"; the call seems innocent and inadvertent but has been carefully designed to give that impression, because it is a signal being sent in secrecy (see *Wait Until Dark* [1967]). Somebody wants to know whether anyone is home to pick up the phone, anyone, not someone in particular: is the place empty? (not that failing to answer a phone could be a clear signal about this, as in drama it is often taken to be). Or it is the receiver making the calculation that the caller has dialed a wrong number because when the phone is picked up there is no normal response to "Hello." The person at the other end is listening hard, trying to decide whether he or she has made a mistake. Or else something more instrumental: a fault on the line, a system transmission problem, broken transmitting equipment, and the silence is both unintelligible and confusing (for an interesting cocktail of these possibilities, see *Dial M for Murder* [1954]). Oddly, when I hear the phone ringing, *Ting-a-ling-a-ling*, I expect that answering will produce a voice, a voice quite discernable as such and rendered with special, amplified crispness (see *The Man Who Knew Too Much* [1956]), and given this expectation, given the

---

[2] Or as in the giant marionettes occasionally displayed (performed) on European streets.

naturalness and thoroughness of it, the very notion of some flaw in the pattern—a wrong number, a bad line, "Doesn't he live there anymore?," whatever—simply does not come to mind. I hear the ring, I reach out. I reach honestly, openly, purely. I do not expect the local character to consider all the ways this could be a non-call and to meditate upon the choice of whether or not to answer. And the interesting dramatic potential for troubles doesn't come up in my calculations, the chance, say, that instead of a successful telephone call this will be a damaged and damaging one. The telephone's ring summons me to human contact, and I act as though at least on the most basic of levels this contact will be normal, routine: routine of etiquette, routine of vocal level, routine in terms of mutually recognized conversational guidelines (such as patterns of voice alternation).[3]

(The phone is still ringing, *Ting-a-ling-a-ling*, answer the phone!)

[15] Through its ring, *Ting-a-ling-a-ling, ting-a-ling-a-ling*, the diegetic telephone, not unlike the real telephone, is both impetuous and imperious. It rings, we race to answer. We do not take the telephone's ring, *Ting-a-ling-a-ling, ting-a-ling-a-ling, ting-a-ling-a-ling*, to be a musical phrase that could "perfume the air" while we went about our business. No, the ring barges in to signal a force barging in. Implicit here is a curious anomaly:

[16] That whatever the pace and schedule of events around us in this present (screen) space, whatever the pattern of action, the rapidity or lethargy of movement, whatever the questions awaiting answers and the shopping lists waiting to be ticked off, the caller has no sense of these things, no information, and no concern *when initiating the call*. One picks up a phone and calls somebody, without having any knowledge or inclination about the state of affairs at the other end. Call as happenstance. Call as trespass, if you will, but no matter; just call.

It may be that in my own life I learned most of this about telephones and telephone conversations early on, at least in the most rudimentary sense. I certainly don't think I was much older than three or four by the time I had figured out what the *Ting-a-ling-a-ling* meant as signal and invitation. And this may be why one of the very first films I saw—it may conceivably have been the first, but on this my memory simply isn't there, repressed, perhaps, for the best of reasons. It was suggested to me (after decades and decades of mystery-bound and, I think, only half-hearted struggle on my part to locate this thing) that the film might have been *The Thirteenth Guest* (1932, with Ginger Rogers!), but of even this I cannot be sure. Nor can I recount the plot or the characterizations. Only one thing remains in mind:

There is a salon (black and white). Upholstered chairs, a floor on which various people stand, perhaps a sofa, and a little wooden table (a Regency table, I now suspect)

---

[3] And presumed agreement about conversational level and focus and requirement for informational detail. See on this Garfinkel, "Studies in the Routine Grounds of Everyday Activities."

upon which stands a telephone. The people are there for some kind of party or civil entertainment, but I have no idea what it is. In the middle of the happenings, the telephone rings. Somebody walks over and picks up the receiver. "Hello? Yes?" And then through the telephone this person is electrocuted to death. This happens more than once, but finally there is a kind of tracking camera shot (as I recall it) where we move across the floor, passing chairs and legs and reach a wall, and then somehow (no memory) we go through the wall and find ourselves in a tiny chamber where we see part of a body, and a hand, and a switch, and a peephole. This person can make the phone ring, and can watch, and by hitting the switch can produce the electrification.

There: that is all I remember. If, Dear Reader, this clue hits the button for you and you can identify this film, I beg, do not tell me. And of course the electricity as connected with the telephone is hardly surprising, as one learns much later in life, because the mechanism operates by electrical impulse. I did not originally know that. I did recognize, both in these characters and in myself, the impulse to go over and pick up the receiver of a ringing phone. (An infant at the doorstep wailing for food.) I recognized already the anticipations, desires, conventional practices that would be in play (although I did not know how to point to them this way), so that it was a sensible outcome that I would find deeply shocking—shocking as though by electricity—what happened in place of these conventional practices in that horrible film: special, diabolical practices the shocks from which, the displacements of which could make one's attentions dissipate.

But displacement may go very deep.

Rules, guidelines, and practices are apprehended, tested, accepted, digested, and in this way incorporated into a body of knowledge. Not only do I have anticipation when the phone rings, the anticipation is *known and already incorporated.* Thus, when I feel the anticipation, I do not recoil in surprise at myself; I am feeling only what I more generally know I will always feel in circumstances like this—in circumstances whose any distinction from this one I cannot, or do not, read. If my learned anticipations are undone by the electrocution scene(s), then my very knowledge is undone. What I know about the world is not about the world at all, it is about my faulty knowing. And now I have to accept that I cannot touch the world, cannot assess the world, cannot understand anyone or anything beyond the shadow of my own speculation. The phone habit was basic, after all—as I say, learned early. It was something that would come up anytime anywhere, and once learned be applicable quite generally, so that I must now—I had to then, after the quivering terror of watching—have a quite *general* doubt as to my learned habit, perhaps all my learned habits, perhaps learning itself.

Ting-a-ling-a-ling!
Hang on, the phone is ringing . . .

16

Unheard Voices

(Left) Winnie the Pooh and the Blustery Day *(Wolfgang Reitherman, Disney, 1968). Digital frame enlargement;* *(Right)* Sterling Holloway.

The ear is sensitive in part by being vectorless. Sight requires positioning and orientation, and so when one is seeing a film image one is always determining where one is, that one could be seeing this particular way; and perhaps even wondering by what rationale one came to be at such a placement, although surely a rationale for point of view is not always felt to be necessary. Sometimes the editor has leapt to a position unexpected and unknown but action is continuing there with such fluid rapidity that both keeping up with it and ascertaining how one can be doing so cannot both be accomplished together; then, not to be lost, one lets go of the need to rationalize how what one is seeing can be seen. I think of the moments—odd-seeming, when viewed from afar—in the celebrated car chase sequence of *Bullitt* (1968) when we jump away from our hero in his car into the front seat area of the vehicle he is following. We certainly get some limited information there: that the thugs are doing up their seat belts in preparation for acceleration, that they have a rifle, that the driver is concentrating hard as he looks around, and although none of this is really crucial to the chase itself we follow it intently, gathering up the crumbs of information. But to wonder how we managed to jump into this position is to lose the thrill of gathering. When in *Lawrence of Arabia* (1962) we cut forward to the attack on Aqaba, knowing we are arriving at the site of an event long planned and carefully prepared for (the story makes this clear), we are so caught up with the charge across the beach that we cannot also wonder how we traveled here. With cinematic space we position ourselves very swiftly, as though all our movements are ordained.[1]

The ear does not need to take a particular *position*—face a certain direction— to hear sounds that are emanating from a nearby source. From ahead, from behind, from the right, from the left, from above, from below, sound reaches the ear with equal directness if the source is within range.[2] Sound systems can be designed to pinpoint positions in a space (say, a theater) from which sounds are emitted, but the ear distinguishes spatial positioning in a much vaguer, less structured way. In most situations, to the extent that one can hear at all one almost always hears a great deal more than one can see; or let us say that the world heard is greater (more variably sourced) than the world seen.[3] When we consider the assertion offered by John Belton that film sound is not the sound of a place represented but the sound of the picture, in short, that film recording concentrates on matching sounds to actions visible onscreen, we must remember how offscreen sounds can work as invasions of this acoustic space, especially if they match in amplitude sounds originating from screen space. One feature of cinematic space that renders it unreal, no matter the realism sought for in performance, décor, and pacing, is its special shaping of sound not associated with what is pictured, since in the everyday real we do not achieve this shaping to such a degree.

Most acousmatic sound finds itself pinned to something onscreen, to a telephone, to a radio, to a bounded room from outside of which the sound is emanating. When we have the omniscient invisible narrative voice, that "room" is the frame of the cinema itself, and the narrative seems to be proceeding toward us from a vocal position distinctively *somewhere yet not here*, and otherwise unidentified and unidentifiable. In his *F for Fake* (1984), therefore, Welles snaps our consciousness when he jumps from presenting an offscreen (acousmatic) voice (the notably orchestral Welles voice) leading us forward, to a sudden screen image of himself talking to us, with the sound now (apparently) organically located in the body we see depicted.

Not only is the invisible narrator surely not on the screen, the voice is coming from a position that is also not in the theater where we see the screen. Yet, since we take our acoustic powers to be blocked by the walls of the (soundproofed) screening space, that voice can also not be outside the theater. Chion has written extensively about how this voice is *beyond* the screen, which is not to say behind it, above it, below it, or in the wings. This opens for consideration the full meaning of *beyond*, applied

---

[1] Lawrence is gazing off from a dune far away and the sound of a bell ringing is heard; then the image shows the bell up close, at Aqaba, signaling the attack. Anne V. Coates invented the sound pre-lap for this cut. More on this in my *Horse* 145 ff.

[2] In *Forms of Talk*, Erving Goffman defines a *social situation* as "any physical area anywhere within which two or more persons find themselves in visual and aural range of one another" (84). Cinema offers us only *virtual* situations, then; and in these, it is interesting to note, the senses can be divided, so that acoustically speaking we can be "in a situation" with the maker of a sound excluded from presence here or in the immediate nearby.

[3] And often restfully. Georg Simmel: "The one who sees, without hearing, is much more perplexed, puzzled, and worried, than the one who hears without seeing" (360).

to matters cinematic and otherwise. One might well conceive of a phantom universe coextensive with our own, surely a phantom screen world coextensive with what is depicted in the film, and posit the narrative presence as an inhabitant of that world. Interestingly, from its position in that phantom world the narrative presence can see well enough what we see onscreen (Welles's animating presence off- in *The Magnificent Ambersons* [1942] is a leading example) because it can offer comment upon it, make fun of it, point out some particular aspect of it to us and in doing this lead the camera forward to an isolation (a considerable feature of *The Hospital* [1971]). It can speak as though it recognizes the identities and expressive postures of the people we see. Further, this phantom voice almost always has—and thus always illustrates that voices of its kind *can have*—a sense of history that far exceeds our own as stimulated by the film. It can know where people have been, how they got here from there, what chain of eventuations led up to the moments it is helping us grasp now. Of the people to whom it introduces us it can know whom they know. It can know people we do not meet, know conditions we do not apprehend, know the world. It is not knowledge itself,[4] it is a personality (a personality, possessing a valuable storehold).

Vivian Sobchack has written interestingly about the "'Voice of God' narration" that was conventionally used for Hollywood historical epics in the 1950s and onward (333), a voice, I might add, that Cecil B. DeMille expressly avoids casting in his *The Ten Commandments* (1956), because he replaces it with his own (American) one. What Sobchack discerns in the high narrative tone, she suggests, is "not so much the narrative accounting of *specific historical events* as it is the narrative construction of *general historical eventfulness*" (338, emphasis original). And we know that a certain height can be gained even by purely human voices, entirely non-general, such as Gloria Stuart's in *Titanic* (1997) as the aged Rose gazing back over time to her experience as a survivor of the catastrophe: any person might age sufficiently to gaze back over a long history but when we have an offscreen narrative voice that is aged and canny we feel introduced to a past far greater than that of the story alone. In *Titanic*, the singularity of the ship's sinking, the magnitude of the technical and human disaster (souls lost) magnifies the size and also the importance of the event, brings it toward the kind of generalization that Sobchack mentions, so that the omniscient *acousmêtre* "Rose," telling us about all of what she experienced there, is simultaneously swollen and shrunken to a pinpoint, a viewer from outside the passage of everyday time yet also, because the memories are starkly detailed, a viewer from within, from the bowels of an event elapsing over a relatively short number of minutes. She was a single person, she was on deck, she interacted, she spoke, but also she can tell us all this now, in another epoch. More than the gigantic ship, imperceivable in detail in a single view, spreading all around, she was the sea that swallowed, the sea that kept, and now, as we learn, the sea that remembered, as well as the little being floating upon the sea. She is involved

---

[4] As conceived speculatively in sci-fi stories including a sentient and all-knowing computer, to which absolutely any question can be asked in surety than an informative answer will come directly. By making this always competent computer "ill," that is, incapacitated, Stanley Kubrick brings a deep chill to *2001: A Space Odyssey* (1968): an unreliable *acousmêtre*.

with a contemporary hunt for the wreckage, scanning into herself. All this happened to "me," she says, but all this shows the kinds of catastrophe that can befall mankind, punishments of the gods.

A wholly contrasting *acousmêtre* brings us in, and then pops up once in a while to guide us around, in *The Maltese Falcon* (1941). This is the presence of the central character, Sam Spade (Humphrey Bogart). Because of the vulgar commonplaceness of his voice, its origins in urban topography, and the details it reveals, we are taken instantly into the relevant small details of a criminal event, a kind of organized happening that contained "dance steps" that the narrative articulates. In *Casablanca* (1942) that same tonality is heard again in the sequence when Rick recollects "Paris" with Ilsa. Here the voice says much less, phrases rather than sentences, leading us to sense that the *acousmêtre* is in pain to speak of this, that the man we see onscreen suffers as he remembers but suffers even more as he is transformed from the inhabitant of his recognizable body into the invisible presence that guides us.

Vocal tonality as narrative element is generally used to more specific, more deeply etched effect than musical performance is. When one is established in a location and hears musical performance offscreen, that performance could inform the present vision much in the way that acousmatic narration does, yet it almost always doesn't, being relegated instead to a decorative assignment performed by obedient and careful underlings whose job it is to support the structure of the storied event, even to paint the walls, but not to give meaningful comment.[5] A singular example is the Lady Dalroy soirée sequence of Cukor's *Gaslight* (1944), where Ingrid Bergman and Charles Boyer will go through a bizarre little masque in the view of nosey Joseph Cotten while a guest artist plays at the keyboard. The staging is tight and overflowing with information about Paula's (Bergman) progressively panicky state of mind, but what goes untreated, either in the narrative or in much scholarly discourse about it, is that the guest pianist (Jakob Gimpel) is busy performing Beethoven's Piano Sonata No. 21 in C, Op. 53, the "Waldstein," a tempest of emotion widely regarded now, and also at the time of the diegetic moment, as *the* signal achievement of the composer's "heroic" phase and notable, also, as a supreme technical challenge. Invoked in the music alone then—one could say, intoned by the narrational presence (almost always offscreen here)—is a heroic stance (the stance that poor Paula will need to summon in herself tonight) and vastly complicated technical maneuvers (such as will be discovered very soon to be motoring the story). Yet in the scene we hear this piano music as just realistic décor, cake dressing, the sort of offering a visiting virtuoso would offer a salon crowd in the upper crust, not something to take seriously as a centerpiece of their sociability or of our drama.

A similar fate awaits the voice that comes through loudspeakers in a public venue. That voice is announcing something urgently important to *only a few* of the many people passing here—"The zero-eight-twenty-eight to Ramsgate is boarding at Platform 12,"—or else announcing urgently something important to all, with the proviso that we are meant to understand the message in the most general terms:

---

[5] Although, in Nicolas Roeg's *Walkabout* (1971), there are some haunting passages where visually engaging material is accompanied by extradiegetic choral music not directly connected to what we see.

Warning warning! Danger danger! Time left before auto-destruction two minutes!—general terms abstractly speaking, because if the auto-destruct goes all the way to zero, which it almost always doesn't, we won't be here listening anyway. One isn't treating this *acousmêtre* as a persona, as a distinctive quality, as a discrete intelligible messenger, but is instead regarding the sound generically as *loudspeaker sound*, generalized sound, public sound, impersonal sound, the voice of a system. In film scenes about classrooms, such as the marvelous lecture theater scene in *Dr. Mabuse, der Spieler* (1922), when the camera turns away from the (brilliant) lecturer into the audience—the stupefied or bored students are checking their lipstick, gawking at their notes, carrying on whispered conversations—the primary voice in the room quickly fades into a disattendable *acousmêtre* so that the subject of the image (as per Belton) can take over. In this audience image itself, the lecturer is both off- and far away psychologically for the students, not part of their immediate world. A film image will speak forcefully through a voice from the invisible if the object most closely associated with sound is focused in the picture: for instance, in a close-shot of the loudspeaker itself (there is such a shot in the finale of Stanley Kramer's *On the Beach* [1959]) or in one of Lang's lecturer's hand drumming his desk while he spiels out his patient Mabuse's symptoms. It is interesting that with music this formula fails to work. Even when the camera cuts to the pianist hard at work in the middle of the "Waldstein," once the character protagonists have been introduced in the scene, they remain the center of attention even when they are not on camera, and the piano sounds, replicated however accurately, are relegated to the acoustic margins.

The piano player can become centrally important in such a scene—the piano player, the violinist, the orchestra, the singers onstage in an opera—only when she has been arranged already as a character of importance and now happens to have seated herself at the keys. Melanie playing Debussy's Arabesque in *The Birds* (1963). It is in order to qualify the character that the music plays centrally, becomes an example of what we might call adjectival harmony. But again, only when the character is already, or is on the cusp of being shown as, a mainstay of the screen picture. If the camera is following other characters in a chamber, and the pianist is somewhere else, the piano sounds are nothing but atmosphere. Notwithstanding that atmosphere is always acousmatic.

When the acousmatic sound seems like a voice very nearby, just behind the camera position, say, or just off to the side, our understanding of its positioning and value depend upon not its quality and amplitude but its (imminent) emergence onscreen, the tenor of which need not be one-dimensional. There is always an option for a character, in mid-speech, to move from off-camera acousmatics to on-camera dialogue by moving into the scene, or becoming visible in some other way, while speaking. This technique makes possible that the viewer discovers the *acousmêtre* as a lapsed *acousmêtre*, an *acousmêtre*-that-was, now become a vivacious speaker. This is what happens with Rose in *Titanic*, albeit somewhat shockingly the very first time we lose that distant (and mature) voice and find the eager (but more jejune) persona of history (Kate Winslet). Various strategic games can be played with transitions of this kind. The voice can be continued, sounding live and present and very close, and shifting, as the camera pans toward it, into sound coming from a device such as a radio or music player (the climactic bedroom confrontation between Waldo Lydecker [Clifton Webb], both live and on the radio, and Laura [Gene Tierney] in *Laura* [1944]; or in *The Passenger* [1975] Locke's taped chat with Robertson). In this case we come to the sharpening realization that the voice transmitted by radio waves was a voice only by transmission, a simulacrum: a "transmission" that really was a transmission (like all voices in cinema!). In the same way, the scene could fade into a depiction of a memory or a dream or a hallucination, where the presently embodied voice onscreen is identified as part of a subject's innermost world, acousmatic in the first place because, yet only because, it is fully interior and in that way off- from the visible surface of things.

If in order to hear it is not necessary to see, if sound can strike us from a position inaccessible to the eye, the voice off- can become a denial of definition. Not a shape, not a color, not a size, not a moving thing, not a personality, yet at the same time a characterization. The vocal timbre will be apprehended and assimilated, the stretches and contractions of a dialect will ring musically, the enunciation and breathing will be yoked to produce instantaneous distinctness. While the listener can "cast" the voice (voice as role) with an actorial identity, still the voice can go as itself, as an immediacy of presence, a pure existence without pattern: the opening passage in *Rebecca* (1940). "Last night I dreamed of Manderley again . . ." To work well in a dramatic context, the off-voice needs be compelling and fluid, capable of an extended range—Joanne Woodward in *The Age of Innocence* (1993). Idiosyncrasies of speech (stammerings, lisps, nasalities, and so on) may work or may block a viewer's comprehension, dependent on diegetic circumstance. For high-toned historicism best to go with the masterful elocution and lulling intonation of someone like Basil Rathbone or Alexander Scourby or Peter Ustinov (British, note). For animations, the vocalizations of which are all acousmatic, go for distinctiveness and tonal fit. Lisping Sterling Holloway as adorable Pooh. Oaken James Earl Jones as lordly Mufasa. Twinkly Whoopi Goldberg as the goofy Cheshire Cat. The ineffable Robin Williams as the ineffable blue genie.

With animations, there is a continuing battle between the owner of the animating voice (sometimes a celebrated personality) and the visual qualities of the screen entity that voice vocalizes to life. Which of the two will dominate? When Holloway did *Winnie the Pooh and the Blustery Day* (1968) and the Pooh films that followed for Disney, he was not a major star and his persona would not have come to the attention of many who watched, certainly not the children. But when Danny DeVito did the dog on *Men in Black* (1997), the opposite was true: the dog instantaneously became DeVito, since the creature itself was nothing but a typical pug whereas the actor had already become well known as a puggish character player. In casting for animation, the balance, and shift of balance, between character and voice constitute a central problem for producers seeking audiences and ratings. In all animated work, viewers come to know that cartooned characters without their own voices—that is, projective voices of any kind—are filled in, dubbed, by people we do not see.

One feature of vocal animation, that the voice comes from nowhere and in this way casts the visual character into a kind of "nowhere," is that we entertain every nuance of it, every breath, every consonant hard and soft, since it is informative both syntactically and harmonically. The voice takes on a rounded, fleshly character, not only giving life to drawings but assuming (caricatured) life itself.[6] In catching the animated voice by catching all of it, in apperceiving it by rounding it, we eschew the act of filtration by which in the everyday we permit sound to approach. In the everyday we do filter the considerable sonic array all around, making a crucial division between the momentarily vital and the momentarily neglectable. Discussing "normal appearances," Erving Goffman points to how ordinarily "the individual mediates between ... placidly attending to easily managed matters at hand" and being "fully mobilized ... with a very pretty capacity for dissociated vigilance ... readings can be done out of the furthest corner of whatever is serving for an eye" (*Relations* 238). Without some method of filtering out the unnecessary-to-watch and the unnecessary-to-hear, a creature would drown in the stimulus array. And because what is heard can come from so many places, even from more than one place at once, acoustic filtering is vital. The bear-eats-Hugh scene in *The Revenant* (2015) is an attempt to replicate a real encounter, and although it is cinematic—thus bearing a feature I shall discuss momentarily—it has marvelous moments in which the real is stretched: we *see* the bear looking at the camera (where Leonardo DiCaprio is positioned), then beginning its rumble forward. But *quite suddenly we can hear the beast grunting up close,* the sound of close grunting being an effect here crafted to make the oncoming animal feel nearer than the eye says it is. Sound against image to produce a sense of danger that will be felt through unwarranted proximity, a quality of presence conveyable acoustically from the margins of the visual frame, indeed from the margins of the narrative. At the same time, the closeness is unmappable.

Watching cinema, we tend not to filter sound. As any sound at all, even an off-sound, is taken in and interpreted to be associated in some way, central or peripheral, with the picture, and as the picture thus takes a dominating position, the sound fills our conception of the frame just as much as the picture fills the frame. Everything that is articulated is heard, directly as sound emanating from a diegetic source onscreen or associated with a screened instant; or else indirectly, because being off- it is not clearly associable with what we see and thus seems eerie to one degree or another. Yet we do recognize that all sound was recorded not in strict accord with the structural principles of everyday life but instead in alignment with purely diegetic considerations, so beyond there being no nuances that one can filter safely one senses that everything has been designed, and so everything must be attended: in this way, the picture as a whole becomes a potential source of peril, something that rouses us to a certain defensive sensory acuity.

However:

Cautionary disattention being a component of attention—keep an "eye" on what's "behind your head"—we need something, some potentially discernable essence, to "turn away from" as we focus on the film, and this something is the circumstance of watching, itself. To concentrate on what is *there*, we concentrate on *not concentrating on what is here.* Sounds around us in the theater space are filtered out if they can be.

---

[6] Maurice Ravel's *Boléro* is a good illustration of the way instrumentation can design a sound for character.

And when such sounds are too distracting, too imposing, too messy to be rapidly cleaned away, we are forced to begin hearing them *in lieu* of the picture. The picture diminishes, and our pleasure is interrupted or ruined. So we notice this diminution, because of its outcome. We bark, "Shushhhhh!" In some limited circumstances, sounds from the audience—that give a cue to the presence of an audience in the first place—can be tolerated, even thrillingly enjoyed, during a film projection: what must occur is that the audience sound not only match the picture, but fill in what can be interpreted (pleasurably) as a gap in pictorial proceedings. *Don't go into that room! . . .*, in *Poltergeist* (1982), for example. *Oy, you're going to get it!*, in *Raiders of the Lost Ark* (1981) when Indiana has the bald Nazi standing obliviously in front of a whirring airplane propeller. How can this participatory energy from partner viewers be misguided and go horribly foul? When it acts to predict a moment that is felt to be suspenseful and exciting *precisely in its* hitherto unexperienced upcomingness, when anticipation is taking the place of perception for viewers. In *Psycho* (1960): *I think you'd better think twice before getting into that shower . . .*

17

Remote Control

Rod Steiger (left) with Marlon Brando in On the Waterfront *(Elia Kazan, Horizon, 1954). Digital frame enlargement.*

Nicholas Ray told his acting students that they should try to say a line as though for the very first time. He was encouraging the achievement of what would be sensed as spontaneity, a springing to life in the moment here, now, before our eager eyes. He knew how performance could have the *look of performance*—the giveaway: the actor aware of acting, aware we are watching that acting, concentrating on how careful one must be to do an act and showing that care. What made actors like Marlon Brando, James Dean, Montgomery Clift, Kay Francis, Carole Lombard, and sometimes Elizabeth Taylor so electrifying in performance was their spontaneity before the lens, the freshness of their moments, their apparent unawareness of where they were and what they were doing as they did it.

But an actor's moments are also generated by a script.

In terms of a displayed continuity of feeling, every moment in the character's being (every effect in the act) is prearranged to flow from something earlier (something quite specific) and leads to something (quite specific) later. When we see the gesture, we will recognize its meaning-in-scene by figuring its origin elsewhere, perhaps in an overall character design set out previously, perhaps in particular actions and responses. We seek a tight weave between what happened, what happens, and what will happen. With the everyday gesture we do not seek this, accepting that any gesture might be engendered by something far off, something to which we have had no access, something outside the present "frame." A cardinal feature of drama (staged and cinematic, both) is that, as seems, either directly or by open reference we are given access to everything. Anything that matters is there for us (a lavish banquet); and anything that is there for us, matters. Histories, to take a case, are handed over as part and parcel of characterizations, there being an inherent logic to the script that characters will evidence. In the text of Albee's *Who's Afraid of Virginia Woolf?* (filmed in 1966), there is an instant in which we are told in passing that George (Richard Burton) earned his esteemed position in the college History Department by marrying the president's daughter (Elizabeth Taylor). The theme of career incest implied here reverberates through the film. Implied but not shown is a strategic line of scenes in which George scans, evaluates, plots, arranges, and finally actually sets up his career path, the path he followed for many years before we meet him as this film (this play) begins. In our everyday lives we do not rely so firmly upon implications.

Because a character's moments are script-logical, the actor's spontaneity is tempered by extrinsic demands, by enforced obedience to the "plan." Since all of what happens will fit into the frame originated and covered by the plan, it will need to be worked to flow *as though it was not thought of before.* The actor's task is to behave as though there is no *before.* To behave *without apparent memory.* We can imagine the daunting challenge presented to the actor who must do a shot fifty, sixty, seventy times to get it the way the director wants, each time working *as though with no memory* of what could ever have gone before for the character, or even for himself. The character will seem to be alive without a memory of self, will gesture with no memory of the thing called "gesture" and no recollection of having gestured before, unless the script is calling for a specific point-to-point reference (E.T.'s finger upon Elliott's temple). In every take of a shot, every instantaneous feeling will be original, will bear no historical trace.

This challenge can be especially fraught in relation to dialogue. One says a line—*I coulda been a contender*—breathing it fluidly because in preparation one has caught the poetry and shape of the line, tasting the syllables on one's tongue. But for the next take there must be no evident memory of that catch, that taste. A fisherman whose every cast is the only cast.

Generally we are rarely called upon to use and show such relentless spontaneity. We will use, and know others will use, phrases that have been uttered before, even with the same accentuations, emphases, and breathing. *How ya doin'?—Fine, fine. You?*[1] Yet,

---

[1] A marvelous study reported by Harold Garfinkel involved his students agreeing to behave with friends as though such casual, gestural comments were not typical and typically meaningless, but instead focused and intended to convey precisely the meaning the grammar held. "What's new?," coming from a passing friend, was to be read as that person wanting to know what it was that had no previous existence, and the student was to press the matter by revealing that "precise" reading and pressing the interlocutor to either explain herself or else. See *Studies.*

even recognizing the limited reservoir people carry, and the need to have constant recourse to old routines, still, we do not expect to encounter robotically rehearsed and programmatic presentation. Even when we find people being hackneyed, we take them to be originating themselves as present and as at least striving for an originality of feeling. Personality is recognized partly in this dimension, and is an accommodation between wholly spontaneous and wholly repetitive behavior. A person who acted in the everyday with supreme and continuous spontaneity, as, say, Brando does as Terry Malloy in *On the Waterfront* (1954), could seem bizarre, egotistically stagey, a performer in a world where performers do not exist except on the special screen. Brando's performativity becomes real by virtue of standing almost too bravely away from habit: that is, from not only his own actorial habits but also the ordinary habits we see surrounding him in the show. Brando and Terry seem to have no habits.

Self-consciousness comes from memory, and characters have no memory.

With a scripted line of dialogue, an actor will find it necessary before opening the mouth to understand how it would be that the character would say "this" "here and now." How it would be, not why. (The "why" is always in the script.) Should the line be mumbled as though being reflected while being spoken? Should it be barked, as though a great force of conviction lies behind it? Should it be uttered with pauses, as though the character is having some difficulty getting it out? There are so many choices. Let us say the actor says, "I coulda been a contender!" with a sigh of loss and disappointment. Now the director asks for another take—the lighting was off. The actor has to say, "I coulda been a contender!" with a loss and disappointment *that is not at all tinctured by* any potentially irritating note that this exact loss and disappointment were felt before. The feeling is ostensibly true only now, but unfortunately not pointedly enough because there lingers an implicit "still": *I still coulda been a contender:* a *still* that is not in the script. *I'm still here, trying to write this.* Or, *I wrote this already.* (No matter the reason for the re-take, the actor must face the event as a problem for him or her; a time travel.)

When a performer is a singer, how touching it can be when a melody seems only to emerge. Emerge, but not be searched for, found, withdrawn, spread out from the files. No matter how many times one has heard this song from this mouth, still, here and now it is being sung directly and as though never before. Liza Minnelli's "New York, New York" solo. Tony Bennett doing "I Left My Heart in San Francisco." Joan Sutherland singing *Turandot*. There are not many singers who manage to get this effect, but acting in front of the camera can be very much like singing in this way. It is as though a spirit wells up and is allowed to flow out. There is no act of searching, summoning, invoking. There is only presence. Straight unadulterated presence (but also hitting your marks).[2]

In *Shane* (1953), there is one shot in which Jean Arthur leans forward, opens an oven door, and withdraws two apple pies, one after another. They are certainly paragons of the American Apple Pie, but it is the way she reaches in and pulls these out, with a simplicity, a directness, a total absence of thought, even a total absence of evaluation. None of the "Oh!, these pies turned out well" (because *we can see that*), nor

---

[2] D. A. Pennebaker's *Original Cast Album: Company* (1970) is a textbook illustration of singers laboring "only to sing."

"Oops, I better not drop these pies" or even "I hope Shane likes apples," or anything *referential to* the action. She has as little self-regard at the moment of pulling the pies out as any homemaker would have in his or her kitchen just trying to get something safely out of a hot oven and ready to serve. Near the end moments of *Donnie Brasco* (1997), Al Pacino is readying to go out for the evening. His character Lefty knows this will be his last evening, and that as he goes out he will be leaving life. He pauses at a closet area near the door, opens a little drawer, drops in his wristwatch and ring. One can hear him thinking, "Leave your wristwatch and your ring for Annette. Just here. Just like that. Done." Talking silently to himself because he is overcome with all the emotions that could end an existence now consciously brought to a conclusion. The actor does nothing at all here to enunciate his actorial presence. He is in part-shadow, his gestures are simple and brief, he gives no facial work to the camera, and before one can breathe the moment is done and he has left.

Some moments, on and offscreen, call up recognitions of spontaneity as we know it. The viewer's feeling is that behavior visible at such times is actually un-"presentable," is just simply emerging, and would not have been, really cannot have been, contrived, arranged, shaped, or prepared. Moments of intimate contact tend to be regarded this way, until, that is, a film like *Klute* (1971) debunks the myth of "intimate spontaneity" in its opening fuck-while-checking-the-wristwatch sequence or, in a coffee shop in *When Harry Met Sally . . .* (1989) Meg Ryan gives off a spectacular fakery that calls "genuine moments" into question. Or mortality: the mortality of the screen is hardly anything but a contrived get-up, since we do not expect actors to die on camera in order to give the impression that the character they play is dying. It is easier in many ways to play a corpse than to expire on camera, since the corpse invokes the viewer's imagination of a death and the imagination will always be more faithful than any direct presentation could be. "Sudden inspiration," something that in the everyday would feel spontaneous enough to the recipient, plays onscreen only because of the unsolved problems that precede it and the successful outcome that follows—all this because thought is invisible. Tears have a tendency to seem spontaneous and some actors know a trick for bringing them up on the spot, a trick so unreferenced, so undiscussed (even actor to actor) that one does not see it operating. As for spontaneous speech: what is said, apparently now and here and with no outside control or choreography at all, is almost always written to be said, and even in filmed moments where an actor improvises a line of dialogue or two the audience will be unaware of the improvisation if the rest of the performance gives the feel of an improvisation, too, a character flailing around in impossible circumstances played by an actor who would ruin many shots if he were in the same boat.[3]

The spontaneity problem, if one might term it that, raises a new head in contemporary film viewing, an affair very different in nature from audience experience in the earlier days of cinema (say, before 1982 and the birth of the Carolco mega-picture with *Rambo*). Audiences now are fully attuned to the back production

---

[3] A supreme example of an actor delivering written lines with a veritable flood of feeling is Ashley Zukerman's performance in *The Code* (2014).

of the presentation they see, the dressing-room trailer, the cameraman choosing a lens, the editor snipping, the make-up artist brushing, the dialogue coach rehearsing lines over and over, the make-up team baking prosthetics. There are, too, more offscreen moments now dramatized as part of the show. There are legion venues outside the theater where discussions abound of film production per se. One sees and ingests interviews with actors, writers, and directors. One reads "reveal" stories in the supermarket line-up. Not that so very much is known of the elaborate system of work behind the screen, but that what little is known is known over and over in many different contexts. Thus, actors' friendships, animosities, and love affairs off the set; special effects makeup and its taxing pains, and so on. The issue of spontaneity can be mooted, then, as audiences look for, find, and take pleasure in finding only contrivance. Even subtle and sophisticated contrivance, as is appreciated here by a brilliant observer considering *Homeland:*

> Details of performance in the two *Homeland* openings complicate any sense of straightforward accumulation. Consider how, in "Grace," our briefly held sense that Carrie is becoming psychologically "linked" with Brody is achieved by a perceptual trick. The scene exploits settled expectations of dream sequence convention to overturn assumptions of privileged access to character interiority. As we cut to Brody in his bed, the camera swiftly pushes in towards [Damian] Lewis as he sits up violently, his eyes wide with panic, darting from one side to another in search of escape while his rigid arms and shoulders appear paralysed, holding him in place. Woken by Brody's scream [as she secretly surveils him from her home], Carrie looks to the monitor to discover its source. But in Lewis's performance of Brody's terror there is no such thing to be found—only the image of a man lost in confusion and fright, overwhelmed by an obscure sense of threat that has no intelligible outer object but which resides everywhere within. (Logan 88–9)

The apparently spontaneous gesture can have alarming dramatic effect, too, real definitional power. At the end of *The Laundromat* (2019), Meryl Streep removing some of her performative surface and then looking straight into the lens to deliver what amounts to a brief political lecture: it seems a moment of startling and unprepared actuality, a meeting of the actor's and the viewer's struggles, through the veil.

Spectator, Watch Thyself

{18} Paranoia

{19} Quote Me

{20} The Magic Touch

{21} Exeunt omnes

{22} Throw It Away

{23} Who Are You?

{24} The Walking Cure

{25} The Picture Dances

{26} Taboo

{27} Only Connect

{28} The Impatient

{29} At the Party

{30} O!

{31} A Sight for Sore Eyes

Paranoia

Keeley Hawes (left) and Richard Madden in Bodyguard *(World Productions, 2018). Digital frame enlargement.*

> *Everyone sits down and watches it; you don't talk as much as you used to. If anyone came in, you used to talk—now you watch the television.*
>
> Elaine Bate, 14, girls' grammar, Stoke-on-Trent, late 1950s (qtd. in Kynaston)

At this writing, binge watching is widespread and popular. The serials fans binge-watch through streaming may not replace films, but will the experience of viewership that is learned through binge watching come to make a new kind of viewership in cinema? The experience of binge watching serial programs (easily made habitual by streaming services like Netflix and Amazon Prime that offer, for the viewer who does not act to interrupt, a continuous flow of episodes) interestingly sheds light on some features of normal (singular, staggered) television viewing and film viewing as well.[1] Characters (actorial characterizations) can begin to infect the viewer, to perdure in the

---

[1] It is convenient enough to think of "television viewing" as the spectatorial experience that is focused on a piece of television equipment.

active mind, in a new way. Even in serial dramas with exotic pictorialism and set in distant historical eras the characters approach and re-approach in stages: they become appreciable, then repeatedly recognized, then known (and then perhaps cherished) by virtue of personality, mannerism, appearance, and scripted personal dialogue.[2] Afforded opportunity to see characters present themselves and interact in multiple, very different social situations, one comes to feel one is following the events close by them, that one has become attached—a sense of approximation to their position in "life" (as the story poses it). This kind of viewer bonding can happen in cinematic screening as well, and in traditional once-a-week tv watching, but with serial drama conceptual "knowing," fleeting and temporary, is one thing and the manifest, unbounded quality of knowing people long encountered and understood, as in binge watching, is quite another. In binge watching, one so-called episode of a show bleeds into another, both diegetically and in the viewer's real time, so that one's exposure to characters at any one viewing is extended in duration—often far beyond what occurs with film.

One walks away from the binge experience, if not smeared with traces of the characterological world (Vienna in 1900, Manchester in 2009, Hollywood in 2015) at least feeling the characters still present and alive. They first whispered and now abide, their facial expressions and vocal tones echoing and re-echoing in memory, their stunning personalities (designed explicitly to stun) displayed with great articulateness over the arc of numerous episodes now seeming to congeal into an amalgam of self one can recognize, affiliate with, and comment upon through a rhythmic, addicting regularity. Raymond Reddington (James Spader) on *The Blacklist* (2013). Eva Geller (Michelle Monahan) in *Messiah* (2020). Kiki Camarena (Michael Peña) in *Narcos: Mexico* (2018). Wendy Byrde (Laura Linney) in *Ozark* (2017). Gordon Clark (Scoot McNairy) in *Halt and Catch Fire* (2014). Harry Bosch (Titus Welliver) in *Bosch* (2014). These are only American shows; streaming cine-fiction is worldwide: Robert Taro (Gérard Depardieu) in *Marseille* (2016); Marcella (Anna Friel) in *Marcella* (2016); Tokio (Úrsula Corberó) in *Money Heist* (2017); Brigitte Nyborg (Sidse Babett Knudsen) in *Borgen* (2010); Seong Ji-hun (Lee Jung-jae) in *Squid Game* (2021). It may well be that owing to the multiplication of characters (often, by hundreds) in serial dramas and viewers' tendency to binge watch even more than two episodes at a time—this conceivably with more than one show within the same period—the exact characterological relations between persons become confounded in memory, blur, slip, and slide. Not only who is A to B technically (sister, wife, ex-girlfriend, stranger at the office) but also who is A to B emotionally and dramatically: what has been happening between them no matter who they actually are? A character in one show might even be associated erroneously with one from another. Meanwhile, as a personality and type, each character being shown and shown again radiates with a glowing persistence that encourages, even stimulates a *persistence of vision*. Serial development can offer actors a chance to plumb the depths of a character slowly and systematically, to build

---

[2] On dialogue as value in itself, a much discussed characterization popularly admired (because of what she says) is Maggie Smith's in *Downton Abbey* (2010).

long arcs, so that one's view of a character through repetition, especially instantaneous repetition, will be deeper and less rational.

In conventional cinematic narratives, characters tend to embed themselves in viewers' perceptions and sentiments as feelingful, attractive, and purposive creatures bent toward what each would consider a logical resolution. They emote with and toward each other, however tersely or in however much repression; they draw our gaze to their luminous selves; and they act ongoingly as though they are trying to accomplish something important and recognize themselves doing so. But they do all this *in the scene*, the revealed here and now. The target of their behavior is, if not directly addressed in the scene at least hinted at as an element in a continuity. In *Money Heist*, every moment is about achieving a spectacular robbery. One is presented with a chain of scenes editorially linked so as to build to a culmination as the story winds out. Once images have left the screen what remains is a publicity trace of the star or of some momentary intensive pose or expression, finally an exaggeration of attitude (in *Heist*, the Professor staring forward expectantly through his thick-rimmed eyeglasses) but not a sense of characters changing during one's submission to their action. Thus, continual surveillance on our part does not help characters grow; it is the scripted contingency that does that. In the binge experience, the scene seems never to end, since the invocation of the story, its places, its characters are extended in incompleteness. Serial characters gain full presence only retroactively because as the series unwinds they are constantly being submitted to an accretion of challenges and perils. Acting a "serial scene," the performer recognizes its place in a very long arc that will extend before and after the boundary of an episode. In standard series television, the character arc is fully contained in each episode; then given gross repetition later, as with, say, Perry Mason (Raymond Burr) solving a case and then solving a case and then solving a case . . . until, as the series expires, there seem to be no more cases to solve.

Binge Bond • Between the binge watcher and select characters an especially perduring bond is established, one that, in conventional stage and screen work, actors know they can effect only for the lapse of a moment however cathartic and that they would not expect to endure outside the theatrical frame. The binge bond has to endure outside the frame, because it is from a position outside the frame that the binger makes a move to plunge back in and find that character again. The film sequel may raise for producers the "hope" of continuing fan affiliation, and films that have been intensively sequelized *with the same performers* may potentially have an effect similar to what one experiences with binge watching, with the proviso that sequelization is known to be both limited in extent and especially hyped in advertising—hyped so that re-commitment by viewers is potentially embarrassing and hardly without a degree of self-consciousness. Further, many cinematic features that have been sequelized, at least to date, involved fantasy characters in wildly conceived fantasy situations, so that re-bonding is like re-entering a game after a hiatus. By contrast, at the end of a streamed series the binge watcher can feel grief at the sudden absence of persons who have stepped markedly toward the real.

Kaleidoscoped Strands • In order that it be made substantial enough to fill the space of a series of eight episodes or more, sometimes as many as fifteen or more episodes per season for several seasons, series action must be fragmented into strands each of which is "kaleidoscoped" in juxtaposition to oppositional, contrasting, incomparable, or radically foreign material, harmonious, comedic, or ironic; in this way, the weight of impressing the audience falls not to events, which have to be seen flickering and shifting, but to characters' personalities. When a loyal fan is asked about some favorite binge watch, "What is the show about?," the answer is invariably incoherent and incomplete as regards story but notably affirmative as regards main characters; indeed describing "what happens" is typically not a simple affair but characters, however complex, can be easily simplified for description.

Characters not as agents for spinning a story, but characters as related to the viewer notwithstanding that a story houses them. Bingeable stories are ramified only to keep a number of interesting types alive and kicking for a very long time (as with traditional television soap operas). In serial drama, the character's demonstrated qualities and attitudes modulate from circumstance to circumstance, just in the way that the colored glass in the kaleidoscope changes its character in relation to the pieces around it. Traditional television casting works differently. It involves a ritual approach to character: no matter what happens and the history of happening, every presentation of main characters has them fully and recognizably themselves, now as always. With a typical "traditional" show, be it *I Love Lucy* (1951) or *77 Sunset Strip* (1958), *The Mary Tyler Moore Show* (1970) or *Friends* (1994), the characterizations are repeated with precision, and in balance. The narrative circumstances change to throw us momentarily off balance. Circumstances must never be scripted to change so very much that the stalwart repeated character suddenly seems lost or out of place.

Actor as Scene • Casting for binge-watchable television must negotiate some obstacles. Many characters, certainly central ones, will be on the screen (however tiny) for quite a long time, so long that, even with variations in setting and distance from camera to shift their visual weight they will become part of the scenery, that is, taken for granted as obviously, naturally, and unexpressively "being there." Very often in dramatic performance, a character will inhabit a setting without seeming to be, or belong, there—the character uses the setting as a station to move through. But binge-watched stars do not do this, they inhabit space. What must be located in casting is the actor who is sufficiently appealing to watch as a visualized form, yet at no point so patently knowable that in successive scenes her presence will seem only repetitive. If she "lives in" the setting, her appearances will be naturalized. The actor must therefore have an opacity. In this way the character can always seem fresh, no matter how many scenes must be played with her or him in an episode. Fresh and pretty, and never quite yet wholly discovered. *Always* never yet wholly discovered. By opaque I do not mean to suggest, invisible: invisibility (to the viewer) is reserved for marginal characters any trace memory of whom could interrupt the flow of ongoing action. Main characters must be acted by performers who shape and restrain gesture, who keep gesture just on the cusp of flowering.

The Malleable Face • The performer is used through a distinct, even dominating, "faciality" that must work lastingly if with systematic variation. In terms of the body and face in its relation to behavior—what Kenneth Burke calls the actor: act ratio—the actor in role must always seem entirely appropriate for what the character is presently doing; the physique must lend itself to some optical filling-out of the character-in-place. Often, casting directors will need to know not only what a character's position is, *generally*, in the story, but exactly what sorts of scenes the character will be in, and the range of what the character will have to do there. In conventional singular visual narratives, the character may be pungent, not easily warping or changing in variant situations and conditions. But in serial drama the character, often binge watched, needs to make numerous reappearances in wildly different settings, and always be a person viewers are eager to see more of because there remains, persistently, something incomplete. The embodiment must host and retain a mystery. The issue in casting, then, is less how powerfully a person can act out a scene than how many different pictures of this person can be loaded and looked at one after the other before boredom sets in. How quickly does one tire of that face, of those soon-to-be-conventional expressions?—because they will go on for some considerable time. How hungry is one for that performer to return, once he or she has walked out the door?

In the Family • What Kenneth Burke calls the "family motive" (*Permanence*) very often comes into play with serial television, because many binge-watched shows fashionably involve family structures. It is ideal that characters should believably seem blood-related. (For extended viewing augmentation of the cast is a principal rule, and bringing in a family is a simple and effective way of doing this.) Family relation(s) will gain multiple demonstrations over time, but the difficulty is that anytime a "family" is invoked dramatically, here, on the stage, in conventional movies, the viewer's suspicion is aroused about the credibility of the characters' "togetherness." An example from *Bosch*: can Madison Lintz, who plays Detective Harry Bosch's daughter growing up over six years, believably seem to be Titus Welliver's offspring, now, here, and ongoingly? In *Homeland*, could Jackson Pace and Morgan Saylor seem believably to be Damian Lewis and Morena Baccarin's? Every invocation of the family bond raises the viewer to some controlled speculation. One has to have opportunity to grow into "membership" in a staged "family" that must seem subject to normal familial variation in attitude, mood, and behavior while never losing its binding form. In straight cinema, it is likely that once a "relation" has been established onscreen, it will persist for the audience, who recognize that in only a short spate of real time they will have to be engaged in events that will eclipse the characterizations.[3] Whereas in serial television a child–parent relationship is likely to survive through a large number of sequential "familial" happenings onscreen and off-.

A Fast Act • To keep up the energy of variegation, binge-watched shows switch frequently from one action thread to another, eventually producing a multiplication of such threads in any one of which characters may differ (slightly or significantly)

---

[3] A typical trope of the mystery drama is a final scene in which it is revealed, surprisingly, that many of the individuals we have been following as discreet persons are now, and always have been, blood-related. *Murder on the Orient Express* (1974) gives an excellent example of the trick. When the blood relation is established only at the finale, it demands the scantest attention beyond its factuality, because the film is soon to close in any event.

from those in another. Any particular scene could be relatively brief, with the show's discursive energy coming from the editing between scenes. "Relatively brief" means that an actor might have to play "a scene" in which only one tiny action point is included, a sneer, a slow smile, a turn of the gaze, a lying back on a bed, driving a car, drinking a coffee. In the *ongoing context*, the tiny moment can have potent meaning, much more than it would in conventionally structured drama. A performer can be challenged to play a huge number of "scenic bits" over a long shooting schedule and must be capable of giving over a quality of attitude, alignment, and feeling in only seconds on camera. The scene itself isn't a development, as in typical visual drama; it's a node in a longer (and often fragmented) phase of scenic developments. Here, an actor's work must be *readable* instantaneously in the smallest of movements made however casually but seen up-close. While there may be long, thoroughly developed speeches in the script, they are more likely to be rare than plentiful (the limited series *Midnight Mass* [2021] being a notable exception in being chockful of long vocalizations). Typically we are stitching narrative pieces together as part of the viewing experience: an old lady sits at a restaurant table clutching a wrapped package containing the ashes of her deceased husband (*Giri/Haji* [2019]): where is she headed with the package?, what might get in her way?; a police chief looks down from a high balcony onto an atrium where a particular other character is making a (surprise) entrance to headquarters (*Line of Duty* [2012–21]): what will happen if they come face to face?; a young man who is hired to protect a politician, older than he, very beautiful, and wise, does not notice in her apartment one night that she has turned to look at him in a new and enticing way (*Bodyguard* [2018]): or does he notice, but not show that he notices? For any mini-event, lines of connection could stretch forward and backward into the series plot, illuminating many other moments and lines, shocking only now, in light of a present gesture.

Producers know that viewer engagement will be fostered if in brief scenes action fragments enacted by the cast have a gripping, stunning, stimulating, tickling, frightening, cautionary, or implicating quality. However mundane it will seem on point of contact, the small expressive scene is calculated to be thrilling ultimately—ultimately: in the viewer's canny reflection—thus important. Indeed, one recurring feature of series drama, taken as law by the binge watcher, is that every element, every moment, every nuance is to be regarded as important, finally. The short scene may be the hardest work of the actor's day.

An Act of Undoing • To assist in ramifying the jolts of binge drama,[4] story threads are typically constructed with challenging and/or confrontational twists and turns, so that in almost any scene, as watchers learn to expect, there may spring an event that will undo any previously settled affair and open the receptive door to dangers yet undreamed. The deeper one goes into this narrational rabbit hole, the more Red Queens there are, finally demons of all kinds located in all sorts of story space and taking all kinds of character form: demons threatening the heroes; demons inside

---

[4] On the importance of the "jolt" in media production, see Wyatt.

the heroes, eating them from within; demons only imagined; demons remembered. In *Homeland* (2011–20), to cite a well-known case, the hero Carrie Mathison (Claire Danes) is a full-fledged "action star" in the realm of international espionage but at the same time suffers, and has suffered since childhood, a debilitating psychological disorder to mollify which she must be on heavy, in some ways disabling, drugs: the drugs interact with the bravery to compromise her judgment and sometimes even her ability to move. To make matters more complicated, her former lover, either a secret American agent who posed as an al-Qaeda operative in order to secure information otherwise unavailable to America or else an al-Qaeda operative in fact (posing as an American operative posing as an al-Qaeda operative: we never find out), finally caught in Iran and executed by hanging, has left her with a baby, who grows up during the ensuing years of the series and becomes, in many different ways, not only her cherished love but also a threat to her freedom, her sanity, and her spying.[5] Our commitment to the show often depends upon feeling part of a game being initiated by the show runner, who revels in outsmarting viewers. One trick is to "unmask" a character, make the identity that a character has been blithely sustaining entirely unsustainable: *Homeland*'s Berlin CIA station chief Allison Carr (Mirando Otto), having an affair with a high-placed CIA associate from Washington (and one of the central figures in the show), turns out to be nothing other than a KGB plant. The viewer is now clued into the possibility that every trusted character is "really" not to be trusted, that plants are everywhere. Of course a viewer's actual distrust would undermine the workings of the show, which does require believing in heroes. "Unmasking" can be like making a U-turn in the story.

Another tactic is having "associated others" suddenly appear from out of the blue: a cousin, a brother, a lost parent, a former lover. The last here, the former lover, nicely opens up chances for a sex scene that is at once plot-marginal and viewer absorbing (see the work between Viola Davis and Famke Janssen in *How to Get Away with Murder* [2014–20]). Still another strategic move is the platform leap: opening a mid-season episode with characters—never encountered in this way before—discussing a carefully organized plan they have been running, a charade, and as we hear more and more, we begin to realize the "plan" is the entire storyline in the series so far (see *Imposters* [2017–18]). In short, we've been hoodwinked and these familiar, much-loved earnest souls are the hoodwinkers. Yet another tactic is the "triumphant wound": a key player, having sustained horrifying and life-threatening injuries at the hands of nefarious others, is now found carefully wrapped up in a hospital bed—white sheets and bandages, bright lights, soft curtains around the bed, flickering monitors; she is interrupted in half-conscious reverie by her boss, who is the only other person aside from her to know that she isn't wounded at all. He contrived this whole thing as an elaborate fakery to surprise *someone else*. Alternately, she is visited by a putative assassin who intends to

---

[5] For a thorough discussion of this program's early days, see Logan, who argues cogently that the issue of "What [her lover] Brody is up to" is quickly turned back onto the series lead, CIA agent Carrie Mathison (85 ff).

fiddle with her I.V. In such a scene, our hero will be on the verge of death and very far from the verge of death, simultaneously.

Staccato legato • Being composed of short, attention-grabbing bursts (*staccato*) but at the same time being constructed to sail over a very broad arc (*legato*), serial drama must find a way to produce not only a rhythmic chain of throbs but also a feeling of building continuity, and binge watchers must learn how to accommodate themselves. *Staccato legato, legato staccato.* Since there will be many characters in many "independent story lines," ongoingness works best through some process of shifting from one character/thread to another, jumping away from a figure we have been raptly following—and in mid-breath—to another attractive type in some distinctively other place: in *Narcos: Mexico* from Javi's lavish urban hotel suite in Guadalajara to Rafa's lush marijuana field hidden in the desert. Without particular care and attention, this kind of track skipping can yield a jumpy, disarming, disorienting, displeasing feel. An overriding concern of the production will be to make jumping never seem jumpy while still clearly announcing itself as jumping, so that the shift to a new locale and new personae will not seem incongruous. *Unjumpy jumping.* Irony underpinning the edit from A to B is a very good answer to the problem. The vision can cut between two depictions, one of them an apparent "echo," "reflection," or "metaphor" of the other. In a small car, a woman is speeding along a highway in flight from some truly horrendous thugs who are trying to find her: will they succeed? In another small car, a young man and his brother are driving to the apartment of a man they wish to interrogate, perhaps with violence, perhaps with courtesy. The cut is ironic because the young man in the second car is the son of the lady in the first car, an estranged son to boot, and he does not know she is in the position she is in, *he being in London and she being outside of Tokyo*, and she does not know anything about him, even that he is alive (*Giri/Haji*). The Einsteinian thought arises, that conditions are the same everywhere.

Gamble • The jump of forward progression as one binge-watches serial drama suggests a certain reliance on a mathematical universe, what Roger Caillois calls "a world of number" (107). The viewer is keenly conscious of watching, at any moment, one out of "x" episodes, which, taken all together, will constitute either the whole work or a single season of it (a phase; an innings). With each progression forward, each reincarnation of character bonding and loyalty, comes a simple accretion. And this idea of accretion, of underlying order, suggests the logic of gambling, which depends upon the belief that chance controls universal operations and can very well control the development of one's satisfaction with the show: each episode is a win or a loss, either satisfying and complete or painfully unsatisfying and suspended; and we know already that in almost every case some form of painful dissatisfaction rules. Now the viewer keeps "playing" the interface, choosing another "roll of the dice," since if one rolls enough there must surely come a moment of intense reward. The merit one displays in order to receive the reward of satisfaction (satisfaction entirely irrespective of what might or might not transpire for the characters) is one's commitment to the process, a long-enduring patience and willingness to continue selection. Caillois emphasizes how in games of chance "anyone can win. This illusory expectation encourages the lowly to be more tolerant of a mediocre status that they have no practical means of ever improving" (115)—that is, the viewer, lower than the events on the screen, must remain content with a powerless status in which no action can be taken to ameliorate dramatic conditions other than pressing forward and "betting that" (hoping that) what is about to come will be liberating. One seeks the "sudden lucky stroke of fortune" (115) in removing to a hazy background the bleak and horrifying episodes one has endured, trusting to an "efficacious magic" (116) that sparks a wholly positive state of affairs in which dramatic resolution and fullness are guaranteed.

Designing force • A visual *acousmêtre* is often invoked onscreen. Of the *acousmêtre*, the telling case in contemporary binge drama is the cellphone call,[6] in which we see a character connecting to an apparent other place, an apparent other person or system of persons, here invoked only by way of the presence of a device that can bring sound from any-space-whatever. In *Bosch*, there is a crucial cell call on the average of once every thirty seconds of screen time. The narrational gift with the cellphone is that such a device can be used virtually anywhere, rather than characters having to locate fixed phone sets. This "anywhereness" of the cell phone makes possible something that is utterly standard in serial drama (and other drama now, as well): the visual excitement of a setting change coupled directly with the sonic pleasantry of narrational continuity; not to mention a certain ubiquity of information, since everyone within reach of such a call can be "in on" the current state of affairs without having to move to accomplish that awareness; information can narratively jump from setting to setting. As information jumps, often through text conversations spelled out onscreen, so does the viewer climb Thomas Scheff's "ladder of awareness." In earlier, conventional drama, knowledge was more or less restricted to those who shared space in a single room, and the viewer had to learn in accompaniment with them, thus within strict boundaries. But the cell screen makes rooms obsolete.

In the case of the *optimêtre*—which I have discussed elsewhere[7]—the situation is different.

With the *optimêtre*, a character who is off-, that is, not explicitly shown, is watching something or someone we do see explicitly shown, quite as though our view is this other's view; we are quickly transported from one spatialized (present and seen) character to the vision of another (present though unseen, seeing what we can also see), but the speed and cleanliness of the jump suggest an echoing, a relation between our sight and the invisible other's sight, a sense that the "other" stands in an extension of the space and reach of the character seen, almost as though the presence (or "presence") of the other co-exists in time and space with—while being dimensionally separate from—the presence of the seen character. But in adopting these points of

---

[6] The timing of binge drama development in mainstream aired and streamed media indicates that all of it is formed after the cultural disappearance of land-line telephones, more or less; and it is a rarity indeed to find binge-drama characters who do not have at least one cellphone apiece (unless, as with *Wormwood* [2017], for example, the show is set in an earlier time).
[7] See *The Film Cheat*, chapter 29.

view—in adopting *any* points of view—we stand with a narrative being of some kind. Here the unseen "narrator," whose point of view we adopt in seeing what he or she sees, however disparate in diegetic geography, somehow inhabits one single "world space" comprehensible to us, a "world space" through which the edit-jump moves. By extension, although the story may take a viewer to many discreet locales, populated by many discreet figures, all of them will seem connected in a tightly woven and invisible web, a web in which unseen forces may be positioned and one a full picture of which we will be given, if at all, only later notwithstanding that its existence and persistence are accepted in advance as a foregone conclusion. In the Japan-London movement I mention earlier (from *Giri/Haji*), we have two small cars, two Asian drivers, two matching conversations, two similar road infrastructures, and the possibility of negative pursuit in both cases. We can easily take the two scenes to be happening at once,[8] either end of the join revealing part of one single tale in a single global space-time, and each end of the join being theoretically capable, while technically incapable, of observing the other. This capability/incapability is the irony stressed in the match cut. To say that in Japan the passengers *do not know* about the passengers in London is to imply that knowledge is conceivably possible, but not present. The *reveal* of the edit, the veiled and powerful suggestion, is that all these characters will meet "someday." But such a *reveal* utters secretly to the viewer that there is to be thought a linking operative behind everything given to be seen, a designing and intentional force.

Climax • Climax and completion are not the same. Completion is the rounding out and full gravitational reduction of all relevant components of a story; one speaks of all the "threads" being tied (as though the narration has been a garment in some elegant *haute couture*). Climax is the point of maximum tension; in music, the highest (or sometimes the lowest) note in the scale. In much dramatic cinema, the story is suspended from climaxing until it completes, the completion becoming the climax in fact, so that the viewer is pulled all the way to the end, and feels the ending with a kind of jolt. (A telling filmic example is given in David Fincher's *Gone Girl* [2014].) In serial television, story suspension works more complexly. A number of intertwining threads are suspended, of differing lengths, and as it were in parallel, each promising resolution after a different temporal interval and with a different outcome for the story as a whole. What is given overall, then, is a weave, with so much of the audience suspension differing in quality and timing that suspense comes to seem unbounded. This is partly due to the sequelization problem: that a show may, or in fact may not, be "renewed" for a subsequent season in which action now apparently "concluding"—but by no means actually concluding—can be progressed. As the watcher does not know whether at the end of the present series an announcement will foretell a second to follow, then a third, and so on, the act of watching involves holding one's breath but simultaneously preparing for an explosive release. Binge

---

[8] In the 1940s and onward, filmmakers used the split screen in convey to viewers "simultaneous" distanced actions in a single image, at once. *Pillow Talk* (1959) is a textbook example, as are *Grand Prix* (1966) and *The Thomas Crown Affair* (1968).

watching aggravates the anxiety associated with this "holding of breath." For those who are binge-watching *mavens*, knowing always to harbor a vague suspicion that something more will follow no matter the urge to exhale, the requirement to hold breath over an end-of-season break and wait for the continuity "next year" can be less than irritating (with *The Crown* [2016–] there are timetabled delays sometimes amounting to a year or more; with *Mindhunter* [2017–19] a long delay broke the first and second seasons apart, and the show ended peremptorily before a third season could be produced). *Mindhunter* is a provocative case here, since the first season ended not with a curtain call but with a breath-gripping "hanging" finale in which a central character appeared to have been knocked out of the action. Dead? Injured? Stunned? The binge viewer had to wait a long time to find out, and the answer was finally insignificant.[9] Shades of the Saturday afternoon serials of the 1940s and 1950s, though for these the temporal hiatus was usually seven days.

Learned Impatience. • As to waiting a long time for a serial to continue, the binge watcher is in an especially precarious situation emotionally because the act of proceeding onward without a break (e.g., binge watching itself) teaches, by instantly rewarding, a certain impatience for the future. Catching a season finale in the knowledge one will not be able to continue the binge for several months at least is depleting, like driving a racing car into a brick wall.

The Tiniest Detail. • The binge viewer left hanging, or tossed off a cliff, is potentially very hungry for whatever will come "next." Because disappointment can breed excitement, excitement stretched too long can breed ennui: "I surely don't need any more of this." Ennui would be weightier the longer the binge, the more emotional resources had been committed to caring about characters, to following story complications, and to never missing the tiniest detail—all this apparently to no avail.

The tiniest detail is important in itself, because in binge drama, broken as it is into small bits that, shifting frequently from spot to spot, steadily gain complication, any slim bit of information can twist the meaning of perceived events and realign the direction of a story. Typical visual drama is not packed so densely, the viewer being assumed to be wavering in and out in order to breathe with the tale.[10] One does not take the liberty of breathing as one binge watches. One also does not hold the breath, as a way of sustaining one's involvement episode to episode. There simply is no breathing, only flow. Binge drama is thus a little like electricity. The charge is unremitting, and this is why the viewer segues directly from the end of one episode to the beginning of the next. It is difficult to sustain involvement thoroughly and faithfully even if one

---

[9] "Serial publicity" was first invoked by George Lucas with the 1977 release of his film *Star Wars*. He gave out to the press that there "would be" nine such films, emerging for the public in groups of three, and that the present film was Number Four. After the first group (which ended six years later with *The Return of the Jedi*) the first three would come, and that would be after a long hiatus (*The Phantom Menace* was delayed by sixteen years!). Later, Lucas announced that he would not be involved with Nos. 7, 8, and 9.

[10] A groundbreaking innovation in conventional broadcast drama (with shows appearing once a week) came with *Alias*, in which the episode complications were designed to accrete over a single expanding story over five years (2001–6).

blinks. Anything might be a vital clue, any object in the scene, any gesture of any body, any casual comment—a clue to the whole picture as it will turn out someday, or a clue making intelligible the shifts and transpositions one sees only here and only now. Clues everywhere, everything a clue.

Clues everywhere, the paranoiac state of mind.

19

Quote Me

Humphrey Bogart with Oliver Blake in Conflict *(Curtis Bernhardt, Warner Bros., 1945). Digital frame enlargement.*

We take it as a matter of course that the grammatical function of "the question" is to open space for a statement of fact or conditions that we call "the answer." Questions beg answers. Answers address questions. A marriage made in heaven, no doubt, and a marriage inviolable. Or is it? What of the interrogative that spurs, engenders, inspires, or tickles meditation and closer looking? What of the prod to wonder, wonder not as an upbeat before the downbeat of the surprise but as a downbeat of involvement, pleasurable in itself?

I want to raise a question that—I think—does not have an answer, but if there is an answer, I am not inclined to learn it because for me the question surpasses all. There are such questions to be found, brave questions, by which I mean to say not that one is brave or wonderful for asking them, only that one recognizes them for the wonders they already are. Let us call them *mysteries*, a term that in the Age of Disenchantment seems dirty.

Question, then, in regard to *Vertigo* (1958):

There is a passage many fans have noticed but few who study the film pause to discuss. Our hero, Scottie (James Stewart), has been obliging an old chum by following his wife around San Francisco (Kim Novak) and finally she has parked in front of a dilapidated old wooden structure, in the Northern California style, which, we learn a little later, is at the corner of Eddy and Gough Streets.[1] She has been leading him a wild goose chase, and now she has drawn him here, to the McKittrick Hotel. She goes in and a few seconds later, after seeing her at an upstairs window, he follows. Gentle conversation with the concierge, who is putting olive oil on her rubber plant (Ellen Corby) and persists in claiming there is no such woman, nobody came in here, he must be mistaken. The woman went upstairs, he insists, and begs her to have a look, so she ascends the staircase only to soon call down, "Mr. Detective . . ." When he goes up to join her, she takes him into the room fronting the street and sure enough, emptiness. There is neither woman nor sign of woman, nor an exit, nor anything noticeable at all. He goes to the window and looks out, and of course her car is gone.

Quite an enchanting scene in its way. Novak's little pause at the window, as though to taunt anybody in the street who might be looking this way to have a gander at her. Corby's quaint excuse about the rubber plant, which is obviously her favorite friend. Stewart's modest perplexity. The staircase, the chandelier dropping just above its newel post. And the central idea above all: that a man following a woman should (a) see her enter a structure, (b) pursue her there, and (c) discover emptiness.

Let us put aside reflection into Scottie's experience discovering emptiness where he hoped to find beauty, affection, and interest—an experience that is revived for him in this film and to startling effect—and examine one other aspect of this scene.

That it can be thought a quotation.

In Curtis Bernhardt's *Conflict* (1945), Humphrey Bogart has murdered his wife and is pursuing her sister (Alexis Smith). But he comes to believe the wife may still be alive, many small clues building and darkening his suspicion. He is mailed a pawn shop ticket and when he goes to redeem it, he is shown his wife's locket and her signature in the register. He goes for help and when he returns with the police, magically the locket has disappeared. The employee who showed it to him has disappeared, too. The signature is gone from the register. Now in the street he catches sight of a woman he thinks to be her and follows, urgently, on foot. She goes into an apartment building. He keeps on her trail. But inside, no one is there.

The tailing of a body that isn't there. The evidence plainly visible that is suddenly gone. The same kind of mounting desire and tension, leading upstairs to emptiness. The same kind of hunter, more than desperate to seize hold of his prey.

And of course a wholly cinematic effect, that when you join any piece of film B to any piece of film A your viewer can find that something very evident in A is suddenly not so evident—not there at all—in B. Méliès Magic 101.

Is Hitchcock quoting Bernhardt? Or Arthur Horman and Dwight Taylor, who wrote the screenplay for *Conflict*? More crucially, can Hitchcock *be thought to be quoting*,

---

[1] One of the few *Vertigo* shooting locations that is no longer there.

and what would be the implications if he were? Quoting not dialogue, of course; not specific decorative details—the pawn ticket, the locket, but instead the structure of happenings, the *appearance and disappearance*, the pursuit that leads to discovery, the male's eager passion to locate and pin down the female but for a reason not made clear, perhaps to identify her, perhaps something else. The camera meticulously following his following, and then the building—hotel, apartment—in which it is apparently possible to make an entrance and then disappear. Or at least possible for a woman, for this woman, for this vision. Of course in *The Lady Vanishes* (1938) we have disappearances inside a magician's cabinet.

The viewer is invoked in both *Conflict* and *Vertigo* as a follower of followings, a creature who tracks after disappearing people and after those who track after them. What is it to watch a film, but this?

Quotation need not be linguistic. As an author once wrote, "Quotation need not be linguistic." If not as a language *per se*, film can be understood as a form that fulfills some of the functions we conventionally assign to language. Here, we must grasp that a form itself can speak, regardless of what it may say. "Speak the speech, I pray you, trippingly on the tongue." The tongue and not the speech. Not that Stewart or Bogart say something important in their scenes—they say just enough to make it clear how it is that they are in pursuit. Some of the deep power of Scottie's pursuit is the silence in which it occurs, a silence made notable by the gentle beat of the Bernard Herrmann score at that point. Nor that we hear the Bogart voice, strained, hoping, fearful of disappointment. But still, in experiencing film we can catch something of an echo. Again, not the thing that is echoed, exact, bounded, implicative, but the very echo itself. Echo *as echo*. The echo and the associated—very directly associated—fact that we can catch it. What does the very echo "say" *as echo* when it is "saying" only for itself? The echo's "saying" about echoing saying.

Central in the echo, and similarly central in the problem of quotation, is recursion, the inclusion within a form of another (perhaps identical) representation of that same form, a picture within a picture, even if that inner picture is only the trace memory of having seen something like it, somewhere before. When I studied with Theodore Newcomb,[2] he taught me that a *self* is an image of an organism held by that same organism. In other words, as I would argue here, the self is already a recursion, a kind of echo, a quotation. A borrowing from the past, or a delivery of the cargo of the past forward toward whatever will come to bring a view of the past that led to this now.

In order to quote, one sometimes feels it appropriate to seek permission—from the very famous, the very political, the very confidential, the distinctively published. And sometimes one makes a ceremony of quoting, gives acknowledgment, as it were, to the "source." Yet there is no pure source, at least no identifiable pure source, anymore than there is language that has never been used before. Ralph Waldo Emerson: "Every book is a quotation; and every house is a quotation out of all forests and mines and stone quarries; and every man is a quotation from all his ancestors" (422). For Emerson,

---

[2] Theodore Mead Newcomb (1903–84), author of *Persistence and Change*, among other works, and cigar lover.

a kind of trepidation is provoked by the possibility that "tomorrow a stranger will say with masterly good sense precisely what we have thought and felt all the time, and we shall be forced to take with shame our own opinion from another" (133). To be quoting, then, and quoting perforce, only because "in every work of genius we recognize our own rejected thoughts"; indeed, because, thinking them, we recognize the choice to reject those thoughts. Stanley Cavell uses this meditation as a vantage from which to observe that "philosophers nowadays tend to associate the experience of [Aristotelian] wonder with the explanations of science rather than, as in Wittgenstein and Austin, with the recognition of our relation to things as they are, the perception of the extraordinariness of what we find ordinary (for example, beauty), and the ordinariness of what we find extraordinary (for example, violence)" (33–4).

The deep point in quotation citing is not some respectful tip of the hat to indicate (and broadcast oneself indicating) deference and recognition, deference however gracile and the obligation to recognize being a matter of arbitrary definition. The deep point is indication of the picture-within-the-picture as such a structure, a structure operationally free from content in that no matter what image is being used here to call up memories of some other placement it is the potentiality of the image to stand in internal relation to another image that is the marvel. The recursion points to itself, to *any* recursion. It points to pointing, then. And in pointing to pointing it calls up acknowledgment of that gesture of *pointing to pointing*, the viewer's ability at least to recognize that a finger is being extended toward that tree on the lawn in the photograph inside the photograph in the oil painting that hangs on the wall in a scene of the film. To catch the pointing *as pointing* is to be conscious.[3]

The meaning of quotation is consciousness.

Consider:

- The hunt with clues that are each, regardless of shape, evanescent. A plant-loving concierge who affirms, "Our clients are entitled to their privacy, you know," and then, in a chill, "No, she hasn't been here at all." Absolute conviction. "I've been right here all the time, putting olive oil on my rubber plant leaves" (this clue giver had been crouching down behind the registration desk, quite invisible: certainly not seeing). A pawn shop proprietor who claims that no, I don't have any such locket and I've never had one, and you won't find any signature in the register, and this person you claim you spoke to earlier standing right here where I am: I have no idea on earth who you are referring to. It's my shop, I've been here all the time. In both cases, at the side of the hunter, who is desperate for clues, *we see* clues, we see the girl draw her car to a halt and walk out and go into the hotel, and we see her in the window, and we see the man notice the locket in the display case, and take it into his hand, and open it, and look at the signature in the register. When he is forced to doubt the clues he has seen he moves us, perhaps, to doubt, too. But then, of course, if we are taking all this seriously and also taking seriously ourselves

---

[3] My "Visit to a Gallery" addresses the importance of pointing in a key scene of *Vertigo*.

taking this seriously: to doubt even what we are seeing now. To doubt is to suspend the spirit at the gateway to consciousness, to wait. Or perhaps more clearly if less assertively: to suspend the spirit at the gateway to the hall of mirrors. "The mirror is the door by which Death enters and leaves," Cocteau affirms in *Orphée* (1950).

- Is it Cartesian doubt that we suffer along with these protagonists? Concern or fear that there could be a Malevolence that is bent on tricking us, doing us out of truth, doing us out of experience; and thus extreme devotion to the belief that there is not?

- And, film being sensual, what of our senses, after all, should we go stepping into the shadow of doubt? If we are to doubt the "evidence" of our senses, the evidence and our method of detecting and accepting it, the evidence must first exist to be doubted and how could such evidence ever come to us? And if our eyes can be fooled, what cannot be fooled? Of what can we claim to be conscious? And if we are conscious, in what way do we accomplish consciousness? Richard Gregory reminds us (re-minds!) that before the Greeks consciousness was thought by some to reside in the stomach, by others in the heart. One "stomached" something; or didn't. If we recognize that every cinematic vision is evanescent, exactly as every clue in the *Conflict* pursuit is evanescent; and, later, pointing to that, drawing up consciousness of that, that every clue in the McKittrick Hotel chase is similarly evanescent, are we being told—now twice—about the fading from vision of things that are seen? About the not-seeing of the seen? What is it that is being pointed to, after all, if there is a cinematic repetition, a quotation, except a condition and a question?

- If every vision is to be thought evanescent, is not the cinemagoer in a strange and indefensible position! Could the cinemagoer somehow watch without seeing? Watch without consciousness? (Or without stomaching what she watches?!)

- Quotation of—duplication of—the idea of a glowing object, the sacred woman, the Grail. A woman seen from behind who may have come back from the dead; or who will soon appear to have come back from the dead; as though there is linear time. One is directed to be *conscious of*, but every *consciousness of* is also, and at heart, a consciousness. Is any bright object, as we see it, temporary?

- Regarding consciousness, the problem of emptiness: if we are to see a body melting into the air—a woman in a closed space; a completely empty closed space—if we are to trouble ourselves with the reflection that, per Prospero, "We are such stuff as dreams are made on," if in two films we are to see a hunter seeing and then not seeing, and if this hunter explicitly rejects that equivocal experience, if he doesn't believe that what he doesn't see isn't or wasn't there to be seen before, if the hunter rejects disappearance and then acts—over his shoulder we must feel ourselves acting—as though his memory of the woman's presence is a solid memory, as though her presence, too, was solid, and also as though solid memories are the fruit of solid facts, solidity being the nub, . . . if all this, then what? Now the hunter (with our accompaniment) must trace solidities to explain the absence, must look around for a physical escape route. A hidden door, a back exit. Something in the ledger that shows erasure. A secret passage. "On the whole people tend to trust too much in the evidence of their senses," writes Stanislaw Lem. And how much is too much?

- In the case of *Conflict* and *Vertigo*, we can find recursion itself doubled. One film is a recursion of the other, yes; but in each film one moment is a recursion of another moment in the same film. The mystery works only with a double visitation. Now one is conscious of being conscious. If the experience of consciousness can shift so radically, a thing turning into a nothing, a person disappearing into thin air, does this mean consciousness has failed? Or does this mean consciousness has no fixation, no certainty, no solidity, and no stasis. If consciousness is in some ways—even in many ways—like film, we can easily understand how "disappearance" is possible, the frames in general offering us an appearance that will always become a dis-appearance with the onset of the next frames. These two chase scenes metaphorize film itself, by pointing to consciousness and our troubles with it. Yet, too, with Bogart every present moment reflects upon some recent past moment that denies it. Also with Stewart. (The way on a film set that every new take disavows, erases, historicizes the rejected takes that came before.)

- For the purposes of storytelling: it would be one thing if the vanishing target—Madeleine Elster, Kathryn Mason—were altogether blank, a person we hear rumors about but never meet, tagged only by name, and also desired by some nameless and uninteresting client (a George Kaplan, say, rather than Scottie Ferguson or a Richard Mason). But here the target is not and cannot be such a neutral form. In *Conflict*, she is the wife of the principal character, slain by him brutally and her body hidden away. If she returns it must mean the "murder" was only an attempted, and failed, murder, and now this has all come to light; also that her distinct being will continue to mar the would-be killer's life, as presumably it marred his life before and provoked him to kill. Or in *Vertigo*, the magnificent wife of a friend, who has been losing herself, taking trips she does not remember, being haunted by a ghost from the past, but also stunningly attractive, radiant, pure, golden, haunting her pursuer now as a ghost would haunt, if only (an ex-policeman) he believed in ghosts.

Is quotation to be reserved only for the esteemed, the special, the sacred? The library as repository and warehouse. "Burn but his books." Or is quotation common? Is every act of consciousness a picturing inside a picture, a tagging of an object in relation to another object placed here once before? Not only the room in which I sit producing these chains of words, a cream-colored room with paintings and books and apples and flowers, but my image of that room, my consciousness of the place, the room that belongs to the self I carry around—carry in my pocket—even as I move my fingers over a keyboard. I know I am here, but this knowing "I" is not the "I" whom I know to be here. I am here picturing myself here, being conscious of myself here, and my comment, "I know I am here," is a quotation of my experience.

Everybody is quoting.

To speak the common code, one can learn only by quoting what other people say, and hoping one gets the circumstances right. Can I please have a chocolate malted without whipped cream? Omigosh, I forgot my belt! Getting the circumstances right, which means knowing more than the words in the script. (Raul Julia's wonderful Calibanos in Paul Mazursky's *Tempest* [1982] keeps trying hard, and failing; or in *Mickey Blue Eyes* [1999] Hugh Grant torturing himself to pronounce the word *fuggedaboudit*.) The words alone are nothing but surface, easy to apprehend if one merely concentrates. Surface not implication, surface not design. An appearance is easy to effect but recognizing when to effect it is not. As a friend of mine said, in a discussion about seeming, "Well, anyone can put on a shirt"—and I quote! He said "Bla bla bla," and then I said, "Really?," and he said, "No, but bla bla bla," so I said . . . And I quote again. And there we were (pictures I am calling up inside the picture I am giving you now).

How vitiating and saddening it could perhaps be, how empty, to be told by a quoter discovered quoting, discovered but at the same time not claiming, that yes, quotation was on his mind, yes yes, a quote is what that was. As I said once, quote, it would be so vitiating if we were to discover that quotation was on my mind. "Quotation is on my mind," I quoted. And she responded, "Oh, my!" (thereby quoting millions of previous speakers). Is there not a piquant vitiation and sadness that come with every honest and proper footnote of reference, every "honest" and "proper acknowledgment" that we must take our meaning from someone else's words, that we must use "words, words, words" not (registered in the property office as) our "own." Ah yes, "Words, words, words": *Hamlet* Act II, scene 2, line 194. And yet the constant interposition of quotations in our speech, that we borrow our tongue, admitting that "borrowing only lingers and lingers"—a quotation out of context, *Henry IV Part II*, Act I, scene 2, line 586—is not the same as an explicit pointing in one work to some spot in another—"my finger, like a dial's point/Is pointing still" (*Richard II*, Act 5, scene 5, lines 2850–2851)—a pointing with scalpel's sharpness, say with the "sharp constraint of hunger" (*All's Well That Ends Well*, Act 3, scene 2, line 1528) to a character now matching, mocking up.

In quoting, I spell out broadly: that I see, that I have heard, that I read the book, that I have access, all of which required me once, just as calling them up requires me now, to point my mind, turn my mind into a pointer. There's the point. I mean, "There's the point" (*Antony and Cleopatra* Act 2, scene 6, line 1248). But what if cinema cannot point the way language points, the way the arm points? What if cinema's pointing is organically different? An obvious feature of cinematic quotation is its limitation to a purely surface-level reference, the fact that in film, superscript and notations being by nature absent (not that they cannot be superimposed), the quoted material resides on the screen in exactly the same way as the framing material within which, and in terms of which, it is quoted. All the facets of the recursion are in the same plane (no "punctuation marks" and also no punctuation marks). As there is no conventional apparatus for signaling it, the quotation is as likely as not to be imperceptible except to the small audience-within-the-audience already familiar with the earlier material and sensitive enough to detect its presence again. With some filmmakers—Godard is a fair example—the viewership may expect quotation, seek it out, and delight in finding and tagging it. With other filmmakers one is less expectant, and a considerable amount of quotation can pass by undetected as such. Maybe quotation is all over the place. In *La mariée était en noir* (1964), François Truffaut has Bernard Herrmann literally quote his own music from *Marnie* (1964). In *Cape Fear* (1991), which is itself, obviously, a wholesale quotation of J. Lee Thompson's *Cape Fear* (1962), even repeating Gregory Peck in a different, a complementary, role, Martin Scorsese quotes *Psycho* (1960). Robin Davis's *J'ai épousé un ombre* (1983) is a remake—that is, a block quotation—of Mitchell Leisen's *No Man of Her Own* (1950). Godard's *Nouvelle vague* (1990) quotes *The Barefoot Contessa* (1954). And on and on, with each "and on" a quotation of some previous "and on," and each "a quotation of" a quotation of "a quotation of."

Given the chance that a single instance of filmic quotation could find but a small audience in the know, harbored inside a greater audience filled with naïfs and naïves, what can be the function of the quotation as information, that is, as *information quoted*? Is information in a quoted state different in some regard from information that is not quoted, begging the question as to whether it is possible to give information without quoting. Does the presence of quotation, even not perceived, make a new lamination in the experience? Does quotation work in and of itself no matter its apprehension? Take two eggs and beat them very well until they are frothy. No no: "Take two eggs and beat them very well until they are frothy." In *F for Fake* (1984), Orson Welles regales friends at table with a Hungarian's recipe for an omelette: "Steal two eggs . . ."

Hitchcock, our "Significant Quoter" here, saw a lot of films without diarizing his experience, films, parts of films, scenes, audition clips. He could probably quote *Conflict* without noticing. Indeed, perhaps he never did see *Conflict* and had absolutely no inkling that his scene was a quotation, which circumstance would not make it not-a-quotation. Would it generally be said of Hitchcock that in *Vertigo* he quoted *Conflict*? Not at all: and that is my principal reason for opening discussion here. Another way to think of this is that some quotations are apt to be seized as "quotations" while others are not, but their identity as quotations and their being apprehended as such, are two different things.

Or more captivating still: if the scene in *Vertigo*, at the McKittrick Hotel, is actually not a quotation of the scene in *Conflict*, with the chase after the pawn shop visit, not a quotation but just another piece of another film, still, here I take up more than three thousand words of your time, dear reader, suggesting the contrary, making a claim which I now admit I could easily be wrong in making (whatever "wrong" can be argued to be). Is my argument, its value of whatever kind laid aside, itself a quotation, a quotation of quotations about quotations, and does it show us that somewhere in a galaxy that lies between this page and our devotions far far away there is consciousness, not mine, surely, but a consciousness with its own life?

20

The Magic Touch

Errol Flynn (r.) with Basil Rathbone in The Adventures of Robin Hood *(Michael Curtiz, Warner Bros., 1938). Digital frame enlargement.*

Earlier I raised for discussion some difficulty in viewers' engagement with the screen image, given that narrative separates away the characters' embodiment while the camera image urges us to believe we are seeing and hearing what characters see and hear. The issue of touch is even more fraught. Film narratives are filled with instances of touch and touchiness, with surfaces and textures, understood only in the abstract.

When an object is shown directly onscreen, under most circumstances it looks as objects look in the everyday, it *is itself*. A pitcher resembles a pitcher, an apple an apple, a finger a finger, and so on. The screen appears not to metamorphose. In viewing, we have no trouble presuming that some apple was taken from a supply, brought in front of the camera, placed with a few fingers next to a pitcher taken down from a shelf, and that is how a shot of "pitcher with apple and some fingers" was made. We watch without stickling, and notwithstanding tiny variations and deviations because of lighting, film stock, lens, angle of view, all such discrepancies are treated as minor and negligible, and being treated this way are neglected. As in the everyday we might claim to be looking at an apple, a pitcher, and a finger, here, too, we would make that claim. Very roughly speaking, when a character speaks and we hear the voice, that voice is comparable, we like to believe, to the actor's voice off-camera, which as a voice is comparable to other people's voices in the everyday, unless some modulation is being consciously effected for the drama: accent, pitch, or enunciation of phrase. The voice itself is a voice, like any voice, and also idiosyncratic like every voice.

When I adduce "the actor's voice off-camera," I mean, as far as almost everybody in the audience is concerned, "the actor's voice off *this* camera and in front of *some other* camera," because this so-thought "backstage" voice would likely be recognizable to us from television or internet interviews. Admittedly, if one knows the actor one knows the unmodulated off-camera voice, but most viewers who watch actors speaking don't know those actors.

But touch, that is something else again.

When a figure of the screen touches another figure of the screen, the material feel, the smoothness, the moistness, the warmth, the roundness of the experience all don't—and all cannot—come across directly as with sights and sounds. He steps over and lifts her free hand, feeling the weight, but when we watch we cannot feel that weight. All we can do with touch is make a guess, based on our own entirely non-diegetic experience. Here inside the theater there is very little to touch except the armrest of the seat or one's own body. Touch is a *conception* in cinema.

"Hear me! See me! Touch me! Feel me!"

Yes. Yes. No. No.

How do we establish and organize our experience of touch in motion picture drama? I am not generalizing here to "haptic experience" but addressing the peculiarity we call touch and only that.

[1] *Displacement touch.* A brilliant, possibly surprising sound effect is made to coincide with the narrative display of significant touch. Given that sound can be synchronized frame by frame, the exact point of contact between one surface and another, as shown onscreen, can be coupled with a downbeat. Here, then, two operative senses—sight and hearing—take the place of tactility. In the most technical of senses, this is ersatz touch. In *The Man Who Knew Too Much* (1956), at the instant we hear a woman's scream we see a plump man in a tuxedo suddenly jerk his hand up to his arm and his face register pain, in this way "feeling" a bullet's impact.

[2] *Cached touch.* The surfaces meant to be understood as touching are kept offscreen entirely. A hand reaching beneath the sheets. A spider that a terrified character claims is climbing up her leg. A cook in a kitchen throwing something we cannot see into a bowl so that one ingredient touches, mixes with, others only because we trust the "chef" isn't mad. A voice on a telephone complaining that the voicer has just jammed his knee into a chair leg: "Oh! Ouch!!!" Here we are led to imagine the factual touch and its outcome(s). Sex scenes very frequently employ this technique of *pose touch*, using facial expression and the muscular movements of, and around, the head to indicate a pleasure being produced elsewhere by "special" contact.

[3] *Retroactive touch.* Touch already happened. Onscreen a person emits an unmistakable sign of reaction to the "touch event," so that we are forced, ourselves, to conceive and "render" the touch that "must" immediately have preceded and create for it an appropriate occasion: a robber's very visible sigh of delight after touching the loot he has purloined; a shriek of withdrawal when a character jumps back from an open fire, effectively to say I *was* too close; an indicative vocal curtailment, as when a doctor prods a patient's arm for a trouble spot and at one point the patient says, curtly, "Ah! There!" The patient's cry replaces the actual touch that apparently produced it.

[4] *The touch of logical coherence.* A situation is depicted onscreen, with which the viewer can be presumed so familiar that the narrative elaboration can be abbreviated: say, a wedding. When the bride kisses the bridegroom, we sense the touch principally because we expected it, a touch of this kind being conventional, even required, in a circumstance depicted this way and with this care. Again, touch *shown not felt.* Placing a ring on a finger. Taking the fringe of a prayer shawl and using it to kiss the parchment of the Torah at a Bar Mitzvah. A dentist's tool touching the inside of a character's mouth (on which the absolutely limiting case is given by Laurence Olivier in *Marathon Man* [1976]). Having learned to expect and accept an operational touch, we use a depiction however curtailed as an estimation of our knowledge, our recognition. What we see is not only a substitute for what we know; it substitutes for what we have known for a long time.

[5] *Projected touch.* If a woman is trudging down a country road by early morning light, wearing tatters instead of shoes, and proceeding along a length of wagon tracks and cow droppings after several days of dry weather (all of these things depictable), we will understand how her feet are wobbling and adjusting with every painful step, especially if the actor produces "painful steps." Any lame character, similarly. When he performed in a wheelchair, one had the distinct sense of Lionel Barrymore's hands touching the wheel, and this is replicated with Tom Cruise as Ron Kovic and with Christopher Reeve performing *Rear Window* (1998, in the tracks of James Stewart, whose hands on his camera gave off the same quality of touch). A character receives an injection, or a slap in the face, or a kick to the stomach, or—fully conscious so as to be able to be responsive—brain surgery with the top of the skull removed, this last a strange circumstance that leads viewers to only the projection of the feeling of touch, since like the spectator watching the patient in fact does not feel the absent skull cap. A young woman, delirious with joy, skims across a vast green sward on a mountaintop, spinning around and looking up at the sky, before singing "The Sound of Music" (1965) and we think we feel the grass beneath us. Or, trailed by machine gun bullets, a man in an expensive gray suit throws himself down into the gravelly dirt at the side of a road (*North by Northwest*, 1959). In *Sound*, Maria's (Julie Andrews) boundless happiness causes the spinning sensation

in her feet as she turns. In *North*, Roger Thornhill's (Cary Grant) throwing himself into the dirt causes the touch of his body in the ditch. These and other examples of "projected" touch all require the viewer to have knowledge of the displayed circumstances, if the feeling is to be direct and receptive. If a viewer knows nothing of throwing oneself into a ditch, any "touch" he tells himself he is sensing is an entirely invented one.

[6]   *Negative touch.* A character extends a hand for a handshake, but the other makes a grimace (of distaste, of disapproval, of rejection and alienation) and quickly draws back her hand so that contact will *explicitly and definitively not be made*. Here, the viewer confronts a challenge in the "cutting off" or "turning aside." If there is no spectatorial tactility to the touch that is being withdrawn, there is also no tactility in the withdrawal itself, yet this is not how it feels.

[7]   *Incoherent touch.* A surgeon reaches inside a body cavity and palpates an organ, indicating verbally that this is happening and receiving acknowledgment verbally or mimically from operating-room assistants. The camera shows the open torso, but not the organ. Here a mirroring is involved, since while the unprofessional viewer no doubt imagines the feeling of something soft, moist, squishy, tender, slippery (for the layman slightly or intensively unpleasant), the character makes no display of attitude to correspond: a surgeon is very accustomed to feeling around like this, and has few surprises. We have a sense of vague, extended, displaced, uncertain touch in a procedure, but a sense that is purely rational. In a great many screened operating-room sequences, dialogue and partial faciality are used to convey dramatic build-up, and the issue of having hands inside someone else's body is entirely elided.

[8]   *Abysmal touch.* A character in a restaurant looks down at a plate of food, the camera following, and we see from offscreen a utensil enter the frame and hesitantly prod at something in the serving. Something that should not be there. Something that perhaps should be there but that the diner is entirely unfamiliar with. Something that is symbolically provocative for a reason highlighted in the story. In *One Day in the Life of Ivan Denisovich* (1970), Ivan (Tom Courtenay) sits to table in a shambles of a room, with other inmates of a gulag, and looks into the tin bowl where his day's ration of soup waits. Then in the close-up, we note that the spoon is touching something inside the soup mixture, something that looks far too much like a human eye. It *is* a human eye! We project feeling into the spoon's contact with the eye, a feeling that ascends from the spoon through the screen up the arm to the self.

[9]   *Playful touch.* A special kind of touch is reserved for game situations, such as when, in a cozy den two teenagers sit side by side on a sofa using remote devices to play a video game in competition with each other, and each presses strenuously on the controls in order to "urge" the game to go her way. Or,

coming off a football field after a touchdown, a player finds himself pounded on the top of his helmet, slapped on the buttocks, shoulder butted by his joyous teammates. The visual display calls up the conception of such touching, which replaces direct sensation. Touch as signal. (In the case of the video game, the strenuous gestures signal intentfulness, zeal, competition. Actual remote devices do not work better when they are used with exertion.)

[10] *Alien touch.* For the best narrative reasons, a character acts at a given moment to take up an instrument he or she must be about to use, but that is relatively rare in the everyday world. In some parts of the Western world, for instance, holding a pistol would not be likely for most people, but holding a pistol is a frequent narrative trope in action cinema. What does the object feel like, and what is the sensation of sliding the finger tentatively toward the trigger? Or, in a First World War narrative, a character is shown gingerly stepping at twilight across a mucky battlefield littered with suppurating corpses of animals and men. Or a young pilot hops into a strange aircraft and prepares to take off quickly, notwithstanding that he has never seen controls like these before (*Independence Day* [1996]). The tentativeness of the touch in such circumstances can be both understood and "felt" by the spectator, "felt as tension" if not felt as tension.

[11] *"Fur."* The touch of the animal in a character's hand is imaginable (thus, substitutable by imagination) for some viewers, depending on the animal. In *The Long Goodbye* (1973) Marlowe (Elliott Gould) plays with a cat. In *National Velvet* (1944) Elizabeth Taylor engages with a horse. In *Treasure Island* (1950) Long John Silver (Robert Newton) walks around with a parrot squatting on his shoulder. In *Manhunter* (1986) Reba McClane (Joan Allen) goes into a protected facility and runs her hand over an anesthetized tiger. A *real* tiger. A chilling scene or a scene inducing squeamishness in the viewer can be fashioned through the use of a creature entirely unconventional, such as we see with the tiny civilians gawking in freaked-out horror at the giant Godzilla (1954).[1]

[12] *"Touch."* But there are legion narrative situations that are depicted onscreen by virtue of a special effect. When the effect is carried off with accuracy and aplomb, the viewer will have a distinct sensation of live presence, and so if any touch is imagined or projected it will be the touch sensation that typically appertains to live presence. Take the basement stabbing of a giant spider with a hat pin in *The Incredible Shrinking Man* (1957), a scene in which the man and giant prop pin were not even in the same space as the (normally sized) spider shot in macro-close-up. In *Star Wars* (1977), when Luke fights with Vader, the

---

[1] See Lennard for an elaborate discussion of the human-animal interface in film.

beams of their two light sabers make hissing and zapping sounds when they "touch" (an acoustic fill-in both on the film plane level and on the conceptual level for the viewer wanting sensation), but these beams are actually matted in. We "feel" the shock of the zapping, or the spider softness where the pin goes in, even while knowing that touch is at a remove.

[13] *Suspended touch.* Beyond situations where a viewer's foreknowledge guides filling in or projecting "touch," an occasion might arise in which it is a viewer's *imagination* aforehand, not her knowledge, that guides. In short, the typical viewer is not expected by the narrative to have had experience in the "touching" that is portrayed. Say, a character is confronted with a corpse. The hand is seen reaching out, coming close. The fingers are seen millimeters from the dead skin of the dead face. But the character holds back. In order not only to hold back along with the character, "not to touch," but also to feel the holding back, to "touch the non-touching," the viewer will play on the "feel of a corpse" as an imagined experience, and will thus hold back from a conception. See the discovery scene in *Blow-Up* (1966).

When the starstruck screen gazer sees a figure reach out and touch or embrace the face or body of a beloved icon—Scarlett Johannson, say, in *Marriage Story* (2019)—there is a suspended touch in this way: if the star icon were thought a person like all other persons, the experience of touching them would be somewhat knowable; but movie stars are usually *not* considered persons like other persons as, in watching the characters they perform, watchers consider them to be, and every smallest exertion of the fan's to elevate the star to appropriate high status (the status that merits the fan's adoration) pushes the figure away and renders the experience of touching him or her remote, even unthinkable.

[14] *Waiting-room touch.* In Hector Babenco's *The Kiss of the Spider Woman* (1985), two men share a prison cell, Luis (William Hurt) and Valentin (Raul Julia).[2] In one scene Valentin has become very ill indeed, and the script calls for a moment when, having involuntarily soiled himself in the bed from which he cannot arise, this man is nursed and cleaned up by his cellmate, this being the principal action of the scene. Beside the fact that the camera shoots with circumspection, and that the scripted language works by circumspection, too, and that the dim lighting makes visibility hard to achieve in any event, the viewer has already presumably turned away from "touching" the narrative, from imagining the experience either man is having and letting some loosely structured imagination fill in. One sits in one's seat rather as though occupying a waiting room, calmly suspended until the next scene comes on. Some will view dramatized execution scenes from a "waiting room" of this kind.

---

[2] As the story goes, the two actors were cast in opposite roles but rehearsing playfully one day decided to try switching, and the switch endured.

Or scenes of horrific tumbling from a great height (*Watchmen* [2009]; *The Hudsucker Proxy* [1994]). Or scenes of abject torture (*The Hill* [1965]; *Casino Royale* [2006]).

[15] *Modest touch.* And, as I have discussed elsewhere at length, while sexual or erotic scenes involve a touch that viewers will have to fill in if they are to "experience" it at all, they can do this filling only to a degree. When the screen action becomes extremely graphic, viewer sensibilities may be withdrawn in the name of modestly leaving other people to their privacies—that is, other "people" to their "privacies." Else the viewer seems (at least to the self) the sort who likes to peep on, even barge into, events like this. Marion Crane undressing before she gets into the shower in *Psycho* (1960) is one thing (a smaller thing today than it was at the time), but a full-fledged, and complete scene of lovemaking (*Devil in the Flesh* [*Diavolo in Corpo*, 1986]) is something else.

[16] *Substituting in for substituting in.* Sometimes a scene is played in which the graphic presentation gives the viewer grounds for substituting-in a sense of touch not otherwise conveyable. But what happens when the onscreen touchers know they cannot touch? Kissing or finger-touching through glass (*Romeo + Juliet* [1995]). Shaking hands by touching elbows, because one or both are infected? Giving a *Mwah!* air kiss, as a way of saying "Lova ya but I wouldn't touch you to save my life!" The viewer *substitutes in* the dramatic touch that is being dramatically, intentfully withheld by characters, the kiss, say, and then, having *substituted in* an idea of it, proceed to *substitute in* for that idea a rationale, while the characters need only *substitute in* for the act.

[17] *Instrumental touch.* A character may touch something or someone by indirect means, using, as extension of the hand, some object or device that does not— that cannot—duplicate the sensitivity experienced through the hand. There may be a reverberation produced, or an inspection of the material "touched" now made accessible by the instrument. This kind of narrated "touching" is unmistakably ersatz in the first place; unless the viewer can call up experience with an identical or a similar tool, the reception of the moment will be abstract. A Parisian sister and brother have some idiosyncratic erotic play by means of an ostrich feather in *The Dreamers* (2003): a "delicious touch" that is not actually a touch by the hand. A doctor inserts a tongue depressor. A live bomb is addressed and worked on by means of a remote-controlled robot. Guests at a fancy fin-de-siècle dinner party are shown, but only after we see a monumental device: the table at which they will dine, notably set with numerous pieces of cutlery they will need (and presumably be at home with), flowers, gilded plates, and so on. The *locus classicus* is swashbuckling swordplay, now parodied (and intensively modernized) by Indiana Jones but made famous by Flynn and Rathbone in *Robin Hood* (1938). For a soft version, consider pillow fights, as with Stockard Channing and her crew in

Grease (1978) in the "Look at Me, I'm Sandra Dee" scene. The typical narrative use of instrumentation in this way is for establishing a tone of negativity or hermeticism since an unstated convention in human interaction calls for directness in body contact. In fighting, where weapons serve instead of hands (the *mano-a-mano* invoked in westerns of the 1930s and onward, then later as a retro fashion in *Fight Club* [1999]), the lethality of contact can be almost too swift to feel, even if characters cry with Laertes (*Hamlet* V.ii.287), "A touch, a touch, I do confess't!"

* * *

In direct experience, a dramatized (emphasized) touch is accessed and comprehended differently than the scenarized vision or scenarized sound, most principally because in watching or hearing a scene, the audience attends to a vision or sound from the screen, and these are vision and sound replicated. The theatrical venue doesn't afford touches and smells that are related to the "touches" and "smells" indicated onscreen.

One may reasonably wonder, with all the "touch" that is not touch, to which an increasingly large spectatorship is ongoingly exposed, whether *the look of touch* and any of its simulacra as detailed above might not come for citizens to replace the vitality—whatever that vitality might be thought to be—of touch as vivaciously felt. Further, whether the thing that we now call touch may come to be replaced altogether, for reasons of hygiene and sanitation if not simply because people no longer find it valuable. Without touch to refer back to, is not the false "touch" on the screen already become touch itself?

21

Exeunt omnes

Dustin Hoffman in The Graduate *(Mike Nichols, Lawrence Turman Productions, 1967). Digital frame enlargement.*

Must I be self-centered in order to survive watching cinematic melodrama? Acutely centered on myself, that is: care not a whit for the beings I have been following, have no concern as to what will happen with them now that the light has stopped revealing them on the screen? The film closes, and I close not only my involvement of the moment, not only my attention but also my devotion, that has been pried open by the story. We do know that the characters must make their exits: Fortinbras must preside as Hamlet's body is borne off, and Officer Krupke as Tony's (*West Side Story* [1961]), and Nobody as William Blake's canoe glides off on the lake of eternity (in *Dead Man* [1995]). But with these disappearances, these slow and majestic disappearances, it is as though the iris of the viewing spirit is slowly drawn shut, a kind of fade to black where the "black" is not absence of color or light but absence of care. The Tony who sang to Maria, with whom I felt involved at the time.

Later, I know, I may remember having been devoted; but the memory of devotion and devotion are not the same thing.

We can think of the way some film narratives play upon their closure, by appending written statements to the effect that so-and-so became a dentist in Idaho and so-and-so suffered wounds in Vietnam, and on and on, quite as though we can legitimately be presumed hungry to know still more than the story has seen fit to tell. As though we are flipping through a family album. As though the story could, and should, have continued to give us more cause for care, because we do still want to care. Yet, oddly, there is no second-level text projected yet later, that comments upon those comments: "... was reported as a dentist in Idaho, *but went off to prospect for gold in Myanmar, where he was attacked by* ____." The film gives "one little thing more," one and only one, that viewers presumably need to know and don't know yet. A good example is *American Graffiti* (1973) but examples abound.

Ilsa Lund and Victor Laszlo walk off arm in arm, with steady pace, toward the last plane to Lisbon. I have been following them closely for the past "twenty-four hours" or so. She is a woman desperately torn and willing to let other people decide her fate. In love with Rick, in love with her husband (whom she thought dead when Rick came along, in Paris), loyal to Rick, loyal to her husband, needing Rick, needing her husband. Rick has the letters of transit and maybe if he is still feeling the draughts of their love (what?—years later?—months later?—nobody says), will he not possibly reach into the hiding place and put them in her tender hand? Laszlo must be allowed to go on, to fight the crusade, "And this time we'll win!" Laszlo is very much alive, and hopeful, and handsome, and brave, and he knows how to wear a white linen suit with impeccable style. And Rick: he could not more evidently be a man destroyed by that Parisian love, thrown into drink, into cynicism, into hardness. What exactly did he offer her, or give her, that has turned to dust (we are never quite shown)? She is hooked to a man a very great number of Nazis are hunting with their trademark gravity and organization: perhaps he hasn't long to go. Or she might release him and stay in Casablanca.

I have been watching Rick slickly manage his American Café, deal with his friends and brokers, handle the police, keep the roulette spinning, and I saw the look on her face the moment she stepped in and realized where she was, whose place this was, who the man in charge, and the look on his face when he saw her. The extraordinary courtesy of sitting the Laszlos to table and giving them drinks on the house—Renault is shocked, this never happens! That horribly agonizing little song, O play it again! (but not here).

And now, as she walks off to that plane (that cardboard plane!¹), and we lose sight of her, beautiful, sculptural, glowing, alabastrine, agonized, adoring and adored Ilsa, lose our *final* sight of her, am I to mourn or forget she existed? We see the plane in the air, we can tell ourselves she and Laszlo are on it, we can say they will be flying to safety, we can imagine them passing through Portuguese customs and walking through a city unencumbered with fear. And then making plans for subterranean travel into the heart of Europe where the fires are burning. Will Laszlo, of necessity, lose his grip on her, cease to be quite so gallant, because now the battle is before him and he is an important player? Will she stand alone when he goes off, alone as we can surmise she was in Paris when he went off before, and will she receive news once again of his death, and will that also be incorrect news? And will another man find her, someone who reminds her of Rick? Or someone who doesn't remind her of anybody? Does she wait

---

[1] For a notably exciting reprise, see Coppola's *One from the Heart* (1981).

with the new lover until war's end, wait for Laszlo, and when Laszlo doesn't return do they marry, Ilsa and the New Rick, and fly off to America, to California? Does she live a long life after the new husband perishes, and become one of those little old ladies from Pasadena, except that every day she takes out her picture of Victor and then has a vague memory of another man, a sweet and troubled man? I don't trouble to wonder any of this or to wonder anything. I don't trouble with her. The film tells me that I should stop troubling with Ilsa, and I comply. Lights up. I stumble up an aisle that reeks of salt. The daylight outside cuts into my forehead like a scimitar. Where am I? Which direction do I take to get home?

Rick and Renault are striding across the tarmac in the rain, and through the marvel of cinema, though we are a galaxy away, we hear Rick promise this could be the beginning of a beautiful friendship. Do I not release them, let them go into the dark without the least urge to follow? For I don't care where they are headed, here, on foot, tonight, the plane having left. Some other aircraft, perhaps, that will fly them to Brazzaville? And what will they do there, these happy two, rent a worn-down villa and redecorate it in the modernist style, banana trees in the foyer? Will Rick give up his memory, his belief, his passion? (Renault never had those.) Will Rick finally start drinking absinthe with Paul Bowles? It's raining hard, I forgot to wear a raincoat, I will be drenched before I get to the subway.

What strikes me as both amazing and intriguing is my ability to be deeply woven into the fabric of *Casablanca* (1942) while it is flickering before me, but then to lift away without affect or effect, just like that aircraft bound for Lisbon. The world must go on, of course, and there are other films to watch—but not when I am in Casablanca. When I am watching in Casablanca there are no other films, there is no such thing as film; and the "world," so to speak, is this café in this confusing time, and the confusing time yawns out with no bound. When Ugarte bleats, "Help me, Rick!!!," one feels the electricity sparking off his little sweaty body, one has a kind of empathy, *being there* albeit imaginatively. And then "there" transmogrifies into nothing more than credits scrolling on the screen. Even Peter Lorre isn't there anymore after early audiences watch him bleat, he is shooting *The Constant Nymph* (1943) for Edmund Goulding, but in the same studio. What is this feeling of proximity that is born at Rick's Café, this piquant eagerness, moment by moment, to experience what will come next, that is, to experience the fate of the characters and the fate of the film? What is this dalliance with fate?

Imagine how dysfunctional it would be to form a genuine relation with screen characters. One comes to the film with a circle of friends. Now one is exposed to some half a dozen fascinating types, each of whom reaches out through a pregnant line of dialogue or an action incommensurate with everyday proportion and sense, and one adopts them into one's sphere. But then another film comes along, and another six. And then another ten. We see, perhaps, a few hundred films, some of us many more, and for each of them there are half a dozen interesting types, all adopted or adoptable, so that soon the skin of our bubble is stretched to the bursting point. Do we start thinking of newcomers to the crowd as duplicates of others (as Italo Calvino suggests: the inability to see new faces), do they become less persons than reminders? This is a difficult position to imagine being in, not only because strain is placed on one's satiety but also because so often, when a character walks on, we find ourselves entranced by something unique, something we seem to think we have never known before.

I recall that when I was a little child, my parents often hosted parties, and to these events there streamed dozens of people I had never seen before. Each man or woman had unique features, a special way of dressing, eyes that regarded me in a particular way (or that avoided regarding me at all), and possessed what I heard at the time as an outlandish name. They were like the characters in Looney Tunes, in that each character had a distinctive and inimitable quality and each had to be recognized, on every appearance, for the being he or she was. I can still, decades and decades later, call up the name-face combinations, but now they are only references. Yet, of course, at the time, almost instantaneously, they had become references, too. People becoming references. When we watch a film and engage with the characters, perhaps we are like children meeting the world. There had been a sheltering period when we lived inside our family and later we picked up sensations of place, forms, colors, lights; but all the human beings were but cardboard ciphers, they had not made connection (that vitality of which Forster writes in *A Passage to India*). It was only the parade moving into our home that initiated my observation of character, and when a film comes onto the screen it is coming into my home: or, through looking at it, I am building a home that includes it. We make the film *Heimlich*.

When I meet and come to know beings like Ilsa and Rick, and then discard them, I am engaged in a process of interactional memory we could call *periodic*. Under such conditions, each character-figure resonates with us then markedly ceases resonance. Our involvement fills a distinct period, and this one, like all periods, is limited, albeit retrievable with a lesser and more diaphanous effect. We could say we are loving within limits, churlish as that might sound. One could think of a *Casablanca* period, within the bounds of which we become involved with Rick and Ilsa and Renault and Laszlo and Strasser and the whole pack, this period eliciting a temporary devotion that doesn't seem temporary until it is over. This is not to fail to recognize that when we go into the film we know our "presence" forms a temporary engagement, we know this of all films, and yet when we are actually inside the temporary engagement we do not feel it as temporary—not during the crisis of sight. Understanding the nature of a periodic attachment, we know ourselves open to repeating it, perhaps each time with a little less enthusiasm (or perhaps with more), and that during our attachments they will seem periodic we perhaps do not remember.

One might have instead a *biographical* attachment and detachment. Something about the characterization harmonizes with a fact of our biographical experience or history. There may be a moment where the character poses in the sunlight on a hilltop, but this is a hilltop on which we have stood, and so we recognize the place intimately and affiliate with the character's *presence* there. We actually know *through stance* what this presence of the character is, in that exact place. It is possible to extend this affiliation through a whole drama, never to forget this "blood bond," so that when the film is finished one must either continue an extended sense of presence—person in place—or else drop it, arbitrarily. Cutting off the character is also cutting off part of our own biography, because now, whenever we remember that hilltop the character who has been vanquished comes back to stand there at our side.

Utilitarian attachment/detachment is based in some functional need to identify with a character while—but only while—a drama progresses, identify so as to follow coherently, follow coherently so as to see where the story is heading and turning. A curiously "unforgettable" type dawdles all through Jean-Jacques Beineix's *Diva* (1981), Le curé ("the priest"), a thug capable of sudden and alarming violence (Dominique Pinon) but also apparently an aesthete, because wherever he goes he has music playing through his earphones. We never hear what the music is until much, much later. What is interesting about him, beyond his slender physique and moist eyes, is his obvious addiction to music, which in some ways mirrors that of the principal character. As form, the character comes to mind after the film is done only as part of a more generalized memory (a calling up) of the film as a whole, where he is positioned in a small galaxy of similarly quirky characters turning out a story. Quirky being, quirky situation, quirky film. But as a unique being who has affected us, he does not linger, nor did he ever truly affect us *as a unique being*, the story regardless.

Negative attachment is complete detachment. Something about the character is so disturbing, so unbalanced or unbalancing, so insidious that the viewer totally erases him, or believes to have done so. Forgetting is repression, of course, so that the forgotten character, and the forgotten scenes in which this character played some signal role, are liable to spring forward upon any ostensibly random trigger. When the film is done, we bid adieu to the character by erasure, certainly by what is experienced as erasure, although because we have no way of actually "taking out the trash" there is no real erasure, only repositioning. Absent a trigger, the "erased" material will remain out of view, perhaps indefinitely, and the idea of *erasure* will itself gain more and more credibility over time (the more credibility the more distant is the material from our field of view). Erasure being taken seriously, then, were one to be asked to exemplify a case of detachment by erasure the challenge would not be met—unless that request for exemplification turned out to be a trigger itself. The erased screen character has the capacity to vanish and to reappear "at will," in this way seeming to be a phantom. When we let go of characters with whom we have been openly and thoroughly identifying, we can sense their exit, even watch them walk away or fall out. With the erased character, we sense nothing at all.

Many screen characters undergo what might be thought a "warehousing." They are available for retrieval at will, lingering in a kind of repository of forms yet not in short-term memory. One digs to summon them, but they can be summoned. When we watch the film we register such forms, freeze them as they are shown onscreen, and "file" the registrations. Retrieved much later, the forms will show the characteristics that appeared onscreen when first we watched. The little girl and boy trapped in the Land Rover while the T-Rex stomps toward them and sniffs (*Jurassic Park* [1993]) will be there still, just as young, just as untried, still fiddling with their infernal flashlight. We can retrieve them; refile them; retrieve them again; but they will not have aged.

We who are doing this retrieving—that is, *not* the persons we were as we watched the film—won't really care to remember, as we concentrate on them frozen in fear and disattend the story all around, whether the beast ate them or not.

The complex arrangement by which one bonds with a character is highly idiosyncratic and will affect one's judgment of the film as a whole, the film being, finally, the laboratory that made possible that bonding. Is it the character/actor who strikes and inspires the vision, or the visual styling, or the spread of a picture before the eye? In developing their characters for the screen, filmmakers will be careful to compound a number of accessible attributes and attitudes—that can be read speedily—and to collect them under a broad and clearly identifiable arc of condition or personality that can be accorded easy reference, given informal as well as formal consideration, shared among friends as well as with a public however large. Take Mike Nichols's *The Graduate* (1967), with its young man fresh out of college and searching for his future, his doting mother, his obsessive father, the father's sluggish business partner and aggressive wife and tender daughter, all in palmy California under the relieving sun. I saw the film within a short period of its opening release, and guised at the time as a novice graduate student who had, in fact, just finished my undergraduate studies only breaths earlier, like Dustin Hoffman's Benjamin in the film. The fact of his being a "recent college graduate" would have been effortlessly apparent to anyone and everyone. That he came from a middle-class family in Los Angeles. That he wanted love and sex and truth and a future. That his parents didn't in any way understand him. That their (crass) world terrified him. That he had no sense of balance as yet, no project, no identity. That his energies and desire were unshaped, thus unbounded, unfixed, and weighty. All of this was in the character arc, and like everybody who saw the film I was able to comprehend the formula, to place it in a broader arrangement of organizations and formulae that had become "known" to me. Because he came out of a college and I did, too, I knew where he had been, and I superficially knew him. But perhaps only superficially.

Not long ago, however, more than fifty years later, I chanced to hear on the radio, while driving through the city (thus with only half a mind), a guitarist playing a rendition of Paul Simon's song, "The Sound of Silence." And as the melody gently flowed, I heard myself singing the lyric, "Hello darkness, my old friend . . ." and had a sudden, distinctly shocking, pointed and electrifying memory not of the film as a whole (that organized laboratory, in which this song was used pre-eminently on the sound track, performed by Simon and Garfunkel), not of the central character in a typical pose, not of the scenario (that I recognized and still recognize to be arch) or the lines of argumentation but—of an aroma and tone that, as I now recollected at a stoplight, I was *synaesthetically* connecting with the screen presentation when first I watched. I could virtually smell the theater of that first viewing, and the aroma that filled my spirit in those college days. In all my viewings of the film in the intervening period, several such, I had retrieved no such memory. But now that it was triggered—a trace, a smell in some nearby room or a vague hint of taste at the back of the mouth: because this song is a sad song, a gray and empty anthem to acquiescence—I could see how very sad the film had originally been for me, in a certain way, how much I had been witnessing myself onscreen as hopeless and alone and uncertain. Standing at a kind of abyss, perhaps, not only with no certain future but feeling as though there was no such thing as a future. Hopeless and alone and uncertain, while gliding forward through life, through my classes, through my days. That sense of hopeless aloneness was the core of *The Graduate*, it was the river of motivation running beneath Benjamin's movements, it was the flow of the narration as one scene melded with another, it was the flavor of the eye moving across the colors, the separations, the whispers. I realized now that in 1967, without having been able to explain or define it, I knew in my flesh, hearing that song, how private was the darkness, how comforting and how cold, what a place of retreat and what a neverland, what a blanketed hollow and what a provocation. I understood the darkness as personal. "This thing of darkness/I acknowledge(d) mine." It was palpable as a tabletop, my grasp of just what the darkness of the song is. Darkness of the self. Truth of the origin of feeling.

Perhaps this darkness is the darkness to which we are especially prone when we are twenty and coming out into the world. Perhaps an echo of some emergence. But the idea that darkness could be present, and as "my old friend," a personification near to me, known intimately by me, treasured by me, jumped stunningly off the screen way back then, even if unrecognized; and now . . . now as I drove, jumped out of my hidden memory.

I had thought Benjamin Braddock was gone, and that whatever person I had been at the time, the doppelgänger who could know and reside with him, had gone, too. But he had not. He was haunting me. And "I," too, had not gone, that "I" whom I had been. "I" was still here, as was I, still able to welcome darkness, my old friend, and able to acknowledge my welcoming, here.

22

Throw It Away

"Hogwarts" in Harry Potter and the Philosopher's Stone *(Chris Columbus, Warner Bros., 2001). Digital frame enlargement.*

At the release of *Raging Bull* (1980), Robert De Niro shared with Michael Parkinson a comment about the actor's method that has been made as well by numerous other actors in more or less the same words. His idea was to prepare a character quite intensively, and work hard practising until the character was very much "with" him; and then, once he came onto the set (set/location), "throw it all away." His rationale was both perceptive and enlightening: that in real conditions, people don't "work at" what they're doing, they merely do. "Work at," as in labor to give the impression of doing, strive to make certain that no observer would come to the conclusion you're not doing. The actor playing a cab driver, for instance, needn't try hard to "be a cab driver" and do the sorts of things that cab drivers do, all that's necessary is to drive the cab (recall *Taxi Driver* [1976]). Not drive: *merely* drive. One could see, too, how the poet isn't "being a poet," she's just making poems; the doctor is just examining the body. "Just" as in *without rehearsal*, without awareness of the action one is accomplishing. Without seeing the action outside oneself.

In order to be able, facing the camera, to execute actions with the ease and unreflectedness that will appear utterly real, De Niro was saying, he needed to work to make those actions natural to him, *just as people actually do* in order to pass through initial discomforts and awkwardnesses into skilled (and unthinking) smoothness.

David Halberstam reports how the teen idol Ricky Nelson spoke of a similar manifesto in 1953, thirteen years old:

> I think the first requirement for a young actor, or any actor for that matter, is to lose his self-consciousness and be himself. People who are ill at ease and self-conscious are people who are thinking too much of themselves and worrying about the impression they are making on others. The best actors lose themselves in their parts. (516)

It is interesting how a director can obtrude in selecting a close-up on the face or upper body when an actor is using the entire body in a way that *is natural for the character* in the situation: when this happens, no matter the actor's labors, the camera is framing a (merely) facial identity, causing it to dominate over (and define) the behavior and/or the moment as a whole. The swelling face could be fragmenting the wholeness of a performed moment. Close-ups might be useful for all kinds of dramatic reasons and a director might feel the need to shoot some (among other versions of the same shot) for use in editing should a contingency occur where, in the flow of the film at a certain point, the sense of the viewing eye would best be shaped up close—a "call" that might not be evident on the set (it often being months or longer before the edit is made; and the viewing eye not being at the center of the actor's focus). A close-up insert can absolutely shatter a fragile performance and have lasting effect: once the actor is identified as "but an actor" in the close-up (so identified because instantly recognizable outside of the characterization now curtailed by the framing) the audience may not be able to lose touch with him in that guise. In theatrical acting, where there are no close-ups, actors can more easily lose themselves inside a role, even much celebrated actors. In drama and opera given widespread screening in theatrical venues, close-ups are being used again today, Don Giovanni suddenly becoming *a singer*, Hamlet suddenly morphing into Benedict Cumberbatch, Frances McDormand into Lady Macbeth.

When one watches a film one behaves *naturally*, too, merely watching and not concentrating on being one of those who watch film. We become engaged by letting go of any and all self-consciousness in regards to that engagement, by seeing what is on the screen, as it were, *without looking*. Only seeing. There is work in this dedication, because to center one's consciousness in the screen events it is necessary to undo attachment to daily chores, local geography, cultural history, and the sense of present placement. In writing about the "onlooker" in his discussion of the theatrical frame in *Frame Analysis*, Goffman actually notes how in watching *Hamlet* the audience "travels to Elsinore." But how, if she is not already in Denmark, does a viewer travel to Elsinore? Perhaps without even the most rudimentary geographical knowledge of where that place would be we hop to the scene as given before us and accept, without question or doubt, the location tag affixed to it. A parapet. Night. Perhaps a howling wind. *This* is Elsinore. In the same fashion, we see an immense gothic palace ensconced upon a shimmering lake by moonlight, with little lights warmly kindled inside and swerving beneath us since, like birds on high, we are circling from above, and we call this Hogwarts. Now we are at Hogwarts. We see an immense toadstool with a hookah-smoking caterpillar half asleep upon it and we say, "This is Wonderland!" We can manage this acknowledgment and identification only if we block away any awareness that could contradict: most principally our seats in this odd dark space, which we have rented (at a continually mounting cost!), and in which we sit surrounded by strangers. Self-conscious watching must go, ours and our neighbors'; and making it go is work. For the actor, his behavior is written in a script, and that he is to move as the script and director indicate is part of his professional understanding: but all that must go, too. He must merely inhabit the body of the character—a body that is not his own. He must be someone he is not. More, he must be someone he cannot see, and we agree to act as though we cannot see him not seeing himself.

In John Frankenheimer's *The Train* (1964) there is a moment when Burt Lancaster, the underground activist Labiche pretending to be a trainee engineer, must (a) slow his engine so that its coupling to the car behind will tighten briefly, then (b) await the moment of skilful decoupling performed by his colleague, then (c) accelerate the engine once more. Lionel Lindon's camera sweeps in to his hand on the control as he makes the move he has patiently, tactically learned before shooting. It's a real move because it's really in the mover's body, and to be this particular mover Lancaster has made himself an engine-driver, not an actor. Bluntly, he has worked hard at learning to drive an engine like this. In *Hangover Square* (1945) Laird Cregar had to perform Bernard Herrmann's piano concerto, so he taught himself to play the piano. Prior to his engagement shooting *Red River* (1948), Montgomery Clift had no talents riding or roping and was disparaged in advance by his co-star John Wayne. What Wayne didn't foresee was Clift spending a month on location before anyone else arrived and learning, learning, learning. Like living, acting is learning.

The theatricality of the venue is only one of the objects of consciousness that viewers must work to lose, and that performers' skilful lack of contrivance helps them lose, before they can commit themselves to a film. Awareness of the film as a *present and viewed thing* signals the fact that its exhibition has been established and elaborated architecturally to facilitate viewing, thus points to all the strangers gathered around as being there to perform a watching similar to one's own. To see without watching we must lose touch with all of this arrangement. We must abandon the lighting of the theater space, which is expressly dimmable and which, bright and homely as we entered, now gradually fades away—fading, although we do not think of the electrical controls, the rheostats, hidden away somewhere. And as to hiding away: if electrical controls can be hidden away so might numerous other features of the environment that might fascinate the student of theatrical architecture but would daunt the would-be viewer of a film. Throw it all away. And the etiquette, exactly because the crowd is a crowd of strangers and the interrelation of strangers in a limited space requires etiquette if it is not to be riddled with violence. Throw away the etiquette, the intolerance of someone coughing or crinkling a popcorn bag, the whispers, the head too large directly in front of the face: it's not there. Some theatrical venues are designed now with winged headrests and stadium seating to facilitate elision of the call for etiquette and make even that very elision unthinkable. And when somebody has to edge out of a seat in order to pee right in the middle of a key scene, somehow we can find that they are not there blocking the screen, and decline to pay them attention: a profound difficulty that must be obviated through learning. The untutored viewer is usually cast out of the diegetic paradise and forced to work her way back, and, of course, when the patron who has left makes a return a few moments later, the entire process of being cast out and struggling back will be irritatingly replayed. Every puff of irritation is a distraction.

And throw away that screen, too, in the sense that it is a construction made to reflect projected light. It is not the reflection but only the light we must detect, the light and its form. Throw away that rebound, that the image was thrown toward the screen—pitched—from a projection booth behind us (Plato's Cave) and is now, as it reaches us, but a second-degree reflection. Throw away the construction of the great rectangular thing, its edges, its being tied to rigid supports, its being draped at the proscenium in some decorative fashion, its tiny holes (Michel Chion calls it a *toile trouée*), its specially prepared surface to increase diffraction. Throw away all of what is outside the film itself and therefore functional—too functional—as an index of the presence of the film as such: the advertising in, and outside of, the theater, the reviews, the hype, the interviews, the backstage "palaver." Throw it all away, or else be afflicted knowing, while attempting to watch, that one is watching-in-order-to-see.

See garb but not costumes. See facial disfigurement but not makeup. Only see.

And then: how can we note *without noting* the swooping, circling, speeding, jumping, shifting, creeping, slinking, thrusting, lifting, dropping, intruding presence of the viewpoint, that is, of the camera? If the camera is nervous, constantly shifting (because of itself or because of the editing); or if it is too languorous; does it jar the viewer out of unreflective involvement by changing point of view before there is a desire in the viewer for a change of point of view, or by not changing when the desire is there? If we look at melodrama of the 1930s and attend to the placid stability of the camera by way of the placid stability we experience in watching without watching, if we can be brought to feel that we are here, that action is playing out in front of the eye so fully and so naturally there is no "action" and there is no "eye," that all spatio-temporal transitions are signalled bluntly through dissolves or fades articulate enough to be caught without being so articulate as to be thought-provoking; if we can do this, and then look at the movement offered us in a typical Harry Potter or James Bond or Marvel action film, it becomes clear that over the decades audiences have learned to watch through increasingly sophisticated spectatorial shifts: shifts of placement and shifts of consciousness of placement. The audience has learned to watch, has worked at learning to watch, has in fact learned so very well to watch, in an ongoing *explicit process* of learning watching, that is exacerbated in rapidity and degree by the incessant onslaught of new technologies, that only watching is impossible. Instead of the sight, we have the education required to absorb a sight such as this. "Oh, that was great CGI!!!" We know enough about how changed methods of filmic transposition are introduced to, and then negotiated with, viewing audiences (see Carey)—this endeavor of introduction tagging an action of the production. But how is it that viewers take a further jump, not only learning to see but learning that they are going to have to be learning to see, to shift their spectatorial modes? Older viewers sometimes find it difficult to watch-without-watching the films that very young viewers are at least claiming to be watching-without-watching, the speed of change being accelerated to a pace the younger viewers find conventional and imperceivable but that the older ones must rehearse, possibly through pain, to experience naturally. Intergenerational discontinuity. Or:

Is there actually no intergenerational discontinuity at all, but with action films viewers have come to expect not to actually "just watch" what is onscreen and instead to always watch in tandem with pointing to the technique by which the watchable is mounted there? Not a new way of watching at all; only something new to see, that didn't used to fascinate anybody.

Nowadays, transitions often involve shifting through narrative "times" in a non-sequential manner and through narrative spaces in a way that is conceptually non-contiguous: going, say, from one scene by jump cut to something that, we will learn only later, took place a long time before, or that in fact is taking place at the same time but somewhere else. This mental agility is part of the framework of watching that must be learned and accommodated to, before one can *see*—more and moreso as I write. Those who are comfortable sweeping through time, bouncing in time, moving from supposedly actual to supposedly conceptual time and space, and who do this without seeing themselves doing it, have learned to grasp an entire (new) mode of apperception and throw it away.

Yet the increased speed of movement onscreen, daunting as it is for those accustomed to more patient narrative action, also works by depending on superficial characteristics of figures and scenes. Nothing else is possible if one is to flit quickly from one thing to another, to dart-swoop through the present moment, in some staccato editing pattern of intense speed. What is onscreen to be recognized must be recognized in the shortest of glances, a blink, and so it will be superficially decorated—extreme color, definitive costume, bizarre makeup or set design, gestural manner—to facilitate. As a style of looking, blinking is Impressionist, "oblique vision, those side views 'from the tail of the eye' which represent the height of disdain" (see Ortega 123). Blinking increases consciousness of surfaces as surfaces. When the screen world is made into a surface that openly claims to be a surface, it must cease to be a surface that claims to be a depth: cease to show not only who a figure is, where they stand, and what line of action they intend but also, and available to patient perception, what contradictory thoughts and impulses they hold, what implications of their presence abound both here in the scene and in other areas that are subtly referenced. All this must go. One can understand how sophistication of movement supplants sophistication of characterization, how the characters of fast film are thin caricatures of the more sensually contrived characters and presences of slow film, how *going* becomes a replacement for *being*, or *being-on-the-move* a scion of *being-in-place*.

Throwing it all away as one watches is in conflict with prevailing exhibition trends in general, however; capitalized cinema has leapt in to advertise itself. In theaters one encounters (a) the proliferation and augmentation of food and drink, as well as the operational complexity of acquiring these; (b) the presence of advertisements prior to film screenings (utterly distracting advertisements, by design, for raising the thought of shopping); (c) the screening of trailers made by specialists to excite and confuse (not only to offer a sharp, optimistic sense that no matter what is on the menu now, *more is to come*, but also to attract attention to *watching that one is watching*) and to raise thoughts at best tangential to the film of which one is promised a view, thoughts that may find harbor and not be casually erased afterward. For home viewing there are distractions, too. Advertisements on dvds and blu-rays sometimes, intruding into the flow. More and more engaging, optically spectacular production-company logos—sometimes a dozen!—that are like tiny films in themselves, almost always involving, in some cleverly designed "universe," the sudden, sanctifying presence of hyper-intense illumination, as from On High. Series episodes that link automatically to ongoing episodes, so that one is conscious of a viewing mode being cultured from outside. Confusing and optically challenging screen menus. Not to mention intensive popular discussion about material viewed—the director commenting on his scene as you watch it—since the collectivity and sporadic fascination of the theater audience must somehow be mocked up in the relatively private world of home screening. To help the viewer throw away all this optical detritus, producers may screen dramatic characters of astounding bizarreness, complexity, and acumen experiencing strange new forms of pain and pleasure and performing actions as yet undreamed by viewers. "Am I really seeing this?" one wonders as one gapes, unconsciously careful not to take a breath to wonder about that wondering.

23

Who Are You?

Carol Lynley in Bunny Lake Is Missing *(Otto Preminger, Wheel Productions, 1965). Digital frame enlargement.*

When I sit in front of the moving images, a certain perplexity invariably arrives, not quite a disturbance and certainly not a pain, yet surely a form of discomfiture, a confusion. And this has to do with doubled facts. First, I am fully aware it is me sitting there watching, using my eyes and my body, being the singular maker of response I have been as long as I can remember, as well as having spent my money for the experience (and "my" time), and feeding myself some popcorn to keep up the energy—popcorn out of my own hand, into my own mouth. Then, second, I recognize that the film is not actually speaking to me as an individual. It is speaking to me as part of a very large YOU, very likely an international YOU but absolutely a YOU made up of various ages, genders, ethnicities, races, historical backgrounds, national affiliations, interests, doubt, queries, and so on. A YOU whom I cannot fully perceive or measure, but suffice it to say that the cost of the film will be earned back more readily the larger the YOU is. Even if it has become divided by censorial (rating) practices, this audience, this gang, is an entity I have addressed elsewhere as *highly amplified*, amplified in that the emission (coming from the screen, in my case in front of my face) is addressed with noteworthy broadness over a massive territory (what Harold Adams Innis called an empire). The greater the amplification the broader the territory. Here am I, situated in this amplified audience as a member, one of a crowd of like enough individual beings conglomerated: together we comprise a vague but certain set of typifications because we are all *here in front of this screen.* Yet, I the gang member am watching at the same time as I the single person watches, he who used his individuality to enter that group. Having a group mind and a single mind at once, in what sense can I understand some elements of the film to be speaking to me?

I surely do apply the filmic content autobiographically. Something happens onscreen and *it reminds me of* something in my life, something I am remembering at that instant, or can conceive. By way of remembering and conceiving I conjoin myself to the filmic content, so that my life and the filmic presence seem reflections of one another. More, I take this reflection to imply personal meaning, say, a road direction, a philosophical hint, an address to some vague query or misunderstanding about my place in nature. It feels as though the film is providing an answer to a question I have silently asked, albeit I am not conscious of having asked a question. I frame the logic of the story as a sermon. (*Shane* [1953]: about moral and geographical hardship and yeoman strengths; *Personal Shopper* [2016]: about the limits of our knowledge and belief.) I exercise the quirkiness of my personal taste when I am powerfully struck by a film (a taste cultivated culturally but the subtleties of which have been modified according to my own, perhaps transgressive need, surely my need for music). My taste guides me to find the thing funny, pleasurable, incomplete, problematic, satisfying, sad. When I use my biography, I am bringing forward elements that I can grasp and hold and understand (as I choose to believe) without bringing into the equation knowledge or speculation about other people in their relation to such things. Something like the taste of my cup of coffee in the morning, which is, I know well, part of a worldwide system involving economical exploitation, capital investment, advertising, and a kind of brainwashing albeit simultaneously *this exact* cup of coffee, *this hot one*, and it tastes the way it registers in *my mouth*. "Coffee" is *this* coffee *now*. My coffee. My coffee is not just an expropriation, an exploitation; it is a drink. But also worldwide commerce.

I think it possible that the last time a complex work was created, rehearsed, and performed for *an audience of one* was the première of Wagner's *Das Rheingold* in 1869, attended, in a theater containing only one (regal) chair, by Ludwig II of Bavaria, the composer's patron (and "Mad King"). Operas, dramas, and motion pictures today are so extraordinarily expensive they can be financially supported only by the purchased attendance of huge multitudes, and so, whichever film one sees one sees as a member of a multitude. (The Bank of America makes its loan to the producers on the guarantee of worldwide distribution rights, typically.) This broad audience is divided spatially and temporally, of course (technically "multiplexed"), and no one need ever feel part of something more than several hundred people strong, never feel—may easily forget— that thousands of cinemas are screening the same images just now, and again four or five times a day, collecting a serious aggregation of watchers. (Film producers talk about "how many screens" they have.)

In order to think about cinema as a mass medium, I need to imagine how people are being brought in "busloads" to the screen, deposited in the dark stables in herds and tribes, opened to reception and thought by narrative keys tooled to fit the perceptive, psychological keyholes of vast audiences simultaneously. These keyholes we all possess by virtue of our class position and historical presence, involving name tags that can be taken to be familiar, aspirations that can be taken to be shared. When, seeing a film, I frame an "idiosyncratic" response, I am struggling against consciousness of my collective membership(s) in order to build an edifice of the self, a self unlike all other selves, standing on the foundation of the secure knowledge that as a living being I both stand alone and unmatched on the surface of this earth; and stand in a vast company, so many people at the same time, with whom I share some features broadly and uniformly.

The "vast company" was not always so dominant. Dean Acheson, a man who believed that a person had to fully be a person, had this to say about the debates between Richard M. Nixon and John Fitzgerald Kennedy:

> Do you get a funny sort of sense that, so far at least, there are no human candidates in this campaign?. . . They seem improbable, skillful technicians. Both are surrounded by clever people who dash off *smart memoranda*, but it is not all pulled together on either side, by or into a man. (From a letter to Harry S. Truman, qtd. in Halberstam 733; emphasis mine)

Smart memoranda from the screen.

So then, this:

Taken for her first day to a new school in London, whither her mother and she have just recently moved along with the mother's brother, a little girl abruptly disappears, as it were into thin air. Tremendous consternation from the mother, the headmistress, the teachers, who scoot around the facility looking in corners and cupboards but find no one. In fact, not only no little girl but also no evidence of her ever having been present. The brother is helpful and tries to console his sister, but agony and grief pervade the texture of the story. A detective arrives on the hunt, turgidly methodical, sane, sweetly mannered. But no: he can't find the girl either. There comes a moment when he has to suspect—and now, testing the delicacies of our own memories, we have to suspect, too—that there never was a girl, that the mother has invented her and the whole scenario, and that this is a far more complicated and shadowy case than first appeared. Otto Preminger's *Bunny Lake Is Missing* (1965), with Carol Lynley and Keir Dullea as the siblings, Suky Appleby as little Bunny, Laurence Olivier as the detective, Finlay Currie as an old dollmaker, Martita Hunt as a retired old schoolmistress living way up in the attic in a closed-off apartment.

Seeing this marvelous film I find that:

[1] I never for an instant care about little Bunny, although surely I wish her to be found alive. Basically she is beyond my perimeter. I do believe that she exists, just as the mother and uncle do, and I would like to know how it is that she became "lost"—but these are all dull mechanics of the plot. I do not have a feeling for her. Were I to be there and stand next to Bunny, would I give her a welcoming pat on the head?—No. Not even a special glance. She is somebody else's little kid; this school has a whole gaggle of them. They all gab and move around and act as little kids do wherever in the world I have seen little kids. I would hate to see any of them come to harm in any way; but I can't claim to care about them. I couldn't in

honesty make the affirmation that Bunny has roused my worry, my devotion, my concern. She is a kind of cipher. The film shows a bunch of frantic adults running around after a cipher. Yet *we* are to be "concerned," of course.

[2] I do care about the mother, some—perhaps as though she and her brother are my kids. By the time I see *Bunny Lake* I already know Carol Lynley from her many television appearances (made later on, but seen by me well before I know the film). I sympathize that it is ineffably chilling to bring a creature for whom one bears the responsibility of care into what appears a trustworthy situation and then lose her there. Shame unutterable. And panic. She has to be here. She *must* be here. Here *somewhere*. Bunny! Bunny!!!! A *school*, after all. Responsible *teachers*. The civilized center of the world, London.

[3] And then springs the riddle of Bunny's "somewhere" as it appertains to narrative cinema: the entire space of action is, and can only be, what is given within the screen frame moment by moment, coupled with what can be adjoined to the margins through our imagination. The onscreen and the off-. If she is *here somewhere*, Bunny must be here where she could be seen, or just adjacent, and like me the mother, the teachers, and initially the detective, like good movie watchers, will take exactly this position, looking in the spaces the camera reveals. To make matters worse for me as a viewer—yet me as isolated from some other viewers in the great YOU, namely British citizens—the spaces also involve streets and houses in London, specifically areas of London with which I have no familiarity at all. While I know London, I do not know *this* London. I cannot map the territory beyond what is given to me onscreen. Bunny is *here* somewhere, *but where is here???* I have to find Bunny, but first I have to find the *here* where Bunny ostensibly is.

[4] The film's being in black and white exacerbates the queer sense I share with the detective that "Bunny Lake is an abstract concept, not a person," that in fact all of the aspects of the story, the characters, their faces, the house in which the school is set, Ann Lake's rented house, the brother's sports car, the children's toys, . . . all are a collection of abstractions, definitions, proprieties, but not quite living flesh. Add to this the flat light on the principals, evening out the topographies of their faces. Noël Coward as a neighbor is especially "dull." And a special "dullness" is to be found in Superintendent Newhouse (new + house, with Bunny and her mother inhabiting a "new house" in a "new city" and Bunny going to a "new school" in a "school house"), a man whose life is a submission to routine, who seems to be all method and no madness. We will see that this is far from the case, but only later. (Script here by John and Penelope Mortimer.)

[5] The London of the story is made to seem both quotidian and familiar—streets, houses, rooms, cars, persons wearing decent clothing—like virtually any urban location with the pleasing add-on (for me, on this side of the pond) of English-

speaking accents (and the especially pleasing add-on of the Olivier voice, without affectation); but then, too, strangely unfamiliar, as in a warren from which one cannot see an escape route, as in a cultural cell of completely incomprehensible people engaged in completely incomprehensible everydays. Uncertain as to where I am, I have as option only following the tale as the thread leads me, and as soon as he comes on the scene Newhouse is the needle pulling that thread. That allocation of responsibility is by convention, of course.

[6] Dullea is performing his very-nice-boy-dressed-properly routine, just as he did to enormous acclaim in *David and Lisa* (1962), and not at all the athletic and smooth creature will see in *2001: A Space Odyssey* a few years later. He is pure, pristine, accomplished, smart, tidy, meticulous, very tidy, very meticulous. The facial expressions are true models of civil behavior. (Dullea an actor, like Lynley, who has never yet had the audience his work deserves.) Steven Lake is not at all unlikeable except in one respect: to like someone, we sense the radiation of their warmth and let it affect us, then make response. For all his prettiness, all his extreme couth, he is as cold as a block of ice. Chalk it up to "good upbringing," to class sophistication and reserve, but his character is a sum of smart memoranda.

[7] Considerable action occurs inside the half-lit or unlit interiors of Ann's place, newly rented and thus mostly unfurnished so that the rooms loom large against the size of the human bodies inside. Windows looking onto the dark garden. Cupboards unused behind shut wooden doors. Echoes when one calls out a name. Not a sooty, mechanical place (like the traditional boiler room of mystery and horror film) but instead whitewashed and clean and untouched, perhaps too untouched. The word "empty" resonates in mind over and over when we are here. Is Ann as a person empty, too? As empty as this place of hers? Is the sibling relationship empty? Was her womb empty? (Set design by Don Ashton.) There has never been a better white onscreen.

[8] And I find that in this strange, rather intoxicating film, there is no sense of tempo at all. At once it both moves forward and stands still. The conversations are polite and logical, yet not leading: they are not vehicular. There is a kind of vacuum in the center here, around which the planets slowly orbit, Bunny, Ann, Steven, Newhouse, Steven, Newhouse, Ann, Steven, Bunny, Newhouse, Bunny, Bunny, Bunny, Ann, Ann. A film full of angularities, not one of which leads off to a haven or a find. The spread of the space, the emptiness, the haunting idea of a child who, as the film winds on, is further and further from consciousness, more and more lost. Lost and irretrievably lost, perhaps in a character's dream. The camera relentlessly leads us not quite onward but only "onward," and, as in a nightmare of terror, we do not sense ourselves moving.

[9] And the motionlessness is made certain, is frozen, by the surrounding panoply of supporting performances, each etched with the sharpest engraving tool, each

fully committed in only a few lines or a few shots briefly touching one another. Not only the aged and supremely wise Currie in his creepy/charming, charming/creepy shadowy doll shop (the porcelain dolls look like Ann and Steven) and Hunt in her charming/creepy, creepy/charming attic but sage and careful Anna Massey prim and repressed at the school, dutiful Clive Revill as Newhouse's bumbly assistant, or obnoxious, effete Coward. Who has the answer to the mystery? Who knows the secret? And we revolve and revolve and revolve trying to find a clue in the faces, the voices, the spaces between the words. The London spaces at once familiar and strange.

I am pushed away from the story space of the film by my strict unfamiliarity with types like Newhouse, my sense of only vaguely recognizing the American Lake family as coming from a part of the country and a social class I don't know very well. (Something about their fresh propriety vaguely suggests San Francisco.) London is a dream city, but this particular London, very residential, very tranquil is just hidden, even from those who stand there. The cinematography affords us a powerful illumination, so much of the film shot in daylight, brilliant daylight, flat daylight; and even the night scenes are brilliantly nocturnal. The school itself seems filled with eccentric types, such as one sees in filmed British dramas and whom one can come to know, of course, once one has spent time in England, but many watchers in this vast audience to which I belong have not spent time in England. Is it I alone who am lost in London here, or is it WE, a problem especially knotty while I am watching, because the vagueness and emptiness of the spaces, the cleanliness, and the throbbing absence (that is Bunny) all fog my relation to the general audience and my independence: fog my way of knowing what I see.

Yet, with a foggy knowing, I do see. And in this I begin to discern how seeing is not knowing.

To comment on this film is one thing formally and quite another colloquially. When a speaker uses the colloquial code for pointing to aspects of, say, *Bunny Lake Is Missing*, she will make use, ironically, of a masqueraded second-person-*plural* referential pronoun when indicating her listener. It has the twang of a *singular* reference pointed right here and now at the listener, but in truth it is not: "So she goes to the school, desperate, and looks everywhere but she can't find her daughter and you're getting really worried that the kid has been taken or something." *You're* getting worried. Meaning explicitly, of course, "I was getting worried at that point, as far as I can remember now." Or, "Right now it strikes me that at a moment like that a person who claims to be the sort of person I claim to be should have been worried." The speaker-about-film tends to want to avoid that too boastful, too proud first-person singular, but also avoid seeming presumptuous and far too familiar, as would happen with the bald second-person singular; the speaker wouldn't make the claim to actually knowing what the actual listener would do. In such conversation, the listener is converted to a member of the broad audience, a typical viewer of the film, and is compelled, if she wishes to hear the statements personally, to imagine ways in which, unbeknownst to the speaker making them, the comments could be practically applicable to a listener's life. The film very interestingly raises this problem of identification and pronoun-assignation to the forefront, since all of the following are happening simultaneously:

[i] British reticence, civility, and punctual language, all used in modest restraint. Nothing onscreen but eloquence, in the extreme.

[ii] Open reference by speakers to others they cannot possibly know, and yet must accept as close connections by virtue of the professional associations they call up. Address to occupational role, but occupational role close by: mother to headmistress, for example; or to searching detective. Something of a bureaucratic structure, then. Relationships between position holders and roles, not human beings; although to be fair to him Newhouse shows great compassion.

[iii] The absolute epitome of pronoun reference in the film is a little girl who either (a) doesn't really exist at all, or (b) is entirely missing from the action, yet a figure who must be referenced because everyone is concerned about *her*.

Accordingly, listening to the dialogue we find a continual skirting about the issue of direct person-to-person address, a grammatical generalization of sorts. You see the film and you hear it somewhat abstractly. I see the film and I hear it somewhat abstractly. I saw the film and I heard it somewhat abstractly. Yet I do not shirk from assuming that you will be just like me when you see the film. The one proposal I don't make, that so many speakers also don't make when they regale their friends about the film, is that watchers all over, upon seeing the film, will have the same response. The idiosyncratic difference between viewers is de-stressed but not negated.

As to Bunny, little Bunny: is she actually missing? She is absent from the space where, as claims have it, she should be. She is the object of claims. But is there anything else to her?

And here we have the conundrum of the divided self watching film. For the audience as a mass, as with any claim offered to and accepted by a mass, Bunny is real because *we* have accepted her. But for the viewer as an experiencing self, Bunny is a mystery. Since both personae of the viewer are present before the film, so must the two Bunny Lakes be present, one of them a fact, the other a phantom.

24

The Walking Cure

Oskar Werner with Julie Christie in Fahrenheit 451 *(François Truffaut, Anglo/Vineyard, 1966). Digital frame enlargement.*

Frequently we see a character walking but have no idea where he or she is headed.[1] We will almost always discover if we hang on, but only when the character arrives at a destination he or she—but not we—anticipated in advance. By stark contrast, when a character announces (to another character in a "three-dimensional" onscreen space or by phone) where she now intends to go, if we see the transit at all it tends to be by vehicle of some kind, most typically a car. For the unmapped future, footsteps. For the mapped future, wheels. Wheels typically including trains, aircraft, and space vehicles, although it is true that in his spectacular *Skaterdater* (1966) Noel Black shows us the movement of wheels upon pave without specific destination (also we see mostly legs and feet apart from a face).

---

[1] In many of their (first) films, studied with care by the researchers, the Navajo who worked with Sol Worth and John Adair included shots of people walking attached to further shots of people walking, sometimes the same people, and sometimes continuing in the same screen direction as in the previous shot. "Going" was a central idea for these filmmakers.

Movement, then, both ambulatory and vehicular.

In both types, dissolve editing that combines a number of shots set in different locations can produce an "image" of the narrative space that is unknowable and confounding, streets coming from and going to anywhere. But there is certainty and comfort to be felt with walking, even when the character is a wanderer, like Harry Dean Stanton's Travis at the beginning of *Paris, Texas* (1984) pacing the desert by foot. Our certainty and repose stand upon the character "aiming for" a destination ahead *somewhere*; and if somewhere then *out there to be found*. If the destination can be found it will be. Gus Van Sant's *Gerry* (2002) upsets this expectation dramatically with two hiking friends (Matt Damon, Casey Affleck) getting lost in a desert, after setting out on nothing more than a casual friendly hike. An epitome of ambulatory movement is the showdown in western films, for which duellists walk into the scene from shelter in the wings. The formula seems to announce that each step is a move toward a future condition, and the future is neither theirs nor ours to see.[2] In vehicular motion, the moving character is usually posed as having imagined the destination already. *I am already there in thought; I know the way.* This, even when the driving is part of a mad pursuit through a warren of streets.[3] A dramatic event can occur to block the resolution, something on the road that interrupts the passage: hold-up, accident, police roadblock, armed border guards, bridge gone out in a storm. The character's problem is instantly that he cannot go forward, though this not-going-forward is shown in the film's forwardness; his movement is inhibited but so is his prediction of success and, by a kind of Law of Natural Expansion, prediction more generally. He is made a kind of fool, who claimed spuriously to know what would be next but is foiled by fate. The blocked walker, blocked driver, victim of a transportation wreck—all these have suddenly fallen off their own maps.

We note how driver characters never seem to search for parking spots, nor do they get tickets when parking illegally (*The Magic Christian* [1969] offering a hilarious exception to the rule with a parking warden [Spike Milligan] lured into eating the ticket he has just delivered). The walker, who tends to be in a trance of some kind—a bubble of personal reflection—walks forward and, encountering a roadway, is magically unharmed there.[4] Walking is not only meditative, it is reflective. The walker thinks things through, turns a situation around and around, comes to a resolution. Go for a walk and clear your mind. But the driver is urgent about arriving, and the entire journey is a struggle for arrival. The walk is typically a passage to the generally unknown, not the previously mapped. The walker uncovers the future, courts possibility.

Various strategies open for depiction, each offering its own connotation:

---

[2] Telling examples are *The Fastest Gun Alive* (1956), *3:10 to Yuma* (1957), and *The Quick and the Dead* (1995).
[3] As in *Ronin* (1998) in Vielle Nice, *The Bourne Supremacy* (2004) in Moscow, *Baby Driver* (2017) in Atlanta, or *6 Underground* (2019) in Florence.
[4] For an interesting epitome, see *Run Lola Run* (1998) where walking is sped up to running, especially the moment when racing Lola sees a van proceed through a gigantic piece of plate glass being carried, invisible, across the road in front of it.

[A] A character walks and the camera is in front of his face, tracking backward as he moves (the opening conversation between Cary Grant and Doreen Lang in *North by Northwest* [1959]). In this way, the character is always moving toward the viewer but never arriving: Zeno's paradox. The territory ahead is presumably glimpsed by the walker, at least partially, whereas the viewer is cut off—like cameras, humans do not have eyes pointing behind them. Involved here can be detailed examination of the walker's face, and in this way potential illumination of the walker's thought. If the walker is speaking, the progress through space and the progress through the utterance can work in harmony or against each other. Consider that opening sequence of *North by Northwest*, with Roger Thornhill walking up Madison Avenue in conversation with his secretary, where the speed of his dictation makes it seem, at instants, as though they are stationary; or think of desperate Szell (Laurence Olivier) stumbling along 47th Street in *Marathon Man* (1976), to the accompaniment of another voice.[5]

[B] The character walks and the camera stands at right angles, from up close or far away catching a profile of the mover. Here the viewer is positioned to adopt an attitude of unconcerned interest, even fascination, a relatively objective measurement of movement that may be predictive beyond what the mover can be thought to experience. A nice case is the finale shot of Truffaut's *Fahrenheit 451* (1966), with Montag (Oskar Werner) so absorbed in his book as he strides that he doesn't see any future outside the words stretched in lines on the page. The character can be objectively interesting— attractive, repulsive, humorous, grave—but our involvement in the experience of his or her forward movement, of *the movement itself*, is elided in favor of a dispassionate observation of his or her character seen passing us. In *Rebel Without a Cause* (1955) Jim accompanies Judy who is walking down a little alleyway near her house, but she doesn't see him because he is behind a high fence; he keeps leaping up to catch brief glimpses of her over the top of it as we see from the side. He is like a jack-in-the-box, charming, innocent, working for that delicious profile view.

[C] Character movement is shown from a backward- or forward-looking angle, so that the mover's "forward" is a diagonal across the screen. Col. Nicholson pulling at the explosive cable hidden under the sand in the telltale CinemaScope shot near the finale of *The Bridge on the River Kwai* (1957), revealing it, revealing it, revealing it, and stumbling forward along the diagonal line. Because the angle shot includes the viewer's position by implication, it is not difficult to comprehend the counterlinkage between the mover's being confounded here and our own foreknowledge of what he is about to find, the detonator. When the angle is from the rear, we can see a mover's forward action coupled with some knowledge of where he is headed; but he and we can be surprised.

---

[5] As to the conundrum involved in seeing where one is going, see Pomerance, *Antonioni* 222-3.

[D] Walking movement can be shown from directly behind, with the camera following the character in a line. This will tend to mean the screen features two distinct elements: the character's back as dominant feature, and the surrounding territory moving past the viewer's peripheral space. Shots of this kind must be made with close attention to the speed of camera movement, since fast-moving peripheral objects bring on a state of nausea in the viewer.[6] In this kind of arrangement, because we are flush behind the character, whatever it is that lies ahead he or she will come to know before the camera does. Photography of this kind is basic to climactic moments in horror film, where our rapt concentration on the character is produced at the expense of awareness of our own surround; objects or beings can suddenly, shockingly, intrude from the off-camera wings, sharply cut off by the frame. That the character cannot sense presence so close is preposterous, but we elide judgment for the pleasure of fear. The emerging intruder trick is easily learned by viewers, who couple relative darkness and this rear camera position with an expectation there will surely be something springing; oddly, as time goes by and cinema matures, the trick is not learned by characters.

In all of these constructions, albeit least in the angular and side shots, a certain tension is produced in the viewer notwithstanding any "emotion" being "felt" by the character, since the comfort of certainty for the watcher is tied to an unobstructed vision of narrative space and the "walking shot" always involves some kind of obstruction, most intensively when the character walks toward us or walks with us trailing behind. The tension gives emphasis to the uncertain quality of walking in general. That every step is necessarily a forgetting of the steps before, an approach to the unimagined. The young child will have a profound sense of discrete adventure in each step. The camera returns us to childhood.

It is also interesting that in the most general way cinematography and editing can work together to analogize both methodical walking and vehicular speeding. When the editing pace is exacerbated, through radically decreased average shot lengths, a certain graphic logic is required to tie the brief shots together coherently, this logic also producing a tranquilizing sureness about direction and outcome. After all, *per* Heisenberg, we cannot worry simultaneously about where we are headed and where we are. The swift-moving passage works as a kind of nervous tremor inside the narrative flow. The narrative world jitters, but will come to rest, we can be certain. Only this certainty prevents us from having a vertiginous experience. In vehicular motion the world stutters by as the protagonist speeds forward through it, but since a planned destination will be reached—catching or escaping from another vehicle, arriving at a spot, getting lost and stopping—the outward arc of the story will continue at a reasonable pace over and above the interstitial moment of high stimulation. The vehicular sequence is essentially (a) "I will go there," (b) "I am quickly going there,"

---

[6] As I learned in a public lecture by Edward T. Hall in the early 1970s.

then (c) "I have arrived." Since (a) and (c) are the structural frame limits, (b) works as a built-in aggravation of sensation, a thrill but not a vector. In *Accident* (1967), Harold Pinter's script turns (c) into a puzzle.

Most frequently, cinema *walks through* its development, proceeding forward, with some methodical motor, through unclarity toward increasing likelihood of resolution in clear light. In a normal non-action shot or sequence, for instance, each character "walks through" the dramatic contingencies of the moment, noting, reflecting, thinking, surmising, wondering, suggesting, arguing, hypothesizing, forgetting, and hesitantly, bravely, wisely, or thoughtlessly going forward. Regardless of the physical movement of any character body, the camera as "narrative eye" walks through the story, moves coherently from one setting to the next, encountering relevant folk and relevant problems along the way. The camera seems not to know where it is headed in the accounting, very much as we (pleasurably) do not know: the camera (as production) *does know* but *seems not to know*. *Gerry*, in which we are offered hardly anything except back-tracking, following, side-viewing, or angular shots of the two principal characters walking through magnificent natural space, is an allegory of the narrative process in film, beside also being, of course, a narrative process in film itself. Now we are here looking at this and going forward. Now we are there looking at that and moving forward. But still, when a point of arrival presents itself, we will find ourselves surprised.

A dominating side feature of walking is disattention. Once the child learns to stand, to negotiate territory, to make progress so that use of the legs has become "natural," he ceases worrying through the action step by step. This attenuation of concern leading to easefulness can be reprised in adulthood after any injury that imperils the walking function; one learns to walk again and having learned to walk, simply walks. If one is heading toward an uncertainty, one incorporates the acceptance of uncertainty into one's sense of the world and one's basic expectations for its continuity—the police agent creeping alone at night into a dark house. Never knowing what the next moment will bring, we nevertheless make no particular effort to speculate or fret. In *Sylvie and Bruno*, Lewis Carroll has a character reflect at one moment that it would be best never to go anywhere one would not wish to be found dead. A logical consideration, to be sure, while at the same time a practical impossibility unless one chooses to remain paralyzed in the cradle. The camera insistently draws us forward, openly promising nothing so much as the furtherance of experience. Furtherance—the ongoing procession, the parade's continuance. There is still more to come.[7] Notably, in the tremors of action sequences this essential hope, the forward gaze toward more forward gazes, is often removed, dissolved, and replaced with an acute sense of the vibration of the instant.

The prominent disattention in walking is often mocked up by the production practice, as when actors only appear to be walking forward when in fact they are on a treadmill against a background suggesting motion. Additionally, the camera must sometimes be affixed to a dolly that rides along a track laid out beforehand, this process

---

[7] R. Barton Palmer helpfully reminds me how with film trailers, the "coming next" posture and tonality have the effect of promising not only an upcoming spectacle but the future of film itself.

requiring the actor to step very carefully along or inside the track. The treadmill functions in the walk to the commissariat passage in *The Man Who Knew Too Much* (1956), and walking along a track in *Day for Night* (*La nuit américaine*, 1973) where it is parodied a little in a recursive shot with the camera pulling back to reveal an actor (Jean-Pierre Léaud) working this way. When the actor can "walk" without normally walking, the character can be free—and will look free—to daydream, chat, look around, or otherwise turn away from the process itself—literally not watch the territory.[8] In any shot closely tracking a character's walking movement, it will be necessary to calibrate and retain focus, and to establish proper lighting all through the passage, so the metricality of the maneuver, on the actor's part, will be essential. In both "careful" and "carefree" walking, the actor ironically does not suffer the character's uncertainty.

The non-diegetic soundtrack can be used both to cover (to mask) and to accompany (as with a pianist accompanying a singer) the vision of movement. In walking, we find unattached musical accompaniment, a setting of pace that the character may seem to follow, and a harmonic intimation of the mood we are to interpret as being cued for the character (and us) by the scene. In driving, the sound masks the necessary edits and lays over a diegetic motor tempo (that in the reality of shooting cannot be matched). An action sequence with vehicles would seem entirely incoherent without the music (rhythm) track, since the splicing would be too obvious and the concomitant apparent fragmentation of what we are to take as fluid speedy movement would ruin the effect. The sound of motors can be musically arranged as a music track. Walking begs for tranquil music. Stepping forward along the surface of the earth: this is tranquility itself.

---

[8] The opening of *High Plains Drifter* (1973) has a man "walking" by using another creature's legs. On horseback Clint Eastwood can afford to check out his surround casually.

25

The Picture Dances

(Top) Robert De Niro in Taxi Driver *(Martin Scorsese, Columbia, 1976); (Bottom) Planetary alignment in* 2001: A Space Odyssey *(Stanley Kubrick, MGM, 1968). Digital frame enlargements.*

From Erich Wolfgang Korngold's swashbuckling, wave-tossing theme for *The Sea Hawk* (1940) to Bernard Herrmann's stabbing violin sounds in *Psycho* (1960) and lazy saxophone obbligato in *Taxi Driver* (1976), from Richard Strauss's prophetic *Also Sprach Zarathustra* in *2001* to John Williams's ethereal Debussyesque chorale in *Family Plot* (1976) and pixie staccato scherzo in *Catch Me If You Can* (2002), the history of film scoring has been, among other things, a progression and complication of onomatopoeias. In literary study, the onomatopoeia is a (musical) sonority embedded in a word pronunciation that imitates or matches the claimed sound of the thing referred to by the word. A bee *buzzes*. In film, the word is replaced by the image of the thing. The musical grounding is a sounding that imitates or matches what the thing seen can be claimed to sound like in the world as known outside of its cinematic depiction. Music can be used, then, to help the visualized world sing, and also *sing appropriately*, since just as straightforward onomatopoeic scoring can be done so can ironic scoring, in which a sound contradicts or flips the presumable sound of the thing imaged.

Take the Korngold. After a brief brass fanfare, the music leaps into a sumptuously rolling 2/2 marine anthem, the forte phrasing giving over the impression of massive rolling waves and allowing for our vision of the pirate's ship yawing upon the glorious, massive swells of the sea. Onomatopoeia operates exclusively in the subjunctive mode. The sea does not sing as the waves rise and fall, splash and recede, but we can grasp a certain metaphor: *if the sea were to sing, it would sing like this*. If we were to hear the sea singing, this is what we would hear. *If we were on the ship, and the ship were singing as it rolled with the sea . . .*

Hearing is affective. We are led not only to enrich our reception of an image but to imagine ourselves subjected to, influenced by the pulsions that the music releases, the charges to feeling, the inspiration of breath. In *The Sea Hawk*, we are joyously on the main, aboard the ship with the pirates and so, thanks to the vivacity and major tenor of the score, we affiliate with Thorpe (Errol Flynn), allowing our hearts to race with his all-expanding passions to the very beat that Korngold sets. In *Catch Me*, we adopt a sprightly acceptance of sprightly Frank Abernale (Leonardo DiCaprio). In *2001*, we see the planets literally bursting into place *tutti fortissimo* with the expansive, trumpeting chords—and coming into position, the heavenly bodies announce themselves in the most magniloquent voices imaginable.

Beyond any music that might directly appertain to the story, does a film require what is called an extradiegetic track? (Virtually every film has one.) When we soar to the mountaintop for the kiss of love, must there be violins? Or, to ask this differently, when we soar to the mountaintop for the kiss of love, and hear the violins, what do we make of the sound and of the kiss? I don't mean, do we recognize and acknowledge that an orchestra is recording a movie score in a sound studio, but, taking our hearing of this score on the same level of appreciation as our hearing of dialogue and our seeing the sights onscreen what can this music be for us and what can it mean, of itself and in combination?

One might wonder whether the very ascent of the story, the climbing up, calls for a musical elevation, an interval leap upward or a chord modulation upward or a melodic ascension; calls for or is conventionally associated with, no difference that makes a difference. And whether the shadowy progress of a truly debased action, performed by nefarious monsters, naturally belongs with an orchestral wandering in the very depths of the celli and double basses, perhaps hooked to a tympani roll. The links between music forms and image contents seem to meld them, so that Travis Bickle behind the wheel of his cab on the streets of New York at night somehow always already merits the jazzy riffs that back up his progress. He is in a jazzy place, the night makes for jazzy neon thoughts, the street filled with lonely strangers is a kind of nest for the birth of jazz. Jazz isn't a track *behind* this film, jazz *is* this film.

The *Zarathustra* fanfare that opens *2001* seems to make proclamation in the tenor of a biblical voice, situated in the court of the Monarch of the Universe. Not just: something is foretold, but: Something is Foretold. Something that Eclipses Space and Time. Something so Huge, so Unquestionable yet so Mysterious, so Fundamental yet so Far Ahead of its Time that further Information will be of no help to us wee folk who stare in awe. The very universe is involved, is implicated, is dancing. And it thunders around us, albeit harmonically. All is pure, as it should be, as it has been ordained to be, as it can only be. Without this musical hit, we would see three planetary bodies slowly moving in relation to one another until they came into alignment; we would witness alignment, slow and deliberate alignment, alignment as per the rotations of the cosmos, like some immeasurably large clockwork. We would see clockwork, and we might even think of clocks—the film will exploit this invocation of time as Time. We would even see the shock of illumination as an eclipse is rounded into happening. But there would be no proud and strident announcement of eventfulness. Strictly formal according to the physics of deep space—a zone already known; or known to onscreen sorts whom viewers can presume to know—the movements would seem perfunctory. We would witness happening, but only in the exact way that such happenings happen, a natural event being natural in its place. What is required, that the music brightly delivers—delivers, in fact, with supreme illumination—is foreboding, the quality of "introduction" which says, in effect, THIS!!!!, BUT SOMETHING MORE IS COMING THIS WAY.

Or in *Jaws* (1975), Quint's boat, *The Orca*. She sails off of a morning, with Brody and Hooper aboard. And viewing through the yawning maw of a shark skeleton mounted in an upstairs room near the dock we hear, as the craft shrinks away onscreen, John William's jaunty sea shanty cue. (Sailors with pipes in mouth, dancing on the deck.) Without this, there is something ominous about the boat drifting away from the safety of shore; the three men aboard are gambling their lives; we are holding our hearts in our hands. But with the music, they are three boys out on an adventure, characters who swim out of a kid's book. The boat is sailing, in fact, toward the music. We will have fun together, we will find the beast and hunt him, we'll have a story to tell. With this initial optimistic tone, the shark hunt (soon later) seems dangerous and shocking because it so fully contradicts—both optically and sonically—the hint of an escapade promoted at the moment "we" sailed.

Alternatives:

2001. What if Kubrick decides to eschew the musical track and simply use the film of the planets coming into alignment, over total silence? Notwithstanding that there is no sound in space, and that therefore the music of such planetary movement would actually be *just this total silence*, still two major problems would arise:

- the footage looks too realistic, but then, instantly, too unbelievable, since how could a filmmaker in 1968 position a camera to get an image like this? Clearly, the image is an animation of some kind, and if this is seen right off the top the later special effects, positioned to be galvanizing, leak away.

- a particular sense of rhythmic climax is dampened, because now there are no musical downbeats to signal sharp changes in the visual display—the sacred alignments. Without the sharp changes, things happen according to the laws of gravity and natural movement but not with drama. A motion picture is all about development, not just representation; drama, not just eventfulness. Natural movements in themselves do not constitute drama.

There is also, without the music here, happening without foreboding. Here are the orbs, here is how they move, here—they are coming into alignment; now they are aligned. Facts described, absent the peculiar clarity of mystery. "There is nothing as mysterious as a fact clearly described," Garry Winogrand said. Every cinematic image is both a revelation in itself and a promise of revelations to come, since in cinema the image endures by moving forward, not only waiting in its envelope of tranquility. Without music, the planets of *2001* are celestial bodies, but not harbingers.

Jaws. Without a musical cue, the boat sailing off in *Jaws* constitutes an event and only an event. One way to see this film, distantly, unfeelingly, is as a chain of events, first harrowing then blood-curdling then nightmarish and ultimately relievingly placid at dawn. A chain but not a propulsion. What would be missing is the anticipatory gesture, the hope of success or of restitution or of a communal therapy. If there is no hope, the boat merely tokens one phase of a bureaucratized process whereby the ravages of a beast can be accepted with seriousness and the perpetrator pegged for justice. If the film is downgraded to no more than a series of events—if any film is downgraded this way—it becomes little more than a record of the daily news. This happened here, that happened there. The witness has no recourse but to tabulate the happenings, perhaps keep score, perhaps calculate advantages and disadvantages, but there is no feelingful embedding in the moment, nor a sense of being alive as one watches people "being alive."

The sense of being alive comes with the belief in tomorrow.

Or the fear of no tomorrow. In *Psycho* (1960), those razor sharp staccato high-treble string riffs, eep, eep, eep, eep, eep. They do not signify. They do not emphasize. They do not shriek to enunciate an orchestra (made up of, as Bernard Herrmann wanted, all strings). They do not mimic, or intimate, or reflect. They are sounds of the filmic universe, singing themselves just as everything else in the film sings itself. That is how and why they can be so frightening, such a cutting interruption—pure modernity.

26

Taboo

(Top) Ingrid Bergman in Casablanca *(Michael Curtiz, Warner Bros., 1942); (Bottom) Vanessa Redgrave being photographed (by David Hemmings) in* Blow-Up *(Michelangelo Antonioni, MGM, 1966). Digital frame enlargements.*

A child sits in a schoolroom day after day, at a desk adjacent a row of windows looking down onto a quiet street. What is there? Two trees, a maple and an elm, very large and very old, and through the seasons the leaves change color, drop off, grow back, change color, drop off. Two houses, one with a green roof, one with a red roof, and attic windows on each, of which the outside frames are painted white. A third house at left is only half visible and has a tall chimney. Every day, day after day, two trees, two houses, a half house. Through addition and subtraction, the History of Europe, the chemistry of bluestone, *The Merchant of Venice*. Poems. Sentences. Additions and subtractions. Two houses, two trees, half a house, the gray sky. The blue sky, the gray sky, the colorless sky. Clouds.

This little street happens to be on the side of the school building opposite the side that contains the door through which this student enters and exits, so that no visit is ever made there. Never to be in the street, only to see it through the schoolroom windows. Two houses, two trees, half a house. A chimney. Always to wonder what else is on that street, where that street leads. Always to wonder who is inside those houses.

This is so much like looking at a movie it could be a child's primer. What we are shown we are shown in sparkling detail, yet it is all that we are shown. This and nothing more. This place and nowhere else.

Terminus. A legendary scene in Antonioni's *Blow-Up* (1966). A photographer has wandered into an isolated park, a haven of green. On an upper level, accessible by a long flight of stairs, is an open space, margined by a wooden fence and a long wall of waving trees. A man and woman kiss, argue, struggle, kiss, argue, struggle. The photographer snaps pictures, and they do not see him. Then the woman does see him and rushes his way as he is making to leave. They are face-à-face, she three or four stairs above him. Consternation, remonstration. Quickly he snaps a photograph. "This is a public place. Everyone has the right to be left in peace." He agrees to give her the roll if she'll come to his place. He goes off. She turns and goes back to the trysting spot, a cleared area in front of a huge bush (the Burning Bush, not at the moment burning). She looks around. We are in long shot; she is small at the back of the space. She runs away, away, over the lip of the edge of the horizon, and disappears from the place.

But where is she getting to, over the lip of that horizon. The ground line stretching laterally left and right, and intercepted by that immense bush. What is that next—that further—zone, the zone she enters that we do not enter? What does she do there, does she pause to reflect, does she keep running, does she stand looking every which way for orientation and direction? And is it a hillside she finds herself on, or another field, or a gateway to a street, or what? We will never know. She runs away.

Yet by virtue of her pausing to think and then her urgent exit over that horizon, by virtue of her vanishing on the other side, we are led to consider that horizon. We have seen it through a series of shots, it has been there, stolid, silent. And now it has suddenly become a locus of movement and thus an interest for us. But our interest is tabooed. The park zone is magnificent in its silence, its greenness, its slow wind moving the green like the breath of something divine, and a perfect trapezoid falling away from the camera (and from the photographer's camera), so that it confronts us with an elegance of form and design. An Arcadian space, but also a cell, as we learn only too late when it becomes clear that there is in this place a boundary across which we cannot go.

To be given a framed image exquisitely composed is to revel in a rich delight, aesthetic rapture, but also, although we may not think it, to be denied. Every offering is a denial. Every cabinet of curiosities has a drawer we are not to open. And we mustn't think of this. To watch a film is to be confronted ongoingly with a denial of which we are not to take account, as taking account would render the experience a construction and the ideal of film-watching is to render every construction an experience. Seeing a scene, noting its spread, its richness of content, its capaciousness for a broad range of action, its tinctures of line and illumination, we travel onwards through and past it, reaching another apotheosis . . . and neglecting to observe how, in being moved, we have been denied the freedom to move ourselves. "We go to the movies instead of moving," Tennessee Williams has Tom say in *The Glass Menagerie*. Swiftly, before we can sense being denied access to what is beyond the frame limits, to what is over the horizon, to what is in the wings, we are transported to another frame with another set of limits. In order to feel no pain in these denials—our denials—we follow the action. Where does she go, this beautiful woman (Vanessa Redgrave)? She goes forward in the story. Look, she is there! Look! And the horizon she crossed becomes something like a splice.

Zoom. In *Blade Runner* (1982) Decker the detective (Harrison Ford) is confronted with a small color photograph taken in a room filled with objects (as in a still life) that are arranged in apparent layers. He is looking for a clue that he believes he can find there. But the photograph is unforgivingly stingy just like—we think—other photographs, those teases. But magic!, he has a special little machine, and he loads the picture into it and projects the image on a screen. This device, a type of computer, responds to his vocal commands. Magnify 50 percent—track right—that sort of thing. And click click click click the machine complies, until we find that Decker is literally entering and then strolling through this flat picture, entering it by way of movements and magnifications, even being able, excitedly, to see in a pane of glass a reflection of someone who is standing behind a wall that faces him. Then, transgression supreme, eclipse!, through manipulations he is able to see that *person standing behind the wall*.[1]

(The sequence is managed through special effects tricks.[2])

The viewer is given an extraordinary feeling of power here, opportunity to believe it possible, on a whim, on a desire, to go past the frame limits of a picture, to enter, as it were, the pro filmic zone where the diegetic picture was made and to move around there, so that the rigid boundary of the picture edge is turned into a permeable membrane and the axial flatness of the image—the fact that all of its diegetic "planes" of focus are rendered objectively into a single pictorial plane, a screen, a piece of photographic paper—is spatialized, given an atmosphere one can breathe, made the setting of an arrangement of objects (of whatever importance) that one can touch and shift around.

---

[1] Assheton Gorton confided to me that Ridley Scott was able to perceive a space—objects, arrangements—from any point of view whatever while remaining stationary; sitting at his desk he could draw upside-down and flawlessly so that someone standing before him would see the picture straight-up.
[2] A mirror, perhaps, of the effects complexities in producing a film like this in the first place.

What Ridley Scott achieves in this little sequence is the suggestion of a philosophical position regarding the screen; something of a notice to the viewer that, because she does not have—and has no way of obtaining—a device like this, her desire is limited, imprisoned in viewing space, pinned like a butterfly in a collection. Pinned, even when not pinned. For the General Motors Futurama at the 1939 World's Fair, Norman Bel Geddes designed a cityscape across which audiences would be conveyed in seats that were attached to a moving elevated rail. In Disneyworld, a stage presentation operates by having an entire scene appear to shift laterally in front of an audience; but it is actually the theater on wheels, silent wheels, slowly orbiting a circular stage. Cinema is static. Through an exacerbation, an inflammation of her desire, the film viewer comes to know the impossibility of desiring fully, or else the satisfaction—it feels full—of desiring within strict limit (the limit already projected). Even the little shadowy room in which Decker makes his technical maneuvers is closed off to us. We see him, the machine, the room space, but we do not and cannot go beyond the leash so as to be, directly, at his side. What is on the other side of the confrontational wall?

One of the marvels of cinematic construction is our being regaled in every designed space with the richness of where we are, this way being eased from the painful ache of wanting to see more. In his *Until the End of the World* (*Jusqu'au bout du monde*, 1991), Wim Wenders poses this desire to see more than is given, this unrelenting hunger to see, in the sad and wearying vision of William Hurt, who by film's end stares out through bloodshot eyes at a world that still, perversely, teases him. It is not only that we can never see enough—because we never can—but that we can lay aside this feature of experience, leave it in the dark. Else every lovely vision would come along with impossible dissatisfaction. Every paradise would stop at the horizon.

The face is a horizon, finally. This motivational zone, the warehouse of calculations and suppositions, altar of estimations and preferences, noticings and forgettings is entirely out of bounds, tucked away on the other side of a plane of expression to which we are given elaborate, even ceremonial admission. When Ilsa walks into Rick's American Café and eyes him, she momentarily freezes in her steps. What at that instant is going on for her? Surprised fear. Joy. Tactics. Dream. That ambiguous face will lead us to a committed attachment based in an interrogation in place of an affirmation. We will patiently follow that face, but whatever we learn about her no light will fall on what she is thinking now, frozen just here, in the brilliant light. Who is behind those moist, glowing, so very Bergmanesque eyes that seem to fill the screen but then, of course, stop at the edges?

Here is a glorious conundrum for the viewer because who could wish for access (by whatever arcane means) to the details of Ilsa's thoughts at this instant if instead one could be gifted so splendid a view of her so splendid face? Who would truly want access to any space beyond any pictorial horizon if the picture that held one back, the picture with its captivating horizon, were pleasingly composed and in its way "beautiful"? If it showed a clean, well-lighted place? In suggesting that we do not tend to complain about not being taken across a horizon, I do not mean to suggest we ought to have been taken there, ought to complain, or that because they constrain as well as engage us there is some deficit in the pictorial arrangements we see. After all, do I not find myself willing, as a filmgoer watching splendid faces, to revel in the splendor and so fully sacrifice my frustrations at not knowing more that they are no longer frustrations? With Decker, even if he did not find his lurker in that photograph would I care? If he looked the way Harrison Ford looks here, beleaguered, confused, hungry, smart, with those weary but unexhausted eyes? One is always challenged with the decision between understanding a character and seeing one. Between knowledge and light.

Tell me more. Not only the face is bordered, but so is the characterological moment altogether, since no character ever says *everything* one wishes to hear from her, nor gives the impression that she would dream of doing so, even were she to know how. The world of pictorial narrative is thus a city of limitations, a repetition of the assertion that this is what we give, this is all there is, there's nothing more.

The continuing desire to taste more, that I recognize in myself, the curiosity about what is not revealed yet, is not the scientific attitude, it is hunger. The scientific attitude, penetrating beyond surfaces, seeks not only to experience compositional forms but to know them by assignation and measurement—yet science seeks without wanting. "In the late 17th century," remarks Susan Owens, "art and science stood side by side to push at the boundaries of visual perception" ("Baroque"). But standing beside science, art remained art. Not the inquisition but the poem.

27

Only Connect

John Cazale (right) with Al Pacino in Dog Day Afternoon *(Sidney Lumet, Warner Bros., 1975). Digital frame enlargement.*

In the spirit of coming to terms with how it is when we make films our own, let us frame a hypothesis:

Films are theories.

Each proposes a logical order that, as we watch, seems right. We thus come to accept what we see and in accepting it learn it as true. This, no matter how realist or fantastic, how futurist or purportedly historical the vision is. The film riddles us with many elements, dividing the matter of our experience into what we perceive as—what we think of as—discreet components positioned and moving, related and interconnected or apparently independent. And it arranges elements in compositions ultimately graphic, ultimately aesthetic, that address our sense of beauty, our sense of order, our sense of meaningfulness, and our sense of completion. The pieces make sense—seem to fit—in terms of one another and in relation to a proposed universe of happenings, here or on another planet, that we inhabit in our viewing.

Take Sidney Lumet's *Dog Day Afternoon* (1975): A young man walks into a neighborhood bank, pulls out a gun, and takes everybody hostage. That is the central proposition. How can this be sensible?

We are prepared to make associations, the aggregation of which add up to a picture of the world, what Freud called a *Weltanschauung*:

- Man + youth: That a young man is not the same as an old man. Our protagonist is a young man; he comes into conflict with institutions run by old men, and with a few particular older men who confront him.
- bank + neighborhood: that this bank is in this exact place, serving the people who live around here including, perhaps, our protagonist.
- gun + tool: that the weapon empowers action of a certain sort, and predictably. Once there is a gun there will be a shooting, real or potential.

All the tellers will seem to be the sort of people who would be tellers in a bank like this one. Sonny's associate Sal will seem to be the sort of man who would associate with someone like Sonny. Sonny's vibrant enthusiasm will infect, more than the other people we see, the film itself. The film will be a trade-off between enthusiasm and rational calculation.

At play in all of this, all of the various elements in all their various linkages, will be Kenneth Burke's [i] act: actor and [ii] act: scene ratios. [i] That events like these events would reasonably be perpetrated by a young man like this one. [ii] That Sonny's actions would be situated in, of all places, a bank. The purpose of the action, the agencies by which it is mobilized . . . all these are in Burke's ratios, [iii] act / purpose, purpose / agency, actor / agency, and so on. Invoked for us to consider, but also for us *to find considerable,* are youth in its relation to crime, crime in relation to socio-economic class, youth in relation to guns, and much more. This young man Sonny (Al Pacino) is not just making an empty gesture (although there is place in the theoretical universe of the film for empty gestures, to be sure). He will want something in exchange for his hostages, typically he will want money, he will want the money for something particular, he will want it badly enough to commit armed robbery. The bank will have connections to the forces of social control, so that sooner rather than later police cars will show up in the street outside. "Police" will mean police cars, blinking lights, uniformed officers, crowd control, megaphone, dictatorial attitude, gruffness. Display of a certain innocence will garnish the action: Sonny is too nervous to seem an experienced robber/kidnapper; the detective is too agitated to show experience with complex situations like this. The action of the encounters plays out like jitterbug.

We will also come to grasp how the dramatic elements are assembled in a narrative "background," else they could not be visible discretely. "Background" includes both setting and minor characterizations. In our case, the Brooklyn street, the scorching midday sunlight, the shabby bank, the bank interior with its desks, its sterile counters, its huge safe. The police vehicles, multiplied and stopped at all angles. The little shop across the street where the detective can be on the phone with Sonny inside the bank. Sonny's pal Sal, the trigger-happy honcho, sweating with anxiety through the whole event and also a man in desperation, entirely beyond being controlled (John Cazale).

The gruff, entirely proactive detective, smart on the job, meaning to save the victims, working without particular antagonism so as to keep the situation lubricated, and yet also nervously at the end of his tether, as we can see by his constant striding back and forth (emphasized through casting the portly Charles Durning, expert at playing common-man parts, especially New Yorkers). The arrival of Sonny's hysterical wife Angie (Susan Peretz), and then, by telephone, of his gay lover Leon (Chris Sarandon), for whose sex-change operation he is committing the robbery to get funds, and finally of the FBI, personified by two agents (James Broderick, Lance Henriksen) who together form a contemporary analogue to an earlier clean-up artist, the villain Wilson (Jack Palance) in *Shane* (1953). They are as hard as steel, these two, and as cold. Methodical as robots. Perfect for stepping above the highly strung emotionality of the interactions we have seen.

Can we say this film depicts *the* world, not just *a* world? It has been made in a realistic manner, with use of a real commercial site as the bank, a real street, real police cars, real citizens standing around gawking (and paid a day rate as extras). Are banks like this bank? Are streets like this street? Are there really malefactors *like* Sonny? (Whether or not a claim is made that this film is based on real events.) Do people talk the way Sonny talks? ("At-ti-CAH!!, At-ti-CAH!!) Would there be a motorcade to Kennedy Airport, seen from a helicopter at night, carting the robbers and their hostages to a waiting aircraft? Would an aircraft be sitting on the tarmac this way, an isolate object in the night lights? These kinds of questions are relevant only if a signal concern—*the* signal concern—of the appraiser is a picture's relevance to the material pictured, the indexical truth of a photograph as indication of a person or situation photographed: the typical Brooklyn street with a bank and passers-by, then this street as given in the film's rendition. Do we, should we take ourselves to be watching a theorization of daily life (in New York)? Do we, should we learn from this how to live?

Theory: a proposition of how things are in a situation, that addresses all things, all parts of things, all participants, all possibilities and natures. "Proposition," not "statement," since a theory will have a source and a source will have its own limits. So much is absent from this film as a theory of the events it depicts: what is to be hunted inside the bank manager's desk drawers; what the detective was planning for tonight with his wife, before this all came up; what Sonny thought he would cause to happen, and what he sees himself causing to happen, and the gap between them. Or take the observers in the street outside the bank, who are surely stunned by how strange all this is but must never seem *so* stunned that they know this is a movie. The theory must offer suggestion, and fullness, but must not strive to convince, since the striving would be visible.

The film theorizes, but does it theorize an actuality or an illusion, a model or a proposition, a memory or a pure imagination? Jump to a science-fiction fantasy, *Forbidden Planet* (1956), in which we have landed on Altair-4. There we encounter host-guest relations, family relations, and the military organization of a ship's crew all borrowed from conventional earthling middle-class arrangements, yet set in a scene that is styled for an alien futurism. The captain (Leslie Nielsen) is sweet on the Professor's daughter (Anne Francis), but he also knows how to fly a starship and use a ray gun. If the planet looked this way, with a green atmosphere, would a ray emitted from this man's gun, and looking as this ray looks, seem coherent and believable instead of hopelessly fake? Will the organizational balance of the film favor a terrestrial melodrama or a sci-fi adventure, in the end? The fakery or authenticity of the technologies, as appears, will be crucial in shifting the film one way or the other.

What we need of a film when we are watching it is that its parts should stand together against the forces of centrifugality. A film must flow, and it must illuminate, *coherently*, but according to the logical principles it states for itself. Consider, with *Dog Day*, only the storyline:

(A) a man tries to rob a neighborhood bank;
(B) the forces of social control are invoked;
(C) he is finally brought to a halt and given "proper" treatment in a justice system.

Or else this:

(AA) a young man is hoping for a sex change;
(BB) his lover goes off and commits a crime to get the necessary money;
(CC) the plan is entirely thwarted and the sex change won't be happening.

Or even this:

(AAA) an agent of the FBI is called out on a job and leaves his office with an assistant;
(BBB) they arrive at a crime scene (kidnapping is a federal crime, thus the FBI) and put in place a number of clandestine arrangements;
(CCC) finally they apprehend the perpetrator and the case is closed.

Or . . . or . . . or. All of these lines of statement, acknowledgment, attribution, and proposition sum to simple principles we generally regard as moral. Crime doesn't pay. Putting your hopes on the improbable doesn't work. A day's job is a day's job. Moral (but coherently moral).[1]

If one watches films in the context of a hypermoralistic environment, say, a society obsessed with Manichean dualism, with retributive justice, with labelling and punishment and, in general, as Mary Douglas suggested, cleansing, one is prone to taking the storyline that glares in a film—the display that glares in a theory—as a *raison d'être*. Being satisfied to have read the moral, "Don't rob banks," one perhaps too summarily condenses something much more complex that itself is the figure worth examining. Not the story, not the moral, but the film entirely. All of the pieces, all of

---

[1] Crime being shown not to pay was a central tenet of the Motion Picture Production Code, in operation from 1933 through roughly 1968. *Dog Day* could not more evidently be a *post*-Code film, yet in some respects it is sufficiently old-fashioned to hold to the "proper" shape of a finale, yet at the same time the earlier requirement that positive light not be shed on perpetrators of crimes is disavowed by Lumet's careful and very humane attention to Sonny and Sal.

the arrangements and juxtapositions and linkages, all of what is finally bounded. That, moralism notwithstanding, the pizza boy delivering to the bank needs to be real.

Consider, too, bounding. With this and all theories, notation will be made of the position from which—the boundary across which—a framer has framed or an observer sees the theory in the first place. Who are the forces behind the starship that approaches, then lands on, Altair-4 in the first place, and what is their purpose? Where do the old professor's ethical precepts come from, and what do they signal? How naïve, finally, is Miranda, his daughter: has she been unutterably lonely here and desperate for a way to get home? *Dog Day* starts with the street and the bank, not Sonny. A city street like all city streets, at least all city streets in Brooklyn. A bank like other banks. The unexciting quotidian everyday. As all theories focus on something to the exclusion of something else, here we have the bank not the citizens watching the bank. The bank is the entertainment (the screen) and the people standing outside are . . . us.

And then, is the coherence of parts a rational coherence or an experiential one? To show the difference between rational coherence (missing) and experiential coherence (present), an exceptionally crisp little clue in *Dog Day*:

Sal is an epitome of nervous wrecks, from the beginning onward. He is far too prone to fingering the trigger of his gun. He is incoherent in his demands to Sonny. He is paranoically anti-social with all of the people in the bank. And he is like a trained dog in the way he follows Sonny's slightest command. We do not really meet Sal. We do not see the story from his point of view, or find ourselves in possession of any information that might help us understand his background, his concerns, his passions, his reason for being involved in all this in the first place. There he is before us. In panic. The panic seems to speak the personality and the history and the condition. When in the film's shocking finale Sal comes into an unanticipated experience, we are as shocked as he is, never having been given a single clue as to his way of seeing. Sal is like a living lacuna traveling through the film, like a conundrum resting at the heart of a theory that makes no attempt to address it, nor any attempt to indicate to us that there is something here it is not addressing.

28

The Impatient

Kinuyo Tanaka (left) with Ichisaburo Sawamura (right) and Masayuki Mori in Ugetsu monogatari *(Kenji Mizoguchi, Daiei, 1953). Digital frame enlargement.*

To fail to observe the distinctly observable is a strange, evocative trope of film watching. The dramatic effect of not seeing can be greater than the dramatic effect of seeing. Not seeing: a greatly affecting whisper of drama, yet one that is constructed, in a way, out of the viewer's own (in)action. Something is presented, plainly, directly, yet arranged so as to beg no particular attention, to not be apprehended or not taken in—left on the table. Later, much later, some particular indication is made, prompting us to perceive this early presentation in retrospect and with a shocking clarity as though with eyes opened for the first time; to perceive and know that when the indication was given earlier, we were looking away. Away or "away."

Consider Kenji Mizoguchi's *Ugetsu monogatari* (1953). Too tersely: Genjurô, a potter, lives with his wife Miyagi and their little boy Genichi in a village, sixteenth century, surrounded by the din of warfare. An army is coming this way. He must hurry to cart his wares into town to sell them, and then, because the army is coming, the army is coming, the army, the army is coming, he must slave to turn out many more pots, turn them on the wheel with his delicate fingers shaping in the rotations his dutiful wife produces by motoring the wheel to spin. His neighbor and friend Tôbei, a tiller of the soil, craves to become a samurai. The army invades, villagers scatter in all directions screaming, the women are raped or pushed aside and the men are hauled off to be underlings. Genjurô escapes to the forest with his family but then panics that his kiln has gone out: the fire must be kept burning so that his cache of pottery will not be destroyed. Pottery is commerce, and he wants to ensure his family's future against the ravages of war. He sneaks back, and the wife and son after him, and lo and behold, the kiln has indeed gone out! But when he withdraws a piece he sees that it has baked perfectly. It is done! It is wonderful! And so are all the pieces, as he takes them out one by one by one. The pots are piled onto a low craft and the potter and family set out on the lake for freedom. But another craft approaches, with a dying soldier who warns that pirates are out there ready to spring. The potter returns his boat to shore and lets his wife and child off. They wave him goodbye, crying dolefully in the dawn. Now we see him thriving in a marketplace, selling his pots zestfully. A beautiful woman approaches with her elderly maid and buys an enormous supply of his wares, asking that he deliver them to her home. He complies, finding a palatial residence, with plenty of servants, and there is the beautiful woman tended by her old maid. Soon it is evident that she wishes to marry him and without him commenting she falls upon him in a frenzy of rapture. They couple by a stream. But it turns out she is a ghost.

Genjurô escapes and returns home. All is in shadow in his hut, all is quiet. The village seems empty.

He calls for his wife, calls for her, calls for her.

She emerges overwhelmed with joy to see him again. "I have made a great mistake," he sighs, but she urges him to drink sake and to rest with her, to be comfortable at home again. She soothes and envelops him. (This is so profoundly relieving to see!) He rhapsodizes on how wonderful, how peaceful, how perfect it is to be with her. The little boy is asleep. The candlelight is flickering gently. The picture is composed for closure, for tranquility, for the end of war. Softly shadowed space, room to breathe, the warm bosom of love. Home, wife, embrace, soft sleep. A fitting culmination.

Once the potter has fallen off, the wife lights a candle and sits through the night patiently darning a kimono.

All is patience, stillness, sweetness.

Dawn comes.

There is a furious rapping. The potter answers the door to the village chief who walks in, sees the sleeping child, and says, "Oh, there you are!" And now, as the potter proclaims how happy he is to be home again with his wife, the elder looks at him gravely and says, "Oh!!! But Miyagi was killed by the soldiers in the war. I have been looking after the child, and when he vanished last night I could not tell where he was."

Only now do we see something that was laid openly before us, yet openly concealed. That the hut when the potter returned to it was not only peaceful and sweet; it was far too peaceful, far too sweet. This is what happens onscreen: in one single-take pan shot we see him enter a house that is both silent and empty, and make a tour around it before walking outside again. As he re-enters, a peaceful domestic scene has been laid before him. We fail to grasp, either grasp by seeing or grasp by intuiting and believing or both, how in this fluid, unbroken moment the place can have changed. Miyagi's voice beckons him to go to his work, and he turns a pot on the wheel, while she says how beautiful it is, the wheel, the work, life.

Outside later, he stokes his kiln, watches his little boy bring a bowl of food to set down on his mother's grave.

Though there is a brief scene during the wartime fighting when Miyagi is stabbed by a soldier, we do not see her die, and the moment passes in the confusing hubbub of antagonism, every image of which is bound to every other image in a continuing flow (Mizoguchi wanted the imagery to imitate the Japanese picture scroll, and one also thinks of the constructions of Uccello, say "The Flood" or "The Battle of San Romano"[1]). So much agony of war penetrates the story, and so much violence is in the charge of the rich princess in her frenzy to possess the potter (she dies before experiencing the pangs of love) that we tumble ahead in the cacophony with our only concern to see Genjurô escape and find his way home again, a new Odysseus. The logic of the story, to the degree that, full of ghosts, it has what can be called a logic, is the ravage of war. Genjurô and his chum are both continuingly fretting over money in this horrible time, worried about the future of their little families. Soldiers are racing and screaming, moving incoherently in all directions, breaking up civil unities. The symbols of peace are broken or put in the shadow of danger. In short, for all the bucolic simplicity of the narrative space, the story is one of conflict, damage, destruction, and pain. Thus, when we learn that Miyagi is but a shade, is "no longer among the living" nor has been for some time, we should not in any way be surprised.

Until its final shots, in the bright morning of hope, there is nothing but anxiety, fear, degradation. The idyll of the homestead that Genjurô finds on his return can be nothing but an illusion.

Indeed, as we sit in the shadows watching him drink, and being coddled, and falling into sleep, we can have only a dim sensation of beguiling and disturbing tension, a separation between the calmness of the atmosphere and action, its pacific nature, and a dark foreboding that something, somewhere is wrong. Something that has always been wrong . . . When Miyagi picks up the little boy to carry him from her lap to his bed, Genichi hangs in her arms like a corpse—perhaps this is the sign. Or her too utter silence. Or the plainness, the whole abjectness of her devotion. Or Genjurô's half-besotted failure to look at her carefully, though she embraces him. Or the long moments at the beginning of the scene when, as he calls out, there is nothing but cold silence returned to him. We do not catch these details of the scene as first we watch it. And then in the morning, in the clear harsh light, when the leader comes in and gives Genjurô the sad news, we are both saddened by the death (on Genjurô's behalf) and

---

[1] On Uccello and his catastrophes of meaning, see Schefer, *Body*.

chastened to realize we were besotted ourselves. He does not weep, nor does he speak, nor does he move, but only stares at the empty space before his eyes, as we have been staring at the empty space before our own.

In this beautiful film, so much passes in our field of vision, so many angry and desperate folk striving—often to no purpose but the release of impulse—so many pots turned and fired and packed in straw, so many pots held up for admiration, so many gestures of groping, grasping, reaching: how can we follow the story so intently and yet fail to see all of this, until it is too late? Miyagi's wifely duty of causing the potter's wheel to spin while he works: round and round and round, only through her touch, the cycle of life and death. The neighbor chum's frantic desire to become a samurai, procure armor and a sword, against all odds, since he is but a bumpkin farmer; his continual dissatisfaction—that we too easily allocate as a condition of his poor existence, his yearning, his hopeless hopes, without noticing that it is also, even principally, an establisher of the film's deep tone of erosion, decay, disruption, demoralizing, and death. That the too-eager princess declares her passion but wears what seems an expressionless white mask or wears a face that resembles such a mask: the hidden truth covered by eagerness and fire.

I note the beauty of the film—it is exceptionally stunning visually and performatively—in order to highlight how seductive is the screen while we watch it, how evocative the sights, how sensitive the composition of forms. The eye is busy at work all through, something that is not always the case in cinema. And yet for all this attention, demanded from us and willingly accorded, we fail to see. We fail to see the fragility of the circumstances as Genjurô himself fails, for it is only in some ways that he is like Odysseus. Odysseus was prevented from returning home by a chain of forces, only one link in which was his seduction by Circe (of whom this film's Lady Wakasa is an analogue). Genjurô is surely held off, but by the bonds of his own craven desires and ambition—ambition for worldly success (rationalized by him through the pottery) instead of the love of family and home. Held off and distracted by the frenzy of war he voyages, as he thinks, forward. The ghost of Miyagi does not reproach him, but only offers the sweet love he abandoned.

Yet, again, how not to see this, until after she is gone? How to miss the startling emphasis of the ambitions, the anxieties, the fears, the discomforts? Do we miss these features by *reading through them*, aiming our considerations at the characters and their futures? Does the film play to the viewer's forward gaze, then? The forward gaze of the viewer, as this film (and any film) teaches, is impatience, impatience and only impatience, because even without our seeking to know what comes next the film, a form in itself, will insist on telling us. The film is a continual forward-moving design, in fact a scroll, to such an emphatic degree that we can sit calmly, observantly, openly taking it in without the least concern for the ongoing action. Ongoing action proceeds without our motoring energy. Yet we bring that energy anyway, or at least have done so for decades now, since evaluations of cinema published in public organs like newspapers and derived from literary studies have focused on moral tales and their outcomes: tales, not pictures. We have learned the cultural habit of watching movies for the plot. And *Ugetsu* teaches that watching this way will bring us to a great lacuna—a foggy lake, if you like—filled with the piracies of interpretive dangers. In this case, we delve into the scenes to fish out the agents of central action, and we have no trouble accomplishing this task; but delving takes our spirits away from patiently watching, patiently seeing what is right in front of us.

Back at home, Genjurô, too, does not see what is right in front of his eyes, so filled is he with anticipation for his wife and child. Anticipation, the storm against which we cover the eyes.[2]

---

[2] M. Night Shyamalan's *The Sixth Sense* (1999) is an homage of sorts to *Ugetsu*, in which, yet again, a ghost is not recognized as such, again with an arrangement for blindering both a character and the audience.

29

At the Party

Dana Andrews (left) with Vincent Price (center) and Gene Tierney (right) in Laura *(Otto Preminger, Twentieth Century Fox, 1944). Digital frame enlargement.*

Frequently enough in contemporary film (but not only there) we see a party scene. To make sense of it, we note that we are sitting patiently in our private seats without cocktails and without the pleasure of interrupting patter. The cinematic party constitutes both (a) style and (b) identification, as well as (c) a license for the characters. What could this mean?

[a] *Style.* Not that a party scene makes use of decorative style, as in colors, ribbons, banners, sounds, and lighting but that party happenings evidence a *style of behavior*, rather than merely a type. What one does at a party can be done

elsewhere, but the setting confers a tonality and moral culturing *to the act itself*. Just as "walking down an alley stoned-drunk" is a variation on "walking down an alley"—a walking style; just as "speaking whilst under the influence of a religious transport" is a variation on "speaking"—a speech style; just as "forming words in the middle of a heated argument" is a variation on "forming words"—a verbal style; here we have a collection of behaviors all renderable under the "party" rubric yet all essentially variants of plainer renditions: "party dancing" derived from "simple dancing," "party drinking" derived from "drinking," "party conversation" derived from "conversation." In learning how to attend a party, a person gains confidence and awareness in re-styling behaviors already learned elsewhere. "Talk like this: . . ." "drink like this: . . ."

We need to wonder how changes of style (from what has transpired so far in a story) add to, or take away from, the scenic effect. If you're a filmmaker, what can you do with a party scene that you cannot do with an untransformed version of the same action—a plain conversation, a plain lifting of a glass to the mouth?

[b] *Identification*. Albeit an intensive decoration in itself, since parties are generally taken as decorative versions of everyday action, the party scene houses dramatic activity: connections, proposals, reactions, and gestures that work for the filmmaker to inform the viewer about one or more protagonists' attributes. How the voice is elevated to clear the cloud of crowd sound, perhaps. The way the body is held either tense or relaxed, indicative of someone's discomfort or comfort at such an event. An individual's particular behavior at a party, here on open display yet, because of the visually complex action requiring a hunt on the viewer's part, tells us what "a party" means for this person. Whether he or she is a "party animal" or a solo adventurer who is very uncomfortable in such situations. Whether the people hanging out at this party are cozily friendly or hostile (the ball sequence in Baz Luhrmann's *Romeo + Juliet* [1995]). A comment can be made about the social class of central characters, simply by virtue of the conspicuous consumption made in order to effect the scene as we see it. Identifications (and the practice of establishing them) available to writers and filmmakers using a party setting may be simpler, more directly apprehended than identifications set elsewhere, yet it might become apparent how the party scene allows for the camera's motility through space in a unique way; that the sound level and rhythm of the music can aggravate the vision; and that, dramaturgically speaking, the clustering of the party attendees makes possible open secrecies of various sorts, hiding in plain sight, as it were.

[c] *Licence*. Here it is permitted—or at least not enjoined—to do what would in other circumstances be withheld or tabooed; to do such things, or to do them with an energy of commitment, an enthusiasm, a fire unpermitted in conventional situations where close social relations force a certain restrictive modesty. Just as the party licenses extreme behavior for the characters, it licences the showing of such behavior for the filmmaker. The audience can feel fine in

the presence of someone twitching, jerking, and spasmodically moving as long as there is musical support (see *Saturday Night Fever* [1977]) when in other circumstances it might feel awkward for audiences to watch (when, that is, the rubric "dance" cannot be invoked). Not only do characters drink more, speak more freely, and move more spontaneously at a party; the camera can show all this, so that the viewer is entertained by imbibing and inebriation, wild talk, extremity of body gesture.

Usually there will be numerous other scenes in which the same characters distinctively do *not* behave this way, our view of the difference demonstrating how the behavior can be modulated over a variety of social contexts.

Nuances:

[1] A narrated party is distinctly and discreetly identifiable as such. Nobody onscreen has a "secret party"—one that the viewer cannot distinguish for what it is. Usually, the signs are a plethora of people gathered in a bounded space, many of whom we have never seen before; some kind of movement, often "casual" and "shuffling"; and some kind of music. Food or no food, a party can be nourishing and entertaining for the participants, and it is typically presumed by characters and viewers that it will be both.

[2] The camera teaches that we are distinctly and discreetly identified as *non*-participants. We are floating through or perhaps above, but we have not been invited as all these people have; invited or cued; we have not cleared the bouncer at the door; and we often don't know what the party is celebrating. Sometimes we never find out. It is the party as dramatic surface that counts, not the party as indication of purpose (see *The Party* [1968]). We experience our presence as a placement at once within and not within; and we experience the party as a scene that is a "scene." When in everyday life people talk about "the party scene" in which they think themselves involved, they are copying this exact sense of the cinematic presentation of parties, a kind of involvement through alienation, because here the scene seems like an entity in itself, a surround that is not an atmosphere.

[3] The party has its own identity separate from its ceremonial function: it is what it is without reference to what is happening. No matter the inspiration or reason for the event, people "lose" themselves, a "rush" is on. In this sense all parties are the same. Even in sombre gatherings, where the loss of self is through an absorption in some horrid or critical action, and where the rush is a chill, we find the predictable separation from the everyday. For the camera it will be necessary that "loss" of the self is made very explicit, visually. In the opening scene of *Notorious* (1946) where we find Devlin at Alicia's party (without knowing yet who he is) we see a perfectly stationary body (from behind) while all around there is inebriated fluttering: he is not *at* the party that he is in.

[4] The screen population is carefully—but for the viewer also unavoidably—split into two groups, those partygoers who command our attention and those who are there only for realistic background. These latter do not play in the story, have only the most elemental dramatic function (they are not even equivalent to the Greek chorus), mostly to fill space. That is:

[5] The camera glides through the party giving us a plain and unmitigated view of some strangers we do not need to meet, who will not act in a way that bears upon anything we have been following. This kind of shot—the glide over a dense social *nothing*—(it is nothing for us)—has become elemental in cinematic party sequences. The party as a thing itself is thus abstracted from the ongoing story, a kind of attraction. Yet at the same time it is designed for the screen never to attract the viewer's eye so much that attention is lost for the central characters who, just as they were in other locations where we watched, are now manifestly here; here and to be shown momentarily if they are not shown now. Further, the viewer is intended to see that the party is "a party," an organization, not just a random selection of folk (such as in a busy street). Thus,

[6] We sense that all of the characters we see are connected to one another in some way that makes sense to them, even if it is not set forth for us to understand. They all got the same "invitation," saw the same poster, like the same band, want to share the same drug, want to meet someone casually just as the others do, and so on. Whatever it is that brings them here has not brought us here. (We are with a police officer, following a lead, as it were.) And further, whatever they would claim brings them here may be nothing more than a polite cover for what really brings them here, as when the cop edging through the crowd discovers a drug deal or a backroom torture or a captive in chains.

[7] What has led us here is not hunger for a party moment but narrative intent, the presence of the camera placed for a reason we will learn only as the film winds on. We may zoom (figuratively or actually) into a table with particular partygoers or we may pass all the way through to find a vital location adjacent (in an alleyway outside, in a back office). "Fun" is what all or most of the partygoers would claim their intent, but what the viewer needs is to make a find somewhere in the hiding, standing, dancing, waiting action, to discover someone or something the protagonist will discover, too, or signally fail to. But most of the people we see are *just here*.

[8] We can fly over a party in a most unusual way, as though hanging from a suspended track with a pulley system. The "world" is down below, throbbing, kicking, screaming, chattering, jittering, sliding, and we glide with the smoothness of a hawk and with a perfect bird's-eye view, except that there is so much movement to see, color, shape, form, and noise, that the aerial view is not especially helpful to any viewing creature who is actually not a hawk,

and very typically after only a single shot from this perspective we cut down to the floor and move about the bodies, nudging dancers aside. The actors are choreographed to move away from the camera on cue.

[9] Sometimes there is an eruption into violence, when an insult is thrown and responded to with a punch or a stab. The floor clears or is taken up with a melée of fighters. The jittering, rhythmic order becomes chaos—yet a chaos not less carefully choreographed. Normally there is no eruption, however, nor a chance for us to linger long enough to catch one. We mingle until the dramatic moment occurs for which we came, usually a moment of interaction. Aside from moments of violence, in which the protagonists can even be total strangers (the typical bar fight in the classical western), the onscreen party is an occasion when (a) background types act individually or in prearranged pairs, with no serious attention to anyone else, and (b) central characters interact only with each other, standing among the backgrounders, even posed artfully among them, but apparently having no interest. This means that when a character we already know meets a character we have never met before, we understand instantly (and automatically) that this newcomer will likely have some centrality to the story, at least here and now. We know the camera will not dally with an uneventful encounter.

[10] Even when people onscreen "mingle" and meet others (with whom they presumably did not come to the party), these minglers and interactors will all have some architectonic placement *for us*, and the mingling can be a direct clue to the upcoming revelation of a character's as-yet-undeclared centrality. The background crowd have been arranged (usually by the assistant director) to function in front of the camera prettily, but not to be touched physically or interactionally.

[11] In fact, one of the striking ironies of cinematic party scenes is the disjunction between (a) central characters' lack of interest and absorption in background characters and (b) the care and expense with which backgrounders have been cast, dressed, and positioned prettily in frame. The background is full of something to look at, but we look, usually, only while moving, and the central figures do not look at all, except for the target of their hunt.

[12] In the filmic party scene something of dramatic importance happens, and the party is the setting, the agency, by which that happening can be triggered and made visible. That is, in films we do not go to a party merely in order to go to a party. While in the everyday world most people go to parties in order to have a good time (and then go home again), cinematic characters do not go to parties for this reason. While they may or may not be entertained there, they brought themselves in order to take part in an accomplishment, an accomplishment

upon which the scripted action turns. It is not interesting for a viewer to see a character *merely enjoying herself.*

[13] Given that the filmic party is therefore a clear focus of attention between people on one hand (central characters), and a clear focus of disattention between people on the other, one has to wonder at the complications of arranging party scenes when simpler organizations would also do to enhance character-to-character dialogue. What is it, we must wonder, that is added to a two-person dialogue when it is set at a party with a distinctive yet unexamined hubbub in the rear or sides of the shot? Thinking only in terms of the film production itself, the film as film, what are parties for? The answer, "Somebody in the film told somebody else to meet them at such-and-such a club tonight," doesn't work, because the writer made the decision to set the action at a party and could have made another decision. I am asking what the role of such a decision can be, what is gained in films that are not about parties by having a party. The party scene involves scores of extras, set design, special lighting, special camera work, considerable choreography, and time: it costs.

[14] One could make a strong exception for films about performances in front of audiences, especially nightclub-style audiences, where some sort of party is required essentially by the production in order that the "entertainment"—the key feature—be shown for exploration. *Top Hat* (1935), *Modern Times* (1936), *The Glenn Miller Story* (1954), *New York, New York* (1977), *Goodfellas* (1990), *Moulin Rouge!* (2001). Sometimes the "entertainment" is present not for highlighting on its own but only to back up central performers sitting to watch it, as in the Club 54 sequence of *Goodfellas* or the film screenings in *Play It Again, Sam* (1972) or *The Dreamers* (2003). I would also argue that the sitting audience we see in films about musicals or plays, where there is intercutting between stage action and audience attention, doesn't function only as a group of party backgrounders but is to be examined as a special category, a cluster of special participants, whose reactions inform our own. And there are cases where the party is itself a dramatic protagonist (*Some Like It Hot* [1959]), yet even here the central characters pay the least possible attention to the more numerous backgrounders.

[15] It is the presence of backgrounders—invisible backgrounders, in effect—that makes the filmic party scene. So, for example, the Saturday dinner is celebratory in *The Big Chill* (1983) but it is not at all a "party" in the sense I am invoking here, there being no crowd, only protagonists enjoying food and drink. A simple gathering is not a party. A party sequence is a variant of the crowd sequence (as in, say, *The Kingdom* or *The Bourne Ultimatum* [both 2007]), cast in so-named "pleasurable" light rather than in an ominous atmosphere of shooting, explosions, and pain. All crowd sequences have invisible backgrounders.

[16] An interestingly recursive party situation appears in the "Michael's Birthday" section of *Tootsie* (1982), his roommate Jeff (Bill Murray) having arranged a surprise birthday bash for him. Michael (Dustin Hoffman) is flabbergasted and flustered with happiness. But as the scene dissolves to "later on," and almost all of the guests have gone, Michael wants to know where all of these people came from, since he didn't know most of them. Jeff says he phoned a few friends and told them all to call people and bring them. In short, what initially looks to the viewer like a normal and healthy party (where one constantly tries to focus on the film's protagonists through a cluster of assumedly warm connections) turns out to be a fabrication, yet a fabrication in which party backgrounders are all not only backgrounders to the camera but diegetically "strangers," people who didn't know each other and didn't know the central players either. In all filmic parties, one presumes the backgrounders don't know the protagonist(s), but not that they have been culled in the first place so as to give the impression that they do.

[17] The party onscreen can be considered a telltale indicator of purported social mores and cultural times, as when in 1954's *His Majesty O'Keefe* island natives ceremonially perform a ritual, or when *Saturday Night Fever* features a disco party or two, or 1933's *Flying Down to Rio* features an elaborate nightclub, or 2014's *John Wick* features a twilight-blue rave, but the party's indications do not function pre-eminently: the party is usually not onscreen to point to a culture. Beyond mores and interactional patterns (rhythmic movement, curtailed speech, sonic projection) the party setting can indicate informative interior décor and clothing. But the filmic party also turns people into décor. What the party arrangement does that no other social configuration can do equally well, or at all, is to present people this way. That is, to select some figures and reduce them to the status of the furniture, wall hangings, even paintings in frames (Antonioni's *Identification of a Woman* [1982] shows this very well). As the camera passes, each figure merits a swift glance, and perhaps piques a slight interest, but nothing further happens. These are figures for literally fleshing out a setting, importantly filling space. This happens under two social conditions, importantly:

(a) In parties hosted by low-grade workers or the poor, say students or even intellectuals (as in *Annie Hall* [1977]), the space will be cramped because it is a low-rent situation, and so the stuffing of the scene with unidentified revelers helps magnify the sense of spatial depletion. In a small room or set of rooms, a very small number of protagonists will seem at home, and naturally so, whereas the party in such a place can make an unstated claim that there really isn't a lot of room here. For *Mystic River* (2003) Henry Bumstead purposefully built apartments on the small side, exactly in order to produce this nuance of "cramping" even with only a handful of characters in them.

(b) By sharp contrast, parties hosted by and involving the upper class tend to be set in extraordinarily designed and mammoth nightclubs (*Top Hat*) or sumptuous apartments in which the rooms are vast and the furniture pieces set widely apart (the opening-night party in *The Band Wagon* [1953]), or boundless mansions set into vastly spreading manicured lawns by moonlight (*La Notte* [1961]). Here one can conceive of how lonely and how shrunken characters would look if they were all by themselves, but the party gives a pretext for loading the place up with moving figurines who both fill space and to some extent block the camera's view but in any event make the place seem fitting for a party's extremities of action.

[18] If the party music we hear is loud and frenzied, it can be used to give aesthetic contrast to other (surrounding) quieter and less action-centered moments. The party display as a physical, optical organization rationalizes the sudden intrusion into the picture of a musical cue of this sort, that is out of acoustical balance with other cues.[1]

[19] Typically, it is only the main protagonist who will be shown onscreen the "morning after," in a state of depletion (a most elegant case being *Blow-Up* [1966]). The depletion will invoke a trace memory of the party that came before, and is typically not intended to convey any other information in itself, such as a state of affairs in the character's physique that requires specific (dramatic) address. Last night was a BIG WOW and this morning is but a tiny reverberation. The tinier the reverberation—the more hung-over the character—the bigger the party looks in retrospect, but no cause for alarm on our part. This retrospective glance may be the clearest picture we get of the protagonist's experience at the party, since while it was on we were only floating, skimming, bouncing, pulsing, and wondering our way through.

[20] Protagonists typically don't reflect back to comment evaluatively on the party: "Great party last night!!" Characters may reference something they heard or something that happened, but for all its expensive frenzies the party vanishes into thin air.

---

[1] And for a performance that can be included on the merchandised soundtrack.

30

O!

Christopher Reeve in Somewhere in Time *(Jeannot Szwarc, Rastar, 1980). Digital frame enlargement.*

Not only a systematic failure of perception but also the act of sight *extraordinaire* can charge a dramatic moment, yet with a curious structural variation: that the special seeing, whether obscuring or illuminating, problematic or revelatory, painful or sweet, is ours only because it is the character's. It is the character who must undergo revelation, see something carefully built into the narrative frame yet hitherto obscured or hidden from view. The audience can never see more than is given onscreen to see, can never see more, say, than is seen by the most observant and best-placed character, lest the spell of the enchantment be dissolved. When we see more than a character sees we are registering an unseeing one, "present" as we are but unobservant, deluded, blocked, fooled in some way. Or perhaps wounded. The artist, Lawrence Durrell famously asserted, is "the one who is wounded in his sex," but for psychoanalysis, already, the optical wound and the sexual wound are conjoined, a person's sex being a lower face (see Paul).

When we see a character fail to see something that will later be shown to have been hidden from him though *we do see it* now, we have jumped ahead of the film's expression, since the point of that expression, in such a moment, is to refrain from indicating the character's vision until a point we can already deem *too late*. The story is following us (not its characters, exactly). In the following chapter, I will discuss a signal rule-breaking case. But in a typical mystery film, for example, the audience will come to learn a hidden secret just as it is revealed to characters onscreen, not before: *just as*, or instantaneously thereafter (and with apparent simultaneity), since the light from the screen must travel to reach us and by the time we see an image it is gone. Just as the secret is *revealed* to the characters, note, even if they are unseeing and catch the point only after we do. Whether an uninformed character onscreen now sees a truth or remains as yet uninformed, still, that "truth," visually arranged, is given to us. The characters wait for the dramatic trigger (the script); we wait for the light.

Consider the most direct statement of the theme, the viewer closely discerning a *moment in which a character is closely discerning*. This can be a deliriously engaging, even thrilling experience, even if the thrill somehow wounds. Two interesting cases, one on either side of the structural "coin":

[A] In Antonioni's *Blow-Up* (1966), a young photographer is strolling around a quiet park on a Saturday afternoon. Virtually no one is there, the place (as I have indicated in these pages already) is utterly bucolic and green. Two lovers are climbing to the upper level, where they tryst for a while on the green green lawn between rows of green green trees margined by a green-painted picket fence. Kiss kiss, hug hug, whisper whisper. He stands far back, behind a tree trunk, and photographs them at leisure (again, just as I have mentioned earlier in these pages). The photographer goes off to his studio and develops his film. Frame by frame he starts to print the pictures, nice hefty 16 × 20-inch black-and-white images. He tacks these up to look at them in a sequential row. Kiss kiss, hug hug. But—there! She is turning her head to look into the woods beside the clearing. The man is oblivious. She is staring.

Inside a cinematographic image, a photograph being looked at of a woman looking at something.

The photographer rushes back to his darkroom and makes other shots. Looking, looking, looking—in vain. He now frames out part of the telltale picture and makes an enlargement, a tiny rectangle now mounting up into a 16 × 20-inch print—a gigantic blow-up. Grainy, like an abstraction. But when he pulls himself back a little, there!—a pistol in a hand, and a face, all behind the picket fence in hiding. And soon later he goes back to the park, nighttime, green green green grass, low wind, and when—without his camera—he approaches a gigantic bush which had been the backdrop for the kissing, O!, there on the ground, cold as ice, is the corpse of the man. It had been a murder set-up, all of it. Kiss kiss.

From a phase of looking without seeing, the photographer moves to a phase of seeing what he is looking at, and seeing that the woman was seeing, too, yet before he could really see her seeing. (Seeing someone looking differs from seeing someone seeing.) At the instant he is positioned in his studio to see the pistol, so are we positioned to see the pistol, arguably just as he does. One pistol for both of us! We discover it with him, he discovers it with us. When he explores by night, he strides ahead of us and we cannot see what is in front of him, what he is striding up to, what it is that he can see as he strides up, until finally he arrives at the terminus and a shot is made, for our benefit, of the corpse. But he saw it first. Secret revealed. (Or partially revealed.)

Much will happen later in the film, just as much has happened already that I do not adumbrate. The punchline for this photographer is that he will come to a mortal realization of the power of the light that hits his lens, that hits all lenses, and also to a conundrum about the relationship between what is real and what is visible—since finally that corpse, which soon enough vanishes into thin air, was accessible to him only by way of his eyes. "Every looking oozes with mendacity," Julio Cortázar wrote in "Las Babas del Diablo" ("Les fils de la vierge"), or "Blow-Up," the origin of the film.

In this case, to see the secret, to come upon what was hidden, is a sight for sore eyes, a revelation, and its fruit is a kind of release from labor into experience, a freeing. With the photographer, we come to know how one sees with the heart.

[B]   *Somewhere in Time* (1980) tells the strange story of a dramatist, Richard Collier (Christopher Reeve), who is celebrating his new play when an aging woman approaches, hands him a locket, and says, "Come back to me." He does not know her, and later that night we see that she dies. Move forward eight years.

Visiting the Grand Hotel on Mackinac Island, and as vulnerable to influence as any creative spirit, Richard becomes obsessed with a photograph (a sight for sore eyes) of a turn-of-the-century actress, Elisa McKenna (Jane Seymour), a photograph that stuns him. Learning more about her, he comes to know that eight years before, it was she who had been his visitor. Now he has a mixture of perturbation, curiosity, confusion, excitement, and fear.

He finds an old college professor, Dr. Finney (George Voskovec), who has discovered a particular form of hypnosis that will not only allow someone to visit another world—a past world, say—but to actually survive and thrive there. But it demands full, indeed the very fullest imaginable concentration and might be very depleting. Concentration is the key, and the subject must be willing to follow the therapist's guidance in investing himself in his perceptions *completely*; relying on those direct perceptions exclusively, every nook, every wrinkle, every flicker of sunlight on a cheek. Richard tries the self-suggestion but fails. Then, in the hotel's guest book for 1912, he sees—his own signature! So again he tries and this time succeeds. He brings it all in, the world that was, he accepts it, transforms reality so that he *is* in the place he is seeing, just as, here in the everyday, we are all in the world we perceive (our presence a vital supporting pillar of the script, since only because she experiences this fullness of apperception on a regular basis would a filmgoer be willing to believe its power in this story).[1] But Dr. Finney issues a warning (that I paraphrase):

---

[1] The machine of Richard Matheson's script and story derives from William James's chapter, "The Perception of Reality," in his *Principles of Psychology*.

There's only one thing. You must bring nothing of your present life to the place I am sending you to. Nothing of this, nothing of this self, nothing of Chicago where you live, nothing which is nothing which comes of nothing and which will come to nothing. FULL apperception, every wrinkle, every detail, taken seriously for what it is. Every doorway. Every horizon. *You will be where you will be, but nowhere else, and there will exist no other places, other moments, other times.* (That is, inside the dream of his past life, Richard will not have any memories of past life, only direct experience, or "direct experience.")

So now Richard Collier is *actually* at the resort hotel in 1912.

A spreading, sumptuous white clapboard structure in a forest of pines. Guests are strolling in happy leisure, the sun is glowing, the lake is twinkly, the folds in the ladies' garments are spectacular. And there!—yes!, there is the woman we recognize as Elise, young and fresh as a flower, and he is easily besotted with her. The more they stroll, talk, joke, talk, stroll, the deeper it goes and the more he is carried into the special not-quite-dream voyage of love. Nothing gets in his way, not even her manager, William Fawcett Robinson (Christopher Plummer), priggish, perhaps arrogant, perhaps entirely detached in the way that manipulators will be. Robinson wants to control Elise's career but she has become Richard's all. She is the emerald in the ring. She is truth, and most certainly reality. He will not be without her, and she is tumbling into love with him.

His cares evaporate. His passion fires up. His energy becomes substantial. His glow returns. His desire is insatiable. And she is the font and fountainhead of his desire, luring, smiling, teasing, smiling, luring. She is all of literature, all of art, she is music, she is the future.

The film proceeds to build in this way, systematically leading us up the hillside to a throbbing culmination of passion, a commitment of bodies and souls, indeed to an eager and intoxicating lovemaking. Love is conquering all.

Love, which is belief, which is sight without doubt, which is the giving over of the upper and the lower eyes.

But not long later Elise is helping Richard try on a new suit, his own being somewhat out of fashion (for the times). Doffing what he is wearing, he reaches into its pocket and feels something odd there. He withdraws the object into the light and now sees—but in a macro-close-up shot of his palm we see before he does—a 1979 U.S. penny. Instantly, the entire hallucination swirls, fragments, and dissolves away—a wholly nauseating transposition, and he is gagging on a bed in Dr. Finney's Chicago office. Shortly thereafter, we learn that he has had a massive coronary, from which he expires.

31

A Sight for Sore Eyes

James Stewart seeing the mirror image offscreen and left of Kim Novak in Vertigo *(Alfred Hitchcock, Paramount, 1958). Digital frame enlargement.*

In *Vertigo*, we come across a sequence that has caused, and that continues to cause, considerable consternation in viewers trying to iron out the folds of the story. Because a great deal of the shock of this film, as well as the peculiarity of its pleasures, is related to the context in which this sequence fits—fits perfectly although the demurring claim is that it doesn't fit at all!—I shall endeavor to get at it in a way that is somewhat mysterious itself, only to safeguard readers who have not seen *Vertigo* from being given too much information outside the frame. (Information can be the acid that swallows experience.)

The sequence occurs several long breaths from film's end, some breaths after film's middle, and notably after an earlier scene in which, somewhat startlingly, *we come to know something the hero does not know*. Simply:

An eager and pleasant man is with a woman he seems to have fallen in love with, principally because she reminds him of another woman with whom he was in love, somewhat before and quite sadly because she died (not only died but, if one can say this, died most dramatically). Now things are looking up, and our two pleasant, healthy, optimistic lovers are about to go for a terrific (celebratory) dinner. She is dressing in front of her mirror, and he is standing behind her, retired, obedient, adoring, ravenous. And then in a *tiny* turn of action, and *without any preparation at all*, even *in the most casual way imaginable*, he sees in the mirror image something that had been tucked away, now brought into the light. Something suddenly, shockingly, uncannily visible. Something that is functioning for this woman getting dressed as only ornamentation—she is literally acting on automatic pilot reaching for it and lifting it up—but that for our charmed fellow functions as a horrifying reminder, a gateway into a truly horrifying darkness involving an event that he will suddenly now (and rightly) surmise happened one day when he wasn't there to look (a surmise to replace knowledge, because we already learned something that he very notably did not learn; and we still know it; and he still does not). Nothing more need be said in order that we may plummet through the nuances of what Hitchcock has done here. The gist of the scene is a vision that reveals something to a character, a central character, *the* central character, that until this moment he did not know.

We can claim to have had what people call "inklings" earlier, in that educational scene, although we certainly cannot claim to have had clear knowledge. Not even we, watching everything. But as the image swoops in, we are not exactly shocked—as he is. So:

The argument put forward, and by no one more pressingly than by Hitchcock's own personal assistant at the time, Joan Harrison, is that the earlier scene was badly misplaced, indeed placed in a most obstructive way. It ought to have come much later, if at all, when in an explosive climax Scottie (our man in San Francisco) learns, sees, knows, explodes—all together. It should have been *the punch*. Since the secret involves the lady (Judy: Kim Novak), such a construction would establish a solid architecture in which she rode very high as the centerpiece of the story. A film about two women, Madeleine, whom Scottie loved and who died tragically, then Judy, whom Scottie grows to love in part because she reminds him of Madeleine. A story about love and thought, love and doubt, love and reflection, love and memory, love and the search for love; where the love object, here and now Judy, should be the diamond in the setting. Harrison wished the offending scene would disappear if it could not be shifted. It marred the diamond. It ruined the setting. She was defiant, Joan Harrison, even scolding. "Oh, Hitchy . . . !"

Hitchcock asked his editor George Tomasini to make a version without the scene, and this cut was screened for a small audience of the key players in the production. "I didn't even look around to see who came to see the picture," executive producer Herbert Coleman remembered:

> Even though I hadn't invited Joan Harrison, I wasn't surprised to see her sitting right beside Hitch.
> There wasn't an audible reaction to anything during the two-hour running. But the instant the screen went blank and the lights came on in the projection room, she jumped to her feet and yelled out, "Hitchy! How could anyone want your picture to be seen any different from this?"
> There was absolute silence from everyone else in the theater. I got up and walked away from the others. After a brief moment Hitch joined me. "Well, Herbie. That's

it." I told him the silence in the room should tell him he was making a big mistake. He didn't like that, and we began to argue.

We were standing face to face. Our voices were rising. Finally, he'd had enough and gave me the first direct order he would ever give me in all the years we worked together. "Release it just like that."

I pushed past him, crossed through the silent group, and hurried out of the theater. Before I'd reached the corner of the camera building, Jimmy Stewart ran after me. "Herbie," he said, "you shouldn't get so upset with Hitch. The picture's not that important."

"Is Hitch right, Jimmy?" I asked.

"No," he said. (Coleman 263–4)

But recutting *Vertigo* Harrison's way was not to prove so very easy. "Prints had been delivered to exchanges all over the country. Every exchange had to return that one reel. I had to find Benny Herrmann and have him come in and adjust the music. He wasn't a happy man when he heard the news" (264).

And worse: after a recut and a remix, "Five hundred prints were shipped to the exchanges, and they were ready to distribute them to the theaters when all hell broke loose":

Jack Karp [Jacob Karp, Paramount legal counsel] called me to his office. I'd never seen him upset before. He was a kind man with his emotions always under control. But not that morning. "Where's Hitch?" he asked.

"Up at his ranch. Why?" I asked.

"I've just had a call from [Paramount Chief] Barney Balaban. I've never known him to be so angry. He wanted to know what you've done to *Vertigo*. He said that after all the great statements he's made about the picture, he arranged a private showing [of the recut] for the top critics in the East. And calls have been coming in from all of them that *Vertigo* is a disaster. He wants Hitch in my office tomorrow morning." (264–5)

Hitch was startled to hear of this. "Have you told Lew [Wasserman, Hitch's agent and financial partner] about this?" Coleman advised him to speak with Balaban first, and this Hitchcock-Balaban conversation was dramatically brief. Dramatically and without report. "H[itchcock] was . . . looking through my secretary's office into mine. 'Put the picture back the way you had it.' He turned away, went into his office, and closed the door. The mental picture of Hitch disappearing into his office was deeply disturbing" (265).

(Coleman's hypothesis is that the overly friendly Joan Harrison by her blurted comment put Hitchcock in an impossible social situation, since they were very close; thus he went along. I would take the supposition even further, Coleman also having made it clear that Harrison was no ally of his: Hitchcock never did intend to cut that scene, and that is why it was there in the first place. But the social relation with Joan Harrison dictated that he put on a show. He knew very well that Balaban, adoring the film as it was, in fact cherishing it as his own (!), would never tolerate the change, and in that short conversation in Balaban's office he no doubt smiled and said, "Of course!")

To emphasize for focal clarity in this present context: what this scene, that raised such a furor and that put Hitchcock in darkness, leads to, bluntly, is a moment in which Scottie sees something. Scottie sees; we see Scottie seeing. And seeing what he sees, seeing him seeing it, involves the little construction Hitchcock established with elegant clarity earlier in the picture (see Pomerance, "Visit"). Everything now hinges on one shot, a visual revelation. A visual eruption. And the victim of this is Scottie, who now ascends to his true position in the film's structure as its indisputably main pillar but who was no pillar at all when he hadn't seen.

Scottie, the retired police detective, the man who looks at details so that he can put together everyday puzzles in the real everyday world, objective, sensible, feet-on-the-ground Scottie (a telling feature, since he is recovered from leg injuries), Scottie who at her husband's heartfelt request followed Madeleine because it seemed she may be haunted, Scottie who came to believe that yes, haunted she was, haunted and haunted and haunted, and who fell in love with Madeleine, in no small part because he was haunted by her being haunted. Scottie, who lost her suddenly, catastrophically. Scottie who lingered ages in a sanatorium unable to grieve, since at least part of what he lost was a ghostly trace. Scottie floating on the surface of the city, faithless, purposeless, hopeless. Scottie who met Judy. Scottie who thought he might be able to love again. Scottie who worked to reconfigure this girl, who called up the ghost image of Madeleine. Scottie, tied to Judy now, and lashed to a post between rationality and fantasy, Scottie who wants to love because he has long wanted to love. Scottie, riding the precarious perch on which Eros archly sits.

And now, Scottie overthrown. Fallen like Humpty Dumpty. Fallen down and further down, down past the limits. Pillar of the story, yes, but a crashed pillar. And all the King's horses. Because he is now aware that his powers of detection are of no avail. And his powers of belief are of no avail, too. He is standing in oblivion as the film ends, at the top of a tower with a stormy sky in the distance and his hands outstretched to offer up nothing, to the void. *Nothing will come of nothing.*

This complex revelation, that both faith and science can desert us, is possible only because in that hotel room, watching her dress for a dinner he is hungry to eat, Scottie sees something in the mirror. Scottie sees and knows because he sees. And we know, too, suppositions aside, because we see what he sees and because we see him seeing it, and because we feared that someday he would. From here on in, we are waiting with breath abated to find out what he will do now. Waiting, now that he knows what we know, to see what will come of it. *Nothing will come of nothing.* Waiting, watching the tomb.

Made available to the viewer in *Vertigo*, as in so many other Hitchcock films, and especially as regards this mirror scene, is the agony of sight, direct confrontation with the ravages and implications of the act on which all viewers are engaged. Scottie has been tasked with viewing, then has grown accustomed to viewing, and finally has become obsessed with viewing, even from the celebrated point so early on when, dangling from a gutter to save his life, he gazes askance and downward into the peril of the street, which is made, through the expression on his face, to seem in another world. He is the man who is asked to use his eyes, to observe someone, to keep someone "under observation," to *surveil*. The surveiller observes. The shocking observation Scottie now makes in front of the mirror not only stuns his present consciousness and forces a recalibration of everything that has gone before but undercuts it, undercuts everything that has happened to him since he retired from the police force before the movie began. And of course, though we are not told this directly in the film, he left the police force out of defeat, too: that while he dangled from a rooftop in fear, he could not prevent a policeman from plummeting to his death; that finally he was unable to catch the criminal they were chasing; that he was a complete failure. To be a failure and recover one's balance, walk the streets again, temper one's painful memory, and even find another love are all one thing; to be shocked to the core in that second love is quite another.

But because Scottie is a surveiller at heart—for Madeleine Elster's husband an ideal choice, who will be an ideal witness to all he sees—because he puts a lot of credence in what his eyes detect, two conditions immediately obtain. First, here as elsewhere in the film, he believes what he sees. ("The mind believes what it sees and does what it believes": Artaud [27].) Second, and for the viewer worse, he shows his affinity with the Others who surveil him from the theater's darkness, because those Others, too, believe what they see. Every new revelation helps dissolve the revelations and knowledge of the past, recasts things, makes new alignments. Every "I see!" is at the same time "I did not know what I thought I knew." And to have one's pivot on the world jostled, to be shaken in the depths, is an affliction that a quiet rest—even time itself—cannot heal.

The One-Eyed Stranger

{32} It's Like This

{33} Taking Off

{34} Topographies

{35} Forget Me Not

{36} Inspired

{37} Shades in the Dark

{38} The Jitters

{39} Irrational Space

{40} Spaced Out

{41} Rabbit

{42} M'm! M'm! Good!

{43} Brotherly Love

{44} The Star's Twin

{45} Wink Wink

{46} Filmic Is Filmic

{47} Read This

{48} Time This

32

It's Like This

Joe Pesci (left) with Robert De Niro in The Irishman *(Martin Scorsese, Tribeca, 2019). Digital frame enlargement.*

Martin Scorsese's *The Irishman* (2019) is a modernist string trio, each of the principals intensely characteristic and their harmonic combinations surprising. Regardless of the storyline, the setting, the aggression, and moral rectitude upon which the film stands (like many other Scorsese films), it is unmistakable to viewers that they are attending the play of Robert De Niro, Joe Pesci, and Al Pacino, three actors who have never appeared as a threesome onscreen before and all three of whom, like their characters (if less discernably), are aging.

Act I is a back and forth between De Niro and Pesci, in some ways calling up *Goodfellas* (1990) and *Casino* (1995) (more than *Raging Bull* [1980]) and showing a ritual of masculine bonding that hovers over a latent miasm of violence. This is the exposition in which De Niro's Frank Sheeran learns "to paint houses" (when a man is shot in the head, the blood spatter colors the wall red). In the De Niro–Pesci interactions, the narrative makes temporal leaps all through the film with the actors undergoing physical modification accordingly, these modifications intended as signals to the viewer about the time settings of the episodes onscreen. De Niro is devoted of purpose but somber, even mournfully afraid, ungraceful, courting physical and psychological fragility. Pesci's Russell Bufalino is tranquil and reassuring, even fatherly, with a storehold of wisdom and uncountable friends. He is joined onscreen for a few marked moments by Harvey Keitel as a mob boss. Russell, childless, has taken it into his head that Frank is his inheritor, and even near film's end, as the two old men sit with some wine and a loaf of bread that toothless Russell can no longer eat, he commands, "Eat, eat my son." If the song played out between these two is dirgeful in part, it is also deeply contenting, offering the effective simulacrum of a familial bond that each, in his way, needs.

Act II is a back and forth between De Niro and Al Pacino, playing Jimmy Hoffa at his most belligerent, sophistic, dynamic, galvanizing. Pacino gives the impression of having a youthful energy under his leathery surface, though in the decades he has been performing—I saw him onstage in early 1970[1]—this energy has been metered some and brought into register (while in his very early work his acting was like electricity). As Russell adopted Frank before, Jimmy adopts him now, bringing him to his side as protector, agent, and stalwart support in quiet moments of lonely friendship. Paced into urgency by the repeated intrusions of Tony "Pro" Provenzano (Stephen Graham), an insistent warmaker even more provocative than he (and to his deep surprise), Hoffa needs Frank more and more as time goes by, and in accordance with this developing complexity of attachment Frank hardens and changes, learning about the conflicting political machinations of the AFL, the Mafia, and the Kennedy administration. Hoffa begins cocky, develops brassy, and finally becomes paranoid.

Act III is a play with all three figures together, Frank torn between two fathers, as it were. In Hoffa's five-year absence by way of a jail term, the union has been taken over by a second-in-command who affiliates with the mob, specifically "Pro," Jimmy's arch-enemy. Russell patiently urges Frank to explain to Jimmy that the world has changed, and Frank patiently fails to make Jimmy see a thing. We flip back and forth between Russell urging Frank, with more and more deeply felt consternation, and Frank trying his damnedest to urge the recalcitrant Jimmy, the Jimmy whose sole proclamation, strident and high-pitched, is, "It's my union!" The climax is slowly made more and more predictable, its moment slowly and slowly made more and more unavoidable, since Jimmy refuses to budge and it has become clear to Russell that the mob is losing enormous sums of money because Jimmy insists on protecting the union pension fund which they have been using as a "bank." Jimmy has to go. And Frank has to be the one to be his painter. "It's what it is."

The film ends with an extended Coda, very gray and slow, in which we learn of the final moments of Russell and then find Frank in old age, both of them winding down their lives in disability and doubt. Russell remembers Jimmy as a nice guy. Frank cannot find the words to show a young priest contrition. The twentysomething nursing-home aide who checks Frank's pulse doesn't have a clue who Jimmy Hoffa was (one can virtually hear Scorsese quietly weeping).

---

[1] Something of a euphemism! Playing Kilroy in *Camino Real* at the Vivian Beaumont (and not yet thirty years old), he was quite literally all over the theater, up and down.

An elaborate plot weaving into and out of historical fact, elaborating backroom connections between social forces of the greatest pith: the Kennedy White House and brother Bobby Kennedy's attack on Hoffa, mob controllers in and around the Midwest and New York, and the AFL-CIO, controlling rig drivers across America. Hoffa: "If you have food, a truck brought it." Typically, marvelous Scorsesean location choices and use of color by designer Bob Shaw and cinematographer Rodrigo Prieto. Perfectly evocative period pop music selected by Robbie Robertson. Predictably astounding editing by Thelma Schoonmaker, never sharper.

And yet—

We must note the instrumentation, or, as musicians would call it, the "orchestration," since no matter the composition, no matter its coloring and phrase, what comes frontally to work on the viewer is the casting. And here, most likely through no fault of their own, De Niro, Pesci, and Pacino simply do not eclipse themselves enough to believably inhabit their characters, not that we do not see them diligently trying. With whatever personality off the screen, each of the three has accreted an actorial persona as impenetrable as a mollusc's shell. Pesci manages to go farther than the other two, yet still there is no moment when he is not Joe Pesci, especially, perhaps, in scenes where his makeup is (obviously) intensive. The more intensive his Russell mask, the more intensively he must work to keep himself from peeking through it. Pacino has done a lot of work here with his physique and vocal pitch, and indeed he has moments when he seems to have sunk into Hoffa, but he doesn't fail to resurface as Pacino, most troublingly in the culminating episode where Jimmy is escorted to his death (in which his presence echoes that of his "Lefty" Ruggiero in *Donnie Brasco* [1997]). As for De Niro, certainly a performer of great strength, he cannot now, nor ever could, gracefully mask himself. The facial gestures are pure tells, no matter his assiduous work on posture and walk and blankness of stare. We keep waiting for the next "De Niro tweak," and faultlessly he delivers it, that deliverer never quite being Frank Sheeran. Therefore, we are never quite in the 1960s. Never quite separated from Martin Scorsese and his camera. There may be no actor of the present era who more crisply shows the debilitation of stardom than the brilliant De Niro, as adventurous a performer as has ever acted in front of the camera, a student of Brando, a model of commitment and seriousness. Yet, at the same time—and I do not mean to disparage or diminish what he does—he has been caged by his publicity, typed as an epigone, held up for interrogation by every sort of interviewer on every sort of subject, in short, he has had his off-camera presence so sharply lit and drawn to the audience's awareness he cannot seem to be anyone else. One sees him incessantly laboring to overcome this pressing debility, and failing, since the devotion to his craft's labor is, indeed, one of the indelible characteristics of De Niro that has been flaunted in advance to the public. The harder he works, the more he is Robert De Niro working.[2]

And yet—

---

[2] See as well Chapter 22.

Viewing *The Irishman*, one swirls into these morphing faces, constantly seeing not only a build-up of makeup but a build-up of time, the person as accretion, and something unanticipated emerges: the actor living through his tenuous relationship with his character, the actor working the character in front of our eyes, and working it breath by breath—like the puppeteer who shows himself. And now for each of these three central protagonists we get a glimpse of two beings, who alternate like the allotropes of carbon. At one pole is the actor face-to-face with his makeup and his script, knowing how he is being layered over, even buried by an attempted masquerade—a masquerade all too easily seen, all too deftly registered—and at the other is the fleshed-out character, if not exactly alive then as close to being alive as any puppet can be, perhaps more alive to the viewer because related so directly to the performer who is alive in the viewer's world. Again: the makeup and performative contrivance induce awareness of time passing; awareness of time passing spurs awareness of aging and mortality; awareness of mortality invokes awareness of life. While such a layering will occur anytime a major star takes on a film role, any star, any role, something is added here through the agency of the "sign-boarded" temporal movement, which process makes decreasingly possible the obscuring of the actor face. But paradoxically, the actor faces here, more visible indeed through fictional time, and their elaborations of make-up quite notwithstanding, are grown aged, too, so that the more they are painted the less they need to be painted, the more they are wrinkled the more the wrinkles are real. Never quite invisible, the actors artfully share the characters' condition.[3] If for contrast we took the Howard Hughes portrayed in Scorsese's *Aviator* (2004), filmed by the 29-year-old Leonardo DiCaprio, we could easily see the startling effect of greeting old age shown by actors who are greeting old age.

---

[3] A circumstance that is entirely elided in computerized "aging" programs used both for entertainment and as assists in retrospective cold-case identifications. To see some artistic rendition of what someone "would" or "could" look like decades hence is a far cry from watching people onscreen whom one has been watching for, literally, decades playing characters in an editorial set-up that gives the feeling that we have been watching them for decades, too.

33

Taking Off

Andre Gregory with Wallace Shawn (left) in My Dinner with Andre *(Louis Malle, Janus, 1981). Digital frame enlargement.*

The idea of discontinuity is born in our experience. Experience prefaces language; experiential thought prefaces linguistic expression of thought. Beyond the fact that every night when I fall asleep I lose track of where I was the day before, I have five times experienced radical discontinuity in my life.

- When I was very young, four or five, I was struck in the temple by a swinging baseball bat. There is still a vestige of a scar. I know that later I was tended by my parents but the period between the baseball bat connecting with me and the walk home is a complete blank.

- When I was about eleven or twelve, I was backing up in a schoolyard to catch a fly ball and the world disappeared. I must have struck a telephone pole. I have no knowledge of what came after, none at all, nor any memory of being cared for, picked up, taken anywhere, or doing anything—although of course at some point I

- must have gone back to school in a normal way. For all I can say, I may have been unconscious for a long time. No one ever mentioned the event to me.

- In my fifty-seventh year, I badly broke my leg in two places and was anesthetized for surgery. I know that I awoke with a cast, but nothing of the surgery.[1] I envision the surgical action vaguely, based on the many instances of it I have seen imitated in the media.

- Twelve years later I had another surgery, to remove an infected gall bladder. In this case I remember the cheery operating-room nurses in dark blue outfits, then nothing until awakening in a warm room under a dull green blanket to tea and cookies.

- Most strangely, perhaps: when I was about fifteen or sixteen I was performing something on a piano before an audience. Suddenly in the middle, I blacked out, lost my place on the keyboard. *My place*: the keys upon which each of my fingers were to press and the progression of keys through which they were to move. I didn't know where anything was. This was but a bar or two of music, and the lapse was, perhaps, two or three seconds. I knew absolutely where I was on the keyboard beforehand and absolutely where I was headed as my fingers found their place once again and raced on. But during that brief hiatus, it was all pitch black and I knew—and still know—nothing.

From my voyages into darkness, my discontinuities, I awoke and moved one. And now I am here.

Time, one can take to be homogeneous and unceasing, no matter the consciousness of it that we may have—which is something else. Time is not time consciousness, it is not the conception "Time," or the word "t-i-m-e" (in English), or any proposition about "time" that could be framed (such as that it progresses in a certain way: "Time flies"). Time, if it even exists outside our ways of thinking and talking about it, is all-present, continuous and boundless. One often hears people speak of this word *continuous*, of *continuity*, meaning an unfolding of time and crossing of space without breaks (whatever a "break" might be imagined to be). It is only under very particular circumstances that we become—that it is necessary to become—conscious of continuity, or for that matter discontinuity, since for the most part our understanding of ourselves in the world, and of the world in which we are, stands upon isolated experiences withdrawn from the flow. Withdrawals may be 1/24th second long, or much, much longer, but between withdrawals, between episodes of awareness, much is likely not caught. Harold Edgerton's famous "crown of milk" photograph, made at something like 1/2000th second, reveals something usually not caught. A person can be conscious of discreet events, indeed one might say that consciousness is a process of gathering

---

[1] Regarding this incident, and in a wholly different light, I wrote about *Rear Window* (see "Recuperation").

and arranging discreetnesses, but any such consciousness (or lack of it) takes place, is set, against a background of which one is not conscious, or at least not conscious of being conscious, and whether there is continuity between the discreetnesses, or not, is something to be conceived. Conceived and only conceived. Surely language can effect a continuity of sorts, but language is not the thing language addresses.

Continuity and discontinuity are vital aspects of cinema.

What happens as we fabricate the idea of *filmic* continuity and the idea of *filmic* discontinuity? Filmmakers, editors, writers, and performers manage such fabrication all the time at work, it's part of the texture of their labor. Continuity people or script assistants are hired literally to attend to "continuity" and to help the filmmaking team avoid unintended "discontinuities": how far down did he smoke that cigarette in the shot that will come previously when the film is edited, so that we can get another very correct half-smoked cigarette for the pick-up? What is this "continuity" that is sought, this "continuity trouble" that is artfully avoided? Between one discreetness and another, the first coming before and the second coming after, a whole daydream could pass.[2]

Whereas film has allowed us to experience movement as a jump across a particular interval, the jump *as jump* is disguised in the speed of the edit. We know how the human inability to detect 1/24th of a second makes possible "magical" edits, as in the prolific work of Georges Méliès. But we also do not detect many of the jumps we make with printed text. In reading, another optical/linear experience, one might seize a word leaping up from a line of text, then, going back, pick up still other words, until finally assembling through linkage what could be called a "meaningful sentence." The eye moving across a printed line seems to accomplish fluid continuity only because as experienced readers we have learned to assemble quickly. It is perhaps true for most readers that the assembling is fastest and smoothest between the end of one line and the start of the next. Consider the semblance of fluid continuity that is created by eliding— even, possibly, thinking of oneself as eliding—the tiny gaps between letters and the slightly less tiny gaps between words. Reading trouble is continuity trouble. We do glide forward when we read, as Orson Welles's camera does in Thatcher's library when Kane scans a text, or when, in François Truffaut's *Fahrenheit 451* (1966), as Montag reads the first lines of *David Copperfield*, the camera-eye moves (continuously, and in homage) past the words on the screen. To follow these so-thought "fluid" camera movements across printed words we *assemble,* and the camera movement is calculated to be patient (slow) enough that assembling is possible.[3]

---

[2] Henry James recollected this about a Christmas when he "was dining with friends: a lady beside me made in the course of talk one of those allusions that I have always found myself recognizing on the spot as 'germs.' The germ, wherever gathered, has ever been for me the germ of a 'story,' and most of the stories straining to shape under my hand have sprung from a single small seed" (119).

[3] A challenging analogue is the close-up of smartphone text in many contemporary adventure films: the editor must decide how long this shot should remain onscreen (in order, in its very remaining, to capture the spirit of instantaneous texting communication). Very often book readers find that these phone-screen shots move by far too quickly—that the text lines on the phone's screen cannot fully be read.

As perceived on the screen, neither "continuity" nor "discontinuity" is real in the sense of mirroring or reflecting some pre-cinematic state of affairs, since both the sense of space and time that we label "continuous" and the sense that is labeled "discontinuous" are constructed out of what Einstein hypothesized as the "ether," an indeterminately (but definably) homogeneous subtending flow, and our constructing is arbitrary. Film guides our sensing continuity. An editor structures the length of the shots a viewer "moves" through, and a shooting configuration has been designed for fixing the camera's exact position and distance from each of two parties conversing (Hitchcock sometimes varies the lens-to-face distance on both sides of a shot). The pauses in speech, the breathing, and the speed of action and response through gesture are all fabricated in performance or finished in editing, yet it is easy to think there is a single dominating happening, *the flowing event as it proceeds*, as long as there are no interruptions that bring us to another space or another time. *Continuity* of onscreen happening is in the regard, and is experienced and understood as the absence of discontinuity. We think of events as being continuous when we do not detect—when we do not believe we have reason to detect—discontinuity.

What is this discontinuity? What circumstance do we not detect?

[1] *Manifest non-contiguity*. One interprets every perceptible shift—of angle, of distance, of location, of indicated temporal moment—as a discontinuity of sorts, yet most of the time, especially with angles and distances, no disturbance arises. A single view of a person's face shifting to a second view of that face tends to present the two faces as identical and the movement as continuous in narrative, even though of course it could not possible be that. On the sound stage or location, a camera angle means a set-up, so that going from angle No. 1 to angle No. 2 involves breaking for another set-up, involving the labor of many people, all of them paid. Editors (successfully) assume viewers will read appearances of spatial contiguity as cues to continuity in time, so that in shifting angles on a character a filmmaker may work to find what will read as a chain of contiguous backgrounds (even, sometimes, the same background!). If shooting is happening on a boat which is bobbing in the sea (as in *Jaws* [1975]), so that the line of the horizon seen against the gunwale of the boat keeps moving up and down, finding contiguity to achieve "continuity" can be a nightmare.

Discontinuity in time can manifest as a lapse in "temporal contiguity," this often indicated in travel scenes with characters moving from a declared point A to an obviously uncontiguous point B, so that the movement could not be accomplished swiftly in the non-diegetic universe. Even a jump from a living room sofa to a bedroom closet. If the view is from one spot and then the other, and if there is no discernable movement between them, there is non-contiguity, and the central issue for the filmmaker is whether or not *non-contiguous* is what this will *appear to be*. Often camera angles are used to "camouflage" the jump by making one space appear to be probable in relation to another. As long as consideration does not go to the distance between spaces, the travel required to leave one and land in the other, there will be a sensed continuity. It is possible to play with the viewer, say by having a woman in medium-shot walk into a room through a doorway that looks like, but isn't, the door she approached in long-shot previously. This *irony of continuity* can itself be pronounced and made the basis of an audience's pleasure.

A viewer's sensing discontinuity does not immediately call for accounting, theorizing, or speculation, or repair, since audiences may well have grown accustomed to a style of storytelling in which sporadic discontinuities play an important part. Further, such discontinuities may be designed to seem intentional and unintentional at once. A marvelous example of the play of conceptual discontinuities is Louis Malle's *My Dinner with Andre* (1981) where, after a brief prologue and before a brief epilogue, the entire film spills out at one table in one restaurant on one evening, between two people eager to speak to each other. All of the shifts of camera position between framing Andre (Gregory) and framing Wally (Shawn) are of course made in discontinuous real offscreen time but are cut together in fluid continuity, with careful matching of both image and sound recording. But Andre is so uncannily provocative a raconteur that while he talks it repeatedly seems as though we have traveled to the locations he mentions, as though we stand and watch the tales' unfoldings quite as though they are films-within-the-film. The film has many of these "voyages." In point of fact, we never leave the dinner table and all our jumps lead to views of conversing faces.

A sense of overriding narrative continuity stands over any other sense of movement. Continuity even over historical time. Even aware of temporal and spatial jumps, still viewers regard themselves as attached to a narrative presence that is powerfully continuous. As all these events take place, take their particular places, the film smoothly, ongoingly tells it all.

[2] *"Remembering."* "Moving backward in time," as narratives pose it, calls up the figuration that is called "memory," a character's memory, the seen or unseen narrator's memory; and memory is rarely thought to be fluid and continuous. Thus, as the storylines recede from a "present" moment through a chain of past moments in reverse historical order, one has a sense of discontinuous jumping and a sense of dislocation, confusion, being lost. One keeps getting lost, then finding a path, then getting lost, then finding another path—and hoping one will be able to keep the paths one is finding embedded in a single map of a single territory (the idea of the coherent film itself, challenged supremely in Buñuel's *The Phantom of Liberty* [1974]). In terms of the mechanics of production, there is an interesting flashback problem: how long, across what distance, and with what poignancy can a flashback be sustained *as such*, before it converts into direct narrative—operationally, before we get to a point where the audience forgets the flashback is a flashback?

In watching a film one takes—knowingly—a few hours out of the continuous progression of a day in order to occupy a dark discontinuity-in-itself, a cavern in a kind of nowhere to which the pathway is strangely unlocatable and from which one returns homeward—if homeward at all—stunned. Schefer notes how as he is watching, at the same time people are killed somewhere—but he does not note this *while he is watching*. One must know, going in, that no matter the conceit of the film, traditional or non-traditional, rational or preposterous, the thing will begin and then proceed from its beginning until it reaches its end, and as it is on the screen the film will be the only importance: that is, knowing what Schefer knows about film in the world, one also knows how to block that knowledge away. We import to the narrative (any and all narratives) an expectation of, a belief in continuity of a kind, and when the actual filmic surface offers jumps, discontinuous passages, leaps across non-contiguities, we loyally maintain the belief in the fundamental continuity of the happenings albeit the narrative presence behind all this (the puppeteer) is outpouring a development that can be aimed outward only in this exact (possibly jumpy) way. Later, in the penumbra, meditating in a café, one loyally maintains the belief that there, events will transpire continuously, movements will not leap—though for all anyone can be sure, in between sips of latte one falls asleep (like River Phoenix's narcoleptic Mike in *My Own Private Idaho* [1991]), falls asleep or daydreams; or gazes off in distraction not recorded and thus unremembered. It is possible to trust in the continuity of experience regardless of hopping around mentally from thought to thought, from theoretical angle to theoretical angle; and for me, regardless of my knowing I can tell you five times in my life I was unconscious; regardless of my own habitation of this singular place and potential meditative dismissal of it. Perhaps in a daydream I travel to a city I lived in years ago and then return. Musing and returning are possible because the place of return can be taken as unchanged from the place of take-off, although of course whilst the film has captured one in private reverie, whilst one was *not there*, many happenings may have taken place one after the other continuously (even eventfully).

One lands "back home," and works to "fit back in," but the work is not difficult, we like to think.

We daydream, we watch, taking a liberty. We take the liberty to daydream. As do characters in the films we love.

With this ability to leave and reinhabit a continuity lies the root of some interesting (usually sci-fi) narratives in which some radical shift in the "natural" continuity of a place makes a traveler who was at home there and who departed, suffer problematic "bends" on return. Usually the condition of "displacement" is negotiated onscreen through a metaphor, since the screen action *as screen action* can only be continuous. *The Return of Martin Guerre* (1982): a young man literally disappears from his tiny feudal village and several years later returns from nowhere. *Source Code* (2011): an operative on an exploding train, seeking a bomber, is "withdrawn" from the action at the vital instant by means of a (rather incomprehensible) scientific process. *Interstellar* (2014): a man goes off into space and when he returns finds that much more time has gone by on earth than has gone by for him in his spaceship (all this no surprise to us knowledgeable sorts, of course, but experientially shocking for him).

The contiguity essential to forward flow need not be especially designed for the screen, nor shown there in a camera configuration that puts spatial or temporal representations adjacent in some novel way (the split screen used in *Pillow Talk* [1959] is a cute example). Contiguity can be opened to the imagination through detailing in the script, as when, for example, a character in a space invokes silently what is just outside the frame, or when, listening to a character talk we imagine what a person like this could have said beforehand and will probably say later. Remarkably, this filling in, of both space and sound, is something managed with regularity. Typically in movie trailers, scenic spaces that are not adjacent in the story as it will be told are positioned across jump cuts, even sometimes with the sound from one scene overlaid upon the other; one expects this special thrill of sharp discontinuity in trailers, either through scenic editing or, as in the "old days," through the superimposition of glaring text over images not directly referenced. The more discontinuous the trailer the more seductive may be the film, since the trailer offers it as a puzzle requiring the viewer's participation, what McLuhan called "cool" (*Media* chap. 2).

[3] *Comedic Discontinuity.* Comedy often works through repetitive discontinuity. In a typical set-up/punchline joke structure, verbal or visual, the punchline works most explosively if it does not flow continuously from the set-up but arrives as the result of a kind of mental leap—yet, of course, always a leap that can be made. Leaps, even when action onscreen is worked out to be continuous in spite of this structural discontinuity. In *The Big Store* (1941) Harpo and Chico Marx play a little duet on the piano at the end, the music sweetly flowing along, with some engaging repetitions to hook the listener. Suddenly Harpo is standing behind his brother and reaching under his legs to get at the keyboard. This move is probable (that is, sensible, logical, thus continuous) only if one knows Harpo already, and many who watch this film may not. This example also works to show how the perception of continuity and discontinuity will have a great deal to do with extraneous knowledge. One could argue about comedy that the more discernable the punchline from a distance, the clearer it is before one gets there, the flatter the joke. A comedian will work like a magician, leading the audience to expect that they do see the punchline coming, a sort of "inevitability," but then deliver something from *off-*: an idea or ideational fragment that was waiting in the wings, another thought altogether, some different conceptualization of time and/or space. In *Duck Soup* (1933), Harpo is repeatedly hilarious using his scissors to snip off parts of people's costumes, even though we recognize that he is the sort of creature to do this. Each snip seems to come out of nowhere because improbable against the vision of a man ogling soldiers' helmets with relish and admiration.

[4] *Discontinuity by Unfamiliarity.* When the viewing public is deeply informed about the subject of a film account, say, in the mid to late 1970s and the decade that followed, about the Watergate Affair in all its details, a film like *All the President's Men* (1976) can seem to flow forward with logical implications and connections all adequately filled in by the canny viewer—in short, a continuous recounting even though there is much hopping around space and time; yet for a younger audience unfamiliar with the historically highlighted details of the

case the film seems patently full of structural discontinuities. Non-contiguity of spaces is detected; lapses between motive and outcome; as well as the main protagonists continually encountering "total strangers" who are treated perfunctorily, as though they are somehow actually to be recognized. If one knows the mystery Woodward and Bernstein are trying to unravel, and their method of unraveling, their movements seem logical, sensible, unalterable.[4]

[5] *Politics of Discontinuity*. Feeling continuity, we bathe in constancy. Not that the world does not change, for it does, but that the figures of the world retain their capacity to impress, in an unimpeded, vigorous manner. One recognizes, even values, the perduring quality of a space, a thing, a body, a horizon, a musical tone. And by "perduring" is to be understood an unmodified, incalculable, even ineffable relationship between the thing itself and the bath of circumstance in which, subject to gravity, it shows and turns. With discontinuity there is (sudden) freedom from the gravity that composes and bounds that constancy. There is no hold. We did have a hold, then we have no hold, then we have a hold again, and it is this interruption of perduring experience by an emptiness that signals the hiatus in experience. In cinema, the hiatus will usually be of the very shortest order, so much so that an illusion of ongoing process will be offered.

But there is also a politique at work beneath surface assemblage. Take, for just one example, the "teacher-student relationship" posed onscreen. First, a film like *Good Will Hunting* (1997) with scenes involving Matt Damon and Stellan Skarsgård; or *Adaptation* (2002) for the classroom lecture by Brian Cox; or Robert Redford's dialogue with Andrew Garfield in *Lions for Lambs* (2007). Here are sedate continuities of visual construction shot to shot and of forward-progressing dialogue. Implicit and deeply foundational is the idea of institutionalized education's ostensible dependence upon conventionality, an idea bluntly (if also somewhat idiotically) parodied with Robin Williams's taking over a high-school classroom from Leon Pownall in *Dead Poets Society* (1989). Yet Williams's performance need not be thought wild and unconventional; teacher-student interactions need not head away from such a model, but there is a virtually hegemonic politique informing educational practice—a politique film may question and try to overturn. In *The Karate Kid* (1984), for example, there is a substantial tutor–student interaction, taking up most of the film, and the pattern there is based on radical discontinuity. Yet that film is generally seen (and screened, if at all) as only a light comedy that can be laughed off.

Most essentially the meaning of the filmic jump is, "And now it's time for a change," but the call for change, development, and renewal is political and economic as well as aesthetic. Dealing harshly with Prokofiev and other composers, Stalin taught us that.

---

[4] Steven Spielberg faced much the same difficulty with his *The Post* (2017) as Sydney Pollack had with *President's Men*.

Topographies

Aerial view of the Bronx (showing Yankee Stadium) from West Side Story *(Robert Wise, Mirisch/Seven Arts, 1961). Digital frame enlargement.*

Nicholas Ray invented the aerial shot for narrative film by using a helicopter to follow a fleeing automobile in *They Live by Night* (1949).[1] The aerial shot was used again, notably, by Hitchcock following Marnie riding off from a fox hunt (1964). The urban aerial shot, showing Manhattan and the Bronx at the beginning of *West Side Story* (1961) was repeated considerably, such as later with Willy Wonka and Charlie in the Wonkavator (1971). The earliest aerial shots were made in daylight, to give a more or less crisp view of organized topographies depending on the height of the camera from the ground. The idea of an establishing shot looking down on brightly lit city streets at night has now become much used, even bordering on the conventional if one wishes to set a story "in a major metropolis." Much as we find with Hitchcock's repeated pattern of moving from the distant to the proximal (see Truffaut 266), the distant aerial shot in urban thrillers, detective stories, and superhero action films tends to "set up" a movement (of some kind) into a close location. In *Story*, Robert Wise takes us from an aerial view of Bronx neighborhoods in what seems to be a fluid zoom (it is a carefully edited grouping of shots) straight down into one area, then one block,

---

[1] Aerial shot: a shot made from the air, not a shot depicting a scenario in an airplane, etc.

then one playground on that block, then, and only then, one group of boys situated on that playground. Needless to say, for its own dramatic purposes the Broadway version of *West Side Story*, staged by Jerome Robbins, could not have required this optical elaboration to place the audience in the company of the Jets. Onstage, when the boys sang "Here come the Jets, yah, and we're gonna beat/Every last fuggin' gang on the whole fuggin' street," they really were coming at the audience, live and pulsing. In the film, the Jets sing the same lyric, but we have been coming at them.[2]

What is it that is given by the aerial shot of the city, uniquely? Beyond informing us as to the general setting of action to come (something is going to happen in *a* city, in *this* city), beyond cueing us to one culture rather than another (New York, not Los Angeles or Paris or London or Tokyo or Rome), beyond operating by convention to give a clarion call that here and now is to be thought the beginning of our experience, and with omnipotence, what does this particular vision offer? Before the late 1940s, after all, films cued audiences about the setting of action, the culture, and that the marvel was beginning, all without aerial shots. What considerations or reflections are deeply embedded in us in seeing from above, specifically seeing *the city* from above? To what deep message do we respond—since our response is our way of seeing?

[1] Surely, first, that we are above. Not above the action (any particular action), because whatever will constitute the meat of the story has not yet been presented or even hinted at (indeed, anything we are given may be a deflection). Usually, we are lifted so high that we can consider ourselves above *all* civilized action, say, the movement of vehicles like tiny mechanized insects on the spider-threads of streets. If we are not above the story because we are *before* the story; if we are not above the characters because at this altitude humans cannot be seen;[3] if we are not above the central idea or conceit of the film because from this view at this moment such a thing is unimaginable . . . then what is it that we are above? One mustn't say *the city itself*, because the city itself, as an organized agglomeration, isn't there; and one mustn't say the *image of the city itself* because this image is before us, not below us. The answer can only be, the film, as a desire and a formation and an idea; the film as an outpouring and unspooling. That-which-is-to-be. That "earth" which we have not settled. We are above the unspooling of daily realities upon streetcorners and in bedrooms, above the social. Albeit everything we see "down there" is knowably social, we will not be confronting the social in this film in this abstract, distal way. We are now above all that, floating as though for a bird's-eye view—movie professionals call it a "God's-eye view"—except that we are neither birds nor gods, and we know that. Nor, exactly, are we human as we watch this way, so we have ascended above our own humanity, too. We are inhabiting a zone dedicated to dispassionate observation, seeing without caring, seeing without feeling or recognizing, beyond that we

---

[2] The "Jet Song" made its first appearance in the April 27, 1960 return engagement of the show at the Winter Garden; it was not in the opening production.
[3] See Harry Lime in the Ferris wheel in *The Third Man* (1949).

can note the difference between the Eiffel Tower and the Empire State Building, between Tower Bridge and the Golden Gate. We are not meant to be seeing in order to taste, then; we are meant to be seeing in order to determine a superiority of perspective, to enjoy space, organization, extension, elaboration, light, and darkness in a special way accorded only to us. Because we are outside human action, we are similarly outside all of the requirements, skills, tactics, and intentionalities of human action, not only outside what characters will know and plan and understand but also outside the very notion of knowing, planning, and understanding. From "up here," we understand human intentionality and motive as only a conceit. We have thus come to reside magically (since we did not lift ourselves) in a place where a purity of vision is all we want, just as it is all that we have been offered.[4] Our look swiftly bonds to the look of the camera, that we take to be cinema's factotum, in fact the viewer becomes something of a camera embodied, a mere discriminatory presence with a point of view that in some ways is optimal.

[2] Yet, the city is also manifested to us as a particular kind of construction and elaboration of form, indeed a construction that from down on the sidewalk is quite impossible to discern (since down on the sidewalk, or the road, we are literally trapped within it). This construction is an enormous, three-dimensional, typically rectilinear arrangement of habitable environments, multiplied into uncountable myriads, and positioned both on top of one another, as the buildings appear to climb into the sky, and adjacent, as the buildings are clearly standing, like soldiers on parade, next to one another in straight or at least uniform lines. How economical this is! That every available cluster of molecules in the air—reaching outward as far as the city limits (which are beyond the edge of our frame but comprehensible nevertheless)—every conceivable position left, right, and up, is neatly occupied by utile arrangement. A zillion offices, all imaginably interconnected. This arrangement is, of course (a) capitalist in the extreme and (b) bureaucratic in organization. In their costliness and shine buildings can evidence the investment of huge fortunes aimed at self-multiplication. Offices above and below one another can constitute a modern military-style hierarchy, with decision-making flowing downward from the top: the top, which is the area closest to us whilst, up here, we gaze. We must adopt the principle of this gridded city, this entirely post-Haussmannized city. Look at some of the photographs Eugène Atget made very early in the twentieth century of unrenovated dwelling nooks still lingering in Paris, or examine Charles Marville's photographs of the street areas of Paris before 1845, and then contrast these crampings and organicisms with photographs of the boulevards the Baron Haussmann put in, the grand design, in which everything and everybody has a

---

[4] Screen savers for Apple TV include traveling drone shots above cities, and satellite shots far above the earth, moving across continents. Watching these one hungers for them go on and on, but they change up.

proper place, and where movement across broad swaths of city territory is made easy by broad straight thoroughfares and a mercantile economy luring new consumers away from their residences in order that they can make acquisitions and encounter strangers. The railway termini were built in the center of the city, so that voyagers could flood out into the grand avenues directly, writes Wolfgang Schivelbusch (*Journey* 178ff). And one can look at John Bellows's "Blue Morning" (1909) and other paintings of the renovation of New York and see the space opening up.

[3] Since most of the urban aerial shots we catch are from a moving camera—quite typically a helicoptered camera, sometimes now a droned camera, gliding past the skyscraper needles—we gain the impression, ongoing and furiously insistent, that we are not just sightseeing but progressing, moving toward an apotheosis. So much more, and such a greater vision is yet to be seen, and we are *on the way*. And on the multiplied thoroughfares we detect below, the invisible myrmidons of the place are on the way, too. On the way to what? Wait, we will see! "I don't know what it is/But it is gonna be great!" Further, up here we can move *without traffic congestion*: no hold-ups, no sclerosis, no road rage. We can rise above a congestion that is nothing but a trace of the human collisions of modernity, all those cars crammed bumper to bumper (the opening of 8 ½ [1963], with Guido magically lifted away from his steering wheel)—and in moving this way transcend modernity itself. Head not into post-modernity but into the Undefined. An ethereal zone, anything but mundane, so that the film itself takes on the character of the ethereal, not the dully routinized. The characters also ascend even before we meet them, lift themselves above some lowly quotidian lockup within a set of boundaries (trailing an origin, aimed only at a terminus), and become "Olympian." ·

[4] Stability and coherence combine to form an issue most people find concerning, both in terms of the continuity of their living experience and in terms of the continuity of their dramatic entertainments: that this entity, the New City, showing me its face, should truly be something of a revelation; that all its pieces should fit together in glorious harmony; that as an environment of the future it should support faith by continuing forward, promising always to continue forward, be whole, wholer, and still wholer as the future approaches. These are wonderful ideals, perhaps, and surely enticing prospects, yet any careful and objective estimation will prove that down on the ground there is no stability and only a scanty hint of coherence, "stability" and "coherence" being pure inventions to pacify and order the shifting mass in the name of particular vested interests. The world is constantly modulating, arrangements are constantly being spoiled or reassessed and changed. Permanences are transformed into changes. Yet, the middle-class audience's felt need for stability does not evaporate (the film audience is predominantly middle class): this need for stability predicts a state of affairs, for the project of watching which one is about to dedicate moments

of one's life. That a world should be depicted whole and unified, concrete and unshifting, elegantly climbing and boundlessly spreading, founded on bedrock not quicksand. That by twilight the untold lights should be twinkling and blinking, neon white and every other color. Founded on bedrock is this City, but ascending into the furthest reaches of the universe. The land down there is designed, sculpted, subjugated by power in order that structures may be placed together in some ideal way. What better invocation of the stable and coherent than the aerial view of a city, its limitless parts harmonized and set in geometric order, its vagrant human fluidities all made solid and comprehensible by being encased in cubes of official space, cubes all rationally aligned and mounted and multiplied. Let us say that in this particular sense, the sense of its addressing a felt need for stability and coherence, the aerial shot is utopian while being also, of course, a dream.

35

Forget Me Not

The Bourne Identity *(Doug Liman, Universal, 2002). Digital frame enlargement.*

In continuous flow is forgetting, too. The action moves onward, and with shot after shot neatly adjoined to—swiftly emerging from—what was immediately previous concentration turns to evaluating the progress that was promised, a progress and a promise that both swell as the movement continues. Nothing better than a chase scene for illustrating this. But as we bring perception to a shot, assimilating its full content, especially, perhaps, the position of one or more protagonists against a backdrop that continually moves along (buildings on a sidewalk, typically), acuteness of sensibility comes at the expense of recalling what went immediately before. To leave each position and glide forward (at whatever speed) with the action, each position is relinquished. The chase is a continuity of relinquishings. And if while watching a film one lets something go, where does it go?

The viewers sitting around in the dark, or watching in their homes and preparing to text their opinions broadly, cannot possibly all forget in the same way, and yet if they are all watching the same action sequence that speeds from shot to shot, and if they are raptly engaged in each shot, as raptly engaged as one can be in quarter-second shots, the material that they must discard, the *field of the previous*, is in fact the same for all. Albeit the emotion invested both in seeing and in relegating is likely a private emotion. Is there only one warehouse for keeping all this sloughed off skin, one collective repository? When one scene or sequence concludes, perhaps a passage opens permitting one to meditate on the thing as a unit, say a hospital room where a figure lies abed and nurses calmly attend to him. But when another action sequence follows, this island of meditation is sunk in the sea, because it is necessary to speed with the vehicle bearing the action or one loses it. *Sunk . . . in the . . . sea.*

Oliver Sacks quotes Luis Buñuel wondering about a "final amnesia" in which everything will be swallowed in loss. Is it not as possible to forget an entire film as a sequence inside it or a shot that came just before this one? If one sees numerous films with but a finite capacity for memory, what happens to the films that must be forgotten because there is no storage space left? One may remember a single feature of a film much later, vividly, and use it to code the passage and meaning of the whole, except that on re-viewing (somehow) one is shocked to discover that one remembered quite wrongly that the wallpaper was blue not yellow, that the heroine drove a green sports car not a bicycle. That the heroine was not a spy but a banker. That memory is a trickster.

Because it is necessary to remember and forget at the same time.

In the action sequence, the flip from shot A to shot B requires that we recall just enough of A to position ourselves and the protagonists inside a fluidly stretching arc. "Oh yes, she is now here." Or, "She is moving *still*." Just enough from the previous shot or shots to read the action plainly—a moped zipping down a busy road, CUT TO close frontal shot of moped approaching camera: we know it's the same moped and that we just saw it speed away from us. How do we know? The rider has the same, or a too similar, helmet? Nothing interceded between the first and the second moped shots, thus the fabled continuity we cherish? A constancy of screen direction, say, left to right? Say one remembers that moving moped, *but remembers only that*. Once the navigation problem is solved—very speedily—the past is dropped away. As to that moped, again: when I recall that I "just" saw it speeding away down a road, from above and afar, can I confess, in all honesty, that I still see the same *it*, as I watch the frontal approach shot? I *saw it a particular way* but can I remember precisely what I saw and how I saw when I was looking? *Can we remember not only what we saw but how we saw when we were seeing? If we do remember, how did we spring from there to here?* Is that springing also in memory? Or is that springing part of the (hidden) mechanism of memory, *that by which* we remember but not *that which* we remember.

Each seeing, each triumph of the eyes, vanquishes the past.

36

Inspired

(Top, from left) Daniel Craig, Eric Bana, Ciarán Hinds, Mathieu Kassovitz, and Hans Zischler in Munich *(Steven Spielberg, Dreamworks/Universal/Amblin, 2005); (Bottom) The Lost Boys in* Peter Pan *(Clyde Geronimi, Wilfred Jackson, Hamilton Luske, and Jack Kinney, Disney, 1953). Digital frame enlargements.*

Steven Spielberg's *Munich* (2006) begins with a tag: INSPIRED BY REAL EVENTS, and many other films "about real life" make such a signal. *The Right Stuff* (1983). *Judgment at Nuremberg* (1961). *JFK* (1991). For those who take the Bible as a real account, *The Ten Commandments* (1956). *Changeling* (2008) and *The Walk* (2015): A TRUE STORY. Gavin Hood's *Official Secrets* (2019): BASED ON REAL EVENTS.

"Real life": the life, occurrences, and experiences—as well as the fears, anxieties, and wonders—of we folk out here in the offscreen world, that world containing this building that holds this screen: that is to say, the world outside not only the frame but the cinema that possesses the frame, a world in which there persists a substantial and reverent belief in what can be found on the screen. Invoked is an ontology with all the morbid and conflicted tissue of, as André Bazin so famously thought, life embalmed.

It is perhaps not especially difficult to imagine what is meant by the word "inspired" and the phrase "based on," since we do know that those who write movies and pay to produce them are interested in a variety of sources, "actual" events just as much as novels and plays. Nowadays at least, there are relatively few original screenplays. We can picture the "inspired" Mr. Spielberg, thinking retrospectively of the Munich Olympics massacre in a state of still-stunned anger (why is he thinking of the massacre?), and feeling the "inspiration" coursing through his veins. What?—Germany?, athletics?, Israel?, Jews?, headlines? Or, with *Official Secrets*, given that the story is all about a claim *based on* a document fallen into the hands of an operative at GCHQ and then leaked in a whistleblower attempt to prevent the Bush–Blair war against Saddam, we can see how the writers, hearing about the real Katharine Gun (played in the film by Keira Knightley) thought her adventure with the British legal system a solid (enough) foundation upon which to *base* her own account (that would lead to a film account), the way an edifice is based upon an excavated site. And we can know, too, that filmmakers are far less likely to be claiming a *basing on* or an *inspiration by* some putatively rich text lying elsewhere—a problem the Writers Guild of America West is fond of taking up—than to be urging potential viewers to come rushing to see their film because it springs out of the same real world of events that customers already inhabit. First your world, events that are read by you, events that you appropriate as yours, and now a film version, a special gilding, there being some unwritten law that when they have been filmed, happenings only gain serious weight. All this did happen, yes, yes, but pay now to come see it "happening" onscreen. Or with an even more macabre tint, it happened gruesomely but you can pay now to see dramatized gruesomeness: *United 93* (2006).

The problem underlying the positions tacitly claimed in these "inspirations" is *the actuality of* "real events," their relevant and crucial distinctness, as it were, from the "made." What, after all, earns the status of a "real event"? Do we not mean by this moniker *events*, what the system in power identifies, holds up, and regards with an appraising eye eager to publicize, for whatever reason. In our social life, there are nothing but events, finally, yet almost all of them fail to be labeled as such, and as "real," and are certainly not treated as foundational or inspiring.[1]

---

[1] A condition that was inspiring for Sigmund Freud.

The label "real" can fit an event past or foretold. Thus, we are comfortable in using the word *real* when we speak of a *really fantastic Super Bowl*; a *real shame*; *Get real!* or boast, *It's gonna be really really wonderful!* We apply the word real when, as William James wrote long ago, many particular criteria are offered for satisfaction,[2] but there are plenty of happenings that would be thought of as *events* and would certainly be worth calling *real* yet would fail to find themselves on a marquee as REAL EVENTS. I line up at a railway station food joint to get some buttered toast and there are twenty-seven people in front of me so that, from my perspective, getting a few pieces of toast before my train comes in is an event; and it is as real as I am; yet it is not the kind of thing that BASED ON REAL EVENTS is pointing to. If someone interrupted me and my fellow queuers-up with a machine gun, well, *that* might get called a REAL EVENT. Just waiting for toast would (probably) not inspire Steven Spielberg to make a movie (even if I could be available to play the role for him!).

It is possible that the kind of real event that deserves to be included among the limited collection of items bearing the name REAL EVENTS in the opening credits of a filmed version, is exactly—however tautological this might seem—one that inspires or underpins a film: when a film says it has been inspired by real events it is assumedly pointing to happenings that could (because did) inspire a film, saying, in effect, "This film is inspired by the sort of thing that inspires films" and here is the sort of thing called, here in the land of film, REAL. If it happened and you can film it, it was REAL. Or, "This film is based upon the sort of thing upon which films are generally based." If BASED ON REAL EVENTS is a less meaningful utterance than I am meaning to suppose, if it doesn't actually point, still, as my son, a true film lover, says, "It adds *gravitas*." Can we inquire into this cinematic gravitas, the substance or condition layered upon a work that could have functioned straightforwardly without it, a work with pith and moment and personality that now climbs to a higher level of importance (weight), esteem (weight), effectiveness (weight)? And then, must we not pursue another query, even more *gravitational*, namely, given the assumption that the Munich massacre was all of horrendous, disgusting, and debasing (non-combatants were slaughtered[3]), what might the filmmakers have been presuming of their potential audience in thinking that beyond the already present gravitas of the event as it was, the addition of filmic gravitas—by means of the identification tag—and only that, would spur them to watch a film about it? What are we presumed to understand if we are told, "Look, everything you're about to see might seem out of this world but it's not, it *actually happened*," or else, "This didn't happen but something very, very like this *did* . . ." The Gun affair in England: it already had massive gravitas, as it involved a violation of Her Majesty's Official Secrets Act of

---

[2] James notes, for example, that "any object which remains uncontradicted [by some other thing of which we think] is ipso facto believed and posited as absolute reality" (289). He adumbrates as "real," "whatever things have intimate and continuous connection with my life" (298); adding that "An relation to our mind at all, in the absence of a stronger relation, suffices to make an object real" (299); and pointing to sensible vividness or pungency (301), among numerous other attributes.

[3] Ironically, non-combatants who were in Munich in order to be "combatants" for a gold medal but who, at the moment of the shooting, as depicted in the film "based on real events," were not competing ("combating") yet. The slaughter was *real* combat.

1989 in the name of preventing an illegal war (a war not legally declared). Is the audience presumed to consider such a thing trifling unless it is augmented by the special gravitas of the label? I ask because indubitably the phrase BASED ON REAL EVENTS does add gravitas, yet one must wonder if there is a foregone conclusion about *adding gravitas*: that if gravitas can be added to a product it should be added. That "gravitas" is worth achieving, then selling. Could we call gravitas *hyperbole*?

For a fiction film, why not a title tag reading, NOT BASED ON REAL EVENTS? Or better, NOTHING WHATEVER TO DO WITH REALITY.

Another issue is more inspiring. Let me take as an example Walt Disney's *Peter Pan* (1953), a favorite of my childhood. Or George Cukor's *The Philadelphia Story* (1940). Neither of these splendid achievements has the sort of gravitas that comes from being based on real events. One source is a fantasy novel from the early days of the twentieth century, the other was a successful Broadway play. In their quite different ways, both films gained real popularity. Audiences were found and made happy doubly: happy with the films and happy to have been found. Consider the thrill offered to viewers who did not at the time live anywhere near the sea with the release in the summer of 1975 of *Jaws*, based on the Peter Benchley book which was in turn based on some for the most part unknown REAL EVENTS at the end of Long Island. So many thrilling films worked without gravitas. What reality were they based upon, what was evidently the sort of real material worth basing films upon but that failed to merit being officially stamped "real"? How do we work through an ontology of narrative, in short. From what in playwright Philip Barry's real life, if not REAL EVENTS, did *The Philadelphia Story* derive? From what does James M. Barrie's tale emerge—his putative relationship with the Llewelyn Davies children gives some characterizations, but the story? The Darling children flying to Neverland—no gravitas?

And I think a short answer to this question about those legion films not BASED UPON REAL EVENTS but wholly satisfactory nevertheless, an answer that will apply in almost every case, is *imagination*. The film is born of a creative imagination or a group of creative imaginations in conference. The film is, indeed, a product of Imagination. *The Towering Inferno* (1974) comes from Imagination but *All the President's Men* (1976) comes from REAL EVENTS. *Rebel Without a Cause* (1955) is INSPIRED BY REAL EVENTS (articles published at the time about delinquent adolescents and the social problems they "cause") but *The Asphalt Jungle* (1950) is from Imagination, operating by way of a W. R. Burnett novel (fictionalization). Biopics claim to be based on real events, but pictures featuring characters who never did live spring from Imagination. A fundamental antimony, then?: Real Events << >> The Imagination. And should we, in a biopic, assume that every single character we see comes from Real Events, that every one of them was there?

Here the vortex begins to spin. The creative artist's imagination seems to flow out of his productive self, directly, unmediated—his hand, his eyes, his postures. But this productive self cannot exist, does not exist, in a vacuum, does not derive its content only from within. The artist lives in a world, exactly as we all live in a world, and is inevitably inspired by events, even if not INSPIRED BY REAL EVENTS or even if the genuinely inspiring events are not real. The material circumstances in which "real events" are produced are the same circumstances out of which imagination flows. And as to "real events": what turns a typical everyday event into a *real* event is an act of imagination by some agency of definitional power, a dubbing. That a "real" event can first be imagined and only then attached to a conceit of "actuality," suggests that the supposed "antinomy" between *real* and *imagined* is not such an antinomy after all.

We have, finally, two kinds of film side by side: those that are BASED ON REAL EVENTS as per a claim, and those that are, merely, based on real events of one kind or another; both emerge from the world we live in. When gravitas is added to a film BASED ON REAL EVENTS, by virtue of some explicit attribution to the Real, we are prone to believing that little or no work has been done to alter, shape, or project the "authenticity" of the demonstrated events. The film is simply, only, merely, casually, effortlessly, unavoidably given to us "as things were." And this, of course, is nonsense. Nothing is ever given as it was. The film that is BASED ON REAL EVENTS is just as imaginative as the film that is based on the imagination. *Munich* and *Peter Pan* are from the same stewpot.

We should not forget Erving Goffman's dictum in *Frame Analysis* about the ultimate importance of the "outermost rim" of the frame. The outmost rim is the one that counts. A televised football championship isn't football, it's television. Here, the outermost rim is that of commercial moviegoing, the selling of moving images, and both *Munich* and *Peter Pan* must contrive to be sold, no matter what kind of events they emerge from. Latent in the claim of being based on the REAL is a serious hypervaluation of *the idea of the unimagined*, the idea that there are in our universe original things, like the Tree in Eden, that simply exist because they have always simply existed. What is BASED ON REAL EVENTS apparently touches the Chalice of Reality, imbibing from it, being saturated with its mysterious content which, uncontrivedly, outflows. In that kind of light, what would we be led to esteem about the self-admittedly imaginative film? Officially unconnected with the real—no matter how tightly connected in the private rooms of the creators—such a creation floats in a zone of frivolities and meaninglessness. Soon enough we will conceive it as an opiate of the masses, the real inspiration for the idea that some but only some films—important films—are inspired by the real, above or glowingly apart from the opioid domain.

* * *

Post Scriptum: Spielberg's *Munich* is a passionate, increasingly violent, and progressively intimate film that makes a very strong impression, pleasurable or not. Given that by the time the climactic scenes roll around one has more or less forgotten that all this is INSPIRED BY REAL EVENTS and has come to the actions onscreen as simply transpiring, elevating, and expanding—filmically—it becomes a question whether a film like this, or any "inspired" film, does not act finally to wipe away, by replacing, the events of real life that gave it occasion, whether, finally, a film called *Munich* is less the Munich—or indeed *not at all* the Munich—that the viewer holds and maybe remembers, but *Munich*. Munich replaced.

37

Shades in the Dark

Matthew Pitt among others, finding a new favorite film (Samuel Fuller's Shock Corridor*) in* The Dreamers *(Bernardo Bertolucci, Recorded Picture Company, 2003). Digital frame enlargement.*

Confession:
On an aircraft one night, in mid-flight across the ocean, I saw the woman next to me scrolling around her little screen in search of a movie, and her finger came to rest on *Strangers on a Train* (1951). "Aha!," I heard a voice in the back of my head, "You should watch this terrific film!" A character in me owned that voice (and shares my mouth); I have never given him a name; and, somehow vicariously delighted by this woman's enjoyment he could babble, to himself at least, without cease. Of course I kept my mouth shut.

How could a viewer have concern for, be interested in, any other person's possible pleasure? On Facebook and other sites I see people listing their "10 favorite movies," or "10 movies they could not live without," or "10 whatevers they'll whatever forever," as though as a surfer I should find this interesting, as though in posting these they think anyone else out there, whom they've never met, should care. Making a list is one thing—broadcasting it is another.

Wrapped as I am in a film, rapt as I am, it is the film I am committed to when I am watching and not the other watchers spread around me in the dark. Another person's rapture would interest me only if she or he were a character in my sight, and now emerged for me, stepped down off the screen to dialogue, as in *The Purple Rose of Cairo* (1985). For Cecilia (Mia Farrow), while she is gazing at the screen, nothing and no one is as real as Tom Baxter (Jeff Daniels); and she must be as real to us as he is to her. It would be disingenuous of me to protest that I care about the reactions to a film of the strangers around me. I might understand or not understand them, but I don't care. This might be uncivil of me; but in the dark we're not quite a civil society.

People who know I write about cinema often ask me, "What is your favorite film?" They ask with enthusiasm, of course, as though they care to hear the answer. This is a wholly spontaneous, sincere question, asked in the spirit of friendship and real inquiry. But why should they know the answer? The question presumes that the films I have seen are indubitably lined up in some kind of ranking arrangement, and one of them has to be at the head of the line at any moment. That is not the case; and also not the case, I think, is that any film I might name would be subtly saying something about me at least as much, if not more, than about itself. Not "What is your favorite *film?*" but "What is *your* favorite film?" If people believed the films they raved about to others did speak about them, would they be guarded, would they think, "Oh, maybe I'd better not mention that serial killer thing I love so much, or people will think I'm a secret serial killer"? And there is a myth, too, that film hierarchies, if they even exist—how could they exist?—are fixed and not fluid. How, in the flux of today, would I wish to answer a question about my favorites? How, tomorrow? How, yesterday?

Some films are more *mine* than others are, as I take it, and the grouping shifts. Today, as I write, I am a little obsessed by *Simon of the Desert* (1965). But a few weeks ago it was *À nos amours* (1983), and before that *Mauvais sang* (1986) and before that *The Cranes Are Flying* (1957), and there is also *Notorious* (1946) and *Nocturama* (2016). Yet, here is the issue to ponder: Why would this affect you, Dear Reader? Why would anyone plumb another viewer's taste? Are we all lost? Perhaps we have become lost in the forests of ourselves, wanting to know about someone else's experience in order to truly have our own. And when I am queried, am I not expected to be civil and fraternal by giving an answer? And would any answer I gave be easily comprehended, easily acted upon? What if I were to cite Jindrich Polák's *Ikarie XB-1* (1963), for example? Would that seem too esoteric? Should I choose from a fairly limited menu of *popular* titles that virtually anyone on the street would swiftly recognize; the new films currently out, whatever the fashion of the moment? Beyond such sanctifications, film runs for the masses as a current flow, the watery images moving swiftly past the bank on which one's feet are set. So quickly do films move as instigations to appreciation or wonder that most people act as though their film experience cannot sensibly be shared; tomorrow will come too quickly.

Yet films are shared, though we may not notice. Our movie-watching offers us to investigate, like Walter Benjamin, the mass nature of the project. Movies are mass produced and always have been (see Gomery): the same movie is being projected all over the world simultaneously (albeit with different language overlays and sometimes with alterations in the edit), because there are at least hundreds of prints in circulation at once. Not to mention electrons streaming. People I have never met or imagined can be sitting watching while I am sitting watching. What is my relation to these "spectatorial partners," since we are all opened to being stunned by the same images arranged basically in the same order? I find that I do not feel warmed by the company. Nor enlightened. And yet perhaps there is something of a social bond, such as is created among cattle or sheep when they graze the same pasture. We have come to use the word "cinephile," *film lover*, for special adepts "deeply into" film, as though ordinary folk, falling in love from moment to moment as they see the screen, aren't really lovers at all, just numbers in a population count.

Cinephilia is often regarded as an attitude toward, and a way of viewing, film as worthy of special reverence, the cinephile privileging a cinematic experience over a culinary one, a literary one, an architectural one. This is essentially a post-romantic falling-in or surrender. But there is another way to think of cinephilia: that, watching, the cinephile is a person with a warmer relation to what is on the screen than to the people around—either while they watch as individuals or, by implication, when they are generalized into the audience. Not, the person who *loves* cinema instead of taking an objective view of it but the person who loves *cinema* instead of the strangers he could mention it to. If films were seen only objectively, as containers holding signifiers, no such involvement would be called for except in a kind of meta-linguistic way, with the kind of passion scholars have for studying words and word usages. But once a film puts a viewer in motion—*moti*vates, makes e*motional*—it strikes in the deepest chambers of the heart.

38

The Jitters

Ryan Reynolds in 6 Underground *(Michael Bay, Bay Films/Skydance, 2019). Digital frame enlargement.*

Spend many years writing and you will gain affinity for the charms of our language, and the deepest irritations for its limitations. The writer wants to say everything, but there is no language to permit that, save, perhaps, music.

    I have been setting words down for almost sixty years but have never found a really appropriate way to convey two things, sound and image. Every address to sound or image has to be a circumlocution or a metaphor or a downright evasion. For years I was convinced it was my own deficiency, but now it does seem that English doesn't go very far as regards what we hear, and it doesn't allow for true discussion of images because the language proceeds inevitably along a line but images, like sounds, do not.

    And there is one utter queerness of authoring, that one wants to do the impossible. The more impossible, the more desperate the desire.

    One finds strategies for getting at sound and at image, strategies in the military sense, or as an engineer or architect would have strategies for building. Finally, the writer is reliant on the reader to go off and try to see the material, and this means confronting the awful depredations of our library. (After Jacques Lacan some writers like to think not of a library but of an *imagin-ary*, a repleteness of the *image*, but I think this is limiting because it would not include sound and even in silent film—perhaps most intensively in silent film—sound matters.) Depredations: (a) so many films are unavailable, totally and hopelessly; (b) films that are available, even in collectible or downloadable formats, are limited in number and very often interrupted by advertising or by glitches caused in some computer; (c) so much attention is directed by purveyors to keeping alive in the market only selections: the most recent or the most popular releases declared worthwhile by a limited "committee" of marketers. If a writer wishes to communicate with his reader about cinema, he is sometimes forced to write about the films people can see, not the films he wishes to investigate. Increasingly, what can be seen are action films, violent dramas, and comic book transpositions—all big blockbuster productions with opening-weekend sales running to eight or nine digits.

The days may have passed when readers would follow an author's choices. Authors must now often follow the choices of their readers. This, I believe, is a serious problem, because the author may be writing mostly because he has something on his mind that the reader hasn't encountered, the reader's exposure to that something being the principal reason for reading and the author's principal reason for giving the reader something to read.

In this muddle, I watched Michael Bay's *6 Underground* (2019). I am aware that Bay has many detractors out there, and that mere mention of his name is anathema for people who would like to think themselves informed about cinema. And, true to "form," he has here (once again) made an action spectacle that races in twitchy circles around a central void, so there is no point at all trying to say what happens in the story, or why. What happens happens so that the end can be made to seem rational, when of course in a piece principally about an aesthetic effect (action) rationality is not a salient criterion. But near the beginning of the film there is a complicated chase, seeing which was one of the truly thrilling experiences I have had. It offered images that produced a sensation of electric lightness, comedic impulsion. Brilliant and unanticipated flashes of someone's lime-green vest. Tall buildings with expansive aerial views. Cars penetrated and flipped, but in quantity, a vehicular smorgasbørd. Youthful drive, drive beyond the limits of thought, with lightning reflexes permitting changes of direction, changes of orientation, changes of attitude, changes of face, changes of purpose, changes of meaning, all in the briefest of flashes, so that to keep up, one had to abandon—completely jettison—the very idea of stable knowledge and balanced thought. One raced, faster than the blood. There was not only no balance here, there was no concept of balance, no notion that balance might be useful, as indeed it never was.

There are numerous tropes of action cinema that have been repeated so many times the only pleasure they can provide is the fulfillment of strict expectations: cars flying through the air and landing on their roofs, gunfire from moving vehicles not succeeding in doing damage, thugs, thugs, and more thugs, often a neo-Cartesian urban setting (of the kind written about, really before action cinema began, by Frank McConnell) in which we see rectilinear grids of offices lined up in skyscrapers reflected in concrete-and-glass walls. And females in tight spandex. And males who grin at the females like randy chimpanzees but are too busy navigating endless traffic (usually driving in the wrong direction on the wrong side of the road, and dipsy-doodling among the oncoming cars to avoid collision[1]) and surviving the wounds they suffer as testament to their purity.

What is it speeding by, here, as an offering on the altar of viewing experience?

- Movement *without vector*. Very typically action film has movement multiplied and heading in many (screen) directions with what appears to be enormous speed, but the lines of movement are meant to be understood as aiming topologically and narratively forward. This notwithstanding that inside the diegesis we see plenty of corners being turned (in shrieks) and quick "changes of direction." In *21 Bridges* (2019), there are numerous nocturnal ballets of aerial shots of Manhattan, the lights atwinkle (especially on bridges). But we have no idea (the police have no idea) where to head, and so the directionality changes with the "wind." With speed driving, we generally see cars heading off in a straight line, and picking up a new straight line in a subsequent shot. The photography is designed to follow these "lines of action," and in order to give a picture of the girth of the drama the editor will have to cut between mini-sequences with some throbbing rhythm reflecting (and reflected in) the score (that is written to reflect the editing!). In *6 Underground*, however, the camera shows us fast movement heading, at once, anywhere and nowhere. Vectorless movement. What results is jitteriness and anxiety—motion not locomotion. This picture suggests the frenzied, incoherent tension of our current life, a pervasive sense that there's no time for anything nor any clear idea of where doings lead. Soon we lose the expectation of actions leading to results, solutions, redeeming destinations; and this loss is, among other things, liberating. The film takes on the character of a traumatic kaleidoscope. But it doesn't build.

- Interruption. The cutting principle for action sequences is that no action should be permitted to continue on its arc without interruption. A car speeding down a street, seen from inside and adjacent to the driver, is suddenly pushed aside by a stationary figure holding a rocket launched by a smarmy but very skillful figure placed on the peak of a high building overlooking the street. Since all figures in the scene are in motion, though in motion along different lines, once a shot has been interrupted one must follow it with more interruptions. The interruption thus produces systematic discontinuities, which become expected patterns of organization. Conversational patterns, too, are interrupted, broken off, lost, filtered, aggravated. One has the sense of a camera consciousness, a camera identity, with which one feels compelled to affiliate but which refuses to rest with any phrase of movement all the way through. A refusal to rest, as though the camera's presence is entirely fugal. So, watching we are put into a fugue state.

This mode of interruption is far more invasive than merely breaking away from an action as a way of holding its progress, of delaying gratification, because the rule of constant

---

[1] A trope that owes much to the flight through the asteroids in *The Empire Fights Back* (1980).

interruption requires that the camera never return to the scene of departure as it was at the time. And the camera must also never show a penchant for stillness, must stubbornly neglect to incite the feeling that the jitteriness of constant shifting will come to a relieving end. There is too much happening in the contemporary world, there are too many agents with conflicting motives. Yet, too, there is too little energy to consummate a move. Thus actions, once begun, are fated to burn out, or explode away, or vanish into thin air, but always, in any case, be turned away from before they resolve. Another view: the actors do not—cannot—succeed, and so after each broken dream, every sloppy failure, they must try again. Constant interruption means constantly trying again. Constantly heading up the "hill" of which one will never reach the top. Never reaching the top of any "hill," the viewer will never attain an ideal point of view; or: blur will become ideal.

Attention deficit thus not only characterizes action sequences, it accounts for their structural form and rationalizes their commercial success.

- A climate of hopelessness. Action cinema is an outgrowth, and a mirror, of modernity. As such it follows the guidelines William Butler Yeats offered in "The Second Coming." "Things fall apart; the centre cannot hold," and:

The blood-dimmed tide is loose, and everywhere
The ceremony of innocence is drowned;
The best lack all conviction, while the worst
Are full of passionate intensity.

The formula calls for destruction and dismemberment, passionately and intensely. No coherent object passes ruin, no space calamity, no body the wounds of accident, no intention disruption. Pathways are confounded, flight is inhibited, machines fail to work while dominating the environment, prayers and hopes are dashed, achievements are mocked, the clean is dirtied. He who drives the speeding car in desperate flight through the incoherent city, the city without a north, finally arrives at a point of rest, which is to say a vacuum, and is instantly skewered. The hero—we have no option but to regard our central protagonist this way, he is handsome, he makes jokes, he remains alive while bodies pile up all around—has no reaction to the chaos, no disappointment or chagrin, not even a wince, because chaos is nature, nature is chaos, once the hand of the aggressor has set its task. Even when the hero has doubt, and he has a great deal of doubt, he seems soothed and prepared by it, readied for pulsation. Doubt is retreat, repose, calm rehearsal. The pulped bodies of the dead are so profuse we could be looking at a battlefield, or perhaps a "battlefield,"[2] and certainly the drama poses the idea of battle, the idea of destroying the enemy. Yet no one has declared war. War simply is. The world simply is at war. War all-dimensional, all conditional.

Frequently, with others, the hero screams at the top of his lungs. But we are not intended to listen.

---

[2] Sam Mendes's *1917* (2019) offers a lengthy and very detailed portrayal of a World War I battlefield in France, far beyond what action cinema tends to show.

Irrational Space

Grant Williams (with pussycat) in The Incredible Shrinking Man *(Jack Arnold, Universal International, 1957). Digital frame enlargement.*

Keeping up with the storyline(s) of a film can involve a certain dedication to rationality. Much as, from the middle of the nineteenth century, the detective was wont to do, and with the same kind of multi-sensorial keenness, the film watcher is filtering for significances of various kinds, prioritizing findings, searching for the clues that will illuminate (notwithstanding that here as elsewhere once one takes a clue for a light one gets precisely the kind of light that could shine from such a clue). Film watching is a kind of hunt for that wild boar, the "true meaning," that hides in the thickets of narration and charges without warning, sometimes violently. Let us say that a principal project of the viewer's is location and retrieval, which implies storage and (somewhat later) examination. Seek and ye shall find. And the viewer will be intrigued, even sharpened, if she learns at the end that there was a creature she neither found nor imagined, and it was legitimately there, and she walked past it; but if it turns out for her that the forest had no wild life at all, that the promise was a sham, she will find confusion, if not disappointment.

As to beasts in forests, the rationalist will want to affiliate every creature with a peculiar status of significance, dependent on its relation to the principles of a story (the principles of the story constituting a bestiary), and will see in gestures, poses, and moves only navigational information as moves a story along. Story, not being. Recounting, not inspiration. Early taxonomy, we so easily forget, was obsessed with taxonomizing, and every creature labeled was examined for its fit with the labeling system. This is what systems are for.

There is a difference in kind between *The Dark Knight* (2008), which ultimately delivers the moral goods yet also baldly professes to do so, and the profound, insightful films of Olivier Assayas (like *Personal Shopper* [2016]), which hold back outcomes and necessities in favor of a spectrum more ineffable. Nor need it always be the task of the filmmaker to be an explicator even in the driest narrative, or to treat every subject through only rational consideration. Indeed, in the balance between (a) what is apparently happening onscreen and (b) the manner in which it is configured for display there is no reason to suppose the filmmaker must automatically choose the former over the latter. A certain disorientation rather than orientation, disturbance rather than balm, questioning and wondering rather than affirmation can energize and move a film viewing experience powerfully, even if through watching we are left with uncertainty, doubt, and confusion. After all, life is uncertain, full of doubt, and confusing. A rich film about life will render it this way.

Here are some questions offered up in films ostensibly about subjects far removed; they are rich reservoirs of inspiration to thought and study, not mere obstacles to finding the prize:

- *The Maltese Falcon* (John Huston, 1941). A strange collection of desperate seekers caught up by a sadly depressed private investigator in the hunt for a fabled article of supreme value. Every act and every moment spelled out in terms of an arcane history, a set of filthy negotiations, a willingness to kill. But through this dazzling rational puzzle whispers, promises, and then dully glows the *thing* itself, that for which souls will be on the selling block. The falcon is a jewel-encrusted bird, but can we say we ever really find it? *The operative term is find, not see.* Do we find it? Or do we watch people hunting and thinking to find? As a thing we begin to care about—to wish we could lay our hands on, even briefly—does the falcon ever become realized for us?, and the answer is no. It is proposed to be, and it remains, radiant and shining, though people wallow in darkness in order to have it.

- *Rope* (Alfred Hitchcock, 1948). Two young flatmates commit an atrocity and then, with a perversity never matched onscreen, hold a soirée to secretly celebrate. The body of their victim, still warm, is in a large trunk being used as a serving table for an elaborate meal at a party including, among others, the boy victim's father, girlfriend, and former teacher. Yet something odd is arranged between the viewer and the story. Every instant revolves around the murder that concludes just at the opening credits, every line of casual repartee a hint or a veiled reference, every step of the dance magnetically seduced by the trunk, but David, whom Philip and Brandon strangle: do we ever learn or care about him for a breath? He is a complete nothing, not even a proud young man since he has gone limp as first we see him. A nothing who is history, one of those legions who went before and lived full lives out of our field of vision. And all the film's horses and all the film's men cannot put him back together again, but eerily invoke him as though he is a musical tune they can't get out of their heads.

- *Kiss Me Deadly* (Robert Aldrich, 1955). Finally after a catastrophic search a treasure box is found and, as in the myth and against all imprecation, someone pries it open. We cut to a very long shot so that in safety we can see the atomic blast springing up and away from this thing. Not explosion, note: atomic blast. A mushroom cloud. How much is destroyed at the end of this film? The beach on which we are treading is surely turned to glass. But as that happens, is history reinvented, too, and is cinema itself incinerated and reborn from its ashes?

- *The Incredible Shrinking Man* (Jack Arnold, 1957). One of the truly great religious films. A young man out yachting with his wife is accidentally exposed to a cloud of seeming fog. Later he begins to grow smaller, and the only possible medical opinion is that something radioactive must have been in that cloud and he is shrinking. He shrinks (vastly complex and thrilling effects sequences involving his perilous journey through his middle-class home as he is hunted by a pussycat, then a spider). He is terribly small, this being only a measurement, of course, and, as the various travails illustrate, a measurement entirely relative; but at the very end we are given a haunting in the key of relativity. The camera tracks toward a basement window where he is about to escape through the mesh of a screen. *Escape through the mesh of a screen.* As in screen door, as in movie screen. And, his disembodied voice lets us know, he is still getting smaller, and smaller, and as we look at the dark night filled with stars we see the true and riddling reality of size. Our own size, our own bodies, now trembling.

- *Vertigo* (Alfred Hitchcock, 1958). An unending riddle. What is it that we can say happens in this film? One watches it over and over, and over and over and over, and the gauzy curtains of implication sheath over memory of what was solid, or was anything solid? A performance that we did not see begin, terminates. A second performance that we did not see begin, terminates. A man wholly caught up as audience is left empty-handed. A woman who was in love with him no longer knows what will heal her world.

- *Blow-Up* (Michelangelo Antonioni, 1966). A hip young photographer happens to see lovers in a park and makes pictures of them. The pictures are more entrancing than the lovers. The pictures of the park bring the park to life. But magically, owing to forces we are in no position to estimate, the park itself, as we see it, ascends over the pictures of the park; the park cannot be pictured. Except that the fact that the park cannot be pictured is pictured. And by the neon radiance of a queer sign at night, does our photographer find a body? Because on the green grass, the nocturnal green grass, the body is all black and white, like a picture.

- *Zabriskie Point* (Michelangelo Antonioni, 1970). In the Arizona desert, a girl discovers her true commitments as she heads away from the lavish hilltop aerie of her employer—a craven real estate speculator. She turns to look back at the house, its windows agleam, the sandy rocks blushing, the universe turned silent. And suddenly the thing explodes, explodes entirely, leaving not a rack behind. And again, a second explosion . . . since after the first one, in a flash, the house has been reimagined. And then a third explosion. And then a fourth explosion. And then . . . . . Again and again the house is restored and destroyed, restored in order to be destroyed, destroyed in order to be restored. Is this explosion really happening (in the story)? Or is it a creation of her angry imagination? Does she *wish* the house would explode, or *has she caused* it to explode, or what? It is simply exploding; exploding simply; exploding into simplicity.

- *Chinatown* (Roman Polanski, 1974). During a 1920s political war about the delivery of Owens Valley water to the City of Los Angeles, a detective falls into contact with a woman who steals his rational capacity with her arrogant beauty and cold wealth. He cannot have her as a man wants to have, yet he can have her if she will talk to him, if she will rebound his uncertainties. We come to see a massive machine, the pressures and lures and secrets and desecrations that make the city, especially this city, which rests upon a foundation of illusory bedrock and builds an illusion—but only an illusion—of paradise. City as Persian carpet, patterned with conceit and deceit, with hunger and hope, with water and with gold. Money everywhere, perhaps nowhere on earth more conspicuously, yet the most important money is hidden where no one will find it, except our detective, who finds everything. We will learn that this enchantress, this Circe, is not the person she says she is, nor even the person she reveals she is, but some still unseen and unknown fairy of modernity, cobbler of dreams.

- *My Dinner with Andre* (Louis Malle, 1981). Two men sit to dine at a posh uptown restaurant in Manhattan. One, a celebrated director of theater, Andre Gregory, regales the other, a budding playwright (and son of the former editor of *The New Yorker*), Wallace Shawn, with fabulous stories in a chain that calls up *Sheherazade*. That invocation is even material, since the content of the tales is decidedly exotic, seductive, mysterious, and incomplete in such a way that another tale can follow afterward to foray more deeply into the darkness. We are taken into a Polish forest, to a woods on Long Island, to a Buddhist flagmaker's. But do we ever actually leave that table? Where can we say we are as this film proceeds, and where do we believe we should be? (Saying is not believing.)

- *sex, lies, and videotape* (Steven Soderbergh, 1989). A young traveler with a video camera comes to town to visit an old girlfriend and begins to make a tape of her sister, then a tape of her, talking in the most private and awkward way about her sex. He apparently has a large collection of such tapes. The interviews are conducted with full assent, and he intrudes only to prompt the evocations with "helpful" questions. This living camera—this man attached to a camera—how does he have the desire not for the touch of flesh but for the touch of light, and for the touch of the voice, that most sexual of organs? Even watching him at work, patiently watching the women open themselves to his curiosity, we are put in wonder of their desire to be known as voices (the voice, not the body, animates his tapes) and in wonder of his desire to encounter the pleasure of hearing.

- *Birth* (Jonathan Glazer, 2004). A young woman suddenly loses her husband. While she grieves she chances to meet a little boy, who approaches her to say he is the husband, now returned—for her. Her friends and family are filled with doubt and suspicion, as, at first, is she. But she grows more and more comfortable with the boy, who seems to know many private things. She is finally in tears with the conviction the boy *is* the husband, and that somehow in dying he was transformed—a process entirely mysterious and unknowable. She accepts him. And after she has accepted him, it is found that the whole escapade was a charade he was playing, and he is actually an unknown. But in the heart of this woman, what battle can have been waged, what rivers grown turbulent, that an eleven-year-old's claims to be her husband could even for a moment be considered true? What forces does she believe are in action all around her? Because these forces, whatever they be, do not dissipate as quickly as this film will.

- *Personal Shopper* (Olivier Assayas, 2016). A girl is living in Paris because her twin brother (i) died there of a heart condition that she shares, and (ii) promised he would contact her after death. Thinking herself especially "sensitive," and reading assiduously about some notable "spiritual" encounters, she comes to believe the brother is *there*. On a train voyage from Paris to London, she is approached and interacted with at length, by way of an iPhone text conversation, coming from she knows not whom. Finally, in Africa, opening her mouth to address the brother, she is given a sign. Here, a delicate and charged performance by Kristen Stewart makes entirely believable the girl's susceptibility to influential effect, her sincere openness, her sensible practicality. But in order to watch the film thoroughly, the viewer must come to the belief that the brother *may* be there. Submitting to the film's command—because otherwise the experience is only mundane—a viewer comes to see his or her believing self, now, in a very new way.

- *A Ghost Story* (David Lowery, 2017). A young man is killed in a car accident but remains to inhabit his home for an unending time, standing in a corner of a room, watching, knowing, expecting. Through his eyes—except that faced with his draping white concealment, or his draping white being, we have no way to know, really, that behind the dark openings in his "head" he has eyes—we see the wife and how she continues her life, her sale of the house and her moving away; the new owners and their lives; and eventually, with surprise while staring through the kitchen window at a neighboring house, a *second ghost* in habitation over there. Back and forth in historical time our ghost moves, always inhabiting the same spot. The film is an unrelenting confrontation with the white-sheathed ghost, the presence with no form, no name, no desire, no need, the mere observer, quite as though instead of seeing what a camera has filmed we are given to see the camera itself, seeing. But seeing in quasi-human form. So unrelenting is the ghost, so peaceful but also so present, that it will not be denied. It exists. There are ghosts, while we watch for them.

These effects are but a small number of possibilities: cinematic invocations of the unseen and unseeable, the marginal feeling or doubtful feeling, insatiable yearning, fraught imagination, seduction by exoticism. Sensible, rational organization of activity is overcome. The reasonable world is left far behind. Is cinema, we may ask, especially capable of not only addressing but inhabiting this zone of wonder and enchantment? Cinema, that not only joins fragments into ostensible unities but also invokes the chasms between the fragments. Cinema, that flows in time while also being able to jump. Cinema that mirrors. Cinema that positions itself. Cinema that sees and cannot see. Cinema that, finally, money can't buy. Cinema that shows us the still pond in which, thinking to slake our thirst, we see that figure beckoning.

Spaced Out

Setting from Blow-Up *(Michelangelo Antonioni, MGM, 1966). Photograph by Murray Pomerance.*

Very near the beginning of *Blow-Up* (1966), a ragged-looking young fellow, who has spent the night in a doss house, steps out of the shadows near a railway overpass. The structure from which he is walking is a very high, red brick arch with a parabolic opening to the road. A sign marks it CONSORT ROAD, something of a wry "comment," since this person is definitely neither a consort nor with one. He is shambling to, as we surprisedly discover, an elegant dark green Mercedes. (He will shortly prove to have been in masquerade, so that he could "fit in" and make clandestine photographs. He is a photographer. He will be publishing a book.)

Any viewer of this scene could reasonably wonder what it would be to follow this person, catch his actions, decode them, note the progression as a syntax, surmise what he plans to do next, and so on; and utterly to affiliate with him as well, to crawl beneath his skin and stand there looking out, with the street sign over one's shoulder. We bond with characters and through bonding adopt a narrative position from which to spy the film. Looking at this young man standing and gazing we are very much not occupying his point of view; he is occupying ours. Bonding can make us see situations through the logic the character uses, thus in principle take on a characterological position for viewing. Most crucially, as we bond with the character we transform ourselves. It is evident that the character knows neither the fact that we are watching him nor the theatrical space in which we watch. We are not available for him as watchers to be watched, indeed as watchers we are available only for ourselves, able to remember, perhaps just vaguely, the architecture of the space we're in, where the exits and toilets are, how to get a bag of popcorn, where we bought a ticket. And able, of course, to discern and fixate upon the space the screen shows.

Our awareness goes further. If we know where to buy a ticket, we know how much a ticket costs, and we know that we can afford it. So we know about money more generally, and our personal economy, too. We know that we get money from some kind of interactional process (labor, inheritance) and therefore that there is a wider world in which we engage with people, pick up resonances, store memories. We know, too, that we have lives, that the body is to be kept clean and well nourished if possible—not like the now relatively dirty body of this fellow out of the doss house; that we were born, that we grow and have grown, that there is nature, that there is time. The character standing at Consort Road knows none of this about us; being a character he is unaware of being in an audience's view. We are not there for him. We might like to imagine that he knows such things about himself, that he operates the way we do, even though if he operates too much the way we do he suddenly becomes unworthy of our special attention.

We are there as hypothetical eyes, figurative watchers who can see him standing, see him move, perhaps note the way he is dressed. Overnight in the doss house he disguised himself to offset the men's wary looking at him, picking him out, keeping their distance. In his capacity as photographer, someone sensitive to being caught out, being gazed at, he plays to figures who are without position or character for him beyond what he will catch for, say, 1/8th of a second; without background or position that he will care about, without commitment of one kind or another: call them his threatening audience, since while he is photographing them he must always take care lest they see what he is doing. And it is not only the character all grizzled and worn who knows others as an audience, it is also, and intensively, the professional actor embodying the fellow for the camera, who knows about some audience in its own doss house.

We transform ourselves when we watch. We take on what the narrative calls for, we travel where we are asked to go.

And now we are at Consort Road.

(Consorts ourselves, perhaps.)

What might it be if we crossed the hidden axis between our dream-caught moviegoing self and the everyday self sitting to view, if we drew away from invisibly being present at "Consort Road" and came back to the theater, came to believe in the actual physical presence of a Consort Road somewhere out there upon the earth, a presence of the same kind we have while watching—occupying real space as we occupy space. Say we left that *picture of* Consort Road behind and, as a venturing, living, walking, hungering self actually proceeded to Consort Road? Actually brought ourselves to stand where that fellow we watched was standing, next to that road sign, beside the grimy bricks, at the lip of the shadowy parabola? What if we transformed diegetic space into trans-diegetic space, the fiction into the reality, his wholly fictional body (as we take it) into an actual body in space, our body . . . there.

As I have noted elsewhere, though without detail (see *Michelangelo*), I did stand there (after having seen *Blow-Up* a couple of dozen times). I walked to the exact spot, I entered the dark passageway, I walked through with the train tracks far overhead, I emerged where he emerged. What was it like to stand there? And to conceive where the camera must have been, helping me gaze at him. Since this was an action embedded in memory of an experience of film, what can be thought about it?

- As with any film location, there is a pressing sense of being in a hybrid space composed of sharply etched surfaces and glaring lacunae, literally emptinesses all round. There is a position one wishes to take, not a territory one explores as the character may have done. One is entering a shot, not a narrative universe. Onscreen one will often see a spot from one side only, so that the entire camera-side is missing and in real experience can be replaced only partially. The peripheries are lacunae.

- My placement is horridly confined to my experiential position, always, so I am standing just as the photographer-character did, my back to the darkness of the underpass as he looked out and away from the place. In order to see the place as I saw it in the film, I must take a few steps further, then turn around, so I am positioned opposite to where he stood, like a camera. And then neither he nor I can be there to be looked at. I was there on a sunnier day than he was.

- Specific details leap out. The bricks are very old, precisely as in the film, but my filmgoer's memory-judgment puts a little more yellow in them. Did they shoot with a filter? The parabolic opening is literally towering, while in the film, from Antonioni's camera position, it doesn't look quite so high. Narrow, yawning upward. There is vegetation at the top, spilling over from the sides of the railway.

- The road sign is there, blessedly. It says what it should say, CONSORT ROAD, and the font is what it should be, and I know that if our photographer came back he wouldn't be lost.

- He merely materialized here, of course, and we made the presumption that on the other side of the tunnel from which he emerged, or even opening into the tunnel halfway through it, was the doss house. But in fact I had to walk several blocks from the nearest bus stop before I could even see the tunnel (on the wrong side) and had to walk all the way through it before I could know it was right. The doss house wasn't really near there at all.[1]

---

[1] Consort Road is in Peckham; the doss house is in Camberwell—the continuity is purely filmic.

- We get very little sense of the surrounding area in the film, but it is predominantly working-class and around the tunnel itself there are no shops.

- Outside, and down the street, no Mercedes is parked.

I tell myself that all of the modulations of this place, from the film rendition toward my experience of it, were owed to (a) adjustments the filmmaker insisted upon, for his own reasons, or (b) adjustments made at Consort Road after the film was made, and in the course of quite normal urban upkeep and development. In this life, one can never go back to any place at all and expect it to be the same. But being able to swear that Consort Road is always exactly, precisely, wholly, and unreservedly the same on the screen, I was of course given satisfaction to see that the screen world stretched out into real life. I imagine to myself how a lens on the camera could have reduced the yawning height of the parabolic opening. And I work to remember the shot as a composition so that I can look out and decide exactly where the camera would have had to be, and equipped with what lens, to make the shot as it looks.

The photographer-character is there first thing in the morning—men who sleep in a doss house are sent away after breakfast; they do not spend the day inside. I could not possibly get to that part of London from my residence early enough for that. But it was morning.

The thrill of standing at Consort Road, that is, of entering if not the movie then the world that stood under the movie's umbrella, being as near as one could be—that thrill was amazingly short-lived and passed before I could seize it. It wasn't so much awareness of occupying the space that had been occupied by David Hemmings that tickled me, the space that had been filled by David Hemmings's body—David Hemmings who had died some years before I stood there, in Bucharest—as it was standing where David Hemmings's character had taken himself, being, for a split second, and only for *that* split second, the character. This is why I suggest "crossing the axis." Albeit I was not going to be sighing with relief at having successfully got away from the doss house with my film intact, nor thinking, "Now where did I leave the car?" But for a few seconds of my life, I came close—I felt I came close—to merging with, let us say, a few frames of film.

The merging:

Yes, perhaps to enliven the film, to give it flesh and blood, my own flesh and blood. That is, to become piquantly aware of the pictorial—and the celluloid—nature of film itself, that in a movie we see pictures of living characters played by living actors yet the forms we see are not alive in themselves even as they relentlessly point to life. And by coming into so close a partnership, perhaps I could share some life with the character, give him a heartbeat—just one heartbeat. But of course, I would not either presume or surrender to give him my heartbeat, or my pound of flesh. If not a heartbeat, the *idea* of a heartbeat. Perhaps it's as a kind of brother that I link to him, or as a close friend. We walked together, he and I, we were and are there together, at Consort Road. He was with some men from a doss house, and they dispersed. Perhaps this makes him feel lonely and he needs my company, even for that tiny spate of time. As well, I have a feeling of not being in the film, of being barred, a castaway, a saddening feeling of having missed the boat, or, if one goes to see a shot being taken, a feeling of being trapped on the wrong side of the camera. This has happened to me many times, this feeling of being locked away on the wrong side of things.

And a linguistic wrapping binds, too. He is standing in a place, and the movie shows bluntly that the place is named CONSORT ROAD. I am standing at the same place, in London (right across the way from the Peckham Bus Garage). The same sign is there attesting to the identity. Very often—for the location fan, far too often—the signs are either missing or entirely different, because the art director mounted signs where there were none or put up signs in place of the ones that were there already. But here is to be found a sign behind my shoulder, CONSORT ROAD, and behind the photographer's shoulder is the same sign. His shoulder, my shoulder. The same parabolic entrance above and around us, quite elegant. The same shabby gray pavement and grime-worn stones. All of the street space, including the pavement, smaller in reality, just as the tunnel opening is huger. The lens alters space.

An odd circumstantial link. As happens in the story of the film, the photographer is only looking for his car, only relaxing and catching a breath, and then he heads away. For him that will be the end of CONSORT ROAD. I catch a breath and inhale the space, and then I, too, head away since, just like him, I have no further business here. What this space is to me is the presence of itself as my surround, my ability to bring the presence of myself into its precinct.

My pleasures of location confound and dislocate more than comfort and orient me. Irony is always in some way displacing. I am not in *Blow-Up*, and standing at Consort Road does not open a portal by which I can enter the film with my body, as I enter this urban place. I am "at the scene" but not "in the scene." The place in which I am standing was collimated off by the camera's framing, and here with my eyes wide open I can see much more of the territory than the film could show (or needed to show, for that matter). This space I am in is not the filmic space, then. Could one say the filmic space is *inside* this space? Part of the charm of the filmic space came, as with all filmic spaces, from one's *not* being able to take it in beyond the edges of the frame, and from a concomitant "filling-in" by inventive imagination of spatial aspects like continuations of line and plane.

I extend the film frame, wildly, but also with constraint, because the film is moving on and my eye must follow. But there is a sky up there, even if not shown.

Filmic spaces do not faithfully represent actuality, and then actuality is powerless to faithfully represent them. Consort Road becomes a memento, an aide memoire, and my memory of the film is more present than Consort Road. The scene in the film ascends to a plane of reality higher and more noteworthy than my presence on the street. Higher because graceful. And because this tawdry imitation, the only real, seems to stand back with humble respect.

41

Rabbit

Moira Shearer in The Red Shoes *(Michael Powell and Emeric Pressburger, The Archers, 1948). Digital frame enlargement.*

Boris Lermontov, the celebrated impresario, will have Victoria Page as the star of his ballet company. But before we can see this happen, Anton Walbrook coddling and nourishing and commanding Moira Shearer, and then finally, perhaps, destroying her, we must see the audition. *The Red Shoes* (Michael Powell and Emeric Pressburger, 1948). He takes himself to the unimposing precincts of the Mercury Theater, Notting Hill Gate, to watch her dance the Swan with the Ballet Rambert, a tiny company with enough money for only a cheap backdrop and an offstage gramophone for broadcasting the score. When she is on, he will beam his eyes at her, a new-age Leeuwenhoek, and she will train her dark glauque eyes back on him.

This is the galvanic moment when souls collide, her passion and his hunger. Her irreconcilable passion and his unassuageable hunger. She would love to become his star, which—she doesn't quite grasp—would mean becoming *his* altogether—in the spiritual sense—and he would love nothing more than to develop this girl's astounding promise into the graceful polish required of those who step onto his august stage. He came to the theater tonight in hopes she might prod his fancy—who can know when this will happen, in life? She is dancing to give herself entirely to art, and when he comes into her sights his is an imposing, even regal, form. For Vicki it is already too late to work on giving an impression.

He is dressed darkly, has wavy brown hair and gleaming brown eyes. She is all in white, with white (swan) feathers on her head. The camera glides assiduously over the stage, in medium-long shot, to show the construction of the dance, and to feature the corps de ballet finishing a move before, like a line of swans, they shuffle themselves off. Now she is alone in the light, living flesh radiant against the pastel backing, the music charging her with feeling. The choreography requires her to launch into a frenzied pirouette, and as she twirls, with lightning rapidity, her view of the gazing audience is given in a series of flash pans. A zone of concentration and a space to be aware of, without a point of concentration. But as she stops in the twirl, we cut to a facial portrait of him, looking forward with discerning eyes and no expression. No expression at all, and eyes that, having seen a great deal of dance, know the route into the dancer's heart.

But then, a close shot of Vicki staring back. Surprised, cold, distant, haughty, poised, regal, supreme, terrified . . . *She has found her point of concentration.*

How is the action of the encounter managed on the screen? The encounter will *make* the film, *this is the encounter!!*, and will provoke the film's tragic end, too. And will energize the young dancer's meteoric rise to glory.

[1] Lermontov having earlier (and carefully) been established as (a) fastidious, (b) demanding, (c) musically and aesthetically informed, and (d) eager manager, we know him to be both familiar with ballet music and sophisticated in his sensitivity while hearing it. Thus,

[2] When we find him in the audience of the Mercury, (a) we are not surprised, and (b) we know he is paying devoted attention to what is onstage.

[3] We have already in the film seen enough of Vicki to determine that she can dance. But can she hold the stage alone, and with strength?

[4] The camera must (a) find her amid the corps, thus dancing in company, with skill, teamsmanship, force (yet not too much force), and shapeliness; and (b) begin to isolate her as a discreet figure worth *special* attention. Yet at the same time,

[5] The *special* attention she gets must come fully and only from the devotion of the viewer, her viewer, and not from any contrivance imported to the diegesis by the filmmaking team. That team is estimating itself as part of the Mercury audience, and that audience taken as a whole cannot leap up to gesture out a close shot. The isolation of the dancer is accomplished onstage

through choreography, and through the isolated lyricism of the score once she begins her solo turn. Thus, the ballet makes her an individual swan and in seeing that individuality we are merely following the directions given by the ballet. But we must have the impression Lermontov's sensibilities have been awakened, or are waiting to be awakened, and so the springing forth for a "close" view of her is *his* idea even more than the film's. Another way to say this: springing forward for that close-up, every viewer believes herself to be the impresario.

[6] Shearer is already an accomplished dancer, working with the Sadler's Wells Ballet (from which company, by special negotiation with Ninette de Valois, Powell has drawn her to work for him). She can do the moves. She can do the moves well. But her Vicki is also somewhat nervous at the thought that Lermontov might conceivably be out there, and to show the frenzy of her anxiety Powell opts for the pirouette to be handled through the flash pans that give *the dancer's perspective* as she spins. It is as though Vicki handles the physical moves on auto-pilot while the perceptual apparatus is concentrated on scanning the viewers. For her, and also for us at this moment, the world is spinning, spinning rapidly and seemingly out of control, spinning on its way toward a trajectory out of the solar system. She is dancing into darkness, dancing to she knows not where in the unknown future. And if the shots can work properly we are spinning, too, that is, having our perspective wrenched away, losing our speed regulator, becoming Dervishes. And of course, *we do not quite manage this on auto-pilot!*, though the camera's fluid movement works to assist.

[7] The facial portrait of Lermontov needs to be lit to do two things unmistakably, (a) identify him quickly and explicitly, so that we are urged to think of the dance that has just flown by as an event witnessed (now, alongside us) by him, thus to know that his sighting is an evaluation and his evaluation has career and commercial tangents; and (b) focus on his eyes, not his face, since it is his ability to view and to retain what he has viewed that counts, not his personality taken as a whole. His eyes, dark as they are, must seem to project beams of—not illumination but—the galvanic light that is the emanation of pure receptivity—"Now the eye is without any doubt the symbol of the dazzling sun" (Bataille 74), when the sun watches us. He must seem to draw her in, yet not with the kind of allurement through which a seduction would happen. Just previously, Powell and Pressburger had filmed a gigantic staircase on which individuals were *drawn up to heaven* (Stairway to Heaven [A Matter of Life and Death], 1946), and here the same power of traction and magnetism is in effect. This is why I use the word "galvanic," from Luigi Galvani (1737–98), the "inventor" of "animal electricity." Lermontov must seem to receive a *charge* when he watches Vicki. And

[8] Vicki must seem to register a *charge* when, right afterward, she sees him seeing. The two charges come more or less at once—the conjoined shots with precise edit match suggest simultaneity. We can think of this as a "meeting" of spirits.

[9] Her facial portrait will be closer than his and more stunning. Stunning partly because of this closeness and the way it causes her face to fill the frame, and partly because we can see the makeup she wears to accentuate her features, that is now augmenting the power of her realizing eyes. At this instant he feels closer to her than she feels to him, thus the size difference.

[10] To be a "swan," she has whitened her face under that white feather-cap, and because the face is whitened other adjustments must be made. She must always appear to be, if not quite actually a swan, of course, a human-bird, or a bird-human, the resultant of some magical transform. Therefore, we will see her boldly reddened lips and her piercing, but artfully made-up, eyes. The eyes have mascara on the lids and underskins, and dark makeup has been drawn over the eyebrows to shape and accentuate them. Over her temples, and springing from the corners of the eyes, the avian look emerges from drawn dark lines. Her eyelashes are long and very black (as she is theatrical, we well imagine they may be false). And, because her white face under the white hat will flatten in our vision, will simply spread without form, the viewing eye must be drawn to a center of the portrait *out of which* her features can believably and bravely leap. Thus, on each side, at the point where the eyelid conjoins with the top of the nasal bridge, the dancer has put a rose-pink dot; and at the outer edge of each eye, amid the black streaks, a slim red one. Now we are focused on the center of her presence and attentiveness, and on her swanishness.

As ballet, unlike cinema, does not possess a close-up, the danced Odile need not be made up to look avian at all, and typically is not.

[11] A sufficient eyeline match must be established between the Lermontov shot and the Page shot so that Lermontov can be known as looking straight "into" her and she can be known as seeing him do this. It is quite as though each speaks with an entirely idiosyncratic voice, and in unison with the other: "The voice is the element which ties the subject and the Other together, without belonging to either, just as it formed the tie between body and language without being part of them" (Dolar 103). But Vicki cannot be seen as naïve, only untried, when she begins with him. And

[12] When she stops her pirouette in the dramatic pose that occasions the jump to a macro-close facial portrait, she needs to use her arms and body to gesture the stop in a show of dramatized abruptness, something perfectly ambiguous, indeed harbinger of an ambiguity we will not really see resolved in the film. Is she (a) merely dancing out the scripted moves for the ballet, and with a

professional polish; or (b) a dancer doing the scripted moves for the ballet, but with a cutting performative display intended exactly to communicate to him as well as to stun him. Officially, the audience is invisible, after all, but now she is not only looking out to see what is happening but demonstrating the looking-out as a willful act. Is it (a) the Swan or (b) Victoria Page who has shockingly stopped for this facial portrait? And since the answer can only be (b), to what degree may we now think of her as not only arranging for but also beckoning, shaping, and extending this man's attentions?

[13] That Lermontov is shown in the dark penumbra of the audience, and that Vicki is shown in the light-infused aura of the stage merely emphasizes what he has claimed to believe all along, that she will be marvelous in front of an audience (timid though she seems to be in offstage life). She must be in the spotlight not only now actually to do this performance of *Swan Lake* (an act-within-an-act), but *now implicitly*, the sort who will always find the spotlight, the sort who has stardom in her blood, try though she might to deny it.

[14] And, too, the seriousness of Lermontov's mien will convey something broader, indeed more institutional, about this moment, a moment that is actually, for all its performative glamor, embedded in institutional requirements and demands. No matter her talent, no matter her drive, no matter her astonishing beauty, no matter her relationship to the wealthy Lady Neston, no matter her youth, no matter her amicability, no matter, no matter, no matter, Vicki Page must audition. Nobody gets with Lermontov until there is an audition. From his point of view, you never know what anybody will do on a stage until you put them on a stage, a real stage, a real stage in a real performance. And from her point of view, since she will always inevitably be something of a nervous wreck dancing for the imperious Lermontov, she must endure the experience as a test, she must move herself here through a commission of the body and mind, not to say the spirit, and the very least wrong "step" could turn him permanently away.

[15] And why, of all possibilities, *Swan Lake* (March 4, 1877, Bolshoi Theater)? Can it be because the ballet is the story of a princess turned into a swan through the curse of a sorcerer? A princess (the sweet young Victoria) turned into a swan (the fabulous ballerina) through the curse (the imperium) of a sorcerer (Lermontov, seducer par excellence)? If she can show that she can go through the routine onstage here tonight, that she can be a princess turned into a swan, then surely as a princess she can be turned into a swan tomorrow. How does Lermontov put it to his designer? "My dear Ratov, even the best magician cannot pull a rabbit out of a hat if there wasn't a rabbit in the hat in the first place." Yet, note. The best magician in the world (and Lermontov is demonstrably regarded as such all through the film) cannot *know* there is a rabbit in the hat until he takes a look.

And can it be, too, because while *Stairway to Heaven* was in production, Moira Shearer was dancing the lead in *Swan Lake* at Covent Garden?

* * *

If we consider how a viewer could be stunned by a screen moment like this one, how it may seem as though a rabbit is being pulled out of a hat, it is apparent that a number of different factors are involved as many craftsmen cooperate to fashion the delight. The actors and their mapped bodily movements. The space of the stage and its peculiar, soft, welcoming light. It must seem an embracing, not a harsh, world up there. The ballerina's swan costume, its pristine whiteness appearing to bleach her face. The cinematographer's key lights sharpening the acuteness of Walbrook's gaze. The meticulous shot construction which facilitates a clean edit that reveals a match of eyelines. The setting of physical moves against musical cues. The echoes of *Swan Lake* infusing the atmosphere of the Mercury Theater in this small-scale performance. The tension of the audition. The careful modulation of the portraiture so we see not only particular characters but each of them in a particular way, guided and shaped by the focus, the lighting, the depth of field. The ballerina's scarlet lipstick triumphing, finally, over every aspect of the vision, and abetted in its boldness by the animation of her eyes.

The animation: that in Vicki (that in Shearer) there is an *animus*. That she has not only a cultured but also an animal presence. And to match it, Walbrook's Lermontov has an animal presence, too, while the others in this little audience do not.

42

M'm! M'm! Good!

Stardust Memories *(Woody Allen, Jack Rollins and Charles H. Joffe Productions, 1980). Digital frame enlargement.*

> *Consider the exact sense in which a work of art is said to be "in good or bad taste." It does not mean that it is true, or false; that it is beautiful, or ugly; but that it does or does not comply either with the laws of choice, which are enforced by certain modes of life; or the habits of mind produced by a particular sort of education.*
>
> John Ruskin

Frequently when I have seen a film I am faced with a very specific quiz. Did I like it? And if I say no, "Why not?" Very little about the filmgoing experience is more typical than this summary judgment, which on my part always feels, by the way, a little like the introduction to an inquisition. If not this one, what film *did* I like, then? And why? And didn't I think that the scene with the . . .

Whether in the popular domain the challenge seems pertinent, of making a serious evaluation of a work rather than an expression of momentary pleasure or displeasure, still, being evaluative about film is more complicated than with some other forms of art. With prose, for instance, it seems readily apparent whether a text is well or badly written no matter what ideals it seeks. Sentences make sense or they do not, again and again. When we read Dickens or Forster, for example, the language on the page is transparent. With painting one can see whether the artist understands foreshortening and perspective, even if he or she is playing with it. The composition either has integrity or it does not. And interestingly, one makes judgments such as these quite free of knowledge of what the writer faces as a writer when he writes; what the painter faces as a painter. A writer, I would surmise, has more to say about good and bad writing than a lay reader. And a painter knows more about good and bad painting than someone who has never taken a brush to hand. One of the really interesting aspects of cinema, especially narrative cinema, is that filmmakers—directors, producers, cinematographers, designers, performers, and so on—have not by and large spoken out about good and bad films, yet they know how to see on the screen much more than lay viewers see.

Also, for the lay viewer (as I pose this character, and oddly, since we have all seen many more films these days than people saw in the 1930s and the decades immediately after), there is a great deal onscreen to distract attention from cinema itself, its form, its agonies: the fame of the performers, the exoticism of the locales, the swiftness of the camera's darting, the slickness of the progression of the story, and so on. Even the story itself will be an immense distraction from the way it is told. Stories have that power to captivate. Unless one is really interested, passionately interested, in the act of *telling stories,* or in this case *showing stories,* one can pay attention to the roller-coaster ups and downs, the twists, the surprises, the quirkiness, the glory—all of which have nothing whatever to do with the fact that a very mediocre film treatment may be showing all this.

There are thus two distinct issues in play. First, is the film as a moving picture better or worse? Victor Perkins takes this up with real seriousness in his book *Film as Film.* The second issue involves the viewer's delight or lack of it when the screening is done. Do we *like* this film? Is it yummy? And clearly a bad film can be yummy; a good film can be yummy; a bad film and a good film can be bad on the tongue. These kinds of questions trouble the popular discourse about film, however.

For me after watching a moving picture there is a penumbra of solitude and lassitude, a half-dream state in which I go about my business with the film drifting around me like a fog. I do not leap to passing judgment. I let it settle. Something will—or something will not—come out of the fog. Almost never quickly, however. The idea of the film festival, in which I can leap through as many as five films a day, is simply preposterous to me—if I am really truly watching, only the last one has any chance of staying with me coherently.

Post-viewing interrogations and judgments tend to be given a peculiar weight, more than judgments about traffic jams, for example; as if now, coming in the (presumed) vacuum after the event, as one stands on the street or in a coffee shop, questions take the film's place in consciousness, even complete it or provide an appropriate coda. As though without the question "Did you like it?" or "What do you think?" and my (presumably forthcoming) answer, the film experience would be incomplete. There is the film, and there is what I think, and the two must be sandwiched. In this way not the film but the post-film dialogue will constitute the proper ending. I find thinking this way nonsensical, since the film is presented at once to many people of different styles, tastes, and education, and usually in many countries, so that the "vote" taken so very seriously as part of a momentary conversation lacks the symbolic significance it proposes for itself. A film *is* what I find it to be, me myself, yes; but it is also what *it can be found to be because of what it is;* and the tension between these two antinomies is filling the pages of this book about the agonies of the viewing experience.

After a film one may surely feel the spontaneous need to talk, and therefore the need to have something to talk about, and the film does very well in this capacity, being recent and provocative compared with so much else. But if the film is a powerful one, I believe it will overtake the itch for chatting.

Perhaps viewers are puzzled, and feel the need to know whether they agree about what they have just seen (moral support), and if not, why not: all a matter of finding one's way out of the Forest of Principles. Interestingly, many viewers do not typically want to know why they agree with one another if they do, because disagreement itself is more urgent and agreement seems to be satisfactory unto itself. It need hardly be said that when a film has been given considerable advance touting ("hype") as being "wonderful," "amazing," "groundbreaking," and the like—publicity departments are formed to do this touting, and they spend big budgets—there is special emphasis placed on the demand for an answer. The waves are crashing into the beach: are you with or against them?

The relation between what is good and what is pleasant (what is likeable) is fraught. I know how to recognize a "good" film as (a) a serious accomplishment against supreme artistic difficulties of one kind or another, (b) a poetic whole, (c) a provocation to fascinating and important philosophical musing, (d) a healthy marriage of aesthetic style and compositional form, even (e) a hoist into giddiness. And I know how to find in a "bad" film a travesty of the talents of those who worked on it, a piece of commercial pap aimed at—not the audience's lowest point but—some widespread yen for superficial gratification. Yet I can like almost anything under the right conditions, and dislike almost anything as well. I would never presume to claim that I like only films that are "good," because I do recognize that I am easily appealed to by what a discerning judge might call trash. A superficial case: Ingmar Bergman's *The Touch* (1971) and Chuck Jones's *Rabbit of Seville* (1950) are both, and differently, good films. The cartoon is indubitably more loveable, but what is good about it has to do with skill and form, not the taste for fun that it satisfies.

I think I "like" a film when some or another aspect of the thing resonates in harmony with specific qualities of my experience, biographical, clearly contexted, or floating in an ether. Therefore, my "liking" is temporally located. Because of the accumulation of my experience by the time I see it, something catches me that would never have caught me twenty years before. Or else—and this is disarmingly frequent—a film that caught me twenty years ago now surprises me with its thinness, and I wonder who that person could possibly have been, claiming to love it back then. I don't suppose this is about "who I am"—my identity—so much as about what I can sense happening and recollect having happened to me, around me, for me, with me, owing to my presence.

I am affected by my experience, sometimes enduringly, even when I cannot bring it to consciousness. A film—more precisely, a moment in a film—can trigger my memory of experience, can make address to it, can possibly even replicate it, can even stimulate me to stretch beyond it, all either with or without that quality reasonable thinkers about film call "artistic value." I love many films that don't merit serious attention. Moreover, I can approach a film seriously even though I do not like it, just as I can back away from a film even though I do. Even as a film can be a "good" film, a "good" example of what film—film and only film—can be, I can sometimes find no feeling for it. One does not explain or justify one's feelings, they derive from the subtle beach of time on which one stands, or once stood, as the waves of affect roll in.

I remember that when I first saw Antonioni's *L'Avventura* (1962), which is a very fine film indeed, I did not like it. I very much did not like it. Later I grew to like it a lot. Like, dislike, dislike, like. All along it was a very fine film, no matter what I thought—the filmmaker didn't creep in during that lapse of time to recut it for me. If one is too green, many hints pass one by.

Feeling about film is often a currency, an interactional counter, that can be shared as a basis for building esteem. One finds words to abbreviate and convey it, it becomes a game piece to be tossed among friends not one of whom has the slightest chance of persuading any of the others. Or it is a handy pick for hoisting oneself higher and higher on the mountain of opinion, putting oneself where it is possible to look down on the miserables who do not agree. Or a way of meeting a new friend. Or a self-direction. I "like" a film by one director so I go to see other films by this director. Or other films starring this actor. Or other films designed by this designer. If I express it loudly, assuredly enough, my judgment powers the vehicle of my self, credits me, erases my self-doubt, helps me breathe. But all the while I am breathing, there is the film with its own life, breathing the way only it can breathe, holding together against the forces of the cultural storm.

43

Brotherly Love

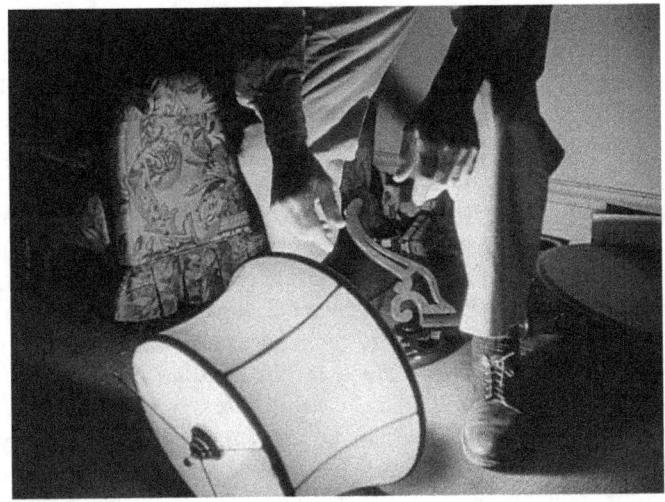

Crossfire *(Edward Dmytryk, RKO, 1947). Digital frame enlargement.*

In the land of the blind the one-eyed man is king.

H. G. Wells

As I watch a film, directly and responsively, it is something like dreaming, in that I do not summon a critical, evaluative consciousness to judge the experience. While I dream, I do not bring forth a theory of dreaming. Outside, afterward, looking back to an experience remembered, I may try to understand and explain and even describe whatever fragments I have been able to retain, but when I am in the middle I float and swim; swim and float. The dreamer cannot know that he is dreaming, although the word "dream" may be sounded around him. And when we are with films, if we are deeply there, it is much the same: only when we have dropped out do we know a film was a film, we know we were watching it, we know it was made to be watched by someone. What is the way we see when we are inside the form? What is our relation to the unknown transparency rendering all this?

The camera, *hypocrite, mon frère*. In an everlasting willingness to go where it bids me to go, even into demonic places whither I curse that I am brought, I wonder and wonder as to its amazing powers not only to glide and turn, to climb and drop, but also to leap through time and space with the grace of a cat. This thing, this alter ego, this brother under the skin, this keeper of secrets has an unparalleled generosity, it hands over what it sees without stint, and without requiring provocation. Before this paragon I submit myself as stranger, so that it may show me the world. There is nothing in the camera's eye that is not offered to me, that I do not take up with hunger and interpret as scripture. It is more than my friend, it is my secret self, I am linked to it by the chain of experience. I never see it make to reveal to me anything that, even in shame, I would be unable to let myself encounter. Nor does it shirk, even in darkness, from penetrating space in order to retrieve and carry back the exact vision that transubstantiates.

This camera-friend, or camera-king, takes the form of a gentle hand holding mine. Its tastes are well known to me, its pleasures I intensively experience, and it gains no recognition from its schizoid sibling, the production camera (about which I know nothing). The production camera, that I know enough to point to but that I do not point to when I am watching, is a dull insensate thing perched on a dull insensate dolly. Its ventrum is popped open so that it can be loaded with stock or with quadrillions of electrons happy and ready. The production camera is a tool, owed to the producer, paid for, serviced and reserviced, loaded, operated, moved in various ways, and always, without end, presumed to be capable of the most articulate renditions of light.[1] My camera-friend, however, invented more or less by me discreetly, becomes the agent by whose doings the "world of the film" is accessible, is warmed and made familiar to strangers, is given as a space with dimension, event, meaning, and gravity, when of course this "world" is no world but only light beams bouncing back from a screen. (Not that light beams are not of our world, or to the world.) As the filmmaker (who may very well know some general audience) does not know me as I watch the work, so his production camera does not recognize the presence of, or interact with, the camera-friend I am following. The director may know where he wishes his audience to go, and arrange for the action to be followed accurately by his production camera, but he can never know what I may wish to see now, and see next, and by offering myself up to the camera-friend I am implicitly stating my hope and expectation that this being will give me the right show. Just as there is an axis between the audience and the director and his team, so there is an axis between the two divided parts of the camera's split personality.

My camera-friend has a viscid gaze, that clings to things and oozes along their surfaces in order that I may breathe and breathe again while I see, and even when, in the throes of panic, it darts like a flying insect.

When I watch what it gives me to watch I bring no books. I make no trades. My pal figures for me accountants, killers, grease monkeys, professors of history, concubines with insatiable hunger, drinkers of tea. I am willing—or claim myself to be willing—

---

[1] The Technicolor camera was in fact returned to the corporation every night after shooting was done, taken apart, cleaned, and prepared for use in the morning—all this by contract with the film's producer who had made the decision to shoot in Technicolor.

to break all the laws of men in order see, without any limit except the limiting form imposed upon me, within which belt I sweetly impose myself in the name of modesty. The images delivered to me, every last one, have a perfect honesty, whether they reveal what appears to emerge from the heart or whether they conceal truths under artificial impositions, because every surface, even every false one, is caught, recorded, offered without modification that I can recognize. In short, contrived or caught, fabricated or found, the images sent my way all look—all are accepted as—complete in themselves. All purport to transmit—and I believe they do transmit—the unexpurgated whole of what is now and here available, and transmit, too, through their working invisibility (that I can taste) the rejection of what may be kept back by a force itself kept back.

There is a great deal I agree to forget in order to put the camera-friend in my embrace. My earthly bindings, all the meat of my transactions, my maps, my need for sunlight. My obediences lapse, my contracts are suspended, the soil on my body fails to register even as, staring ahead in the darkness, I find glowing before me the face of people who never travel, never desert this holy space, and "[do] not seem much the worse, except that they are all fantastically dirty" (Orwell 3). Or polished like mirrors or burnished like gold, running like the desert with sand, wetted by the sea, but all, each, in every way, everywhere, incessantly fantastic. I forget how I came into the thing's company, my desire for the experience, my trek to the Odeon, my forfeiture of the proper token, my stumbling to find a private place in the salt-ridden ancient bouillabaisse of the seats. I forget the curtain with its fronds of colored light (very, very 1950s!). I forget everything but promise.

I will go where I am led by this brother, this *cicerone*, this alien. Doubtless, should I believe I am seeing the thing itself—unlikely—it would fail to resemble a camera but would seem instead a person slightly taller than I am, with a hand reaching back to take mine. It reveals the world to me while at the same time revealing nothing. I never find out why it picks some forms to follow, others to disregard. Its delight in spatial depths, in sparks of light will always be inscrutable. On and on it knows the way, as though following a chart that does not exist. Yet, still, it has a profound sensitivity to my moods, it not only services me but offers companionship, so that if I hesitate in fear or reach forward in eager curiosity it moves as I hope it will, back or forward, and in this sense it is my company, like the best of companions.

My presence as an onlooking viewer of the film is made possible, made bearable only because I eagerly agree to take the hand of this one-eyed companion, and it lasts as long as I permit the thing to linger by me, to tickle my impulses, to catch my eyebrows raising when it shows me someone uttering a magical word. This camera-king has full access to every aspect of the film's universe, hands over the material with the greatest sureness and confidence, the most replete responsibility. It exists as the spirit of the film. It exists to represent and stand in for the spirit of the film. Nothing that is to be given is left out. No one who is to be known remains unseen, unmet, unchallenged, untouched, unborn.

The house lights come down and the screen lights up, and already I am stood on a promontory overlooking the world. I become the creature who would stand on such a promontory. This creature whom the camera presses me to know myself as having become—at its behest and in its always ultimately comforting company—I cannot claim to know; and without doubt I would never recognize him in the street. Actually, he is multiple. I am shifted and transmogrified into a myriad aliases. I do what one has to do to see; I become the person one has to become, any number of such persons (on this becoming, see Gibson).

And that becoming involves surrender, submission, vulnerability, above all relaxation of demand, because my position is that of the creature who receives and accepts the fruit of his own desire, not the navigator who works out strategies. Leap out of the film if you dare, and work out strategies to your heart's content. Strategies, alternatives, weighted decisions in place of other decisions, references to cultural affairs. But to grasp such booty no viewer will be caught up in the act of viewing, having eclipsed that act, even temporarily, and operating as a figure closer to the kind generosity of the production staff than to the dream-judgment she had a moment before, while being swept away.

An odd situation, surely. And here is an odder one:

I watch a team of commandos lurking in the dark water beneath a cargo ship in which Allied prisoners of war have been locked in a brig. A number of these prisoners, bearded, unbearded, are interchangeable game pieces without identities, pawns. One, tall, healthy, and handsome, is a major (played by a movie star). The boarding party produce explosions and gunfire, race to the brig, and retrieve the major. Then, leaping into the water, they are in the process of swimming toward a waiting boat with him while gunfire sprays out from the deck. A number of the heroic fighters (whoever they are we do not know) are shown swimming, struggling in desperation, and suddenly one takes a bullet, is dead, and turns into a mere object floating in the water. When the rest get away, having left this unfortunate behind, we, too, leave him behind mentally and experientially. He was surely there, he helped take over the ship, he ran, he shot, he grimaced, but now he is entirely without not only "life for himself," diegetically speaking, but existence for us; and our vision, the vision our camera-friend has been sliding our way, proceeds onward uninterrupted, undamaged, untrammeled. The camera is always moving on.

Sometimes even our camera-friend can be tricked.

In a bar we follow a man having a soothing drink with a woman and going to a hotel room nearby. He is the definitive center of our attention. Not long later, we come into the knowledge that a murder has taken place in a hotel, and of course it is this hotel, and of course our man is the victim of the murder. Like a sack of produce his body lies slumped on the floor—this is only minutes after the film begins (*Crossfire* [1947])—and a pipe-chewing detective enters to take over the central light. The camera was ready to find and acknowledge this new center, the detective (Robert Young), just as it was ready first to center and then to relinquish our original character (Sam Levene), to toss him away. To move from the corpse to the figure who intends to identify his murderer seems like a natural progression of action. We discover, because the camera is entirely willing for us to discover, that this smart decoder of mysteries is not only the hero but also the camera's treasure, treasured because heroic?, heroic because treasured?, and through a process like oxidation and reduction he becomes our hero, too.

Not that my camera-eye could help itself earlier, for a frenzied second, from leaping close to the dead man, his form condensed into a pallid black-and-white gauzy plate like tarnished pewter, and long afterward we gazed piteously, my friend and I, I and the friend of my heart, . . . gazed at the carpet and the object upon it and then into the cold police eye, cold and colder, more truthful, and noted THE END on the screen. We separated perforce and walked in two apparently unlike directions, the one of us into obscurity and the other into memory, and I knew I had lost a brother.

44

The Star's Twin

Cate Blanchett *in* Lord of the Rings: The Fellowship of the Ring *(Peter Jackson, New Line Cinema, 2001). Digital frame enlargement.*

But the star lives within a kind of chemical bond very like the viewer's with his friend, his king, the "camera eye." An existence absolutely perfunctory qualifies her star life. Like every other person, and without status or admiration, she breathes—thin air here, more congested air there. She thinks, she forms opinions political and otherwise, she has preferences—*latte macchiato* not *cappuccino*. When she travels she is subject to jet lag, and as she comes off the plane with a gentle smile her eyelids are heavy. When she uses a toilet she prefers privacy (and when, in *Eyes Wide Shut* [1999], she performs a character using a toilet, she is not using a toilet). When she walks she feels the muscles in her legs—perhaps she even trains or takes exercise. When she sleeps she dreams. She dreams the way people dream.

What dreams does a movie star dream? Is she acting in a film where the props or the set are repeatedly, endlessly malfunctioning? Is she having a fight with a director about whether she or another actor should get most of the light? Is she warding off advances from someone whose face she cannot see, who smells of onions, and who bears the name of a person she believes she adores (but a name of course entirely nonexistent outside that dream)? Or does she have that familiar work nightmare: waking, realizing she is late, rushing naked out of the house and racing naked down the streets where—horror of horrors!!!!!—no one at all notices her. She cannot find the right building to enter. There is a complicated set of lines she must learn immediately, in a language she does not understand, and she keeps getting the end at the beginning and the beginning at the end.

She walks as a citizen, perhaps a mother, surely a daughter, maybe a sibling, a cousin, an aunt. She drives an old yellow Citroen, merely because she likes to. Her favorite movies—because of course, normal citizen that she is, she goes to the movies—are by Jacques Tati and by Mervyn LeRoy, once in a while by Olivier Assayas, an odd combination but there is no accounting for taste, hers no less than yours, dear reader. She went to college at the University of Wisconsin, degree in English literature for which she read dozens of books only a few of which are still in her possession, cherished treasures: *A Room with a View*, *The Portrait of a Lady*, *The Good Soldier*. Then she studied theater briefly but intensely at Eastern Illinois University and transferred to the acting school at Yale on the recommendation of Prof. Terigus. Or was it Prof. Smarsväl? Or Prof. Jones? College chums still reside in her address book, she will drop in out of the blue and sleep over a few nights. Talk about nothing so much as talking about nothing. She pays her taxes; she has bought a charming little place with date palms and two giant yuccas on Meadow Drive in Coldwater Canyon. She speaks to her agent once a day, like taking vitamins.

And to this living civilian is firmly attached now a creature who was born explosively in 2003 with a film everybody knows so well we need not name it. For this creature the word "star" is far too diminutive. She is virtually embossed on coinage, has spread herself languorously not only in countless swimming pools but also on the covers of more than two hundred magazines in more than two dozen languages. Everybody wants to touch her, everybody stretches. She must sign their hands, their notebooks, their post-it notes. Everybody but everybody wants to . . . touch her.

There are three dozen or more fresh Instagram posts showing her, every day.

Everybody wants to touch her skin, rub her skin, shake her hand, kiss her hand, hold her in their arms, give her an affectionate squeeze, solicit her opinion about puppy dogs and the Presidency. There is no end to the crowd who amass in order to be near her, pushing near the limousine doors. Infection is a constant possibility, ruining a rayon dress is another. She has learned quite well how to smile without pain, enduringly, in long overly drawn-out photography sessions where every single photographer lives in the belief that he is copping the ultimate picture of her, the one that reveals it all.

The one that . . . reveals . . . *it all.*

The name of the star and the name of the person who became converted into the star are one and the same name, finally—it is all perfectly Kafkaesque. The conversion, once finalized, is repeated in brevity and on a daily basis, it being potentially necessary at any moment for the star to make an appearance in such a way that the person beneath is wholly masked away. The star face requires a repetitive pattern of makeup and emphasis, the star wardrobe will attest to distance and specialness. The perceiver will see exactly and fully what she expects to see, what she has been led to expect to see by publicity images prepared with the greatest care albeit constructed to show a natural presence that looks like this merely by the magic of happenstance. As the person enacts, mobilizes, plays out the star image she is conscious of contributing to the apparent existence of a simulacrum who inhabits a place in her stead. The actor, a professional, and the star, a character of sorts, cannot together occupy a single body at one time but must alternate, much like twin roommates bent on convincing the landlord that only one of them is living there. The star is never wholly unaware of the person whose hands reach out from her wrists to fix her eye shadow, never quite distant from the human. What is distant, and distancing, is the marking and warping of the plastic face, and the trace residue of the action of separation. The star is relentlessly alternately both herself and the person out of whom she was born, yet—as with many characters onscreen—no reference to that mothering self is ever made. The star is effectively motherless, the result of a virgin birth. Motherless twice. Absent the citizen from whom she sprang; absent the maternal presence that gave that citizen life.

Vocal pattern, physical posture, technical facility—all of these will have to be cultivated confidently and silently. But when we see the star we are also seeing the cultivation, just as in seeing the cultivation we are seeing the cultivator. The star's "mother originator" knows how she will look under various patterns of lighting, under pads, under makeup, under the thick pretenses of the foreign. The star face, built to be recognizable on the instant, is a specially formed version of the person's, with pronounced cheekbones (heightened by light) instead of bones in the cheeks. And the star knows that this schizoid personality, the two-headed giant, can play to two audiences conceptually very far apart. The character is read and appreciated in a tempest of feeling that floods over moviegoers in their engagement, but the person is seen only by familiars, most of whom do not find themselves watching so carefully and do not—or are not presumed to—flood over with feeling when she drops in.

As a star but not as a person the actor is hungry to meet an audience, and it is through a double agency that this can happen. By way of the role, a character will be fashioned who is seen and remembered, who is made palpable through seeing. The role and character thus act as agency between the actor and the public. But to slip into a part, the actor must have an agent put her up for audition and perhaps negotiate a contract, and she assents to this agent. As the person assenting, mobilizing her acting participation, then, the figure we know as a star must work to solidify relations with helpers of various kinds, to put herself out, to be ready for both acceptance and rejection, glorification and denigration.

The star is neither entirely let go nor entirely embraced in the working environment, so that (1) almost every effect of gesture or nuance of personality is designed to be attributed as a star gesture or star nuance, and (2) in professional interactions around, behind, and in front of the camera there is conveyed no arrogance that could suggest a star who (idiotically) really believes in herself as such. Stars know they go home to normalities, and that it is through business arrangements hinging on financial considerations that their stardom is effected. See *Honey Boy* (2019), a film that points to this star split. On the set there is courtesy. The glamorous face in the mirror is never far from the plain face beneath it, the face of the shopper looking for breakfast cereal at Gelson's, so that, vitalized in the morning, and recomposed in the afternoon, she can still breathe to become that entity beyond becoming, that creature of the everyday specially visible only when she becomes a sacred puppet within the aura of a sacred glow.

It is not so much that the star and her producing substance address each other, because they do not, both being telepathically sensitive and neither taking time to examine the duplicitous surface of the mirror in hopes of finding a trace of the other. "I am. I am alone," each thinks, the one facing one direction, the other facing another. But the bonding cannot occur unless each facet of the split personality subtends the other, exists to form accompaniment, a gentle lead, to embody a confidant in whom one might find the wisest advice and the warmest capacity for receiving agony were one only to speak it, whereas one does not. The star is never alone, the star feels always alone. And though on the screen we may find her in a lock of endless self-imitation, so that in each appearance she can be swiftly recognized and therefore featured to a profit, she is at the same time never really known. Never known because the familiar star body in performance is the unfamiliar personal body in real life. And never known because even peeking out through a rigid and celebrated mask, the essence that waits in hiding between her eyes is inscrutably alive.

45
Wink Wink

(Top) Ann Robinson and Gene Barry in The War of the Worlds *and (Bottom) with Justin Chatwin in* War of the Worlds *(Top: Byron Haskin, Paramount, 1953; Bottom: Steven Spielberg, Paramount/Dreamworks/Amblin, 2005). Digital frame enlargements.*

It is not only in the flexibility of a watcher's optical demand, the suppleness of her wavering, the sharpness of her emotional inhalations, and the depth of her journeying that the film-watching experience is like a dream. The world as it is presented has dream characteristics as well, so that we could say we are watching, are absorbed in, dream pictures. A sparkling face, silky blond hair, teeth painted snow white, wide-open (and archly made up) green eyes, a mannikin face without line or blemish; and behind this sylph the background is a flicker of unspecified darkness, as though this frontal grandeur actually exhausts the capacity of the eye. In Elizabeth Banks's *Charlie's Angels* (2019) we frequently spot and glide over the sparkly eyed and blemish-free hillsides of Kristen Stewart's conniving face: she puts on one thing but is laboring as another, a covert operative of a strange little company called the Townsend Agency, which trains and uses "Angels." Avenge, chase, punish, torture, avenge, chase, grin. But her forward motion, often athletic and swift, and her way of standing out from the background combine to feature certain aspects of her face—identifiable and admirable aspects—against a vague and indeterminate surround, vague even the villain's mansion lair in which there are sixty rooms only one or two of which we see with any detail. Wounds that require tending but do not reveal organ structures. Violent death—a thug in a stone crusher—is a mere flicker.

The "editorializing" involved in the dream vision differs from political sculpting, which uses power to hack out evidence of any progression the dominating class wishes to override. This kind of selectivity in design, focus, and angling is always a presence, to be sure, but even when a single point of view is being emphasized (at the expense of the competition), even when a grand speech thunders, the effects highlight, advance, and draw focus to some central agency of purpose and accomplishment and drop a myriad other details into the hazy alley of the unseen.

There is yet another way in which, its *politique* and its *optique* to the side, and like so many other films, *Charlie's Angels* functions as a dream: it dream-invokes a particular—and very unpredictable—sub-audience, one that as time goes by shrinks and shrinks further, entrenched in its own self-confidence and nostalgia. Here are viewers who see particular improbable doublings and ghostings on the screen, watching, as they do, in two separate time zones: the present moment and the long-lost days of youth now sharply and briefly recalled. A figure emerges from the past . . . . Consider, just in this particular film, a glancing but offsetting little moment:

The finale of an extended chase narrative involving many hideous and cold-hearted types. We know that all through the picture we have seen, in a chain, racing tiny visions, all camouflaged, of a female force who is the Power behind the Agency, clandestine controller of the action on view: a finger on a keyboard as a slinky voice energizes a computerized voice scrambler, a hand moving toward a telephone; a hand withdrawn from a telephone; smooth skin to match the smooth voice. Now stepping past one of the film's protagonists who has just earned her stars as a full-fledged member of the Angels team, a smartly dressed woman exits a building, throwing out a passing "I'm Kelly Garrett, director of the Townsend Agency. Welcome." This is all barely three seconds of screen time. This is of course the figure hidden all along, emphatically and arcanely, the person and personality behind the whole show, the one with the identifiable slinky voice and suave controlling manner—we are to note the female-centered action scenario, the males in this film being either scurrilous or weak or liars or entirely discardable. This woman is not only the female "boss" hiding inside the story, she represents the female power behind a story such as this one in Hollywood, a female guiding hand and directorial force, a female pulling *all* the strings.

But she is also, in a kind of charged halo, something else: if onscreen a dream power figure with a dream identity, in the sub-audience's mind a dream-memory brought to life, clothed to the hilt, coiffed with perfection, made up to radiate. This Kelly Garrett is knowable—but only to the few who are in the know—as Jaclyn Smith. Not only that but *the* Jaclyn Smith, who, from March 21, 1976, until June 24, 1981, when her character was shot, appeared as Kelly Garrett, one of the original Charlie's Angels ("original") in 110 episodes of the (relatively sexist) Spelling-Goldberg Productions television show that gained immense popularity and introduced her to public opinion. A former Breck Shampoo model, and subsequent to the show a player in numerous television shows and made-for-tv movies (including in the role of Jacqueline Bouvier Kennedy), Smith skyrocketed in *Angels* and is, therefore, now in her early seventies, and to an audience who will not forget her youth or their own, instantly and ineradicably visible onscreen, albeit she races past the camera. A cue looking back to dream history. Another such cue is the film's frequent deployment of the name "Bosley" to cite various "lieutenant" characters on the team, a reference to the assistant played by David Doyle originally. And a third is the imitation of Charlie's (the deceased John Forsythe) "unforgettable" voice on the phone scrambler (by Robert Clotworthy). To grasp Forsythe's "Charlie" as the origin of Charlie's Angels, to catch the wit of the numerous Bosleys currently employed (including Patrick Stewart and Djimon Hounsou), and to catch Jaclyn Smith's quick comeback are perquisites of the dream loyalty that audiences of the 1970s show, show in seeing this film now. But the references are knowing, if winking, and at least in Smith's case made at the expense of employing much less expensive because still undiscovered serious acting talents. The producers also know that most of their audience, the thick and raving envelope surrounding the tickled sub-audience, is hip and young, hot to see not Smith but Kristen Stewart and her cronies at play.

Still one more reference—yet something that will be lost on novitiates—calls back to the original Angels' long hair, worn as a dream trademark by Smith, Kate Jackson, Farrah Fawcett-Majors, and Cheryl Ladd. Here the long hair is a "wink wink" put-on, literally a coiffe used to seduce and disorient male figures (who are generally *not in the know*) and one easily discarded, as we see in a dramatic little moment with the blonde bombshell Stewart of the opening sequence ripping off her wig to reveal a butch cut ideal for accompanying her eager eyes.

What Jaclyn Smith has been hired to do in this picture is a "walk-on," in point of fact, speaking informally, a "famous actor walk-on." This is a type of performative appearance, like a "fan convention signing" or a "commercial spot." It has some formal implications of its own:

- Because the audience becomes divided between those who do, and those who could not possibly, recognize the performer and find pleasure in that recognition, a brief screen moment exists in which a star both is and is not a star. Indeed, because of the brevity and succinctness of the "walk-on," for the ignorant viewer it is "Extra" work, not even significant enough to be character play. The star—highest placed worker in the echelon of Hollywood labor—is demoted, and as a working performer must be willing to be regarded without particular attention when earlier, well-known for being well-known, as Daniel Boorstin has it about celebrity, this person could not escape public attention.

- The division of the audience also means that attendees watching the film together in a single room are seeing, in respect of this performance, two different films, and are thus unable to fully share the experience. It is possible for the celebrity "walk-on" to take place early in a film, definitively; or all the way through.

- The actor doing the "celebrity walk-on," frequently in retirement, is given opportunity for a return to the screen, for playing out "really"—and absent the pathos—the touching little fiction we see with Norma Desmond's (Gloria Swanson) return to Paramount's Stage 18 to visit Cecil B. DeMille as he works. From the gaffers in the rigging, from the older of the extras in front of the camera there is cooing delight to have her among them again, to have her "back." In *Charlie's Angels*, by comparison, the pretext is that nobody inside the story has a clue that "Kelly Garrett" was around a long time before they were. The famous actor famously "walking-on" is returning, after a distinct absence, to the company of partners in the filmmaking venture. Special gestures of respect may be accorded off-camera. Youngsters will gather around to sit at the feet, and take lessons from insider anecdotes about "the business." The convivial warmth of film production activity will present itself again, this time without the fears and competitive aggressions that bona fide film workers perpetrate and suffer every day since it is understood that with retired "walkers-on" there is no competition.

- Yet at the same time the performer will be surrounded almost exclusively by actors, technicians, and creative folk generations younger, in some way hard to grasp. They will not share the same life assumptions or the same lingo. They will not know the same people current in practice today, and some of them—shockingly with young actors—will actually never have heard the names of celebrated performers of yesteryear (upon the plinth of whose work their own work hopes to stand). Labor itself will thus be both alienating and, because production methods have been streamlined, strange, all this while the performative talent, now matured in the actor's blood, will be "astonishingly" accomplished and swift.

- Because the new production is set apart in time so very far from the original in which the performer played a key role, it will predictably be styled in very contemporary terms, with design, storyline, and shooting tactics notably fresh. Especially noteworthy will be the cast, now for the viewers distinctively young, in reflection against the original cast represented by the "walker-on." The film viewer most likely to recognize and appreciate the presence of the performer in the "walk-on" is exactly the person least likely to find motivation for seeing the new film, a product she knows will be aimed at her children or even grandchildren, who demand of movies thrills she does not either require or fully perceive. The "walk-on" will be a kind of special treat for her, notwithstanding that the old performer is acting in a sort of vacuum. A special sub-audience is profitably present yet at the same time fails to get some of the punch.

- In the very act of casting and placing a performance-within-the-performance of this kind, filmmakers knowingly emphasize a special feature of the show they are working to mount, namely, that it is taken from an earlier work. It is a sequel, or most likely a remake. This means at least two things: (a) In using material already on the books as "successful," they are hedging bets against a loss by offering what can be sold as "already certified." This re-use cuts production costs some, since the rights to the material upon which the original production was based need not always be paid for again; (b) The "re-made" character "walked on" in the present work can be figured in advertising, thus providing an energy kick for those who contemplate seeing it. While the nature of the "walk-on" is not typically part of this advertising strategy, the name imports a type of quality guarantee (think of Gregory Peck in both versions of *Cape Fear* [1962; 1991]).

- Because a character from the old film is apparently long-lived, the production gains proximity to the real, since embedded within it—again, for some critical eyes—is maturity itself, the passage of real time now configured as a transformation of characterological appearance and identity. The actual proportional size of the newly informed audience group is irrelevant; the point is that the older character, or character type, is presented again through whatever difficulties and with whatever seriousness of intent. The production goes to the lengths of seeking the senior's presence, as though for its survival the film *itself*, in this case a kind of vampire, needs the blood of a very specific old (read, older) person.

- The "walked-on" character notably has no memory whatever that the actor today existed in relation to this title and this self-same character before; indeed, the typical scene has the character so deeply lodged in the narrative present that there is no displayed memory of anything. Thus, even if the audience can look back there is no backward look from the "walker-on." In effect, the performer of the "walk-on" is winking at the audience's predictable recognition. The current "walked-on" character may well have the same name as the earlier one (that this actor played) and some viewers might imagine a characterological memory, some slight reference to an earlier situation. If the new Kelly Garrett has experienced a long chain of happenings, however, she has also erased her past.

- The many (younger) audience members who catch the surface of a performance that is in fact a star "walk-on" but who regard it as only another (and smaller) performance, are put in the position of noticing and at the same time not noticing. They miss a significant part of what is in front of them, experience a structured visual impairment. But if many evasive aspects of a film can be debated afterward—the theme; the meaning of an object; what a character was *really* doing in a scene—this aspect is prone to sliding past debate as well as perception, since if viewers in the know make mention of the name of the "walker-on" innocent neighbors will have no recourse but to nod without comprehension. A deeper tissue of significance, that is formed by the "walking-on" and its placement, is absent for the current viewing organ.

- As happens with Jaclyn Smith in *Charlie's Angels*, the "walk-on" may be characterized *as a quotation*: our Kelly Garrett today is still Kelly Garrett, her "source." She has moved on and up in the world (some would see). She has lost none of her glamour, her appeal, her self-presentation. And the blunt invocation of her name is already a forewarning that an actorial reprise may be in the works. The faked recording of the Forsythe voice also captures the full essence of his "Charlie," the twang, the vocal pitch, so that it is possible to believe he may not be present in the current narrative spaces but he does exist somewhere, in the intestines of the vocal scrambler at least. What is invoked is supreme continuity of form, produced through the agency of narrative and filmmaking technique.

- Vital if unperceived plot innovations can be phrased through the "walked-on" character; she may call back to something over and above, or deeply below, the invocation she makes now. Here we have a film celebrating women's power, women's talent, and women's bonding with one another—what could be called a liberated film—but our "walked-on" Kelly Garrett has been showing a telltale weakness: that even if she is the new puissant head of the Townsend Agency, even if she exemplifies a canny woman with power in the marketplace, still, in order to communicate with other characters she utilizes nothing other than the scrambled male voice of Charlie—just as Charlie used to do. Effectively for participants to the action, this "canny male" is at the top; and even if the final surprise (for all viewers) is that a smart woman, not a man, is running everything, part of her savvy comes from using the male voice as a badge of authority.

- Young cast members who witness the operation of the star "walk-on" from "the wings" learn something more than what they can pick up in private conversations: that the format of the "star walk-on" exists, and works, and therefore that one of the rewards they can look forward to themselves, after their careers seem to have set like the California sun, is similar treatment, perhaps in yet another remake of this same story.

When we reflect that the "star walk-on" operates through a kind of hypervisible invisibility, that it energizes a story (vitally) while at the same time glossing past the action, that it invokes a gone time palpably without drawing that history forward into the moment, that it is a directly accessed moment lost in time, we can see that it constitutes a dream in itself.

There are substantial cases to be considered, most notably, perhaps, the small but vital character role played by Lillian Gish in Charles Laughton's *The Night of the Hunter* (1955). That Gish was a pillar of Hollywood performance culture under D. W. Griffith, that, in short, she is one of the models upon whose screen persona a very great volume of later acting work is based is given no reference of any kind for the viewer who does not recognize her name. Thirty-five-year-old Edward James Olmos played a key character part in Ridley Scott's 1982 *Blade Runner*; and in Denis Villeneuve's remake, *Blade Runner 2049* (2017) he appears again, now sixty-nine and invisible except as the character Gaff to anyone who is approaching the *Blade Runner* universe for the first time. Indeed, as he had a starring role in *Battlestar Galactica* (2004), he may well be much more familiar to viewers for that. Charlton Heston (1923–2008) was one of Hollywood's mega-stars in the late 1950s and 1960s, appearing as the star of *Planet of the Apes* in 1968 (among many other films). In Tim Burton's 2001 remake, he plays the old philosopher Zaius *and without screen credit*, hiding thrice, once behind the ape make-up (which by 2001 was more thorough than before), once behind his present unknownness, and once in the absence of his name from the credits. In *Mary Poppins Returns* (2018)—a film whose title signals the earlier presence of an avatar—Dick Van Dyke, one of the 1964 film's central stars (and a byword of television and film acting) has a modest walk-on. Byron Haskin's 1953 *The War of the Worlds* starred Ann Robinson along with Gene Barry, heroic earthlings finally able to survive the Martian attack, and in Steven Spielberg's 2005 remake she and Barry are the grandparents of the children most centrally threatened. In Spielberg's 2021 remake of Robert Wise's *West Side Story* (1961), Rita Moreno, who for Wise played the central role of Anita (originated on Broadway by Chita Rivera), makes a reappearance in a notably less central role. There are numerous other cases. As in so many other ways, the material of film goes forward untouched, a dream extension of a dream past, never to die.

Filmic Is Filmic

Harry Hamlin with Gorgon's head (by Ray Harryhausen) in Clash of the Titans *(Desmond Davis, Charles H. Schneer Productions, 1981). Digital frame enlargement.*

> *We shall at any one time define the perceptible by what we ourselves actually perceive or what can be demonstrated to us by others.*
>
> V. F. Perkins, *Film as Film*

It has become commonplace for a great number of those who discuss cinema to refer to what is onscreen as a *text*. "The cinematic text." "The text of the film." "The film's textual strategies." "Cinema as meaningful text."

But there are no modulations on the word "text" that do not pin it to words. An author's spoken words, the content of an author's manuscript or published work, the act (a verb) of using an iPhone to type out a message. "I'll text you." "The text avers that . . ." "This is one of the supremely accomplished texts . . ."

Cinema is not words.

This of Max Ophüls' *The Earrings of Madame de . . .* (1953), with Danielle Darrieux walking toward Charles Boyer and away from him, with her spinning with

Vittorio De Sica and spinning again, and all the accounts and stories and lies and prevarications spieled out at soirées, in bedrooms, in carriages, in Constantinople . . . and always glittering here, provoking, retiring, hiding themselves, suddenly appearing, passing from hand to hand, going onto the ears, coming off the ears, hiding among the white gloves, finally resting in the cathedral what have we but the diamond earrings themselves. The earrings always present, always *as a present,* never leaving anyone in peace, and all the words about them of no avail, going off into the wind of desperation.

Yet, in discussing cinema one does require words, at least conventionally, because one is *discussing*. Perhaps it is because we are hooked on words that we use cinema as a pretext for *discussion* instead of, say, a dance, or a choice of light. Finding the right words is no easy task. If we were to call cinema a *pretext*, a multi-dimensional rendition of experience that *must lead to the use of words*, there would be some, but only some, sense; because the cinematic frame is a decisive selection, not a unity. *The framed image* has far too much resonance as a still picture, and the word "image" is harder to tie to a visualized movement, certainly a visualized movement with sound. We sometimes say "the cinematic image," intending a very broad meaning, yet we have not found a word to gather up what happens in a cinematic moment.

One can say *shot*. That is almost always brutally incorrect because what one sees and retains in a cinematic moment is not by definition a shot at all. It may be only part of a shot; or it may be several shots edited together. Shots are not for the audience, they are for the production team, so that work can be organized.

The penchant for using the word "text" to address issues in cinema can be attributed to literary scholarship and that stream of philosophical consideration that is partial to literature and its forms. The film, in this kind of treatment, is more or less equivalent to a book or a story, and the *auteur* is the creature who *wrote* it, notwithstanding that in the early days of cinema much was done to adapt classical literary material for the screen. So easy was it, and so easy does it remain, to think of adaptation for the screen as a re-statement or re-formation, as a way of handing over a story, say, without forcing subjugation to the book. But adaptation for the screen is transformation. And as to what is written for the screen, adaptation or not, in point of fact we almost never experience the writer of the screenplay directly, nor is there a clear way to be sure, even if the screenplay is in our hands, how exactly something written there was modified in front of the camera during shooting. One can collect published screenplays until the cows come home, but never get close to what is onscreen. Even the words of dialogue are not infallibly reproduced, in part because some actors will modify the script as they do a take. Published treatments that derive from recordings of what was onscreen do tend to get dialogue exactly right, but the authors or editors of these transcriptions— "movements into writing"—were not the writers of the film, and do not reflect in their work what the written script actually called for and what the spoken moment actually, for any subjectivity, is. And at any rate they do not come to terms with how a film looks and sounds.

"Textual" analysis has been a major agency in the discussion of film, philosophical and otherwise, principally because Departments of English or Literature sponsored most early academic study of cinema and continue, all over the world, to sponsor—and dominate—study now. The sponsorship was, of course, imperialism; appropriation. Scratch the surface of a great many fascinating critiques and valuable studies and one will find the language, postulates, assumptions, and worldview of literary studies. At its root, this kind of film study is essentially literary criticism. Films, I would maintain, are not literature, and literary-style criticism is helpless, finally, to approach them.

One subtle inheritor of the "literary" approach to film is adopted even by screenwriters themselves and in this way becomes embedded in much filmic fiction: the indicator that not only analysts but also the filmmakers themselves have adopted the *story* as basic structure, have made the story as it can be spelled out in textual terms the motor and foundation of the work. Anyone can see that, productively and experientially for the viewer, the motor and foundation of a film is the image itself, something words fail to spell. In those legion stories set in an urban context where some investigator type must journey to a new city in search of a key player there—political figure, banker, drug lord—we find a repeated trope: the main character we are following is shown in physical proximity to another character who "knows the terrain" and knows the name of the hidden person who must be found. Next, the protagonist is brought into contact with this hidden person, this Baron in his castle. A series of clandestine encounters; a meeting in a major hotel; a kidnapping followed by delivery to the important figure. But cinema itself plays out this trope in its address to the viewer, bringing us to some "city of possibility" and then introducing us to a cicerone who will show us the way. How does the intelligence of the cinema (the camera-mind) know where to bring us? Presumed, always, is that our film-as-inside-source knows everything there is to know about the Place, and through this knowledge cues both us and our protagonist as to where the crucial action will be. Onscreen the arrival of the protagonist is almost always shown in explicit visual terms and his passage to his important meeting almost always shown as narrative magic. The image cannot convey that journey, except, perhaps, by way of interior photography of a vehicle bearing the protagonist forward, with a black bag over his head so that he cannot see. We can see the outside world flash by, yet without knowledge of the cityscape the flashing eludes meaning. Diegetic drivers always know where they are headed. The film as driver has our total reliance, too.

Total reliance upon: the film's driving; our riding in the film, or with it; the limited world as it speeds past us or as we settle into it; the strangers who seem familiar; the familiars who seem like strangers; the implicit contract by which we agree to accept terms; the names that riddle us in a catalogue the title of which is never made manifest; the startling presence and startling absence of light; the sound of the voice, by which we might mean that Barthesian "grain of the voice," and which includes timbre and accent, tonality and pitch; the grain of the image; the camera's nerves . . . .

Here are a few interesting features of viewing the purely filmic, that which works only on the screen:

[1] *Filmic Authority.* While "inside" the film, the viewer is willfully caught up with a certain acquiescence to the shapes and constraints of the filmic world as given. Absorption requires a yielding of control, principally the special control that comes with defining space: near and far, proximal and distal, special and general, and so on. Various beings one meets by way of their postures and gestures. Even the (musical) phrases through which feelings mount and decline are put forward in the tacit assumption we will feel them in sympathy. Our feeling is both wish and capacity.

Accepting the film's authority is part of the viewing contract, an arrangement that can be broken at will but only at the expense of loss. Every flicker of disattention, every calculating withdrawal engenders a beastly lacuna we cannot now fill. Nor ever fill, since, just as cinema stresses, time is flying and the viewer who pauses to consider her own pause for consideration is already not the same person she was.

[2] *Filmic Muscularity.* Our optical and acoustic sensitivities, subject as they are to impression, to being pressed with affect, register the staunch muscularity of the film's visual and sound nuances. In almost every case, it is not possible to tell the exact causes of an impression, but the tonal or color formation will be part of it, as will the quality of movement or (apparent) stasis, the timbre of sound and its duration and amplitude and register, the depth of field, the focal precision (especially challenging for the eye during camera movement), the absolute size of the image. So much more attention is paid, critically, to relative than to absolute size: relative—the size of some central object seen in relation to other objects around (Sabu smaller than the elephant he is riding [*The Jungle Book* (1942)]). Absolute size is something different. When we watch films on a large screen, the figures are larger than we are, giants inhabiting a world of gigantism, and everything about their existence seems augmented as well: the grandeur, the potency, the intention. Through its various qualities, the film impresses itself on the viewer's dedicated attention, and the intensity of the impression is registered subtly and unspeakably.

Consider, for example, how inside a filmic image the bright spots will have been arranged through the lighting plan in a complex arrangement whereby one focal node has the most light in the scene and another just a little less, and so on. As the eye is attracted to light, the positioning and movement of the viewer's attention through a film passage can be spotted and guided by the lighting. At that crucial instant in *Rebecca* (1940), when the camera slowly moving forward shows in close-up the twin doors to the dead Rebecca's chambers as the new Mrs De Winter approaches with hesitation, the two doorknobs are keylit as though they were the twinkling eyes of some famous actress. The twin puckers of light seize the eye, draw the viewer forward toward the doors just as the young woman is being drawn forward. This is not words, it is image.

[3] *Filmic Recursion.* Notwithstanding that the engaged viewer will swim in the narrative flow without meaning to step away, still the modes by which a cinematic moment passes forward into successive ones—the form of movement—will have conventions and these will have been accepted in advance without hesitation. I refer to the passage from one setting to another by way of a dissolve or a cut, the interchange between conversants by way of the shot/countershot setup, cinema's occasional dip into extreme grandiosity—as with, for a relevant example in historical film, the destruction-of-Atlanta aerial tracking shot in *Gone with the Wind* (1939). Characters may sometimes merely be in place, but very often they make notable entrances and exits (Elizabeth Taylor's clumpy entrance in *Who's Afraid of Virginia Woolf?* [1966]). Viewing positions are clearly calibrated to provide ideal perspectives, some of which would be impossible outside the cinema; and cameras, such as the Steadicam, are built to facilitate forms of uninterrupted motion over tricky terrain. All of these effects, and more, have their own token visibility, yet the watcher will be speechless about them, very much as though not noticing.

Certain telltale moments of cinematic exposition, witnessed by cinemagoing wannabes growing into an identity as filmmakers, might form the basis of a quotation much later on, and this quotation can be as unrecognized as the original self-display. One good example is the long sequence (involving untold extras) of the Israelites marching away from Egypt in Cecil B. DeMille's *The Ten Commandments* (1956). A vast background of sand and sky merging. Diverse and legion weary trekkers across the desert. The point is to show the magnitude of the Exodus, not simply the fact of it. That magnitude (here shown in the additionally magnifying VistaVision ratio of 1.85: 1), divorced by time from the event it qualified, is in cinema an authoritative feature in itself, an enunciation of the seriousness of the cause and the historical imperative of the action. In his *Empire of the Sun* (1987), Steven Spielberg, who would have seen *Commandments* at the impressionable and hungry age of ten, moved to quote that sequence in the march of the prisoners toward the stadium. The same vast perspective, the same huge array of wearied bodies pushing forward, the same patient investigation, as though, very like DeMille's, this filmmaker's camera was unaffected and unwavering in its stolid appreciation for the spread of the event. But all this artful recursion is wordless.

The recursive self of film is quite a different being from the recursive self of literature. Because one holds a book (or an e-book), the passage of the eye across the lines of text is steered subjectively, and the alignment of words makes possible retreat, rereading, leaping, and even jumping forward. In cinema one cannot jump forward, one can only survive the illusion of being jumped forward. The speed with which a reader moves across a text line is learned and controlled by that reader, with the text remaining in place patiently while the action occurs. We can note this in (silent) recursion when text is applied to the cinematic screen. The filmmaker and editor must always confront the daunting challenge of how long any piece of text should remain visible before being shifted away

(Jean-Luc Godard is a master). In deciding this, presumptions about the viewer's reading speed are put in place, often inconveniently. As we shall see immediately below, cinema also does not permit the watcher to dwell upon an image or a moment with the written material held in place (except, of course, when dvds or blu-rays are watched in a system with a pause function; but such a system is extrinsic to the work).

[4] *Filmic Memory.* Cinema must function with two memories in operation at once, always. The first is the viewer's personal and actual memory, part of her viewing equipment and personal experience, and this dictates the extent to which, as the film winds on, material that graced the screen can be retained rather than being pushed away by new material. Involved here are numerous aspects of cinematic storytelling. A character once introduced may well have to be introduced again later, perhaps with subtlety but with some clear pointer to that character's place vis-à-vis other characters and situations gone by. A name may be created to be susceptible to musical pronunciation, the tiny melody of the name repetition acting to keep the character in the viewer's mind as the filmic events speed along. "Ashley" in *Wind.* "Mr. Bond" in any James Bond film. "Rick" in *Casablanca.* "Marnie" in *Marnie* (1964). "Dorothy" in *The Wizard of Oz* (1939). Settings will have to be designed and decorated so that no matter the angle the cinematographer uses for showing action, they will be identifiable as belonging to the ongoingness in some distinct way. Sometimes, even during a single filmic routine, the camera moves across a large setting in such a way that later depictions seem incongruous with early ones, and the designer's task is to unify space. Watch the "Cheek to Cheek" dance number in *Top Hat* (1935) for a fascinating trip, *in one place*, through what seem many different topographies. In reading a book, one requires a similar kind of memory of the short past, but the text need not provide it, since the reader can go back to check. The text need not stimulate a memory of the short past, that is, cause the reader to jump back to what came just before, that is, only a moment ago. In film, such constant going back would make for a situation in which the future never came except, more existentially, as itself. As we watch film, the future tends to come as noteworthy event.

A further complication of the viewer's memory is that there are far too many images and sounds in a film for anyone to be able to retain all of them in syntactical order. Thus, the memory of a film once it has been experienced is likely to be incomplete, privileging some aspects over others. Nor is the memory to be assumed faultless and incapable of inventing characteristics that did not appear onscreen. Moments that are felt as indelible, too, get reworked as time goes by.

The second memory of cinema is its own self-recollection, acknowledgment in the happenings of a late scene of the happenings of an earlier one. Say, when Kane meets Susan Alexander coming away from her dentist he is already disenchanted with his wife; not the other way round. Diegetic memory makes certain for the idealized viewer that the events taking place in serial order are arranged in such a way as to form and deliver some large picture, sensibly. Not only must there be coherent forward flow, but the territory to which one comes to have access must be coherent, *as narrative territory*, with the place one left in order to travel here. This means, technically, that the cinematographer will have a single overriding model (often a painterly one) when shooting a picture, and all of the images will have a kind of lighting, a kind of texture, and a sense of space that, however variable for narrative contingencies, remains coherent. Curtly, there is one and only one cinematic "eye" seeing and sharing all this.

[5] *Filmic Display.* Textual materials, being inventions in themselves, can take us inside, outside, around, and below characters and moments. Every word is an author's invention. What is required for the watcher's benefit is constancy and relative proportion. In cinema, we are faced with a world that gives us only its surface, even in those spectacular moments when we ostensibly see "what a character thinks," or "what a character sees," or "what a character remembers." Past these "texty" labels, what we have is pictorial rendition or dialogic claim, or both. The inside life of the moment, such as it is, is in us.

At the same time, over and over, the vision on the screen is astonishing, elevated to marvel, as saturated as pulse. One is swept away, not only by sweeping camera movements (during the "Singin' in the Rain" dance, the camera suddenly flying up and circling the street) or singular perspectives (the Swiss mountains in *Murder on the Orient Express* [2017]) or throbbing close-ups (Kane's lips) but by the sensation of a moving composition, a constantly ordered kaleidoscope. Text of course must be limited to parts of speech in order to give a qualitative sense of the narrative, but the parts of speech are all codes, not things; to transpose Yeats, not the "things that [words] are emblems of." Film is not limited this way; let us say that gestures invent their own grammar.

In what Tom Gunning has called the "cinema of attractions," and in the replay of that cinema in action thrillers of today, the very look of the screen is the lure, entirely without reference to the story point momentarily at hand. This kind of allure attests to what is always in cinema, the palpable vision. But allure is worldly and experiential, not in itself a system of signification, a working of text. There is no limit to what can be analogized as "text": every wildflower meadow, every posture in a boxing match, every nuance of ballet, every kiss . . . but these are not texts as we live them, or even *textes;* they are in the world, indeed they are the world, and we, too, are in the world. The world is not communicating *to us.*

[6] *Filmic Magic.* Only the briefest word here about a very complex and fascinating aspect of cinema, its artifice. Most who watch films have no thought at all for the laborers whose extreme talent and devotion came into use making them. Stop-motion pioneer Ray Harryhausen invented the idea of giving his Medusa a bow and arrow for *Clash of the Titans* (1981).[1] Mythologically speaking, Medusa has

---

[1] I am very grateful to Ariel Pomerance for bringing Harryhausen's ingenuity here to my attention.

no bow, and she has no arrow. But one can understand the adaptive move if one sees the technical challenges that accompanied the idea of filming the Medusa in combat against Perseus (Harry Hamlin). Harryhausen could not have the two of them onscreen together in a single shot (and therefore she could not be close enough to touch him), because the Medusa was a doll, considerably smaller than the life-sized human performer. With that relative proportion shown, she could hardly have seemed anything but comic. Then, the motion of the Medusa was going to be effected through stop-frame animation. She was made of malleable clay and her parts could be adjusted frame by frame as the camera was stopped. You cannot stop-frame a human being in a match that will work, since the number of frames shot at one time for the Medusa—perhaps as many as twenty-four or fewer—would have to be applied to Hamlin as well, yet while the Medusa's *next* move could be calculated and shaped the actor's could not.

Another problem, subtler and to my mind more interesting still, is the conviction that having the animated character and the human one together in a single shot would highlight the artificial quality of the monster in relation to the human body, which is taken by default as being unadorned and unmanipulated *in its very embodiment*, as a natural reality. Somehow, in intercut point-of-view shots, the battle could flow forward without the audience being distracted by the Medusa's not seeming quite as real as Perseus. Cutting back and forth between monster characters thus vitiates filmic realism far less than one might have supposed, and the real problem of identification arises when a human steps into the same shot.

Proceeding through the 1980s, after Ridley Scott's *Alien* (1979), it became an important challenge for effects artists busy designing monsters to decorate them, and for cinematographers to light them, in a way that matched the look and lighting of human characters who would be nearby or in apparent contact; but concentrating as he was on the stop-motion animation that was his métier Harryhausen needed to keep a sharp eye on the graphic balance between images of a clay creation and those of a person intended to match in editing.

With text, of course, this kind of problem does not arise, is *unimagined,* since every word, no matter its meaning, has the same fundamental visual quality as every other word and the writer is therefore in a position to place words together in close proximity and with almost limitless variation, without interrupting the onward flow.

47

Read This

Writer at work. Omar Sharif in Doctor Zhivago *(David Lean, MGM, 1965). Digital frame enlargement.*

Cinema cannot quite manage to show the writer writing. The words that flow out and mark the page or the screen, the *writing*: these can appear, and be crisp and definite, thus almost definitive. But where do the words come from but an invisible—always invisible—zone, *the writer*, and what is their relation to life at large, the author's and ours?

If we regard the imagery as indicative, we can learn from it what in our society the writer apparently is, just as, with any occupation at all, filmic representations give indications about ostensibly real conditions, attitudes, and tactics.

Thoughtful muscularity. The writer is pensive. We see him seated at a desk or table, head lifted (toward the inspirational forces who abide in the heavens) and body at rest. The agility in question here will be purely mental, and the body will not display it. The eyes have a fixed stare, not the stare of having found an object in the vicinity that demands serious attention but the stare that tells of null focus, daydream, rapt concentration on the otherwhere. Is the mind of the writer configuring persons in places and moving them around like pieces on a chessboard, or is it sounding out phrases of verbal melody, trying to work out the best order for laying the brickwork of language? Given that no clue can be put forward, unless we are shown the glyphs on the page—so often are we shown the writer inscribing, looking, crumpling, and throwing away, over and over—what we are left with is the pensivity itself, its stark contradistinction to the groping fingers and strained spine of the action hero climbing a crane's crosspiece or dangling from a bridge or being hoisted into an airplane already in flight. One could say the action hero thinks with his body, that he demonstrates an uninterrupted flow of muscle knowledge. The flaccid body of the writer gives no hint of muscle knowledge or any other sort of muscularity, because the writer's muscularity is in the language itself and the language is still unformed, something he is thinking about forming.

Eloquence. It is only occasionally in film that the writer is discovered in the actual act of writing or in preparing to write (arranging properly the paperweight and little bouquet of flowers on her desk). In normal discourse, she moves about the social scene interacting with relevant others and doing fundamental chores of living as "any person" would. But when this character speaks, it tends to be in a particular way: (a) very grammatical, and notably so because positioned against others who speak with much more slang and show more casualness about the rules of speech; (b) high-toned, with careful diction and honorable harmony, as though the language of the gutter, even if it is something this writer will recreate in a piece of work, is personally unknown. The writer will seem (relatively) educated, interestingly so, as though the urge to write was born in an educational setting and as though the method and means were inculcated as part of an instructional regime. As to education: the writer writes because he or she has learned to write, has learned that writing is a worthwhile, indeed superior, accomplishment, has learned that writing demands concentration, patience, endurance, and intellectual strength. Thus, while a writer with an intense conviction can be momentarily addle-pated or harebrained, he or she will be nailed as consummately brilliant at some key plot point, brilliant in the way that only the "very special" mind is brilliant, and in the way that might lead other minds to follow (the vast and eager readership). Physical quirks may qualify the personality, too: lisps, stutterings, twitches, and various speech tics like malapropisms and arcane references, all of these catering to the idea that the purest consciousness comes into application only when the writer is hard at work, later on but not here and not now. This present coffee-sipper is the person who has relaxed her strengths into the river of the everyday. When she writes she rises above all this, easily, swiftly as a bird on the wing. When she writes she is a faultless mind in frictionless labor, never sweating over a word.

Order. The braver the writer and the more "important," the more creative, the more articulate, the more profound, the less will she have need for physical order in the everyday sense, this to counterassert the pure conditions surrounding the mind and emphasize the pure quality of thought that empowers the writer's text. In real life she is a slob. One will see apartments crammed with books and papers, coffee mugs, clothing, food half eaten. Here is a personality that is always carried away from the mundane, or always vulnerable to being lifted away. The writer is a flyer. The landing strip, therefore, need be nothing but a place to lay the head, nothing but a space without affect. Even if the writer uses a personal library larded with books, she will almost invariably have trouble finding the one she is looking for because they are laid on shelving in no discernable order—importantly, in no order discernable to her, *thus to us,* as she desperately searches. The writerly habits will be exotic: up all night, awake in the afternoon, eating only odd or arcane foods, not talking to strangers, not taking telephone calls, muttering, never straightening a sloppy pile of books since the creativity is picked up, by contagion, from the sloppiness itself: picked up, shaped, polished. William Holden's Paul Verrall in *Born Yesterday* (1950) is a model of dignity but wholly unbelievable as a writer in a movie.

Face. Because the writer writes not so much as an occupation as out of a spontaneous sensitivity to the problematic, the real, the noteworthy, the immediate, or the anxiety-producing, the person will be shown as exceptionally prone to stimulation, touchable by circumstance, and these qualities will imbue the pattern of the face with special design. Soulful eyes, mournful lips, sharply attuned brow, mussy hair because who has time to worry about the presentation of the self when the true "Self" is the text? No matter the specifics, the writer will appear distinguished against the other characters of the story, will seem a peculiar sort, someone markedly special. Star casting doesn't hurt this process, but even the most easily recognized of stars needs some performative trick to lure the viewer's eyes away from those recognizable features and pinion them to the writer's delicate agency: in *Finding Forrester* (2000), the much recognized Sean Connery works at standing stock still, staring, relaxing his facial muscles so that his eyes do the work. Though he is tall and well built, this Forrester sees too much to be an action man.

Mundanity. The author will frequently be shown onscreen to receive a package containing a single copy, or multiple copies, of his or her own book, just newly published. The hands fumble to rip open the bindings, remove the paper, discover The Thing. In brave terror trembling hands pick It up to hold before the eyes, sometimes the pages are gently turned in wonder. In nineteenth-century depictions, some attention is paid to the careful, curling orthography of the address label. Earlier scenes will have shown the delivery of a telltale letter from a publisher indicating intention to publish, this accompanied by the writer's disorientation (as in surprise, shock, wonder). In the actuality of it, a writer would open a carton and recognize that, as predicted, the thing existed in more than one copy at once—was in fact *published*—but the book itself would be somewhat less than wondrous because the writer would previously have seen it in galley (as well as the cover design) and would have gone through it more than twice with a fine-toothed comb. The writer knows—knows exactly—what is inside. But in the filmic design, the writer responds to the newborn book as though it is a newborn child.

Inspiration. Films are not above taking a quick breath for a cut-away that shows, with exceptional plainness and directness, some objective "inspiration" for the writing act. Yuri Zhivago turns his head and lo!, there is a delicious pattern of frost on the winter pane by night, or else a field of shimmering daffodils in spring. The nineteenth-century Creative Spirit, fascinated, as we are to believe, by classed persons and their bizarre interrelations, sexual and otherwise, would float in some social gathering, pause and stare, and we would be given a tableau shot indicating some "interesting" bodies in a moment of notably demonstrative action—a head leaning over to whisper in an ear, a hand offering another hand something wrapped up. Oh yes, all this is going into the book! The viewer shares in the moment by first being inspired as well, made curious, jogged out of complacency, such an action easing the adoption of the writer character as similarly being made curious, jogged out of momentary complacency, subjected to INSPIRATION. It is curious that the writer's exceeding sensitivity, as depicted, would lead one to conclude that the very slightest of tremors could set off a creative fit. But when the audience is handed a vision of the inspiring subject slight tremors of delight hardly do; the inspirational subject is contrived for special display: lit with particular glory, caught at some apogee of feelingful movement, poised in an elegance of focus, laid over with a color palette all jewels and riches and desires. This is so that the viewer, only a commonplace sort, can feel the inspiration before the writer does; so that, finally, the writer's moment of inspiration will follow the viewer's. If the writer follows us, how easily then might we bond! (And how creative is our watching!)

Unity. And a fascinating division—that in literature inheres in the writer's working self, a division by which the person who picks up the writing implement (quill, iPad) is transformed into the "voice" of the text (see Gibson)—is magically undone in cinema, where all aspects of the writer's personality, in labor and in ease, are brought together and made one. The writer always behaves like a writer. We will see a political opinionist cornered at a pub or social gathering after publishing a diatribe, and here confronted and antagonized by a character who's nonplussed that his chum could have written such a piece: the writer growls defiantly, and somehow manages to reassert if not the argument at least the tone of the published piece, as though now, here, in the pub, being a drinker of ale, he is also, still, unremittingly, the presence behind that text. As though the authorial presence behind the "speaker" of the text, that everyday person with conventional social bonds and understandings, could never for a breath be separate from the persona he adopted while writing. *There is no falsehood in writing,* in short. Not only is this author expected to be as articulate and formal in everyday speech as the voice of the text, he or she is required to continue to hold the same opinions even while quaffing a half pint. One can easily leap to the presumption that in her dreams the writer is still on a soap box preaching the phrases of her text, that never in any circumstance is hers other than the voice she has made out of words.

Splintering. And the writer's work, the writer's inspiration, the writer's Writerly Being onscreen is just splinters patched together by a heroic genius. Patched, but splinters. And since splinters, unproblematically interruptible. The most telling portrait of a writer I have ever seen onscreen was Doug Salter (Hal Holbrook) in *That Certain Summer* (1972). Living in a huge house with numerous artists in other media around him, Doug is trying at his typewriter to get a sentence or two down, but he's interrupted, first by one friend, then by another, then by another, and another, and another, always coming back, in between his helpful forays "outside," and trying again to get that sentence or two down. He apparently only works in little flashes like this. There is no problem for him if you interrupt, drag him away, cry on his shoulder, whatever. His work is always the least important thing going on.

48

Time This

Monica Bellucci in Irréversible *(Gaspar Noé, 120 Films/Canal+, 2002). Digital frame enlargement.*

Can you take me back where I came from?
Can you take me back?

Paul McCartney/John Lennon

The answer to the Beatles' question is a resounding "No," not that fervent hearts the world over do not yearn and yearn for return and further return and that cinema does not hesitate to present us with a past.

Cinema has four times: playtime, diegetic time, edited time, and epochal (setting) time:

Playtime: of principal interest to theater owners; measured usually in minutes, from the start to the finish, credits included; helpful in calculating the number of shows one can have per day, that is, the box office take upon the rental expenditure for the print. For a filmgoer, practically this means one can know whether one has the time available for seeing all, or only part, of a film—especially if one is streaming it. But more elementally, it signals that the film unspools (at 24 frames per second, or 1,440 frames per minute) for a certain number of minutes, and that, if it is not interrupted, it does this predictably and repeatably, "eating through" a certain spate of time as the narrative advances. The film leads us into the future, inexorably, always, incessantly, slowly, madly, deeply. We are always older at the end of a film than we were at the beginning. The beginning of the film is always moving further and further into the past. The events onscreen are receding even as we catch them, receding, receding. Everything recedes.

Diegetic time: an arrangement of script logic as enacted physically before the lens. One thing happens "before" another, in a certain specified syntax. The story leaps forward or backward, almost always with some specification for the viewer's help in self-positioning. Events are sped up or slowed down, are repeated or are presented with blank lacunae. There are myriad variations on what the cinematic form can do with diegetic time. When we agree to be film watchers we give ourselves over to the gorgeous, illusory world negotiated in terms of these varying manipulations. We expect that in part we will undergo a temporal adventure, that we may indeed be lost in time, perhaps even archaic but surely fictional time, yet safely so, and that we may think ourselves experiencing the temporal in a wholly new way (although we are not).

Edited time: to do with the way pieces of film are spliced together, that one screen moment happens *actually* before another because it comes at a point earlier in the film's unspooling. Clearly diegetic and edited time can be both confounded and contradictory (see *Memento* [2000], *Betrayal* [1983], *Citizen Kane* [1941]).

Epochal time: in which we find ourselves situated narratively in a particular historical moment, say, the American West in 1865 or inside a space vehicle a thousand years hence. Regardless of how a film moves through diegetic time, or whether it even does move much (consider *My Dinner with Andre* [1981] or *Carnage* [2011]), we may find ourselves moving through epochs, *2001: A Space Odyssey* (1968) being a limiting case and *The Tree of Life* (2011) something of an homage. Again, this is a matter for the script to specify, and when an epoch is defined the film will identify it carefully in several ways beyond the text tag giving place and year: the costumes will be specifically contrived, the setting will be specifically built (see *The Time Machine* [1960]). Props will have been studied by the production and will be reproduced with sufficient accuracy that a general (but most probably uninformed) viewer would not find discrepancies. The lighting is often contrived to reflect historical accuracy, as with Kubrick's mid-eighteenth-century *Barry Lyndon* (1975), a film shot entirely by candlelight. Worth considering: regardless of the epochal setting of a film, even a setting in the "present day," there is actually no way for us to travel to it from where we are as we watch. A past or a present or a future is configured and imagined, but inaccessible. Perhaps things were, are, or will be like this, perhaps not. Historians give us accounts (the production researchers boned up on them), but history is always written by the survivors, often generations upon generations afterward. The future cannot be reached until we reach it. And even the "present day" is something that has slipped away from us as we watch, that is always slipping, and that, at any rate, we cannot access as we sit inside glued to the screen where it is being portrayed. Think of a film's epochal time as a claim, carefully substantiated. And think of diegetic time, too, as requiring constant affirmation by claims. Edited time assists in claiming but does not claim itself, usually. Playtime, if things go well, is beyond the viewer's consideration, certainly while watching: if she looks at her wristwatch the film dies like Alice's Red King.

By means of visual detail and linguistic reference, a film must make constant allusion to its temporal placement not only because it may seek to alter that placement but also because the viewer cannot be expected to have followed every frame carefully and may be "tuning in" suddenly at a point after an action has begun. A setting having been introduced at the top of a sequence will be seen again in successive shots, for example, not simply given over and presumed understood. Characterizations have temporal continuity, too: by their intonations actors will offer what is tantamount to evidence of, or reflection upon, what they said before, again as though the viewer/listener needs repositioning.

The cinematic "past" must be such as to distinguish itself easily and plainly against the cinematic "present," else there is no point invoking it as a past. If things in the "past" look and sound exactly as things do in the cinematic "present," the temporal point of reference won't appear to have changed and certain purportedly delicious confusions can be created in the viewer. When the "past" is constructed arbitrarily to be different, it is another diegetic world tagged with a label that reads *past*. In all events, what we are presented with is a situated enactment attached to a localizing label.

When in cinema we move into "the past," the screenwriter will know the need to invoke a certain innocence, in the particular sense that knowledge and awareness "back then" will exhibit lacunae, notable as such: informational emptinesses, questions without answers. There is an implication that knowledge lives in the cinematic present, and "we are not there yet." Thus, a repeated diegetic trope: the character unaware of something the viewer—who has seen the diegetic "present"—does know, sharp irony owing to situations where what the innocent character doesn't know is something everyone on earth does, such as in the familiar historical epic where Abraham Lincoln is dressing to go to the theater, or where Isaac Newton lies down for a nap beneath an apple tree, or where in her laboratory Marie Curie says, "Je pense que peut-être j'ai trouvé quelque chose!" These are all only tags, reminding us not to forget where "we are" and that the folk we are watching *do not yet know what the narrative knows that we know*: another proclamation of the character's ignorance of the narrative that has caught us.

Biopics are notoriously susceptible to temporal rearrangement, as subjects tend to merit the biopic treatment only because of an action, a life, committed in the *always already*. We are taken back to the undistinguished "beginning" of a life that has turned out to be, as people say, significant (Grand Irony); and this beginning will show an as yet insignificant character showing what we would deem "telltale signs" of developing significance. Cole Porter (Cary Grant) tooling through a melody at a piano. Chuck Yeager (Sam Shepard) flying a jet before the advent of the space program. *Halt and Catch Fire* (2014) repeats this trope many times over with regard to computer design. The pleasure on offer is a chance for us to see biographical development directly placed before us, as though we can retreat to an early point in someone's life and follow their growth onward until they *become* what we knew from before the beginning they would have to be, what, in fact, they did become to general acknowledgment (of one kind or another). We do this retreat-and-follow from a stable reservation outside the events, neglecting to note how as we watch all this we are *becoming*, too. This neglect we have agreed to. We perform it with assiduity.

Time as we know it—cinematic playtime is but one of its agencies—cannot be experienced outside of action; it is always *the time within which* or *through the duration of which* something is done. Though we can pretend to stand objectively apart, in order to make measurements, we can record only the playtime in which measurements are made. Diegetic and epochal time in cinema are posed in edited playtime, since there is no alternative, and very typically they do not make reflection on the playtime in which they are posed. John Badham's *Nick of Time* (1995) purports to align its diegesis precisely with its playtime, both occupying one and one-half hours precisely. But the diegetic time matches up with the viewer's engagement with the screen; and lost in the action, especially in the ninety-minute countdown featured there, the viewer has no sense of real (play-)time at all. The diegesis is presumed to be stretching, in a way analogous to the stretches of parallel-edited climactic action scenes where, for instance, a bomb is ticking down while some hero races against time to abort it. The only way a viewer could have certainty that Badham's story is proceeding at the rate of one second per second, would be to withdraw from the screen and watch his clock.

Yet, the very idea of being delivered backward in time is a pure fascination, and founds considerable pleasure for eager watchers. Backward watching is very largely a matter of logical calculation, a kind of meta-reading of the script, in which one asks for causes in each scene and subsequently finds them delivered afterward. A paradigm is Gaspar Noé's *Irréversible* (2002), which, very like Christopher Nolan's explicitly named *Memento* and David Hugh Jones's *Betrayal*, embeds itself in a constant teleological investigation that comes to an end only through the filmmaker's arbitrary action. The point of each scene, as written, is to be expressive and evocative but simultaneously inexplicable because apparently springing out of nothing—"nothing," that is, what we learn—as we go along—happened before, and will be shown happening next. Each dramatized moment begins to constitute a gateway "backward" to origins. In detective stories, although they proceed in a forward direction (perhaps with occasional flashbacks—as in *Still of the Night* [1982]), the "smart" protagonist's progress through a case only appears to be forward-heading, as each revelation is a reference to some past event we did not see, perhaps could not see since it came before the story began. It is perhaps for this technical impossibility that flashback replays, while illustrative seem so tawdry and out of key with the story they aver to light.

We are always to presume, when the detective finds what she is looking for, that we, too, who have been detecting, now find our own treasure. Some past event happened just this way, and it led to the chase we have been following, and the chase led to this resolution, as though every comment and every fact shared with the detective by every single member of the overelaborated cast of characters was and could only have been too accurate for comprehension. Everyone we see is either inventing or remembering what was, no one is going back to it: back to the time when the victim, now no longer going forward, was going forward without a thought of going back.

Cinematic time games involve logical construction—statements based on claims, hypotheses, guesses, accounts—craftily illustrated by way of astute performances, gay costumes, amazing sets, and haunting music. Logic but not time travel. None of the "facts" of the mystery, as we find them, involve a character's looking at something as directly as, caught up by that character as lure, we look at the looking. We already have a time machine, the human body, and it moves in only one direction while its senses are oriented in another. Our only hope of traveling back is by way of the eye and ear, every looking, every sounding a search in the past.

How confounding, then, as well as charged and thrilling and brave, to emerge from a screening into the streets and alleyways of the everyday, aware with some sharp pang that in one's vacation events took place that cannot, and will not, be recaptured. The memory of the film, meanwhile, is its own unique flashback to a past that never was clearly set in time, that had no mortality to speak of, a very epitome of the uncanny that shone with untenably strange brightness, posing a question we do not answer.

Postscriptum:
Must I Know What I See?

Ronan O'Casey (left) and David Hemmings in Blow-Up (Michelangelo Antonioni, MGM, 1966). Digital frame enlargement.

It's the same old story all over again.

The Passenger

In a helpful distinction, William James mentions two types of knowledge, knowledge of acquaintance and knowledge-about. "In minds able to speak at all there is, it is true, *some* knowledge about everything" (I, 221). Yet, with the world at large, with nature, with electricity, with love, with touch, with harmony, with red and green, we have acquaintance. I have the ability without doubting or questioning myself to put a name-label on many things I see today that I have seen before, and my naming is an announcement of the seeing-before. Yet, of these things, I might never claim to have knowledge-about. I make do, I move without knowing-about. I sleep and I breathe and I write without knowing-about. I can recognize the field with the fence, and the bed with its sheets, and the wind blowing through the trees, and the words, each, one by one, that march together, but what is a word?

When I see the screen image with its superficial array, when I see posited through narrative principles some situation of concern, what can I say I know about the things that are displayed? My ability to recognize something, for instance, can be compromised, teased, played with through the agency of "lifelike" models, where it is in fact a thing standing in for another thing or person I am seeing without recognizing that—without being acquainted with the fact that—a standing-in is happening. Or, with fascination I can watch the action and development of a character, affix myself "knowingly" to the goatee, the high collar, the scarred face, yet have no acquaintance, since this being has never been anywhere else before and exists, in fact, in no place now except, by virtue of the camera and various effects, in front of me now. "This thing of darkness/I acknowledge mine." Acknowledge, not know. Accept, not feel acquaintance with. Or I see a character I have seen many times before (even with pleasure), or very like some other character I have seen many times before, and I think to recognize her, although she is pure light. Of course, I do affiliate with light; but also with forms floating by light. With ghost forms.

When I see a narrative film I follow the story without knowing it and also without knowing my following. Often as I try to know the technical features of what I see, say, the way a shot could have been made, I am stymied, and in being an unknowing viewer of this sort I am, perhaps, adept at researching the technical aspects of cinema (yet far less adept than some[1]). Even knowing that something was optically printed and knowing about the workings of Linwood Dunn's optical printer still I am unacquainted with the exact device, and have never met any of the geniuses who made such devices work in the classical age. When I see optically printed flirting, flitting, flashing on the screen I cannot claim to know-about it, albeit I can discern. Or motion capture: I can utter about it without ever having seen a "Volume" with my eyes.

I believe we come to cinema without knowledge, in either of James's senses, and we do not know what we see. What we watch is believed, to be sure, and accepted, imbibed and considered, remembered and remembered again, expanded and warped and miscolored and repositioned and sometimes even recast by us, but we do not know it. What we can know, perhaps, is its ineradicable flow, its ongoingness, its hope. And then it is gone and we are left alone again.

It is here. It is gone. We are left alone again.

To close, a personal anecdote. I have seen *Blow-Up* (1966) dozens of times and been gobsmacked again and again by that body in the park. Was it there? The photographer crouches down but does not quite touch it, although even if he did, what could that tell him—or me? He sees it the way he could not have seen it with his camera, and now with no camera in hand, so that the only picture of this thing we can have is the one Antonioni gives us of this picture-maker unable to make a picture. The corpse is on the greenest grass in the universe, but he is all in tones of black, white, and gray—the face was covered with a green-gray make-up to effect this—so that he will look like a black-and-white photograph of himself. And we know already about photography and

---

[1] I do not ascend to the plateau where Adrian Cornwell-Clyne, Raymond Fielding, Barry Salt work, among many others.

manipulation. To go further, but only a little further, as the corpse has no actual story function—the man does not do anything we need to care about—the very situating of it on the ground here is an imposition, a placement, a contrivance. I sought long and hard for some knowable truth about this. With film, one always finds oneself seeking. To visit the place. To be inside the performance, or standing by, like the crouching photographer! To help mow the grass! To search through the night for that eerie neon sign by which all is illuminated. Striving and struggling and stretching all the fibers of my mind I came no closer to knowledge about that corpse—that corpse; *the* corpse— and surely no closer to acquaintance. And it is a very strange truth that every time I saw the film, every time I see it still, at the moment when the photographer comes upon the corpse I am as surprised as he is.

References

Arnold, Matthew. *Culture and Anarchy: An Essay in Political and Social Criticism*. London: Smith, Elder & Co., 1869.
Artaud, Antonin. *The Theatre and Its Double*. Trans. Mary Caroline Richards. New York: Grove Press, 1958.
Bataille, Georges. *Visions of Excess: Selected Writings, 1927–1939*. Trans. Allan Stoekl. Minneapolis: University of Minnesota Press, 1985.
Bazin, André. "The Ontology of the Photographic Image," in *What Is Cinema?* Vol. 1, trans. Hugh Gray, Berkeley: University of California Press, 1967, 9–16.
Becker, Howard S. *Outsiders: Studies in the Sociology of Deviance*. New York: Free Press, 1963.
Benjamin, Walter. "Interior Decoration," in *One-Way Street*, trans. Edmund Jephott, ed. Michael W. Jennings, Cambridge, MA: Harvard University Press, 2016, 52–3.
Boorstin, Daniel. *The Image: A Guide to Pseudo-Events in America,*. New York: Harper & Row, 1961.
Bordwell, David. "Intensified Continuity: Visual Style in Contemporary American Film," *Film Quarterly* 55: 3 (Spring 2002), 16–28.
Borges, Jorge Luis. *Dreamtigers*. Trans. Mildred Boyer and Harold Morland. New York: E. P. Dutton, 1970.
Boulding, Kenneth. *The Image: Knowledge in Life and Society*. Ann Arbor: University of Michigan Press, 1961.
Burke, Kenneth. *A Grammar of Motives*. Berkeley: University of California Press, 1969.
Caillois, Roger. *Man, Play and Games*. Trans. Meyer Barash. Urbana: University of Illinois Press, 2001.
Callow, Simon. "Laughton as Quasimodo: Epic Agony," *New York Times* II (May 15, 1988), 28, online at https://www.nytimes.com/1988/05/15/movies/film-laughton-as-quasimodo-epic-agony.html. Accessed February 23, 2020.
Cavell, Stanley. "Emerson," in *Cities of Words: Pedagogical Letters on a Register of the Moral Life*, Cambridge, MA: Harvard University Press, 2004, 19–34.
Carey, John. "Temporal and Spatial Transitions in American Fiction Film," *Studies in the Anthropology of Visual Communication* 1: 1 (1974), 45–50.
Clark, Danae. *Negotiating Hollywood: The Cultural Politics of Actors' Labor*. Berkeley: University of California Press, 1995.
Cortázar, Julio. "Blow-Up," in *Blow-Up and Other Stories*, trans. Paul Blackburn, New York: Pantheon, 1967, 114–31.
Cortázar, Julio. *Cronopios and Famas*. Trans. Paul Blackburn. New York: New Directions, 1969.
Davenport, Guy. "The Head as Fate" in *Objects on a Table: Harmonious Disarray in Art and Literature*. Washington, DC: Counterpoint, 1998, 25–51.
Doane, Mary Anne. *The Emergence of Cinematic Time: Modernity, Contingency, the Archive*. Cambridge, MA: Harvard University Press, 2002.
Dolar, Mladen. *A Voice and Nothing More*. Cambridge, MA: MIT Press, 2006.

Douglas, Mary. *Purity and Danger*. New York: Routledge, 2002 © 1966.
Emerson, Ralph Waldo. "Plato; or, The Philosopher," in *The Essential Writings of Ralph Waldo Emerson*, ed. Brooks Atkinson, New York: Modern Library, 421–45.
Feuer, Jane. "The Self-Reflexive Musical and the Myth of Entertainment," in *Film Genre Reader III*, ed. Barry Keith Grant, Austin, TX: University of Texas Press, 2003, 457–71.
Forster, E[dward] M[organ]. *Howards End*. London: Penguin, 1989.
Garfinkel, Harold. "Studies in the Routine Grounds of Everyday Activities," in *Studies in Ethnomethodology*, Englewood Cliffs: Prentice-Hall, 1967, 35–75.
Gibson, Walker. "Authors, Speakers, Readers, and Mock Readers," *College English* 11 (1950), 265–9.
Goffman, Erving. *Relations in Public: Microstudies of the Public Order*. New York: Basic Books, 1971.
Goffman, Erving. *Frame Analysis: An Essay on the Organization of Experience*. Cambridge, MA: Harvard University Press, 1974.
Goffman, Erving. *Forms of Talk*. Philadelphia: University of Pennsylvania Press, 1981.
Golding, William. *To the Ends of the Earth: A Sea Trilogy*. London: Faber and Faber, 1991.
Gomery, Douglas. *Shared Pleasures: A History of Movie Presentation in the United States*. Madison: University of Wisconsin Press, 1992.
Gregory, Richard L. "Consciousness," in *The Encyclopedia of Ignorance: Everything You Ever Wanted to Know about the Unknown*, eds. Ronald Duncan and Miranda Weston-Smith, New York: Pergamon, 1977, 273–81.
Gumbrecht, Hans Ulrich. *In 1926: Living at the Edge of Time*. Cambridge, MA: Harvard University Press, 1997.
Gunning, Tom. "The Exterior as Intérieur: Benjamin's Optical Detective," *boundary 2* 30: 1 (Spring 2003), 105–30.
Halberstam, David. *The Fifties*. New York: Fawcett, 1993.
Haralovich, Mary Beth. "Selling *Mildred Pierce*: A Case Study in Movie Promotion," in *Boom and Bust: American Cinema in the 1940s*, ed. Thomas Schatz, Berkeley: University of California Press, 1999, 196–202.
Hugo, Victor. *The Hunchback of Notre Dame*. London: Collector's Library, 2004 © 1831.
Innis, Harold Adams. *Empire and Communications*. Toronto: University of Toronto Press, 1972.
Iser, Wolfgang. *The Implied Reader: Patterns of Communication in Prose Fiction from Bunyan to Beckett*. Baltimore: Johns Hopkins University Press, 1974.
James, Henry. "Preface to *The Spoils of Poynton*," in *The Art of the Novel: Critical Prefaces*, Chicago: University of Chicago Press, 2011 © 1934, 119–39.
James, William. *Principles of Psychology*, in Two Volumes. Mineola: Dover, 1950 © 1890.
James, William. "The Perception of Reality," *Principles of Psychology* II, 283–322.
Jay, Martin. *Downcast Eyes: The Denigration of Vision in Twentieth-Century French Thought*. Berkeley: University of California Press, 1993.
Jaynes, Julian. *The Origin of Consciousness in the Breakdown of the Bicameral Mind*. Boston: Houghton Mifflin, 1976.
Kafka, Franz. "The Hunger Artist," in *The Metamorphosis and Other Stories*, trans. Willa and Edwin Muir, New York: Schocken Books, 1995 © 1948, 243–56.
Kirkegaard, Søren. *Repetition and Philosophical Crumbs*. Trans. M. G. Piety. Oxford: Oxford University Press, 2009.
Kynaston, David. *Modernity Britain 1957–1962*. New York: Bloomsbury, 2015.

Lem, Stanislaw. *Tales of Pirx the Pilot*. New York: Harcourt Brace Jovanovich, 1979.
Lennard, Dominic. *Brute Force: Animal Horror Movies*. Albany: SUNY Press, 2019.
Logan, Elliott. "Faces of Allegiance in *Homeland*: Performance and the Provisional in Serial Television Drama," in *Television Performance*, eds. Lucy Fife Donaldson and James Walters, London: Red Globe, 2019, 84–100.
McConnell, Frank. *The Spoken Seen: Film and the Romantic Imagination*. Baltimore: Johns Hopkins University Press, 1975.
McLuhan, [Herbert] Marshall. *Understanding Media: The Extensions of Man*. New York: Signet, 1964.
Morrison, Philip. *Powers of Ten: A Book about the Relative Size of Things in the Universe and the Effect of Adding Another Zero*. Redding: Scientific American Library, 1982.
Ortega y Gasset, José. "On Point of View in the Arts," in *The Dehumanization of Art and Other Essays on Art, Culture, and Literature*, Princeton: Princeton University Press, 1968 © 1948, 107–30.
Orwell, George. *Down and Out in Paris and London*. New York: Harcourt Brace Jovanovich, 1961.
Orwell, George. *Diaries*. Ed. Peter Davison. London: Penguin, 2010.
Owens, Susan. "British Baroque," *The World of Interiors* (March 2020), 153.
Parsons, Talcott. *The Social System*. Glencoe: The Free Press, 1951.
Paul, Robert A. "The Eyes Outnumber the Nose Two to One," *Psychoanalytic Review* 64: 3 (1977), 381–90.
Perkins, V. F. *Film as Film: Understanding and Judging Movies*, Harmondsworth: Penguin, 1972.
Petronius (Petronius Arbiter). *Satyricon*. Trans. Sarah Ruden. Indianapolis: Hackett, 2000.
Pomerance, Murray. "Recuperation and *Rear Window*," *Senses of Cinema* 29 (November-December 2003). Online at http://www.sensesofcinema.com.
Pomerance, Murray. *Johnny Depp Starts Here*. New Brunswick, N.J: Rutgers University Press, 2004.
Pomerance, Murray. *Michelangelo Red Antonioni Blue: Reflections on Cinema*. Berkeley: University of California Press, 2010.
Pomerance, Murray. *The Eyes Have It: Cinema and the Reality Effect*. New Brunswick, N.J: Rutgers University Press, 2013.
Pomerance, Murray. "Visit to a Gallery: Hitchcock, Painting, *Vertigo*," *Film International* 16: 4 (December 2018), 51–8.
Pomerance, Murray. *The Film Cheat: Screen Artifice and Viewing Pleasure*. New York: Bloomsbury, 2021.
Pomerance, Murray. *A Voyage with Hitchcock*. Albany: SUNY Press, 2021.
Ruskin, John. *Modern Painters*, Vol. II, New York: John Wiley & Sons, 1889.
Schefer, Jean-Louis. *The Enigmatic Body: Essays on the Arts*. Trans. Paul Smith. New York: Cambridge University Press, 1995.
Schefer, Jean-Louis. *The Ordinary Man of Cinema*. South Pasadena: Semiotext(e), 2016.
Scheff, Thomas J. "Audience Awareness and Catharsis in Drama," *The Psychoanalytic Review* 63: 4 (1976), 529–54.
Schivelbusch, Wolfgang. *The Railway Journey: The Industrialization of Time and Space in the 19th Century*. Berkeley: University of California Press, 1986.
Simmel, Georg. "Sociology of the Senses: Visual Interaction," in *Introduction to the Science of Sociology*, eds. Robert E. Park and Ernest W. Burgess, Chicago: University of Chicago Press, 1921, 356–61.

Slavin, Neal. *When Two or More Are Gathered Together*. New York: Farrar, Straus & Giroux, 1976.

Sobchack, Vivian. "'Surge and Splendor': A Phenomenology of the Hollywood Historical Epic," in *Film Genre Reader IV*, ed. Barry Keith Grant, Austin: University of Texas Press, 2012, 332–59.

Sobchack, Vivian. "Being on the Screen: A Phenomenology of Cinematic Flesh, or the Actor's Four Bodies," in *Acting and Performance in Moving Image Culture: Bodies, Screens, Renderings*, eds. Jörg Sternagel, Deborah Levitt, and Dieter Mersch, Bielefeld: Transcript, 2012, 429–46.

Solomon, Matthew. *Disappearing Tricks: Silent Film, Houdini, and the New Magic of the Twentieth Century*, Urbana: University of Illinois Press, 2010.

Sontag, Susan. *On Photography*. New York: Farrar, Straus and Giroux, 1977.

United Artists. Pressbook for *A Night in Casablanca*. Available online at the Media History Digital Library from the Mary Pickford Foundation.

Worth, Sol and John Adair. *Through Navajo Eyes*. Bloomington: Indiana University Press, 1972.

Wyatt, Justin. *High Concept: Movies and Marketing in Hollywood*. Austin: University of Texas Press, 1994.

Index

Numbers in italic denote images.

Accident (Joseph Losey, 1967) 179
Acheson, Dean 170
Adair, John 175 n.1
Adam, Ken 100
Adaptation (Spike Jonze, 2002) 230
Adventures of Robin Hood, The (Michael Curtiz, 1938) *147*, 153
Affleck, Casey 176
AFL (American Federation of Labor) 220
AFL-CIO (American Federation of Labor and Congress of Industrial Organizations) 221
Africa 254
Age of Innocence, The (Martin Scorsese, 1993) 117
A.I. Artificial Intelligence (Steven Spielberg, 2001) 85
Aida (Giuseppe Verdi; Khedivial Opera House, Cairo, December 24, 1871) 99
Alfie (Lewis Gilbert, 1966) 104
Alias (2001) 137 n.10
Alice in Wonderland (Lewis Carroll) 26, 301
Alice in Wonderland (Tim Burton, 2010) 72
Alien (Ridley Scott, 1979) 72–3, 90, 93, 98, 294
Allen, Joan 151
Allen, Woody 85, 93
All the President's Men (Sydney Pollack, 1976) 229–30, 230 n.4, 241
Almendros, Nestor 81
Alonzo, John A. 54
Also Sprach Zarathustra (Richard Strauss) 181, 183

American Graffiti (George Lucas, 1973) 156
American in Paris, An (Vincente Minnelli, 1951) 15, *82*
   musical numbers
      "American in Paris" ballet 78, *82*, 86
      "By Strauss" 15
Anderson, Judith 98
Andersson, Harriet 65
Andrews, Dana *200*
Andrews, Julie 149
Aniston, Jennifer 77
Annie Hall (Woody Allen, 1977) 206
À nos amours (Maurice Pialat, 1983) 244
Antonioni, Michelangelo 258, 305
Appleby, Suky 170
Apple TV 233 n.4
"Appointment in Samara, The" (W. Somerset Maugham) 102
Arabesque No. 1 in E (Claude Debussy) 116
Arcady 186
Arizona 252
Arnold, Matthew 24
Arnolfini Marriage, The (Jan van Eyck, 1434) 75
Arthur, Jean 122–3
Ashton, Don 172
Asphalt Jungle, The (John Huston, 1950) 241
Asphalt Jungle, The (W. R. Burnett) 241
Assayas, Olivier 251
Astaire, Fred 77
Astronaut's Wife, The (Rand Ravich, 1999) 73–4, 86
Atget, Eugène 233

Atlanta   176 n.3, 291
Auer, Mischa   103
Aviator, The (Martin Scorsese, 2004)   222

Baby Driver (Edgar Wright, 2017)   176 n.3
Bacall, Lauren   41, 65
Baccarin, Morena   131
Bach, Johann Sebastian   100
Bad Seed, The (Mervyn LeRoy, 1956)   68
Balaban, Barney   214
Bale, Christian   80
Ball, Lucille   19
Ball of Fire (Howard Hawks, 1941)   103
Bana, Eric   *238*
Bancroft, Anne   38
Band Wagon, The (Vincente Minnelli, 1953)   15, 77–8, 207
  musical numbers
    "Dancing in the Dark"   78
    "I Guess I'll Have to Change My Plan"   15
    "By Myself"   15
    "That's Entertainment"   15
Bank of America, The   169
Barefoot Contessa, The (Joseph L. Mankiewicz, 1954)   146
Barrie, James M.   241
Barry, Gene   *280*, 286
Barry, Philip   241
Barry Lyndon (Stanley Kubrick, 1975)   71, 300
Barrymore, John   17, 65, 80
Barrymore, Lionel   103, 149
Barthes, Roland   59, 289
Bataille, Georges   57
"Battle of San Romano, The" (Paolo Uccello)   197
Battlestar Galactica (2004)   286
Bazin, André   239
Beatles, The   299
Beautiful Mind, A (Ron Howard, 2001)   66
Becker, Howard S., and moral entrepreneurship   29 n.5
Becket (Peter Glenville, 1964)   69
"Being Alive" (Stephen Sondheim), *see also Company*

Being John Malkovich (Spike Jonze, 1999)   109
Being There (Hal Ashby, 1979)   65
Bel Geddes, Norman   188
"Bells of Hell Go Ting-a-ling-a-ling, The" (British airmen's song, World War I)   105
Bellucci, Monica   *299*
Belton, John   113, 116
Ben-Hur (William Wyler, 1959)   66, 72
Benjamin, Walter   25, 106, 244
Bennett, Tony, *see* "I Left My Heart in San Francisco"
Bergman, Ingrid   22, 66, 115, *185*, 188
Bernhardt, Curtis   140
Bernstein, Carl (as played by Dustin Hoffman)   230
Betrayal (David Hugh Jones, 1983)   300, 302
Bible, The   239
Big Chill, The (Robert Zemeckis, 1983)   205
Big Night (Campbell Scott and Stanley Tucci, 1996)   41, 87
Big Red One, The (Samuel Fuller, 1980)   41
Big Sleep, The (Howard Hawks, 1946)   80
Big Store, The (Charles Reisner, 1941)   229
Birds, The (Alfred Hitchcock, 1963)   39, 103, 116
Birth (Jonathan Glazer, 2004)   80, 253–4
Blacklist, The (2013)   128
Black Narcissus (Michael Powell and Emeric Pressburger, 1957)   6
Black Orpheus (Marcel Camus, 1959)   56
Blade Runner (Ridley Scott, 1982)   39, 80, 187–9, 286
Blade Runner 2049 (Denis Villeneuve, 2017)   39, 286
Blake, Oliver   *139*
Blanc, Mel   109
Blanchett, Cate   *276*
Block, Irving   101
Blonde Venus (Josef von Sternberg, 1932)   39
"Blow-Up" (Julio Cortázar)   210

Blow-Up (Michelangelo Antonioni, 1966)   152, *185*, 186, 207, 209–10, 252, *256*, 256–60, *304*, 305–6
"Blue Morning" (John Bellows)   234
Blyth, Ann   *64*, 67
Bodyguard (2018)   *127*, 132
Bogart, Humphrey   22, *36*, 38, 80, 101, 103, 115, *139*, 140, 141, 144
Boléro (Maurice Ravel)   118 n.6
Bonham-Carter, Helena   12
Boorstin, Daniel   283
Bordwell, David   46
Borgen (2010)   80, 128
Borges, Jorge Luis   53
Born on the Fourth of July (Oliver Stone, 1989)   66, 149
Born Yesterday (George Cukor, 1950)   297
Bosch (2014)   39, 128, 131, 135
Bosschaert, Ambrosius   24
Boston Common (Boston)   98
Boulding, Kenneth   17 n.1
Bourne Identity, The (Doug Liman, 2003)   46–7, *236*
Bourne Supremacy, The (Paul Greengrass, 2004)   65, 176 n.3
Bourne Ultimatum, The (Paul Greengrass, 2007)   205
Bowles, Paul   157
Boyer, Charles   115, 288
Brady, Alice   40, 103
Brando, Marlon   *120*, 120, 122, 221
Breck Shampoo   282
Bridge on the River Kwai, The (David Lean, 1957)   177
Bright, Cameron   80
Bringing Up Baby (Howard Hawks, 1938)   15
Broadway (theatre district, New York), *see* New York
Broderick, Helen   40
Broderick, James   192
Brown, Norman O.   1, 6
Bucharest (Romania)   259
Bugs Bunny cartoons   109
Bullitt (Peter Yates, 1968)   112
Bullock, Sandra   86, 98
Bumstead, Henry   206

Bunny Lake Is Missing (Otto Preminger, 1965)   *168*, 170–4
Buñuel, Luis   237
Burke, Kenneth, ratios   130, 131, 191
Burr, Raymond   129
Burton, Richard   18 n.3, 69, 121
Bush [George W.]-Blair [Tony], war against Saddam Hussain   239
Butler, Austin   86 n.3

Caillois, Roger   134–5
Caine, Michael   104
Callow, Simon   20
Calvino, Italo   157
Camera Lucida (Roland Barthes)   59
Camino Real (Tennessee Williams; Vivian Beaumont Theatre, New York, January 8, 1970)   220 n.1
Cape Fear (J. Lee Thompson, 1962)   146, 284
Cape Fear (Martin Scorsese, 1991)   2, 146, 284
Carnage (Roman Polanski, 2011)   300
Carolco Pictures, Inc. (Mario Kassar and Andrew G. Vajna)   123
Caron, Benjamin   11
Caron, Leslie   *82*, 86
Carradine, John   17
Carrie (Brian De Palma, 1976)   69
Carson, Johnny   61
Cartwright, Veronica   39, 103
Casablanca (Michael Curtiz, 1942)   115, 156–8, *185*, 188, 292
Casino (Martin Scorsese, 1995)   219
Casino Royale (Martin Campbell, 2006)   153
Cast Away (Robert Zemeckis, 2000)   107 n.1
Cat Ballou (Elliot Silverstein, 1965)   41
Catch Me If You Can (Steven Spielberg, 2002)   181, 192
Cavell, Stanley   142
Cazale, John   *190*, 191
Cézanne, Paul   31, 34
Chalamet, Timothée   19
Changeland (Seth Green, 2019)   39
Changeling (Clint Eastwood, 2008)   67, 180 n.8, 239

Channing, Stockard   153–4
Chaplin, Charlie   77
Charade (Blake Edwards, 1963)   18 n.2
Charisse, Cyd   15, 77
Charlie's Angels (1976)   282
Charlie's Angels (Elizabeth Banks, 2019)   281–3, 285
"Cheek to Cheek" (Irving Berlin), *see Top Hat*
Chicago   211
Chinatown (Roman Polanski, 1974)   54, 64–5, 253
Chion, Michel, *acousmêtre*   108, 113, 165
Chopin, Frédéric   55
Christie, Julie   *175*
Christmas in Connecticut (Peter Godfrey, 1945)   101
Churchill, Winston   9
Cincinatti Public Library (Cincinatti)   99
"Circus Animals' Desertion, The" (William Butler Yeats)   293
Citizen Kane (Orson Welles, 1941)   55, 65, 84, 99, 225, 292, 293, 300
Civil, François   *89, 96*
Clash of the Titans (Desmond Davis, 1981)   *287*, 293–4
Cleopatra (Joseph L. Mankiewicz, 1964)   18 n.3
Clift, Montgomery   77, 87, 120, 164
Clooney, George   17, 57, 86
Close, Glenn   25
Clotworthy, Robert   282
Clucas, Barbara   18 n.4
CNN (Cable News Network)   17
Coates, Anne V.   113 n.1
Cocteau, Jean   143
Code, The (2014)   123 n.3
Coleman, Herbert   213–14
Collette, Toni   41
Colman, Olivia   *9*, 9–15
Colman, Ronald   66
Command, The (Thomas Vinterberg, 2018)   90
Company (Alvin Theatre, New York, April 26, 1970)   70

Conflict (Curtis Bernhardt, 1945)   *36, 38, 139*, 140–6
Connery, Sean   37, 86, 100, 297
Constantinople   288
Constant Nymph, The (Edmund Goulding, 1943)   157
Conversation, The (Francis Ford Coppola, 1974)   109
Cooper, Gary   103
Cooper, Gladys   66
Corberó, Úrsula   128
Corby, Ellen   140
Cornwell-Clyne, Adrian   305 n.1
Cortázar, Julio   1, 53, 55, 210
Costello, Dolores   66
Cotten, Joseph   67, 115
Courtenay, Tom   150
Coward, Noël   171, 173
Cox, Brian   230
Craig, Daniel   *238*
Cranes Are Flying, The (Mikhail Kalatozov, 1957)   54, 244
Crawford, Joan   17, 37, *64*, 67–9
Cregar, Laird   164
Cries and Whispers (Ingmar Bergman, 1972)   65
Cronenberg, David   63 n.4
Crossfire (Edward Dmytryk, 1947)   *271*, 274
Crowe, Russell   66
Crown, The (2016)   *9*, 9–15, 137
Cruise, Tom   65–7, 149
"Cry Baby Cry" (John Lennon, Paul McCartney)   299
Cukor, George   45
Culkin, Macauley   39
Cumberbatch, Benedict   163
Curie, Marie   301
Currie, Finlay   170, 173
Curtis, Tony   84
Curtiz, Michael   68

Dalí, Salvador   26
Damon, Matt   38, 46, 80, 176, 230
Danes, Claire   133
Daniels, Jeff   244
Daniels, William   54 n.1

Dark Knight, The (Christopher Nolan, 2008)   251
Dark Passage (Delmer Daves, 1947)   38, 39
Darrieux, Danielle   288
Das Rheingold (Richard Wagner; National Theatre Munich, September 22, 1869)   169
David and Lisa (Frank Perry, 1962)   172
David Copperfield (Charles Dickens)   225
Davis, Bette   103
Davis, Viola   133
Day, Doris   66, *105*
Day for Night (*La nuit américaine*; François Truffaut, 1973)   180
Dead Man (Jim Jarmusch, 1995)   155
Dead Ringers (David Cronenberg, 1988)   63 n.4, 66
Dean, James   65, 120
Debussy, Claude   181
Dee, Sandra   75
De Heem, Jan Davidsz   24
De Hory, Elmyr   81
DeMille, Cecil B.   283
De Niro, Robert   2, 37, 38, *58*, 61, 162, *181*, *219*, 219–21
Depardieu, Gérard   128
Depp, Johnny   18, 37, 73
Descartes, René   143, 247
De Sica, Vittorio   288
De Valois, Ninette (Dame)   263
Devil in the Flesh (*Diavolo in Corpo*; Marco Bellocchio, 1986)   55, 153
DeVito, Danny   117
De Wilde, Brandon   68
Dhiegh, Khigh   47
Dial M for Murder (Alfred Hitchcock, 1954)   109
DiCaprio, Leonardo   39, 81, 118, 182, 222
Dickens, Charles   268
Diehl, August   86
Dietrich, Marlene   39, 99
Dinner at Eight (George Cukor, 1933)   65
Dirty Dozen, The (Robert Aldrich, 1967)   41

Dishonored (Josef von Sternberg, 1931)   84
Disneyworld (Florida)   188
Diva (Jean-Jacques Beineix, 1981)   159
Doctor Zhivago (David Lean, 1965)   80–1, 90, *295*, 297
Dog Day Afternoon (Sidney Lumet, 1975)   *190*, 190–4, 193 n.1
Dogville (Lars von Trier, 2003)   25
Don Giovanni (Wolfgang Amadeus Mozart, October 29, 1787, Estates Theatre, Prague)   66
   Don Giovanni character   163
Donnie Brasco (Mike Newell, 1997)   123, 221
Douglas, Kirk   18
Douglas, Mary   193
Douglas, Melvyn   65
Down and Out in Paris and London (George Orwell)   24 n.1
Downton Abbey (2010)   128 n.2
Doyle, David   282
Dreamers, The (Bernardo Bertolucci, 2003)   153, 205, *243*
Dreyfuss, Richard   74
Driver, Adam   *64*, 67, 70
Dr. Mabuse, der Spieler (*Dr. Mabuse, the Gambler*; Fritz Lang, 1922)   116
Dr. No (Terence Young, 1962)   100
   as typical Bond film   292
Duck Soup (Leo McCarey, 1933)   229
Dullea, Keir   170
Dunaway, Faye   40, 54
Dunn, Linwood   205
Dunnock, Mildred   66
Durning, Charles   192
Durrell, Lawrence   208

Earrings of Madame de . . ., The (Max Ophüls, 1953)   288
Eastern Illinois University   277
East of Eden (Eliz Kazan, 1955)   65
Eastwood, Clint   180 n.8
Edgerton, Harold   224
Edward Scissorhands (Tim Burton, 1991)   85

Egyptian, The (Michael Curtiz, 1954)   99, 100
8 ½ (Federico Fellini, 1963)   234
Einstein, Albert   134, 226
Eisenstein, Sergei   46
El Dorado (Howard Hawks, 1967)   40, 86
Elgort, Ansel   17
Ellsworth, Robert   74
Emergence of Cinematic Time, The (Mary Ann Doane)   27, 27 n.2
Emerson, Ralph Waldo   141–2
Empire Fights Back, The (Irvin Kirshner, 1980)   248 n.1
Empire of the Sun (Steven Spielberg, 1987)   80, 291
Enemy (Denis Villeneuve, 2013)   51
Entertainer, The (Tony Richardson, 1960)   69
Errand Boy, The (Jerry Lewis, 1961)   109
E.T. the Extra-Terrestrial (Steven Spielberg, 1982)   69
Evelyn, Judith   75
*Everything You Always Wanted to Know About Sex * But Were Afraid to Ask* (Woody Allen, 1972)   93
Eyes Wide Shut (Stanley Kubrick, 1999)   276

Fahrenheit 451 (François Truffaut, 1966)   *175*, 177, 225
Family Plot (Alfred Hitchcock, 1976)   181
Fanning, Dakota   67
Farrow, Mia   *243*, 244
Fastest Gun Alive, The (Russell Rouse, 1956)   176 n.2
Fawcett [-Majors], Farrah   17, 282
Fellini Satyricon (Federico Fellini, 1969)   57
Ferris wheel   232 n.3
F for Fake (Orson Welles, 1973)   55, 81, 113, 146
Fielding, Raymond   305 n.1
55 Days at Peking (Nicholas Ray, 1963)   84

Fight Club (David Fincher, 1999)   154
Film as Film (V. F. Perkins)   268, 287
Finding Forrester (Gus Van Sant, 2000)   297
First Blood, see Rambo
Fitzgerald, Barry   58
"Flood, The" (Paolo Uccello)   197
Florence (Italy)   176 n.3
Flying Down to Rio (Thornton Freeland, 1933)   206
Flynn, Errol   *147*, 153, 182
Foley technique, *see* Hollywood
Fontaine, Joan   50
Forbidden Planet (Fred McLeod Wilcox, 1956)   101–2, 192–4
Ford, Francis   58
Ford, Harrison   39, 80, 187, 189
Ford, John   58
Foreman, Carl   62
Formosa Café (Hollywood)   60 n.1
Forms of Talk (Erving Goffman)   14, 113 n.2, 118
  footings   14
  social situation   113 n.2
  vigilance   118
Forster, E[dward] M[organ]   78, 79, 158, 268
Forsythe, John   282, 285
Foy, Claire   12
Frame Analysis (Erving Goffman), theatrical frame   163, 242
France, and World War I   249 n.2
Francis, Anne   192
Francis, Kay   120
French Impressionism   15, 78, 83
Freud, Sigmund, *Weltanschauung*   191, 239 n.1
Friel, Anna   128
Friends (1994)   130
From Russia with Love (Terence Young, 1963)
  Istanbul Basilica cistern scene   26

Gable, Clark   3–5, 39
Galvani, Luigi   263
Galway (Ireland)   58
Garbo, Greta   17, 54 n.1

Garfield, Andrew 230
Garfinkel, Harold 110 n.3, 121 n.1
Gaslight (George Cukor, 1944) 115
Gaynor, Janet 77
Gay Shoe Clerk, The (D. W. Griffith, 1903) 48
GCHQ (Government Communications Headquarters) 239
Gelson's 278
General Motors Futurama (1939 World's Fair) 188
Gentlemen Prefer Blondes (Howard Hawks, 1953) 37
Gerry (Gus Van Sant, 2002) 176
Ghost Story, A (David Lowery, 2017) 254–5
Gielgud, John 48, 49
Gimpel, Jakob 115
Giri/Haji (2019) 132, 134, 136
Gish, Lillian 67, 286
Glass Menagerie, The (Tennessee Williams) 187
Glenn Miller Story, The (Anthony Mann, 1954) 205
Godard, Jean-Luc 146, 292
Goddard, Paulette 77
Godzilla (*Gojira;* Ishirô Honda, 1954) 151
Goffman, Erving 118, 242
Goldberg, Whoopi 117
Golden Gate (bridge, San Francisco) 233
Gone Girl (David Fincher, 2014) 31, 136
Gone with the Wind (Victor Fleming, 1939) 291, 292
  burning of Atlanta sequence 291
Goodfellas (Martin Scorsese, 1990) 205, 219
Gooding, Cuba Jr. 17
Good Soldier, The (Ford Madox Ford) 277
Good Will Hunting (Gus Van Sant, 1997) 38, 230
Gordon, Peter 11
Gordon-Levitt, Joseph 98
Gorton, Assheton 187 n.1
Gould, Elliott 151
GQ (magazine) 17

Graduate, The (Mike Nichols, 1967) 38, 87, *155*, 160–1
Graham, Fred *71*
Graham, Stephen 220
Grand Canyon (Arizona) 98
Grand Prix (John Frankenheimer, 1966) 98, 136 n.8
Grant, Cary 15, 18 n.2, *43*, 44, 45, 51, 60, 149, 177, 301
Grant, Hugh 40, 145
Gravity (Alfonso Cuarón, 2013) 86, 98
Gray's Anatomy (Henry Gray) 53
Grease (Randal Kleiser, 1978) 153
  "Look at Me I'm Sandra Dee" scene 153–4
Gregory, Andre *223*, 227, 253
Gregory, Richard 143
Griffith, D[avid] W[ark] 286
Groundhog Day (Harold Ramis, 1993) 26
Guess Who's Coming to Dinner (Stanley Kramer, 1967) 103
Gun, Katherine 239
  Gun affair 240
Gunning, Tom 293
Gyllenhaal, Jake 51

Halberstam, David 163
Hall, Edward T. 178 n.6
Halt and Catch Fire (2014) 128, 301
Hamill, Mark 40
Hamilton, Murray 74
Hamlin, Harry *287*, 294
Hangover Square (John Brahm, 1945) 164
Hanks, Tom 54
Hannibal (Ridley Scott, 2001) 66
Haralovich, Mary Beth 32
Hardy, Tom 41
Harlow, Jean 3–5
Harrison, Joan 213, 214
Harryhausen, Ray *287*, 293, 293 n.1, 294
Harry Potter and the Philosopher's Stone (Chris Columbus, 2001) *162*
Haussmann, Georges-Eugène (Baron) 233
Hawes, Keeley *127*

Hawking, Stephen   77
Head, Edith   75
Heart of Darkness (Joseph Conrad)   57
Hemmings, David   *185*, 259, *304*
Henriksen, Lance   192
Hepburn, Audrey   18 n.2
Hepburn, Katharine   15, 31, *43*, 44, 45, 103
Herrmann, Bernard   141, 146, 164
  piano concerto   164, 181, 184, 214
Heston, Charlton   286
High Plains Drifter (Clint Eastwood, 1973)   180 n.8
Hill, The (Sidney Lumet, 1965)   153
Hinds, Ciarán   *238*
Hirschfeld, Al   19
His Majesty O'Keefe (Byron Haskin, 1954)   206
Hitchcock, Alfred   60, 81, 213–15, 231
  as architect   213–14
  and conversational distance filmed   226
  as film watcher   146
  locations
    Eddy and Gough Streets (San Francisco)   140
    Podesta Baldocchi (San Francisco)   86
    and quotation   140–1
    San Juan Bautista (near San Francisco)   81
Hoffa, James ("Jimmy")   220, 221
  antagonism with Robert F. Kennedy   221
Hoffman, Dustin   38, 62, 87, *155*, 160, 206
Hoffman, Philip Seymour   65
Holbrook, Hal   298
Holden, William   297
Holloway, Sterling   *112*, 117
Hollywood
  CGI, use in   72
  CinemaScope   177
  cinematographic techniques   54, 73, 95, 103, 179–80, 263, 265–6, 291, 293
  editing techniques   82, 88, 178, 180, 226, 263, 265, 291, 302
  labor practices   283
  make-up   77, 95, 305
  meal scenes   85
  motion capture   305
  musicals   77–8
  production politics   282
  publicity   5
  screen ratios   28
  sound and sound effects techniques, Foley   85
  special effects   73, 151, 187, 187 n.2, 252
  stardom in   285, 286
  stereotypes in   75
  Technicolor   272, 272 n.1
  VistaVision   291
Hollywood studios
  MGM (Metro Goldwyn Mayer)   3, 60
  Paramount's Stage   18, 99, 214, 283
  RKO (Radio-Keith-Orpheum)   101
  United Artists   33 n.2
  Warner Bros. Hollywood (Santa Monica Ave., now defunct)   60 n.1
Holm, Ian   41
Home Alone (Chris Columbus, 1990)   39
Homeland (2011)   131, 133, 133 n.5
Honey Boy (Shia LaBeouf, 2019)   278
Hopkins, Anthony   79
Horman, Arthur   140
Horsemen, The (John Frankenheimer, 1971)   84
Hospital, The (Arthur Hiller, 1971)   114
Houghton, Katharine   77, 103
Hounsou, Djimon   282
Howard, Ron   65
Howards End (E. M. Forster)   78, 79
Howards End (James Ivory, 1992)   76, 78–9
How to Get Away with Murder (2014)   133
Hudson, Rock   19
Hudsucker Proxy, The (Joel Coen and Ethan Coen, 1994)   153
Huebner, Mentor   101
Hugo (Martin Scorsese, 2011)   54
Hulk (Ang Lee, 2003)   25

Hunchback of Notre Dame, The (Victor Hugo)   20–2, 22 n.9
Hunchback of Notre Dame, The (William Dieterle, 1939)   *16*, 20–2
Hunt, Martita   170, 172
Hurt, John   72
Hurt, William   152, 188
Hussain, Saddam, *see* Bush-Blair

Identification of a Woman (Michelangelo Antonioni, 1982)   206
Ikarie XB-1 (Jindrich Polák, 1963)   244
"I Left My Heart in San Francisco" (George Cory and Douglass Cross), as sung by Tony Bennett   122
I Love Lucy (1951)   19, 130
Image, The (Kenneth Boulding)   17 n.1
Images (Robert Altman, 1972)   108
Imitation of Life (Douglas Sirk, 1954)   75
Imposters (2017)   133
In a Lonely Place (Nicholas Ray, 1950)   103
Incredible Shrinking Man, The (Jack Arnold, 1957)   151, *250*, 252
Independence Day (Roland Emmerich, 1996)   151
In Harm's Way (Otto Preminger, 1965)   38
Innis, Harold Adams   168
Inside Daisy Clover (Robert Mulligan, 1965)   67
Instagram   20 n.6, 277
Interstellar (Christopher Nolan, 2014)   228
Invaders from Mars (William Cameron Menzies, 1953)   57
iPhone   254
Ireland, John   87
Irishman, The (Martin Scorsese, 2019)   *219*, 219–22
Irons, Jeremy   25
Irréversible (Gaspar Noé, 2002)   *299*, 302
Iser, Wolfgang   62 n.3
Istanbul, Basilica Cistern   26, *see also From Russia with Love*
Ivory, James   78, 79

Jackson, Kate   282
J'ai épousé un ombre (*I Married a Shadow*; Robin Davis, 1983)   146
Jamaica (West Indies)   100
James, Henry   225 n.2
James, William   210 n.1, 240, 240 n.2, 304, 305
Janssen, Famke   133
Japanese picture scroll   197
Jaws (Peter Benchley)   241
Jaws (Steven Spielberg, 1975)   62, 74, 75, 183, 184, 226, 241
Jaynes, Julian   2
"Jet Song" (Leonard Bernstein and Stephen Sondheim)   232
JFK (Oliver Stone, 1991)   239
Jingle All the Way (Brian Levant, 1996)   41
Johannson, Scarlett   19, 152
John Wick (Chad Stahelski, 2014)   206
Jolie, Angelina   17, 67
Jones, James Earl   117
Journal of Fahrenheit 451, The (*Le journal de Fahrenheit 451*, François Truffaut)   13
Judgment at Nuremberg (Stanley Kramer, 1961)   239
Julia, Raul   145, 152
Jung-jae, Lee   128
Jungle Book, The (Zoltan Korda, 1942)   190
Junior (Ivan Reitman, 1994)   41
Jurassic Park (Steven Spielberg, 1993)   159–60

Kafka, Franz   37, 277
Kaminski, Janusz   54
Karate Kid, The (John G. Avildsen, 1984)   69, 230
Karp, Jacob   214
Kassovitz, Mathieu   *238*
Keach, Stacy   39
Keitel, Harvey   220
Kelly, Gene   14–15, *82*, 86
Kennedy, Jacqueline Bouvier (as played by Jaclyn Smith)   282
Kennedy, John Fitzgerald, administration   220, 221, *see also* Nixon-Kennedy Debates

Kennedy, Robert Francis ("Bobby"), antagonism with Jimmy Hoffa 221
Kidman, Nicole 80
Kindergarten Cop (Ivan Reitman, 1990) 41
King, Barry 16
King, The (David Michôd, 2019) 38
Kingdom, The (Peter Berg, 2007) 205
King of Comedy, The (Martin Scorsese, 1982) 38, *58*, 61
Kirby, Vanessa 12
Kirkegaard, Søren 2 n.1
Kiss, The (Edwin S. Porter, 1900) 84
Kiss Me Deadly (Robert Aldrich, 1955) 252
Kiss of Death (Henry Hathaway, 1947) 66
Kiss of the Spider Woman, The (Hector Babenco, 1985) 152, 152 n.2
Kleeb, Helen 47
Klute (Alan J. Pakula, 1971) 123
Knightley, Keira 239
Knudsen, Sidse Babett 128
Kohner, Susan 75
Kominsky Method, The (2019) 39
Korngold, Erich Wolfgang 181, 182
score for *The Sea Hawk* 181, 182
Kramer vs. Kramer (Robert Benton, 1979) 62
Kubrick, Stanley 73, 114 n.4, 183
unreliable *acousmêtre* 114 n.4

La belle noiseuse (Jacques Rivette, 1991) 55
Lacan, Jacques 246
Ladd, Alan 68
Ladd, Cheryl 282
Lady Vanishes, The (Alfred Hitchcock, 1938) 141
La mariée était en noir (*The Bride Wore Black*; François Truffaut, 1964) 146
Lancaster, Burt 164
Lang, Charles 54 n.1
Lang, Doreen 177
La Notte (Michelangelo Antonioni, 1961) 207
"Las Babas del Diablo" (Julio Cortázar), see "Blow-Up"

Last Action Hero (John McTiernan, 1993) 41
Last Temptation of Christ, The (Martin Scorsese, 1988) 66
Laughton, Charles 16, 20 n.7, 20–2, 67
gassed in World War I 20 n.7
Laundromat, The (Steven Soderbergh, 2019) 124
Laura (Otto Preminger, 1944) 98, 117, 200
L'Avventura (Michelangelo Antonioni, 1962) 270
Law, Jude 80, 103
Lawrence of Arabia (David Lean, 1962) 112–13, 113 n.1
Léaud, Jean-Pierre 180
Leave Her to Heaven (John M. Stahl, 1945) 66
Legend (Ridley Scott, 1985) 71
Lem, Stanislaw 144
Lemmon, Jack 84
Lennon, John 299
LeRoy, Mervyn 277
"Les fils de la vierge" (Julio Cortázar), *see* "Blow-Up"
Letts, Tracy 54
Levene, Sam 274
Lewis, Damian 131
Lewis, Jerry 37, 38, *58*, 61
Life (Daniel Espinosa, 2017) 72
"Life Lessons," part II of *New York Stories* (Martin Scorsese, 1989) 55, 81
Lili (Charles Walters, 1953) 109
Lincoln, Abraham 301
Lindon, Lionel 164
Line of Duty (2012) 132
Linney, Laura 128
Lintz, Madison 131
Lions for Lambs (Robert Redford, 2007) 230
Liotta, Ray 66
Little Big Man (Arthur Penn, 1970) 38
Livesey, Roger 20
Llewelyn Davies children, George and siblings 241
Lockwood, Gary 86
Lombard, Carole 4, 80, 120

London 11, 171–3, 232, 254
    Blow-Up locations 258 n.1
        British Museum (London) 53
        Camberwell 258 n.1
        Consort Road 256–60
        Notting Hill Gate 261
        Peckham 258 n.1
        Peckham Bus Garage 260
        Tower Bridge 233
    civilized 171
    nocturnal 26, see also *Night and the City*
Lonedale Operator, The (D. W. Griffith, 1911) 48, 80
Long Goodbye, The (Robert Altman, 1973) 30, 151
Long Island 241, 253
"Look At Me I'm Sandra Dee" (Jim Jacobs and Warren Casey) 153, see also *Grease*
Looney Tunes 158
Lord of the Flies (Peter Brook, 1963) 107 n.1
Lord of the Rings: The Fellowship of the Ring, The (Peter Jackson, 2001) 276
Loren, Sophia 17
Lorre, Peter 157
Los Angeles 160, 232, 253
    Meadow Drive (Coldwater Canyon) 277
Lost in Translation (Sofia Coppola 2003) 19
Loy, Myrna 3–5
Lucas, George 63 n.4, 101, 137 n.9
Ludlam, Helen 85
Ludwig II of Bavaria (the "Mad King") 169
Lumet, Sidney 193 n.1
Lynley, Carol *168*, 170–2

Macchio, Ralph 69
Mackinac Island 210
Madden, Richard *127*
Mafia, the 220
Magic Christian, The (Joseph McGrath, 1969) 176

Magnificent Ambersons, The (Orson Welles, 1942) 66, 114
Magnificent Obsession (Douglas Sirk, 1954) 99
Magnolia (Paul Thomas Anderson, 1999) 65
Malleson, Miles *23*, 28 n.4
Maltese Falcon, The (John Huston, 1941) 115, 251
Manchurian Candidate, The (John Frankenheimer, 1962) 47–8
Manhunter (Michael Mann, 1986) 151
Manichean dualism 193
Man Who Came to Dinner, The (William Keighley, 1942) 66, 103
Man Who Knew Too Much, The (Alfred Hitchcock, 1956) 55, *105*, 109, 148, 180
Man Who Shot Liberty Valance, The (John Ford, 1962) 40, 41
Mara, Rooney 41
Marathon Man (John Schlesinger, 1976) 149, 177
Marcella (2016) 128
Marnie (Alfred Hitchcock, 1964) 146, 231, 292
Marriage Story (Noah Baumbach, 2019) *64*, 66, 70, 152
Marseille (2016) 128
Marvel action films 25
Marville, Charles 233
Marvin, Lee 40–1
Marx Brothers 33 n.2
    Harpo and Chico duet 229
Mary, Queen of Scots (Charles Jarrott, 1971) 65
Mary Poppins (Robert Stevenson, 1964) 286
Mary Poppins Returns (Rob Marshall, 2018) 286
Mary Tyler Moore Show, The (1970) 130
Mason, James 60, *97*, 100
Massey, Anna 172
Massey, Raymond 65
Matheson, Richard 210 n.1
Mature, Victor *30*, 31–2

Mauvais sang (*Bad Blood*; Leos Carax, 1986)   244
Max Rose (Daniel Noah, 2013)   38
McCartney, Paul   299
McConnell, Frank   247
McCormack, Patty   68
McDormand, Frances   163
McKellen, Ian   18
McLaglen, Victor   *58*
McLuhan, [Herbert] Marshall   229
McNairy, Scoot   128
McQueen, Steve   84
Mean Streets (Martin Scorsese, 1973)   37
Méliès, Georges   225
Memento (Christopher Nolan, 2000)   300, 302
Men in Black (Barry Sonnenfeld, 1997)   117
Merchant, Ismail   78, 79
Messiah (2020)   128
Mickey Blue Eyes (Kelly Makin, 1999)   145
Midnight Cowboy (John Schlesinger, 1969)   39
Midnight Lace (David Miller, 1960)   66
Midnight Mass (2021)   132
Mildred Pierce (Michael Curtiz, 1945)   *64*, 67–8
Miles, Vera   50
Miles, Yan   11
Milligan, Spike   176
Mindhunter (2017)   137
Minnelli, Liza, *see* "New York, New York"
Misfits, The (John Huston, 1961)   39
Mitchell, Thomas   40
Mitterrand, François   12 n.2
Mizoguchi, Kenji   197
Modern Times (Charles Chaplin, 1936)   205
Modigliani, Amedeo   81
Monahan, Michelle   128
Money Heist (2017)   128
Monroe, Marilyn   *16*, 18, 19, 37
Moore, Juanita   74
Moreno, Rita   286
Morgan: A Suitable Case for Treatment (Karel Reisz, 1966)   56
Mori, Masayuki   195

Morita, Pat   69
Mortimer, John   171
Mortimer, Penelope   171
Moscow   176 n.3
Most Wanted Man, A (Anton Corbijn, 2014)   98
motion capture, *see* Hollywood
Motion Picture Production Code   193 n.1
Moulin Rouge! (Baz Luhrmann, 2001)   205
Munich (Germany)   242
Munich (Steven Spielberg, 2005)   *238, 239*, 242
Munich Olympics, massacre (September 5, 1972)   239, 240, 240 n.3
Murder on the Orient Express (Kenneth Branagh, 2017)   293
Murder on the Orient Express (Sidney Lumet, 1974)   131 n.3
Murray, Bill   206
My Dinner with Andre (Louis Malle, 1981)   *223*, 227, 253, 300
My Man Godfrey (Gregory La Cava, 1936)   103
My Own Private Idaho (Gus Van Sant, 1991)   228
Mystic River (Clint Eastwood, 2003)   206

Nalder, Reginald   39
"Naming of Parts" (Henry Reed)   52
Narcos: Mexico (2018)   128, 134
National Velvet (Clarence Brown, 1944)   151
Navajo, as filmmakers   175 n.1
Neeson, Liam   40
Negotiating Hollywood (Danae Clark)   16
Nelson, Ricky   163
Newcomb, Theodore M.   141, 141 n.2
Newman, Paul   17
Newton, (Sir) Isaac   301
Newton, Robert   151
New York, New York (Martin Scorsese, 1977)   205
"New York, New York" (John Kander and Fred Ebb), as sung by Liza Minnelli   122

New York City   182, 192, 221, 232, 234
   Astoria (Queens)   58, 59
   Broadway (theatre district)   232, 241, 286
   Bronx, The   *231,* 231
   Brooklyn   191, 192, 194
   Empire State Building   233
   47th Street   177
   Hudson River   101
   JFK (John Fitzgerald Kennedy) Airport (Queens)   192
   Madison Avenue   177
   Manhattan   231, 253
   Museum of Modern Art   98
   Plaza Hotel   15
   Times Square   34
   World Trade Center   98
New Yorker, The (magazine)   253
Nicholson, Jack   54, 64
Nick of Time (John Badham, 1995)   302
Nielsen, Leslie   192
Night and Day (Michael Curtiz, 1946)   301
Night and the City (Jules Dassin, 1950)   26
Night in Casablanca, A (Archie Mayo, 1946)   33 n.2
Night of the Hunter, The (Charles Laughton, 1955)   67, 286
1917 (Sam Mendes, 2019)   249 n.2
Nixon, Richard Milhouse, *see* Nixon-Kennedy Debates
Nixon-Kennedy Debates (September 26–October 21, 1960)   170
Nolte, Nick   81
No Man of Her Own (Mitchell Leisen, 1950)   146
North by Northwest (Alfred Hitchcock, 1959)   51, 56, 60, 149–50, 177
Notorious (Alfred Hitchcock, 1946)   66, 202, 244
Nouvelle vague (Jean-Luc Godard, 1990)   146
Novak, Kim   81, 140, *212,* 213
Now, Voyager (Irving Rapper, 1942)   66, 103
Nutty Professor, The (Jerry Lewis, 1963)   37

O'Brien, George   77
O'Casey, Ronan   *304*
O'Connor, Donald   14
O'Connor, Una   40
O'Donnell, Cathy   66
Odyssey, The (Homer)   197, 198, 253
Official Secrets (Gavin Hood, 2019)   239
Official Secrets Act (OSA, 1989)   240–1
Olivier, Laurence   66, 69, 149, 170, 172, 177
Olmos, Edward James   286
Once Upon a Time . . . in Hollywood (Quentin Tarantino, 2019)   86 n.3
One Day in the Life of Ivan Denisovich (Caspar Wrede, 1970)   150
One From the Heart (Francis Ford Coppola, 1981)   156 n.1
On the Beach (Stanley Kramer, 1959)   91, 116
On the Waterfront (Elia Kazan, 1954)   *120,* 122
Orff, Carl   94
Original Cast Album: Company (D. A. Pennebaker, 1970)   122 n.2
Orphée (Jean Cocteau, 1950)   143
Ortega y Gasset, José   28, 83
Osment, Haley Joel   39, 85
Otto, Miranda   133
Outland (Peter Hyams, 1981)   86
Owens, Susan   189
Owens Valley (California)   253
Ozark (2017)   128

Pace, Jackson   131
Pacino, Al   123, *190,* 191, 219, 220, 220 n.1, 221
Padilla, Juan José, gored by bull   56
Palance, Jack   192
Pallette, Eugene   40, 103
Palmer, R. Barton   179 n.7
Pan's Labyrinth (Guillermo del Toro, 2006)   57
Paris   21, 46, 47, 153, 156, 232, 233, 254
   Eiffel Tower   233
   pre-Haussmann   233
Paris, Texas (Wim Wenders, 1984)   176

Parkinson, Michael   162
Party, The (Blake Edwards, 1968)   202
Passage to India, A (E. M. Forster)   158
Passenger, The (*Professione: Reporter*; Michelangelo Antonioni, 1975)   117, 304
Pattinson, Robert   17, 38, 77
Paul, Robert   65
Peck, Gregory   41, 91, 146, 284
Peckham Bus Garage, *see* London
Peña, Michael   128
Pereira, Hal   101
Peretz, Susan   192
Perfume (2018)   85–6
Perfume: The Story of a Murderer (Tom Tykwer, 2006)   85–6
Perkins, Victor (V. F.)   268
Persistence and Change (Theodore M. Newcomb), *see* Newcomb, Theodore M.
Personal Shopper (Olivier Assayas, 2016)   38, 169, 251, 254
Pesci, Joe   *219*, 219–21
Peter Pan, or The Boy Who Wouldn't Grow Up (James M. Barrie, Duke of York's Theatre, London, 27 December 1904)   101, 241
Peter Pan (Clyde Geronimi, Wilfred Jackson, Hamilton Luske, Jack Kinney, 1953)   *238*, 240, 242
Phantom Menace, The (George Lucas, 1999)   137 n.9
Phantom of Liberty (Luis Buñuel, 1974)   227
Philadelphia Story, The (George Cukor, 1940)   *43*, 44–5, 241
Philadelphia Story, The (Philip Barry; Shubert Theatre, New York, March 28, 1939)   241
Phoenix, Joaquin   39
Phoenix, River   228
Picasso, Pablo   81
Pidgeon, Walter   101
Pike, Rosamund   31
Pillow Talk (Michael Gordon, 1959)   136 n.8, 228
Pinon, Dominique   159

Pinter, Harold   179
Pitt, Michael   *243*
Planet of the Apes (Franklin J. Schaffner, 1968)   286
Planet of the Apes (Tim Burton, 2001)   286
Plato   165
Play It Again, Sam (Herbert Ross, 1972)   205
Plummer, Christopher   211
Point Blank (John Boorman, 1967)   41
Poitier, Sidney   77
Poland   253
Polanski, Roman   64
Polglase, Van Nest   101
Pollack, Sydney   230 n.4
Poltergeist (Tobe Hooper, 1982)   119
Pomerance, Ariel   293 n.1
Portrait of a Lady, The (Henry James)   277
Portrait of a Lady, The (Jane Campion, 1996)   48–9
Post, The (Steven Spielberg, 2017)   54, 230 n.4
Potente, Franka   46, 65
Powell, Michael   263
Powers of Ten (Charles and Ray Eames, 1977)   27 n.3
Powers of Ten (Philip Morrison)   27 n.3
Pownall, Leon   230
Predator (John McTiernan, 1987)   46
Pressburger, Emeric   263
Price, Vincent   98, *200*
Prieto, Rodrigo   221
Principles of Psychology (William James)   210 n.1
Prokofiev, Sergei   230
Psycho (Alfred Hitchcock, 1960)   34 n.3, 50, 57, 85, 85 n.2, 119, 146, 152–3, 181, 184
Psycho (Gus Van Sant, 1998)   57
Public, The (Emilio Estevez, 2018)   99
Purple Rose of Cairo, The (Woody Allen, 1985)   *243*, 244

Quick and the Dead, The (Sam Raimi, 1995)   176 n.2

Quiet Man, The (John Ford, 1952)   58

Rabbit of Seville (Chuck Jones, 1950)   269
Raging Bull (Martin Scorsese, 1980)   37, 162, 219
Raiders of the Lost Ark (*Indiana Jones and the Raiders of the Lost Ark*; Steven Spielberg, 1981)   119
Rains, Claude   40
Rambaldi, Carlo   93
Rambo (Ted Kotcheff, 1982)   123
Random Harvest (Mervyn LeRoy, 1942)   66
Rathbone, Basil   117, *147*, 153
Real Thing, The (Tom Stoppard; Plymouth Theatre, New York, January 5, 1984)   25
Rear Window (Alfred Hitchcock, 1954)   66, 75, 84 n.1, 224 n.1
Rear Window (Jeff Bleckner, 1998)   149
Rebecca (Alfred Hitchcock, 1940)   50, 117, 290
Rebel Without a Cause (Nicholas Ray, 1955)   98–9, 177, 241
Redford, Robert   102, 103, 103 n.2, 230
Redgrave, Vanessa   65, *76*, 79, *185*, 187
Redmayne, Eddie   66, 77
Red River (Howard Hawks, 1948)   40, 87, 164
Red Shoes, The (Michael Powell and Emeric Pressburger, 1948)   *261*, 261–6
Reeve, Christopher   40, 149, *208*, 210
Relations in Public (Erving Goffman)   118
Rembrandt (Alexander Korda, 1936)   67
Renoir, Pierre-Auguste   77
Return of Martin Guerre, The (Daniel Vigne, 1982)   228
Return of the Jedi (Richard Marquand, 1983)   137 n.9
Revenant, The (Alejandro G. Iñárritu, 2015)   118
Reversal of Fortune (Barbet Schroeder, 1990)   25
Revill, Clive   173

Reynolds, Debbie   14, 15
Reynolds, Ryan   *246*
Ribisi, Giovanni   41
Richard III (Laurence Olivier, 1955)   66
Right Stuff, The (Philip Kaufman, 1983)   239, 301
Rio Bravo (Howard Hawks, 1959)   40
Robards Jason Jr.   65
Robbins, Jerome   232
Robbins, Tim   67
Roberts, Julia   17
Robertson, Robbie   221
Robinson, Ann   *280*, 286
Robinson Crusoe (Luis Buñuel, 1954)   107 n.1
Roddenberry, Gene   96 n.1
Rodin, François Auguste René   79
Rome   232
Romeo + Juliet (Baz Luhrmann, 1995)   153, 201
Ronin (John Frankenheimer, 1998)   176 n.3
Room with a View, A (E. M. Forster)   277
Rooney, Mickey   17
Rope (Alfred Hitchcock, 1948)   251–2
Rose, Irwin   74
Royal Navy, and tin cans (1813)   92
Run Lola Run (Tom Tykwer, 1998)   176 n.4
Ruskin, John   267

Saboteur (Alfred Hitchcock, 1942)   73
Sabrina (Billy Wilder, 1954)   101
Sabu   290
Sacks, Oliver   18 n.5, 237
and FRA   18 n.5
Sadlers Wells Ballet   263
Salt, Barry   305 n.1
Samson and Delilah (Cecil B. DeMille, 1949)   *30*, 31
San Francisco   91, 98, 173, 213, *see also* Hitchcock, Alfred
Big Basin redwood forest near   98
Sarandon, Chris   192
Saturday Night Fever (John Badham, 1977)   85, 202, 206
Satyricon (Petronius Arbiter)   25

Sawamura, Ichisaburo 195
Saylor, Morgan 131
Schallert, William 99
Schefer, Jean-Louis 227, 228
Scheff, Thomas J. 135
Scheider, Roy 62, 74
Schenectady, New York (Charlie Kaufman, 2008) 25
Schivelbusch, Wolfgang 234
Schoenberg, Arnold 46
Schoonmaker, Thelma 221
Schwarzenegger, Arnold 41
Scorsese, Martin 54, 146, 220, 221
Scott, Martha 66
Scott, Ridley 187 n.1, 188
Scourby, Alexander 117
Sea Hawk, The (Michael Curtiz, 1940) 181
Searchers, The (John Ford, 1956) 40
"Second Coming, The" (William Butler Yeats) 249
Sellers, Peter 65
77 Sunset Strip (1958) 130
sex, lies, and videotape (Steven Soderbergh, 1989) 253–4
Seymour, Jane 210
Shakespeare, William, plays
　All's Well That Ends Well 145
　Antony and Cleopatra 145
　Hamlet 66, 145, 154
　Hamlet character 163
　Henry IV Part II 145
　Lady Macbeth character 163
　Macbeth 66
　Merchant of Venice, The 186
　Richard II 145
　Tempest, The 143, 144, 161, 305
Shane (George Stevens, 1953) 68, 122–3, 169, 192
Sharif, Omar 80, *295*
Shaw, Bob 221
Shawn, Wallace *223*, 227, 253
Shearer, Moira *261*, 261–6
Sheherazade 253
Shepard, Sam 301
Shootist, The (Don Siegel, 1976) 65
Silence (Martin Scorsese, 2016) 56
Simmel, Georg 113 n.3

Simon of the Desert (Luis Buñuel, 1965) 244
Simon [Paul] and [Art] Garfunkel 160
Sinatra, Frank 47
Singin' in the Rain (Stanley Donen and Gene Kelly, 1952) 14, 293
　"Broadway Rhythm" ballet 14
　"Good Mornin'" number 14
　"Singin' in the Rain" number 293
6 Underground (Michael Bay, 2019) 176 n.3, *246*, 247–8
Sixth Sense, The (M. Night Shyamalan, 1999) 39, 66, 199 n.2
Skarsgård, Stellan 230
Skaterdater (Noel Black, 1966) 175
Slavin, Neal 60
Smith, Alexis 140
Smith, Dick 38
Smith, Jaclyn 282, 285
Smith, Maggie 128 n.2
Sobchack, Vivian 13 n.3, 114
Some Like It Hot (Billy Wilder, 1959) *16*, 20, 84, 205
"Something's Coming" (Leonard Bernstein and Stephen Sondheim) 234
Somewhere in Time (Jeannot Szwarc, 1980) *208*, 210–11
Sonata No. 21 in C for piano, Op. 53, "Waldstein" (Ludwig van Beethoven) 115
Sondheim, Stephen 69
Song to Remember, A (Charles Vidor, 1945) 55
Sontag, Susan 55
"Sound of Music, The" (Richard Rodgers and Oscar Hammerstein II) 149
Sound of Music, The (Robert Wise, 1965) 149
"Sound of Silence, The" (Paul Simon) 160
Source Code (Duncan Jones, 2011) 228
Spacek, Sissy 69
Spader, James 128
Spellbound (Alfred Hitchcock, 1945) 55
Spelling [Aaron]-[Leonard] Goldberg Productions 282

Spencer (Pablo Larrain, 2021)   10 n.1
Spielberg, Steven   230 n.4, 239, 240, 291
Spirit of St. Louis, The (Billy Wilder, 1957)   98
Spy Who Came In from the Cold (Martin Ritt, 1965)   18 n.3, 69
Squid Game (2021)   128
Stagecoach (John Ford, 1939)   40
Stage Fright (Alfred Hitchcock, 1950)   99
Stairway to Heaven (*A Matter of Life and Death*; Michael Powell and Emeric Pressburger, 1946)   26, 80, 263, 266
Stalin, Josef   230
Stanton, Harry Dean   176
Stanwyck, Barbara   37
Stardust Memories (Woody Allen, 1980)   *267*
Star Is Born, A (George Cukor, 1954)   16
Star Trek (1966), franchise   96 n.1
Star Wars (George Lucas, 1977)   39, 63 n.4, 102, 137 n.9, 151
  serial publicity and   137 n.9
Star Wars: The Rise of Skywalker (J. J. Abrams, 2019)   39
Steadicam   291
Steenbeck (editing console)   14
Steiger, Rod   *120*
Stewart, James   66, *71*, 81, *105,* 140, 141, 144, 149, *212,* 214
Stewart, Kristen   17, 38, 77, 254, 281, 282
Stewart, Patrick   282
Still of the Night (Robert Benton, 1982)   302
Strangers on a Train (Alfred Hitchcock, 1951)   *52, 55,* 243
Strauss, Richard   181, 183
Streep, Meryl   62, 124
Strong, Mark   57
Stuart, Gloria   114
Stuhlbarg, Michael   54
Suburbicon (George Clooney, 2017)   39
Sudnow, David, *see Ways of the Hand*
Sunset Blvd. (Billy Wilder, 1950)   99, 283
"Susannah and the Elders" (apocryphal tale)   56
Sutherland, Joan   122

Swan Lake (Peter Ilyitch Tchaikovsky; Bolshoi Theatre, Moscow, March 4, 1877)   261–5
  1946 Covent Garden production with Moira Shearer   266
Swanson, Gloria   283
Sweet, Blanche   80
Sylvia Scarlett (George Cukor, 1935)   31
Sylvie and Bruno (Lewis Carroll)   179
Symphony No. 3 in E-flat, "Eroica" (Ludwig van Beethoven)   2 n.1
Syriana (Stephen Gaghan, 2005)   57

Talented Mr. Ripley, The (Anthony Minghella, 1999)   80, 103
Tanaka, Kinuyo   *195*
Tandy, Jessica   103
Tarnished Angel (Leslie Goodwins, 1938)   101
Tati, Jacques   277
Taxi Driver (Martin Scorsese, 1976)   162, *181,* 181–3
Taylor, Dwight   140
Taylor, Elizabeth   17, 39, 77, 120, 121, 151, 291
Taylor, Rod   104
TCM (Turner Classic Movies)   17
Technicolor   272, *see also* Hollywood
Tempest (Paul Mazursky, 1982)   145, *see also* Shakespeare, William
Ten Commandments, The (Cecil B. DeMille, 1956)   114, 239, 291
Tenniel, John
  illustrations for *Alice in Wonderland*   26, 72
Terminator, The (James Cameron, 1984)   41
That Certain Summer (Lamont Johnson, 1972)   298
Thelma & Louise (Ridley Scott, 1991)   98
Theory of Everything, The (James Marsh, 2014)   66, 77
Theron, Charlize   73
They Live By Night (Nicholas Ray, 1949)   231

Thief of Bagdad, The (Michael Powell and Emeric Pressburger, 1940)   *23*, 28 n.4
Third Man, The (Carol Reed, 1949)   67, 232 n.3
Thirteenth Guest, The (Albert Ray, 1932)   110–11
Thomas, Henry   69
Thomas, Jake   85
Thomas Crown Affair, The (Norman Jewison, 1968)   84, 136 n.8
Thompson, Emma   *76*, 79
Three Days of the Condor (Sydney Pollack, 1975)   102–3
3:10 to Yuma (Delmer Daves, 1957)   176 n.2
Tierney, Gene   66, 98, 117, *200*
Time Machine, The (George Pal, 1960)   300
Titanic (James Cameron, 1997)   114
Tokyo   232
Tomasini, George   213
Tootsie (Sydney Pollack, 1982)   206
Top Hat (Mark Sandrich, 1935)   205, 207, 292
  "Cheek to Cheek" number   292
Total Eclipse (Agnieszka Holland, 1995)   81
Touch, The (Ingmar Bergman, 1971)   269
Touch of Evil (Orson Welles, 1958)   40
Tracy, Spencer   103
Train, The (John Frankenheimer, 1964)   163
Treasure Island (Byron Haskin, 1950)   151
Tree of Life, The (Terrence Malick, 2011)   300
True Grit (Henry Hathaway, 1969)   40
Truffaut, François   13–15, 146
Turandot (Giacomo Puccini [and Franco Alfano], La Scala, Milan, April 25, 1926)   122
Turner, Lana   75
Twentieth Century (Howard Hawks, 1934)   80
21 Bridges (Brian Kirk, 2019)   248

20,000 Leagues Under the Sea (Jules Verne)   93, 101
20,000 Leagues Under the Sea (Richard Fleischer, 1954)   93, *97*, 99–101
Twilight (Catherine Hardwicke et al., 2008-2012)   38
Twins (Ivan Reitman, 1988)   41
2001: A Space Odyssey (Stanley Kubrick, 1968)   73, 86, 114 n.4, 172, *181*, 182–4, 300
Tyler, Walter   101

Uccello, Paolo   197, 197 n.1
Ugetsu monogatari (Kenji Mizoguchi, 1953)   *195*, 195–9, 199 n.2
Un chien andalou (Luis Buñuel and Salvador Dalí, 1929)   56
Under the Skin (Jonathan Glazer, 2013)   19
United 93 (Paul Greengrass, 2006)   239
University of Wisconsin   277
U. S. S. Enterprise   96 n.1
Ustinov, Peter   117

Van Dyke, Dick   286
Van Huysum, Jan   24
Vanity Fair (magazine)   17
Van Leeuwenhoek, Antonie   261
Varndell, Daniel   84 n.1
Vaughn, Vince   77
Veidt, Conrad   *23*
Verne, Jules   83
Vertigo (Alfred Hitchcock, 1958)   *1*, 6, *71*, 81, 86, 139–46, 140 n.1, 142 n.3, *212*, 212–16, 252
  mirror scene   212–16
  and pointing 142 n.3
Vickers, Martha   80
Vicky Cristina Barcelona (Woody Allen, 2008)   19
Vielle Nice   176 n.3
Vienna (Austria)   99
Visions of Light (Arnold Glassman, Todd McCarthy, and Stuart Samuels, 1992)   54 n.1
VistaVision   291, *see also* Hollywood
Vogue (magazine)   17

Volume, in motion capture, *see* Hollywood
Von Sternberg, Josef 40
Von Sydow, Max 102, 103, 103 n.2
Voskovec, George 210

Waiting for the Barbarians (Ciro Guerra, 2019) 37
Wait Until Dark (Terence Young, 1967) 109
Walbrook, Anton 261–6
Walk, The (Robert Zemeckis, 2015) 98, 239
Walkabout (Nicolas Roeg, 1971) 115 n.5
Warden, Jack 65
Warner, David 39
War of the Worlds, The (Byron Haskin, 1953) *280*
War of the Worlds (Steven Spielberg, 2005) 67, *280*
Warrick, Ruth 84
Washington, Kerry 17
Wasserman, Lew 214
Watchmen (Zack Snyder, 2009) 153
Watergate Affair (June 17, 1972 and onward) 229–30
Wayne, John 38, 40, *58*, 60 n.1, 65, 86, 164
Ways of the Hand (David Sudnow) 54
Weaver, Sigourney 98
Webb, Clifton 117
Weekend (Jean-Luc Godard, 1968) 56
Welles, Orson 65, 67, 84, 113, 114, 146, 225
Welliver, Titus 128, 131
Wenders, Wim 188
Werner, Oskar *175*, 177
West Side Story (Leonard Bernstein, Stephen Sondheim, Arthur Laurents, Jerome Robbins; Winter Garden Theatre, New York, September 26, 1957) 232, 286, *see also* "Jet Song"
West Side Story (Robert Wise, 1961) 155, *231*, 231–2, 286
West Side Story (Steven Spielberg, 2021) 286

When Harry Met Sally . . . (Rob Reiner, 1989) 123
When Two or More Are Gathered Together (Neal Slavin) 60
Whishaw, Ben 86
White House, *see* Kennedy, John Fitzgerald
Who's Afraid of Virginia Woolf? (Edward Albee, Billy Rose Theatre, New York, October 16, 1962) 120
Who's Afraid of Virginia Woolf? (Mike Nichols, 1966) 39, 121, 291
Wife vs. Secretary (Clarence Brown, 1936) 3–5
Wilding, Michel 99
Williams, Grant 99, *250*
Williams, John 181, 183
Williams, Robin 117, 230
Williams, Tennessee 187
Willis, Bruce 67
Willy Wonka & the Chocolate Factory (Mel Stuart, 1971) 231
"Windmills of Your Mind, The" (Michel Legrand) 84
Windsor, Elizabeth (Elizabeth II), Queen of England 12, 12 n.2
Winnie the Pooh and the Blustery Day (Wolfgang Reitherman, 1968) *112*, 117
Winogrand, Garry 184
Winslet, Kate 116
Winslow, Pippa 9
Wiseman, Joseph 100
Witness for the Prosecution (Billy Wilder, 1957) 39
Wizard of Oz, The (Victor Fleming, 1939) 292
Wolf's Call, The (*Le chant du loup*; Antonin Baudry, 2019) *89*, 96
Wood, Natalie 66–7
Woodward, Bob (as played by Robert Redford) 230
Woolley, Monty 66
World War I 20 n.7, 249 n.2, *see also* Laughton, Charles
World War II 89
Wormwood (2017) 135 n.6

Worth, Sol   175 n.1
Writers Guild of America West   239

Yale University   277
Yeats, William Butler   249, 293
Yeoh, Michelle   17
You Can't Take It With You (Frank Capra, 1938)   103
Young, Mary   15

Young, Robert   274

Zabriskie Point (Michelangelo Antonioni, 1970)   253
Zaragoza (Spain), *see* Padilla, Juan José
Zellweger, Renée   40
Zeno's paradox   177
Zischler, Hans   *238*
Zukerman, Ashley   123 n.3

www.ingramcontent.com/pod-product-compliance
Lightning Source LLC
Chambersburg PA
CBHW052144300426
44115CB00011B/1515